A PRINTMAKER'S WORLD
JACK McLARTY

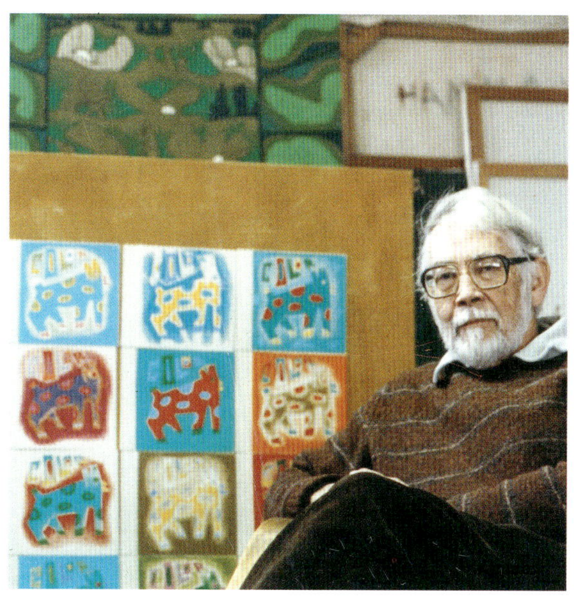

A PRINTMAKER'S WORLD
JACK McLARTY

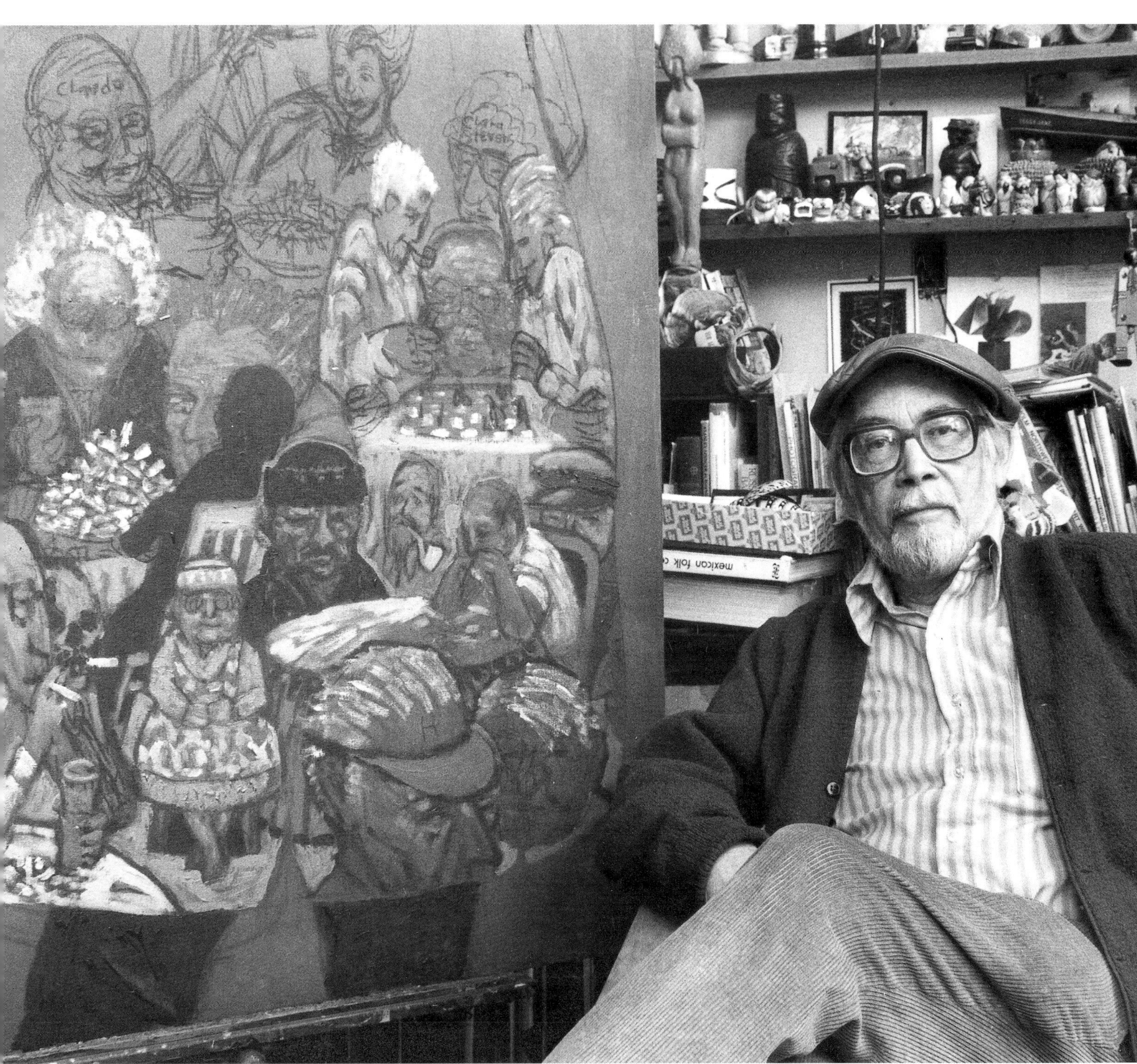

ANGEL SPONSORS:

Carol and Seymour Haber
Charles and Hiromi McLarty
Hugh and Lisbeth McLarty
Mayo Rae Rolph Roy

PRINCIPAL SPONSORS:

Carol and Wayne Bridges
Nick and Judy Chaivoe
Maribeth Collins
J. Michael Deeney
Ken Edwards
Gordon W. Gilkey
Lillie H. Lauha
Laura McLarty and Keith Thompson
Neil J. Moore
Francis J. Newton
Muriel K. Oliver
Michael Parsons and Marte Lamb
Judy and Edward Peck
Roger Saydack and Elaine Bernat
Allen Tooke
Mary Louise and John Uchiyama
Bob and Martha Warnock
Judith Wyss
William F. Yee

SPONSORS AT LARGE:

Stuart and Jill Asbjornsen
Robert Dozono
Jennifer and Douglas Goe
William Gordon
Hanne and Harry Greaver
Jane and James L. Hansen
Irv and Evelyn Lamon
Sarah E. Lapham
Kathleen McCuistion
Eloise J. McGraw
Deborah L. Martin
Ray and Ruth Matthews
Henry S. and Marian Lee Mears
Dan and Fern Momyer
Jane Huston Rawlins
Elinor Shank
Nancy J. Snow
Jacob and Elizabeth Van Staaveren
Arthur and Margaret Wasser
Jack and Janet Witter

Cover. "The Heart of John Donne" (color woodcut) No. 121
    (*see page 56*)
Fly leaf. The Artist (1990) in his studio with handpainted book
    covers for Sponsors of "The Book of Color."
Title page. The Artist in his studio (c. 1985) with "An Unfinished
    Life" (acrylic)

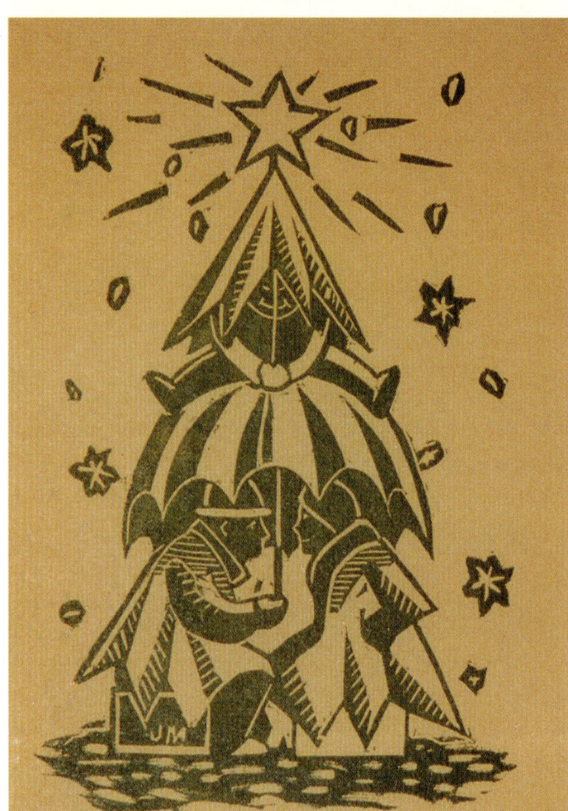

PUBLISHED BY McLARTY'S CHOICE
Portland, Oregon

Copyright © 1997
All Rights Reserved

Editor: Barbara Lever McLarty
Designer: Chas. S. Politz/Parabola, Ltd.
Production Assistant: Carol Hilborn Bridges

Edition of 1000 copies

Library of Congress Card Catalog No. 96-095351

Clothbound ISBN No. 0-9644916-2-1
Paperbound ISBN No. 0-9644916-3-X

CONTRIBUTORS:

John and JoAnne Booth
Angela Cappelli
Patrick and Christine Chan
Elaine and George Chandler
Margaret Henderson
Jean Kavanaugh
Rodney Keyser
David Lindenberger
Grace McDonald
Eleanor Milne
Dennis and Shirley Schiller
Kelton Walston

10

PRINT COLLECTIONS:

Benoit College
Bowdoin College
British Museum
Bucknell University
California Palace of the Legion of Honor
Davidson College
Dayton Art Institute
Drury College
Erb Memorial Student Union, University of Oregon
Gilkey Collection, Portland Art Museum
Henry Gallery, University of Washington
Huntington Public Library (New York)
Indiana State University
Kalamazoo Art Museum
Kohler Art Center
Library of Congress
Linfield College
Mesa Community College
Michigan State University
Montana State University
New York Universities at Brockport, Buffalo
Museum of Fine Arts, Springfield, Mass.
Nasson College
Pacific University
Portland Community College
Princeton University Library
Ringling Museum
Rockford College
Salem Art Association
Salem Public Library
Smithsonian Institution
Southern Illinois University
Southern Oregon State College
Southwestern Oregon Community College
University of Georgia
University of Maine
University of Mississippi
University of Nebraska
University of New Mexico Museum
University of North Carolina
University of Oklahoma
University of Oregon Museum
University of Utah
Wittenberg University

ART CENTERS AND GALLERIES REFERRED TO IN THE NOTES ON THE PRINTS

Art Space is located in Bay City, Oregon.

Bush Barn Gallery is the gallery of the Salem Art Association, Salem, Oregon.

Cawein Gallery is located on the campus of Pacific University, Forest Grove, Oregon.

Carlin Galleries were located in Ft. Worth, Texas.

Erb Memorial Student Union is at the University of Oregon, Eugene, Oregon.

Graven Images Gallery was located in Ashland, Oregon.

The Henry Gallery is on the campus of the University of Washington, Seattle.

The Image Gallery, Portland, established in fall 1961, operated for more than thirty years.

Keller Gallery was located in downtown Salem, Oregon.

Kharouba Gallery was situated in downtown Portland from 1947 to 1953.

The Little Gallery was located in Raleigh, North Carolina.

Maude Kerns Art Center continues as an active art center in Eugene, Oregon.

Lakeside Studios is situated in Lakeside, Michigan. Established as a center for printmaking by John Wilson in the sixties, it has had a long, strong influence on collectors as well as printmakers. John circulated traveling print shows and drawing shows of the highest quality. He offered studio space and workshops for artists, commissioned original prints, arranged their distribution by securing collectors who would underwrite the whole process. Having served as their most knowledgeable and effective field man for Ferdinand Roten Galleries of Baltimore, John was singularly well equipped to open his own Print Studio.

Renshaw Gallery is located on the campus of Linfield College, McMinnville, Oregon.

Rogue Gallery is the showroom for Rogue Valley Art Association, Medford, Oregon.

Ferdinand Roten Galleries, Baltimore, were, for a generation, one of the most notable influences in the graphics world in this country. Their many traveling educational shows, including the work of Old Masters as well as contemporary American and European printmakers, went out to every college and art center/museum in the U.S. A whole generation was introduced to the pleasures of print collecting through them.

Salishan Lodge is located in Gleneden, Oregon.

Sovereign Gallery is located at 716 SW Madison, Portland, Oregon.

Statewide Services was a long-established educational arm of the University of Oregon Museum, providing fine shows by Oregon artists to downstate art centers and schools.

Tahir Gallery was located in New Orleans from 1966 to 1986. Abe Tahir, the Founder and Director, continues to work as Art Consultant in Metairie, Louisiana, and to serve as Adjunct Curator of Prints and Drawings at New Orleans Museum of Art.

The recent publication "Worldwatcher: Jack McLarty" surveys 50 years of McLarty's life and career as a painter. Now, all of us who admire his graphic art are grateful for the timely publication of this catalog, "A Printmaker's World." Along with "Worldwatcher," it provides an overview of the full range of his creativity.

Born in Seattle, McLarty moved to Portland with his parents at the age of two. The central city has been and remains his operational base.

In 1940 McLarty went to New York for studio classes at the American Artists School and additional work with Anton Refregier and Joseph Solman.

He has found inspiration in the condensation and structure of ideas often used in medieval religious murals. The art of the two Breughels and the fantasies of Hieronymus Bosch continue to interest him. He admires the prints of Daumier and the woodblock prints of 20th century Japanese printmakers, the graphic art of the German Expressionists. He is also much affected by the work of the French Impressionist painters and that of the great Mexicans, Rivera and Orozco.

In 1945 he began a long association with the Museum Art School (now Pacific Northwest College of Art). He served as a teaching assistant to Dean William Givler's lithography classes and worked in the medium himself. He then worked in serigraphy with colleague Louis Bunce. In 1947, he joined the instructional faculty of the school.

During the early fifties he began to make drypoint, intaglio and woodcut prints. And, inspired by Glen Alps (Seattle), he worked in the collograph medium. In 1964, with wife Barbara, he visited France, Italy, Switzerland, and spent time doing some etching in Paris with Paul Franck.

During the summer of 1969 he attended the studio workshop taught at Oregon State University by distinguished Visiting Artist, Junichiro Sekino of Tokyo. In 1978 he worked with another great Japanese printmaker, Akira Kurosaki, this time at Kala Institute, Berkeley. The following year he made his first trip to Japan. Periodic, extended travel in Mexico with Barbara has continued to enrich his visual experience.

Of note is the fact that the history of printmaking in the Western World started with the use of woodcuts as illustrations for books. McLarty has four limited edition collaborative books to his credit, each with relief embossments or woodcuts included. He is a book lover who reads widely and finds in literature a source of great inspiration.

Gordon W. Gilkey
Curator of Prints and Drawings
Portland Art Museum
December 1996

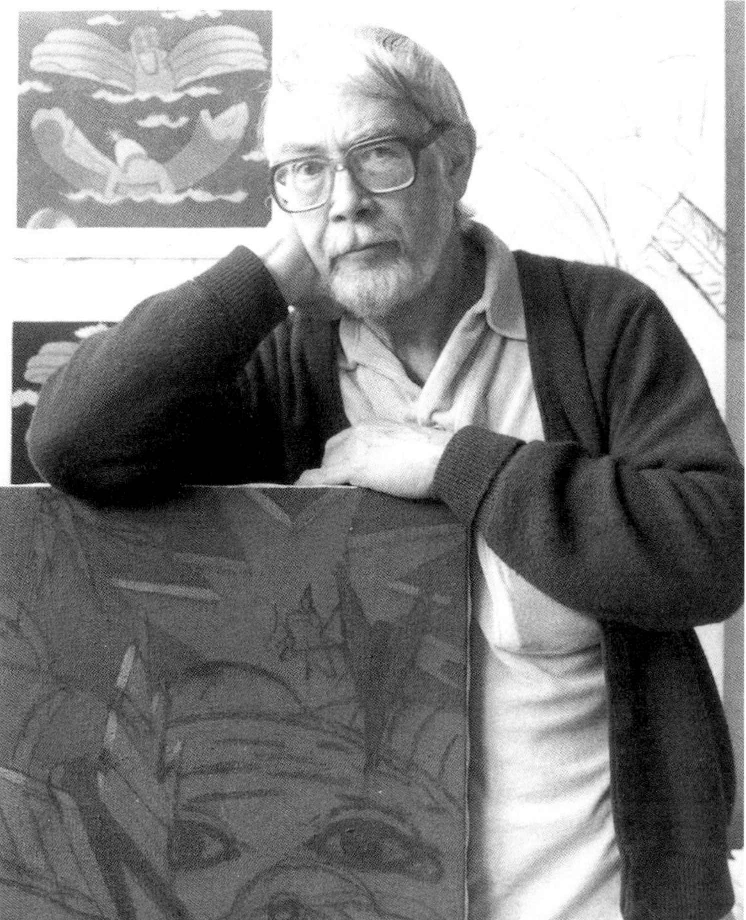

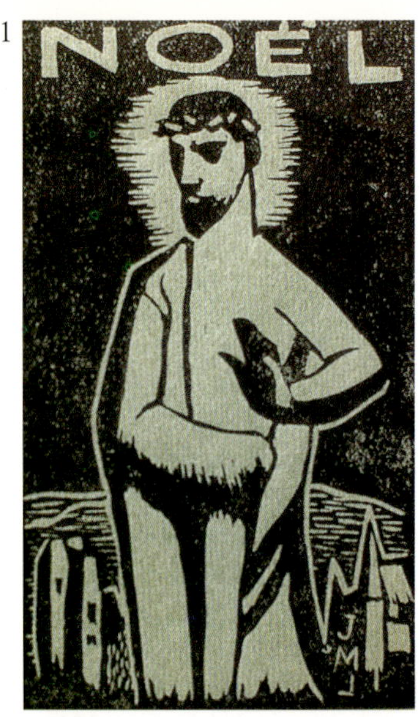

1

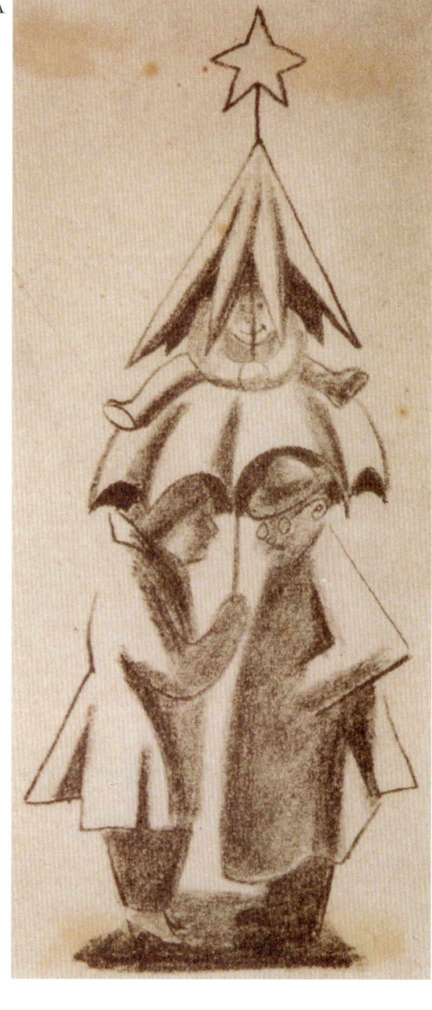

3A

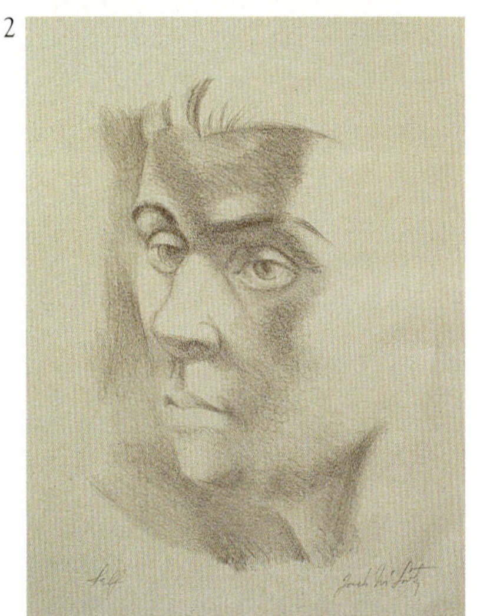

2

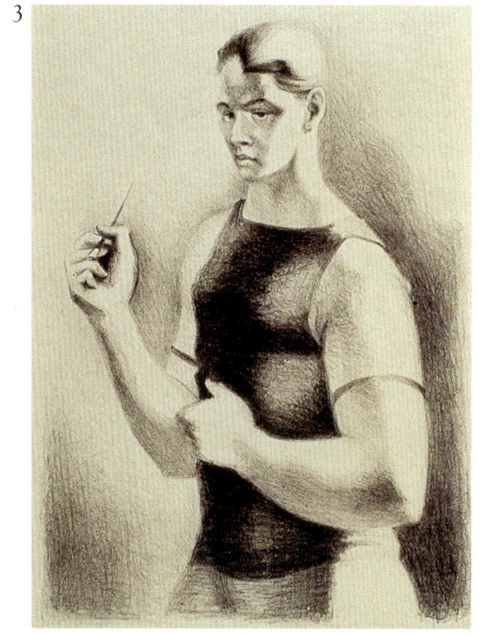

3

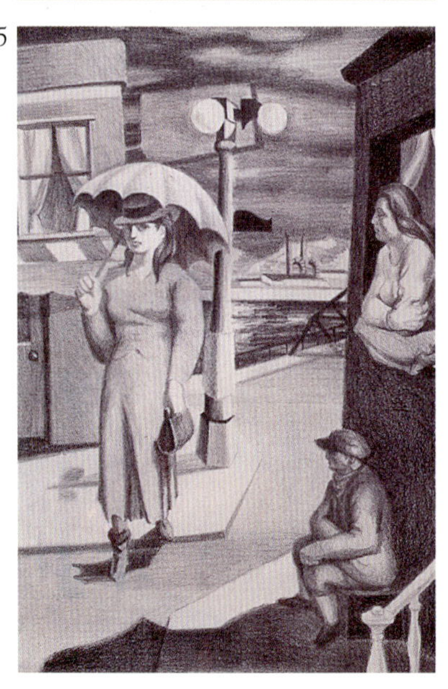

5

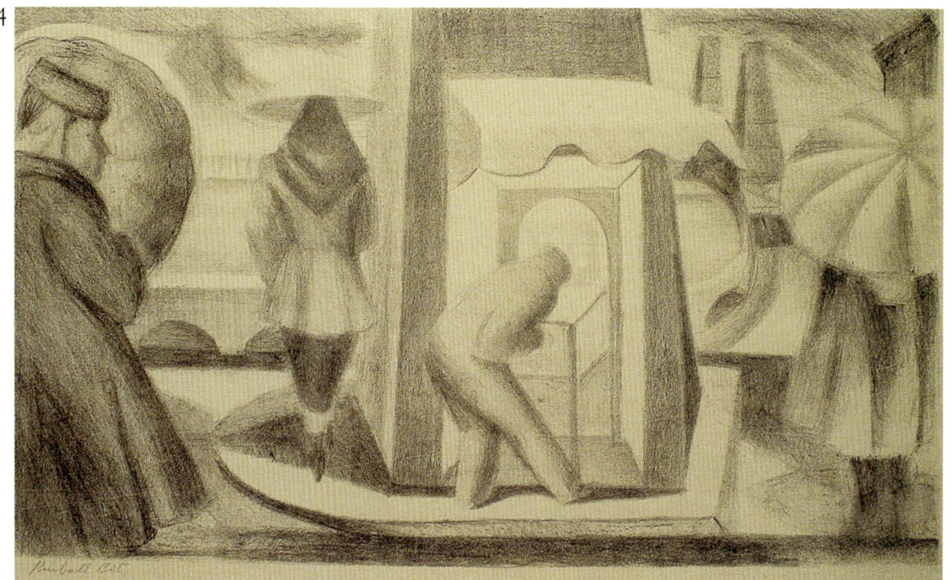

4

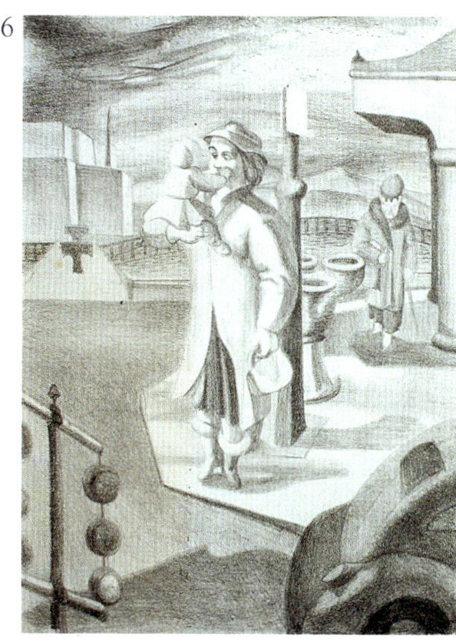

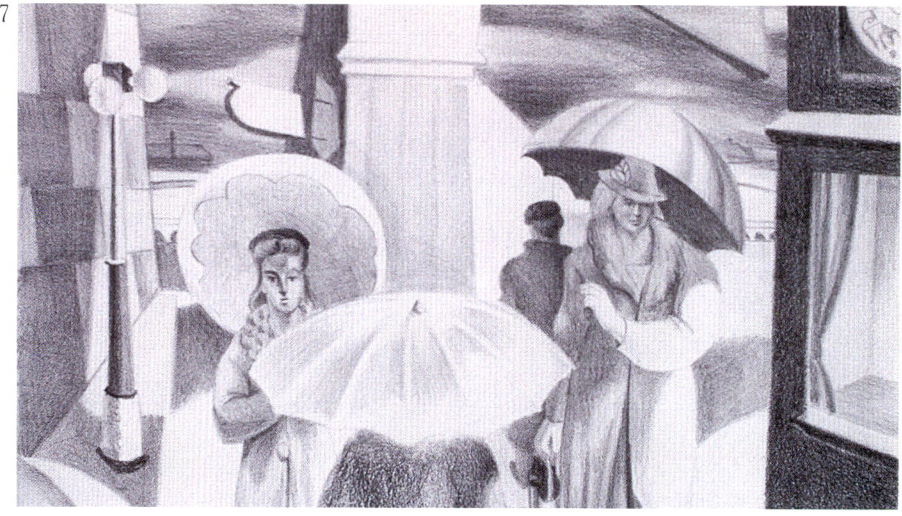

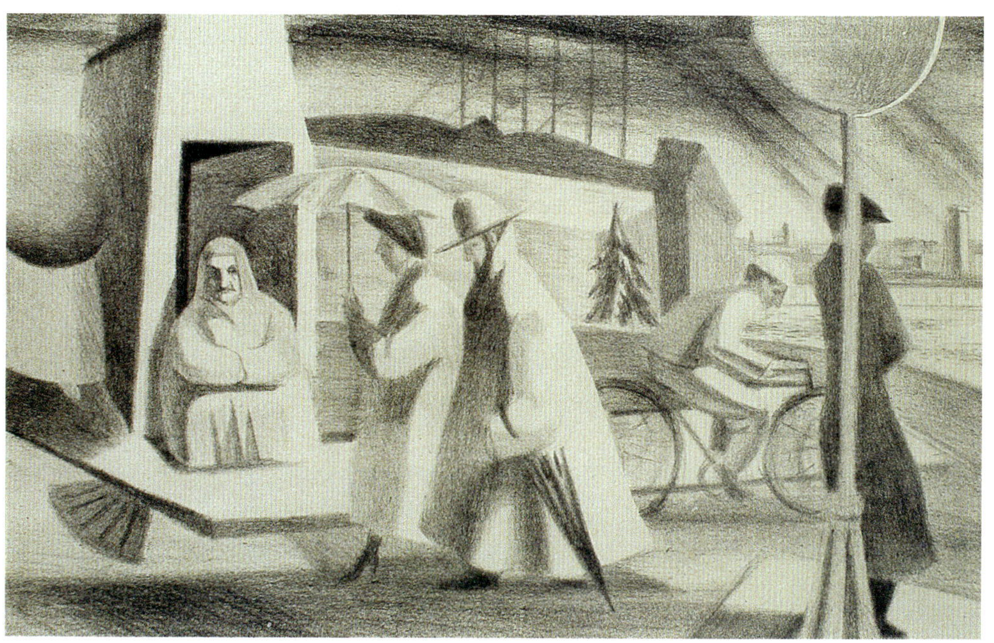

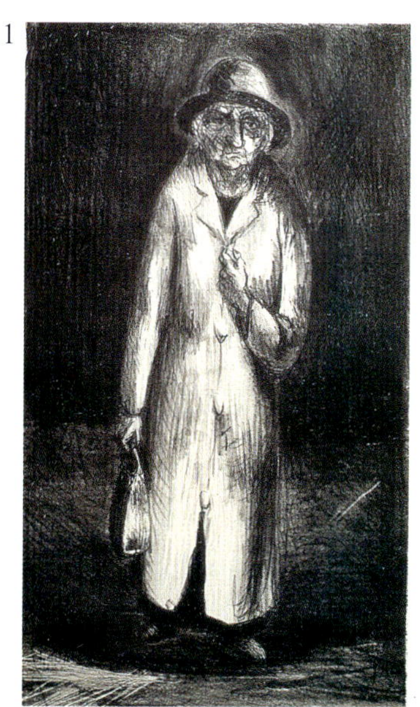

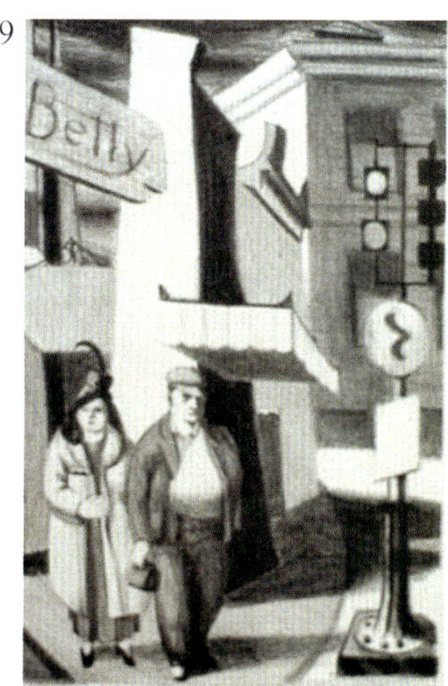

1. Noel (linocut) 1941 5 x 3
2. Self (lithograph) 1942 7¾ x 5
3. Painter (lithograph) 1942 8½ x 6
3A. Christmas Umbrellas (lithograph) 1943 7 x 3¼
4. Pinball City (also titled "City") (lithograph) 1943 9½ x 16
5. Summer (also titled "Portland '43" and "Woman with Umbrella")
   (lithograph) 1944 12 x 9¼
6. Street Corner (lithograph) 1944 13¾ x 10
7. Street (lithograph) 1944 9 x 12
8. Winter (also titled "Night City") (lithograph) 1945 8½ x 13
9. Betty (lithograph) 1945 12 x 9
9A. Christmas Umbrellas (linocut) 1945 6 x 4 (*see page 4*)
10. The Bridge (lithograph) 1946 14¾ x 10 (*see page 5*)
11. Old Woman (lithograph) 1946 17 x 10

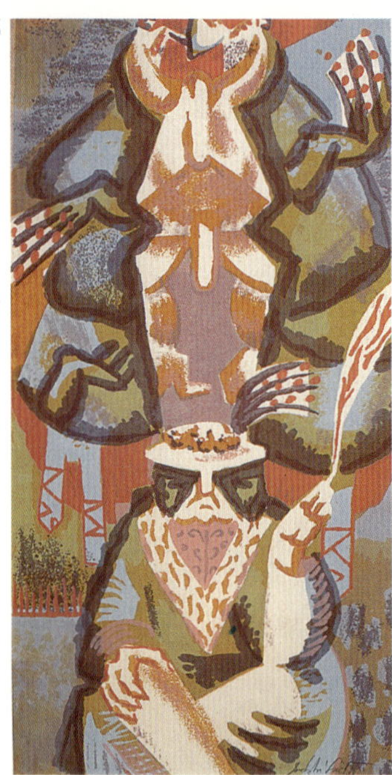

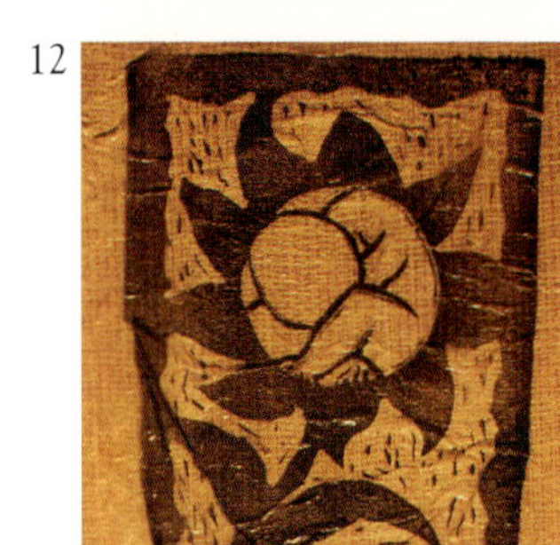

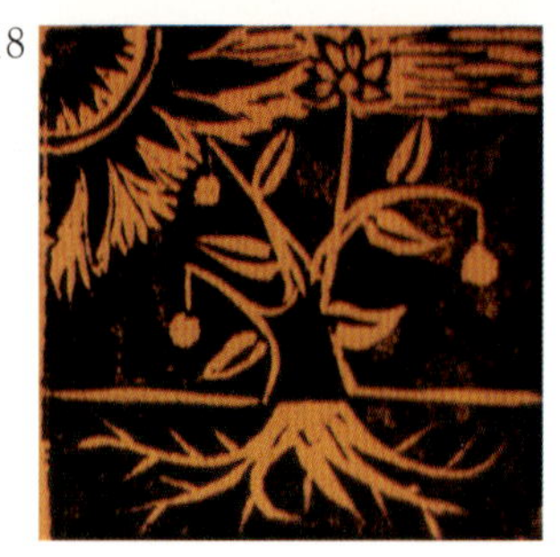

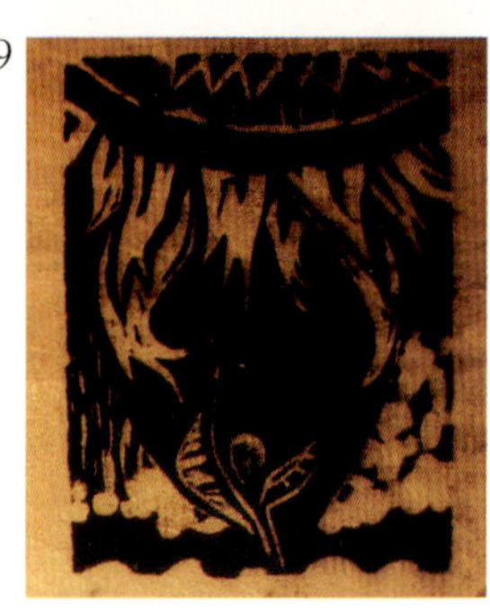

12. Birth Announcement: Polly Harrison McLarty May 1949 (linocut) 4 x 3
13. Polly with a Book (linocut) 1950 2½ x 2¾ (*see page 12*)
14. Rose Parade Rider (also titled "Festival Rider") (serigraph) 1951 16½ x 5¾
15. Old Woman with Turkeys (earlier titled "Turkeys" and "Old Woman") (serigraph) 1951 15½ x 7¾

16. Birds in the Hedge (originally titled "The Hedge") (serigraph) 1952 9¾ x 16
17. Merry-Go-Round (Oaks Park) (woodcut) 1953 9¼ x 18½
18. Birth Announcement: Hugh Jensen McLarty (linocut) June 1953 2 x 2
19. Birth Announcement: Charles Malcolm McLarty March 1955 (linocut) 2 x 1½
20. The Shop (also titled "The Butcher") (woodcut) 1955 12 x 9¼

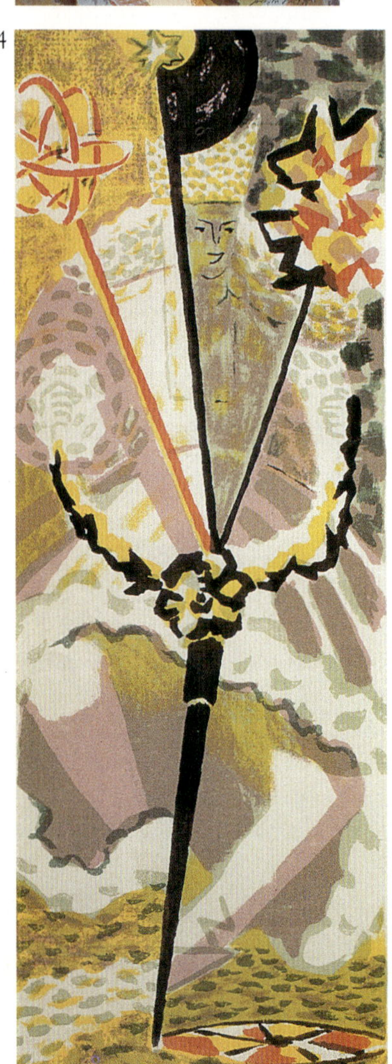

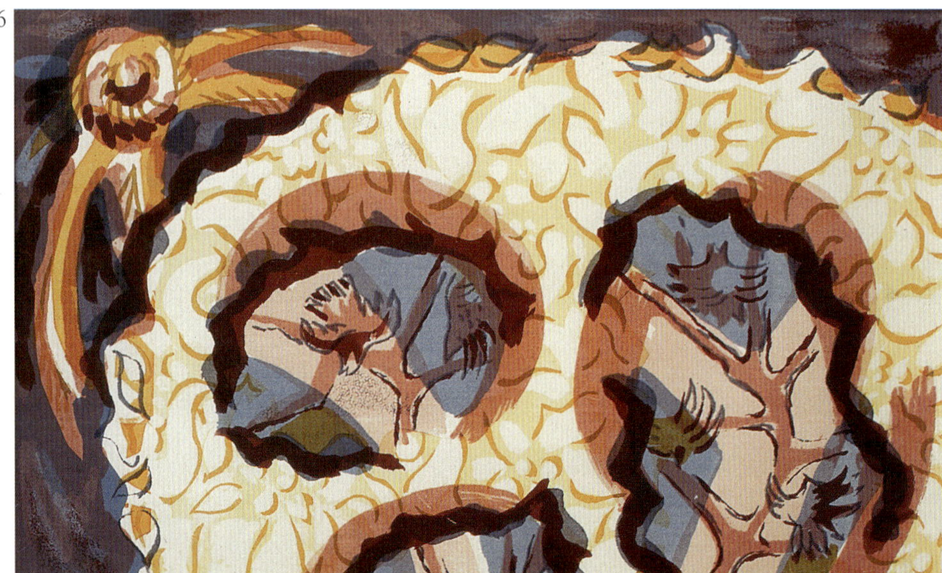

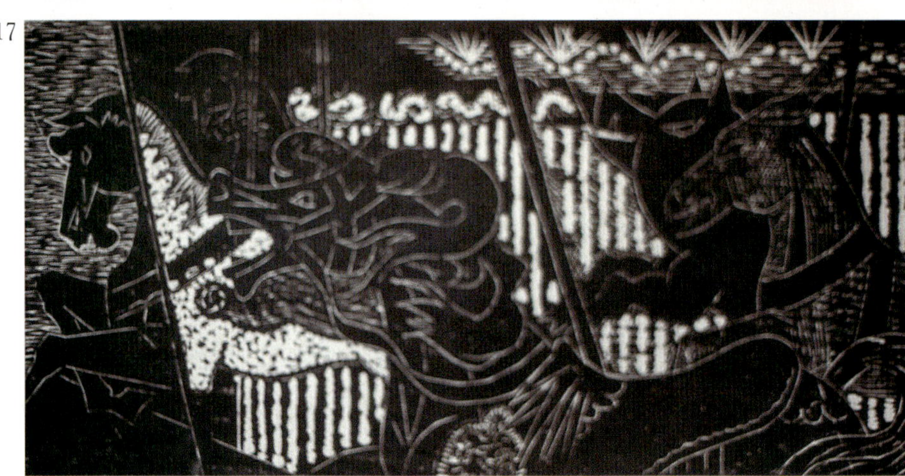

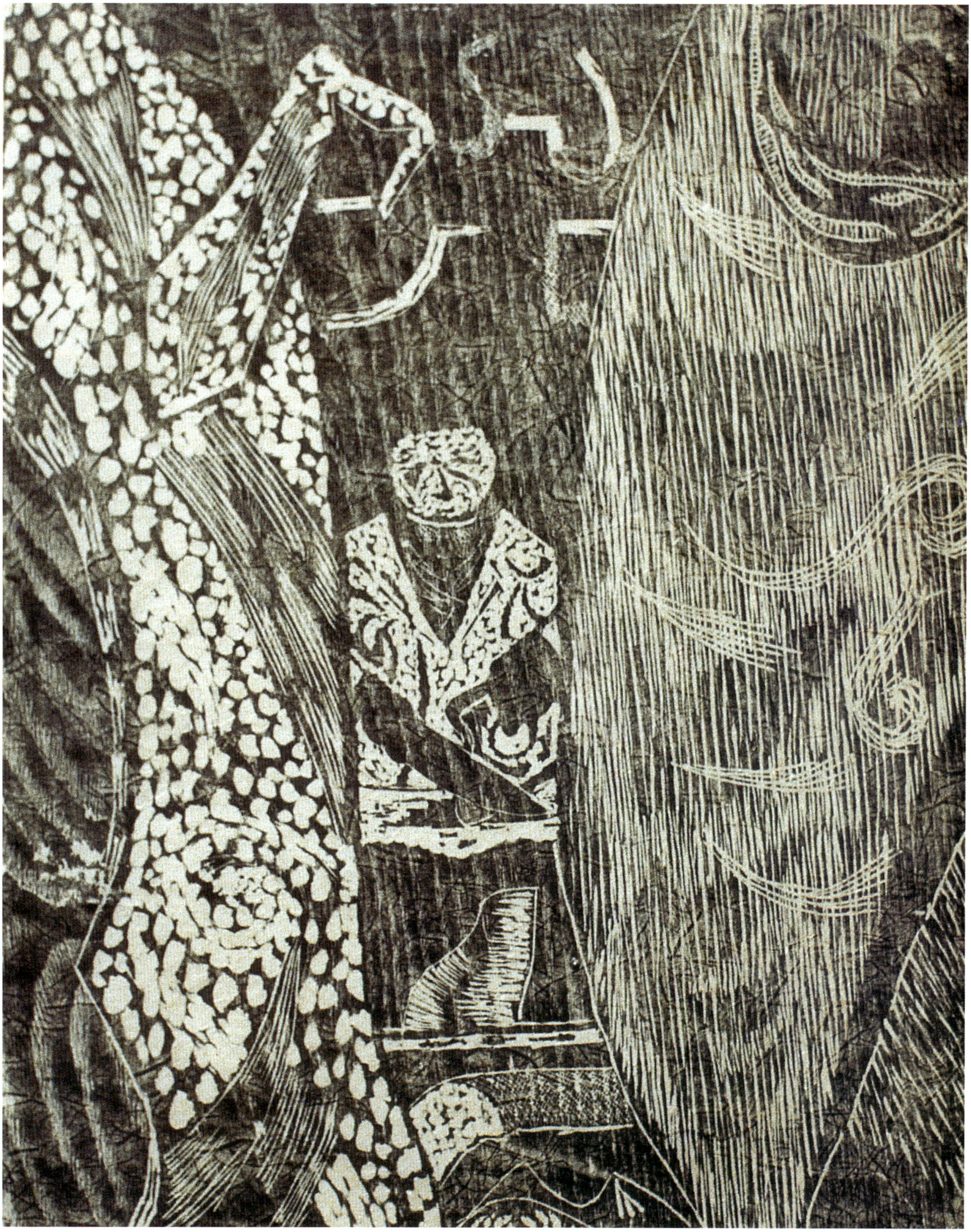

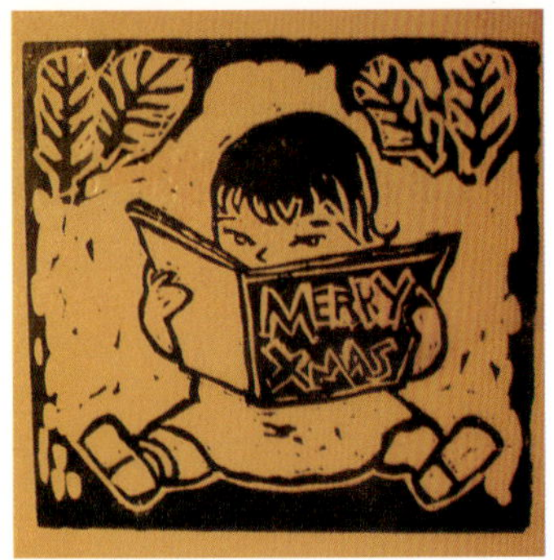

13

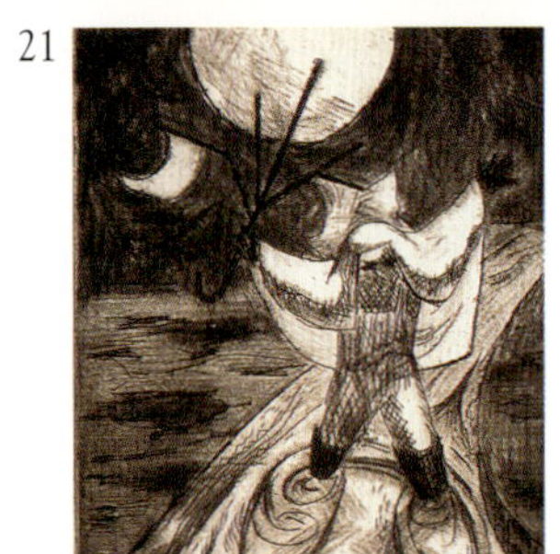

21

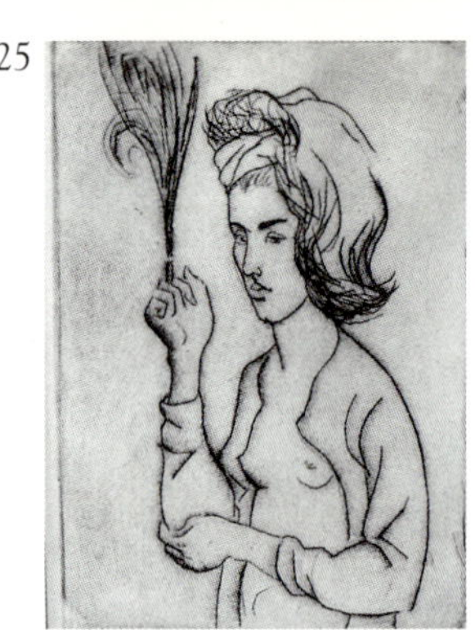

25

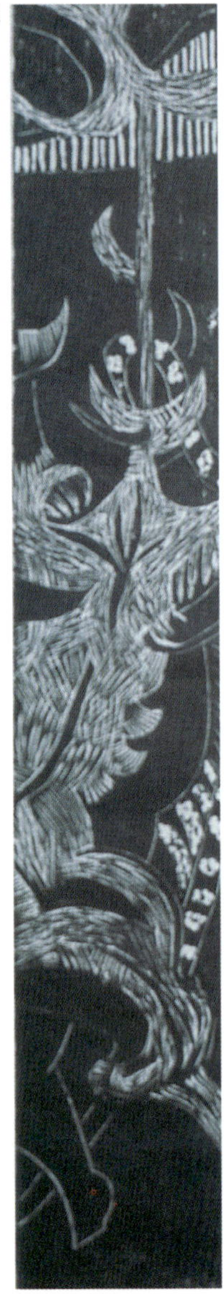

22

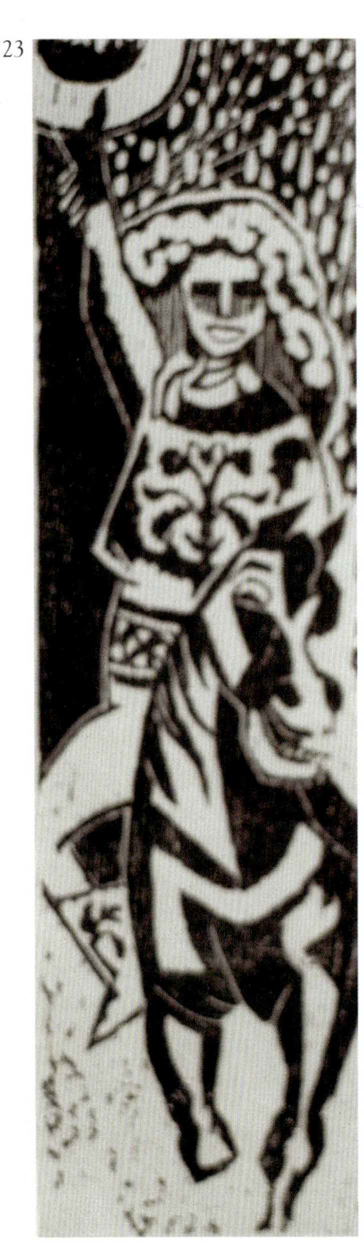

23

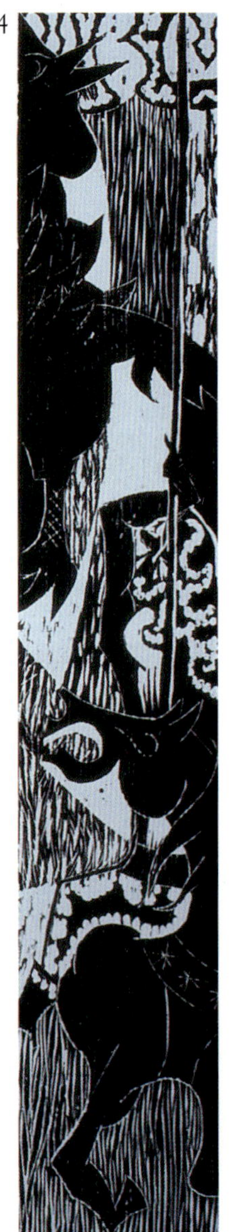

24

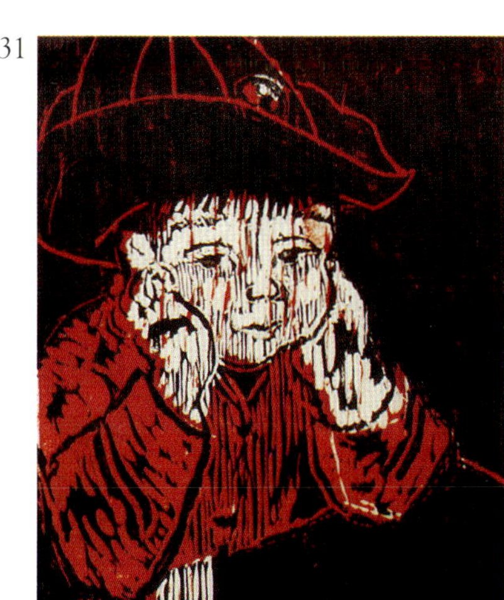

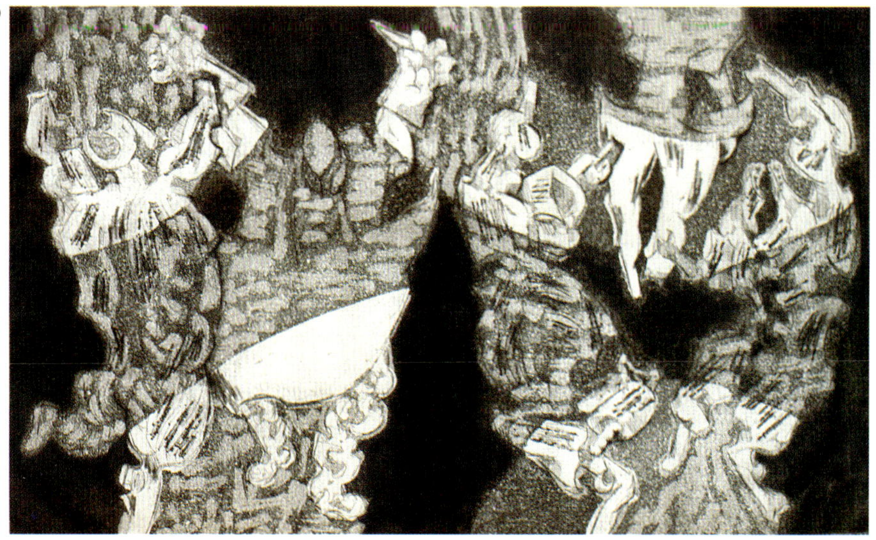

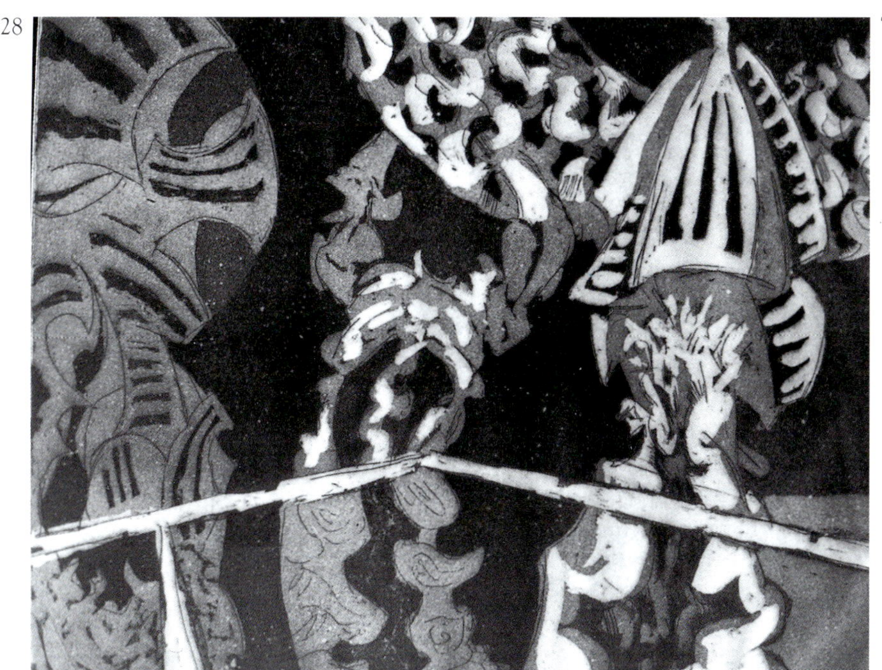

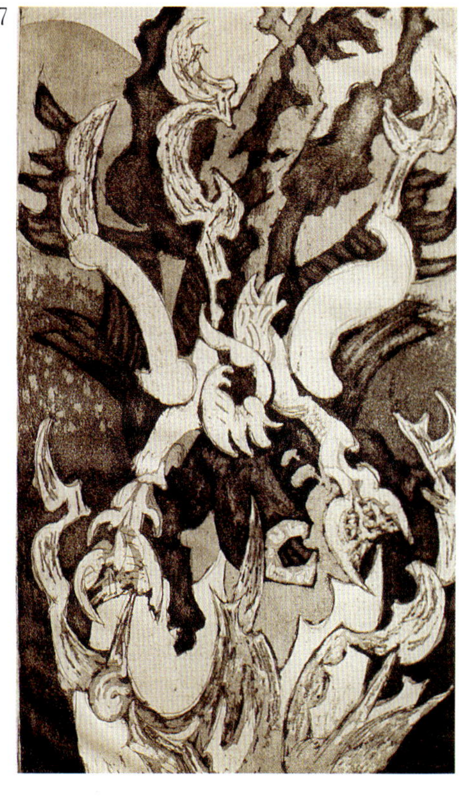

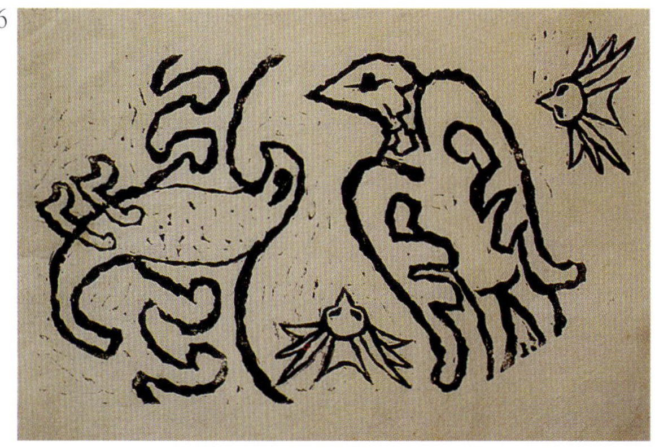

21. King of the River (etching) 1956 6⅜ x 4⅜
22. Beef (woodcut) 1956 18 x 3
23. Rodeo Princess (woodcut) 1956 12¾ x 3½
24. Merry-Go-Round #2 (woodcut) 1956 20¼ x 3½
25. Barbara (drypoint) 1956 7 x 5
26. The Birds (linocut) 1956 6 x 9
27. Persephone (aquatint) 1957 15 x 8¾
28. The Market (originally titled "Butcher Shop") (aquatint) 1957
    9 x 11½
29. Butchers' Ball (aquatint) 1957 9 x 14¾
30. Rodeo (woodcut) 1958 16 x 12 (*see page 19*)
31. Hughie (color woodcut) 1958 7¾ x 6

My great interest and love of prints is based on the print tradition as a popular art medium. Most of the print processes started as ways to produce cheap copies that could be sold at reasonable prices. This is still true—and it makes art, *sometimes great art*, available to almost anyone perceptive enough to make good choices.

I like the fact that prints put art on a taste basis rather than on a money basis (emphasis added). I love the fact that I can touch something (with clean hands) that Goya, Toyokuni or Baskin made with his own hands. But we don't need to touch a work of art to be touched by it. Art speaks to us across time and race and religion and culture. It helps to bring the human race a sense of community.

One of the great pleasures of printmaking is the social aspect. Prints are mostly modestly priced so they enter many more homes and collections than paintings do. They become part of someone's visual life. They are truly a piece of the artist's mind and feelings, so they set up a social conversation. They become a part of other minds and continue into the future of other lives. They are seldom thrown away if they are really art. They are sold (a way of recycling them), given to friends and schools and museums. They become a part of the world mind and world culture. Quite something for a modest work of art!

Prints are a way to talk with other people of whatever color or class or economic level. That is why I love them and sell them as reasonably as possible.

One of the problems in doing a catalog (like this one) is tracking down edition sizes, etc. The whole attitude of "collectors" has to do with money. Limited editions, full sheets, hand-torn paper, archival papers, have nothing to do with the voice of the print. Because I dislike this attitude, I have never made prints with a "precious" intention but have made them and printed them solely to connect, to talk—to others. I love the printmakers who made lots of prints and/or printed many of them: Daumier and Piranesi, Goya and Chagall, Watanabe and many of the old and modern Japanese artists and Mexican artists. I've enjoyed conversations with all of them immensely. *They have so much to say, and I have tried to talk back.*

So I have been casual about edition numbers, the number of artists proofs, with records of where they were shown and where they traveled. I apologize for this but believe I would do it the same way next time. Usually, whenever a print edition of 40 or more is indicated, it can be assumed that the actual number of impressions pulled would number no more than 25. The only exception, and these are clearly indicated, would be for a Special Edition.

PRINTMAKING TECHNIQUES AND
THE WAY I APPROACHED EACH METHOD

The common term for printing in the printmaking world is "pulling a print" or "pulling an exhibition." I'm not sure where this expression comes from, but probably from the act of pulling up on the paper after the print is, in fact, printed. The paper is lifted carefully from one end to avoid smearing the wet ink.

My first prints were lithographs. After two years as an art student in New York, I returned to Portland. I worked a year in the shipyards at the end of World War II. Bill Givler offered me a chance to teach in the Children's Classes, paint a mural for Laurelhurst School, and help to print lithographs in the night school classes. Wonderful!

I had been doing paintings of the city, and I began doing lithos in a carefully drawn and graded tonal style. Litho crayons come in several degrees of tone and can be very gradually graded through a long range of greys to blacks. The limestone surface was like a very fine sandpaper and was a lovely light grey color. The litho stones were thick and often had been used for years. Some had wonderful old designs and lettering left from when they were used to print stocks, bonds and certificates, etc. Each had to be ground with a series of carborundum granules (from coarse to fine) until the old image was removed. The stone was then ready to use again.

How anyone ever discovered the complex process of printing lithographs still astounds me. A lot of divine tinkering had to go on. The crayons have a grease content. The drawing on the stone is coated with a resist film. The drawing color is washed out. The grease remains. The film is removed. The stone surface is kept wet. The ink roller is rolled over the surface and the ink adheres to the rest of the wet stone. The paper is damp. Well, you get the idea. A tricky and difficult medium. Beautiful and cranky and capable of an enormous range of effects. In the hands of a very skilled printer or artist, of course! It is a medium that many artists love for its challenge as well as for its rewards.

The series of lithos that Bill Givler has produced over his lifetime is certainly one of the major art statements about this Oregon Country. Mostly in black and white and greys, they express a love of nature . . . the beaches and mountains, and the people—small in this natural world! Oregon before all the cars and houses and telephone poles. Windswept clouds, dark lakes and deep forests. No one else that I know has made a comparable statement about our State in our time.

WOODCUT

After doing a series of city scenes (lithographs), I ran into a series of disasters. A drawing I had worked on a long time turned black on the stone because I failed to keep the stone surface wet enough while printing. (Black as in gloom!) Next I lost two more prints when earlier images on the stone rose up and came through my drawings. All of this was my own fault, but it discouraged me. At the time, I was helping to print editions for the lithography students in night classes, and I found that I was printing for others and not getting my own lithographs done.

Time to try something else. *While technique interests me (and I am quite competent), it is not my main concern. What I want to say as an artist is the main thing.* As a lithographer, I made some technical messes, but I was to find ways to make woodcut difficult, too.

Woodcut is simple, in its simplest form. Even there, my choice of wood made the whole enterprise very difficult at first—hard is a better word. I chose, out of love, to try to cut oak planks. I fell for the greys that the open grain of oak wood will produce when printed. So I could not get deep blacks. Worse than that, I could hardly cut the stuff with the woodcut tools.

"Merry-Go-Round" (from Oaks Park). Was that a subconscious choice? And a series of butcher shops and a rodeo came out of this series of blocks. I still love the greys and their light and air tones.

WOODENGRAVING

After squashing some small zinc plate etchings, I decided to return to woodcut. I had intended to use the etchings for a book with poetry, *17 Love Poems.* The woodcuts I made for the book were small. Somehow, Baskin and woodengraving put me to thinking how appropriate this scale of print was with type size.

I taught myself, very badly, and mostly from books. The old woodengravers seemed quite incredible to me and still do. Most of the commercial engravers were fantastic craftsmen but not artists at all. The English engravers were either academic or over-stylized and empty. Blake was not so good as a craftsman and much better as an artist. He managed to make monumental pictures in very small engravings. This reminds me of Charles Heaney. Heaney painted vast landscapes in very small pictures.

ETCHING

I made quite a few etchings and liked this medium also for the drawing and tone quality. Worked in Paris one summer with a Belgian named Franck. He liked a strong etch solution—half water, half acid. The etch pan smoked when he put the plate in. He had a friend's press that he was using. This press, well, except for a steel roller, was just like the press I had seen in Rembrandt's house in Amsterdam! Franck's studio was in a group of old, frame buildings where Modigliani had had his studio. His girl friend's father had been a friend of Modigliani and had tried to paint like him. Terrible paintings, though!

Originally I learned etching from Bill Givler, and I did my best work in this medium in night classes on the Museum Art School press.

COLLOGRAPH

Glen Alps probably got me into this. At the time, a new printmaking medium. Not like monotypes these days, for that was an old medium renewed and not really prints anyway, but painting on a press.

Collographs are like collages that are inked and printed. Usually, a heavy cardboard plate with all sorts of things glued on the surface. I used ground walnut shells, sandpaper, etc., and mainly glue. I found that the glue, in one or several layers, gave me a range of tones. I liked it very much but found that the press squashed the plates rapidly and thoroughly.

SILKSCREEN AND SERIGRAPH

The same thing, but because, like most print media, silkscreen was used for a great deal of commercial work, the artists wanted to change that reference.

Serigraphy developed as a print medium during WPA days. The first artist's group was formed in New York, and Louis Bunce was an early member. He was doing serigraphs before I met him and roomed in the Bunce flat in New York. I had no interest in the medium at that time, and it was only later, back in Portland, that I attended a night class of Louis' and produced a few silkscreen prints. What I remember most was mixing one can after another, trying to get the color right, and ending with buckets of useless ink—the wrong color.

HANGA (COLOR WOODCUT)

Long admiration for the Japanese traditional block prints, and then the modern Japanese extension of the woodcut technique brought me to study first with Sekino and then with Kurosaki. The pleasure of learning an ancient craft and its renewal as a contemporary art form is hard to explain. Painting—the Western world thinks oil, the Oriental world thinks water. The same is true of printmaking. Everything is as different as forks are from chopsticks. An old craft grows and becomes complex in all its parts. Ink, paper, tools, printing—all must be learned all over again. Like learning a foreign language. Kurosaki's imagery was highly attractive to me, and he is also a superb technician and modern experimenter.

I learned so much about Japanese printmaking and the history of the exchanges with European art. The reason Japanese printmaking was not practiced and could not be practiced in the West was due to the lack of correct supplies. Even today such supplies are available in only a few places (and Portland is one of them, with McClain's). Paper (it's not rice paper), brushes (not rollers), blocks (they are not construction plywood), and, of course, one must know how to use them.

If I left this technique to return eventually to my old woodblock ways, it was only because I felt it suited what I had to say better. Harsher, sharper, and with a kind of bite—harder to get in a subtle, delicate and fluid system.

I left that world with considerable regret but with immense gratitude for what it taught me and for the enormous pleasure it gave me.

November 1996

FINE ART: THE CURRENT SITUATION

Jack McLarty

Oregon Higher Education, Vol. I, No. 3, Spring 1958

Recently the *Oregonian* ran an editorial on the death of Diego Rivera. The editor praised Rivera's accomplishments as an artist and forgave him for being a communist. . . . But in trying to make a further point, about how well-treated the artist is in the free world, the editor raises quite another issue. "Words are not required to delineate the chasm that exists between the treatment of the creative artists under communism and in the free world, respectively," says the editorial.

How is the artist treated in the *free world* (emphasis added)? Is this chasm so big and deep as it sounds? *Freedom of expression* is what the artist has in this country, but he has practically nothing else. Is he kept from working? No, but he cannot make a living at art so he must "work" at something else. This other job may leave him some time to play around at art after he gets through work.

. . . Sometimes, in the past, I have thought that [the] line between commercial and fine art was breaking down. I have thought that good design was showing up in everything from billboards to chairs. Yet, the truth is that *if good design sells, it is used; but, if bad design sells, it replaces good design.* So we see cars and clothes that are well-designed replaced by those that are badly designed simply to out-date the earlier models.

The sales of reproductions of old and modern masters is another encouraging sign. Or is it? Do those prints that intelligent and educated people buy simply take the place of original paintings? Is anything safer, indeed more conservative, than buying a Picasso or Van Gogh reproduction?

And what about amateur art? That enormous interest in "do-it-yourself" painting and sculpture has increased the business (and the profit) of art supply dealers everywhere. But how has it affected the professional artist? These people who paint for fun or for therapy somehow get the idea that *they are artists* (emphasis added). They put their own pictures on their own walls. Eisenhower and Churchill have both contributed to this folly, yet neither seems to have any real interest in art. *Relaxation is not art* (emphasis added). The real artist is doing just the opposite. He is working as hard and as seriously as he possibly can.

The idea that art should be entertaining is just a part of our overall focus on entertainment itself. We have come far from the basic ideas of clothes and houses to keep us warm, transportation to get us from one place to another, and food to keep us alive. We have "progressed" into an entertainment culture far greater in scope than we like to admit. Our cars have extra chrome, extra lights, extra heaters, extra speed, extra size. *This is waste on a grand scale* and it means that our cars are a major entertainment, like our expensive TV sets, cameras. . . . Filling up the public's time has become very profitable, and industry makes every effort to see that we do not get a quiet hour to ourselves.

A very small fraction of this activity and this material is of any real value. What percentage of television, radio, movies, magazine or newspaper material is worth remembering or retaining? Should we say 5%? And can minds filled with 95% nonsense be expected to look at, listen to, or think about anything with more substance?

There is still a great deal of lip service being paid to the arts, and many people sense that radio, television and the movies do not take the place of art. *Why accept the artist and reject the art?* (emphasis added) In this richest country in the world, it seems that people can find money for everything except art. And does this not reflect the teaching situation? Do our teachers, themselves, consider art important? Most parents want their children to "get a little art," but art is not something to be added on if one has the time or money for it. Art extends its influence all up and down our culture. If we accept the bad taste and bad design of tract houses, of cars, of most clothes, of middle class magazine literature and illustrations, of Walt Disney's various productions, then we acknowledge our bad taste on many levels. Many of our schools have art rooms and art teachers but, again, no art. There are no original paintings or sculpture by professional artists in the classrooms, in the corridors, or on the walls outside. Has the "learning by doing" drifted into "busy work" and therapy, on the one hand, and "anyone can paint," on the other?

How would today's students react to a straight art history course? Would they learn more about art, more respect for the past? It wouldn't be as much fun, of course, and they wouldn't have the false illusion that they, too, are artists. Does not the concentration on contemporary design give the students a very nearsighted idea of who and what they are in relation to history?

These questions arise from the central fact that art and artists today are dislocated. Why they are and what is to be done about it are the problems. Are artists worth worrying about? And, are the things they reject in our society worth rejection? Are the values for which they stand worth retaining? It is certain that the artist gives up many things that most Americans can see no reason for giving up. If his values are worthy of support, it is because he stands for ideas that are basic to man. The way to understand art is to understand that it puts beauty and integrity before disorder and falsehood, love and emotion before cruelty and machinery. This is not a matter of style, nor is it a matter of skill. It is not what any individual picture means.

It is important to recognize that if we accept commercial art, we accept its values, and if we reject or fail to support the fine arts, we reject the values they stand for. This is what should concern us and make us reconsider our current situation. . . .

CATALOGS/BROCHURES, EXHIBITIONS AND MUSEUMS:

Eugene, Oregon. University of Oregon Museum of Art. *Pacific Northwest Art, The Haseltine Collection.* Initial showing of the Collection. December 1–31, 1963.

Eugene. Erb Memorial Student Union, University of Oregon. *Fourth Pacific Northwest Art Annual.* A print invitational. April 21–May 24, 1964.

Eugene. Maude Kerns Art Center. *1st Annual Printmakers in Oregon Invitational.* 1965.

Eugene. Erb Memorial Student Union, University of Oregon. *Ninth Pacific Northwest Art Annual.* An invitational show that includes printmakers. April 21–May 16, 1969.

Eugene. University of Oregon Museum of Art. *Statewide Services Traveling Exhibitions for 1971–72* and *Prospectus Supplement for 1973–74.*

Eugene. Statewide Art Services of the University of Oregon Museum of Art/The American Revolution Bicentennial Commission of Oregon/The Oregon Arts Commission. *The Bicentennial Exhibition of Oregon Artists, General Exhibition.* January 1976 to December 1977.

Eugene. Maude Kerns Art Center. *Jack McLarty: Early and Late, A Survey of Drawings, Paintings and Prints (1943–1986).* July 11–August 1, 1986

Forest Grove, Oregon. Cawein Gallery, Pacific University. *Jack McLarty, Retrospective Exhibit of Printmaking and Selected Paintings.* September 1–30, 1985

Hilo, Hawaii. University of Hawaii. *Northwest Print Council Invitational.* December–January 1994–95.

Indianapolis, Indiana. John Herron Art Museum. *American Prints Today.* March 17–April 21, 1946

McMinnville, Oregon. Renshaw Gallery, Linfield College. *Jack McLarty, 50-year Retrospective, the Collection of Mayo Rae Rolph Roy.* April 5–30, 1993

New York, New York. Pratt Graphic Art Center. *1st International Miniature Print Exhibition.* Shown in New York City, the show then travels the U.S. for two years, 1964–65.

New York. Pratt Graphic Art Center. *2nd International Miniature Print Exhibition.* Shown in New York City, it travels the U.S. for two years, 1966–67.

New York. American Institute of Graphic Arts. Catalog of the annual AIGA Book Show, 1977.

Portland, Oregon. Portland Art Museum. *Prints by Oregon Artists 1952.* November 18, 1952–January 4, 1953.

Portland. Image Gallery brochure/catalog. *Prints by Jack McLarty 1943–1972.* February 2–March 2, 1972.

Portland. First National Center. Catalog of the Collection of 1st Interstate Bank. Circa 1975.

Portland. Portland Art Museum. *The Process of Woodcut & Woodengraving.* 1976

Portland. Image Gallery brochure/catalog. *Recent Paintings, Woodcuts & Woodengravings by Jack McLarty.* March 2–May 16, 1980.

Portland. Portland Art Museum. *Northwest Prints '82.* The inaugural exhibition of the Northwest Print Council. October 12–November 21, 1982.

Portland. Portland State University. *Sapporo-Portland Print Exhibition.* An exchange show with the Sister City, Sapporo, Japan. November 17–December 3, 1984.

Portland. Portland Art Museum. *Western States Print Invitational.* July 23–September 15, 1985.

Portland. Northwest Print Council/Oregon Arts Commission. *Forty Oregon Printmakers.* A catalog of limited edition prints. Summer 1988.

Portland. Northwest Print Council. *The Art of Printmaking.* A handbook for the serious print collector. 1990.

Portland. Image Gallery brochure/catalog. *Jack McLarty: Recent Paintings and Selected Prints (1974–1990).* May 5–June 1, 1991.

Portland. Northwest Print Council/Friends of the Gilkey Center. *101 Prints.* A major benefit for the two organizations. April 2, 1993.

Portland. McLartys' Choice. *World Watcher: Jack McLarty 1943–1993.* Summer 1995.

Portland. Sovereign Collection brochure/catalog. *Revisiting the Fifties: Jack McLarty.* June 1–July 31, 1996.

Salem, Oregon. Bush Barn Gallery. Salem Art Association. *Sixth Annual Printmakers in Oregon Invitational.* 1971.

Salem. Oregon Arts Commission. *Art for People with More Taste than Money.* A traveling exhibition. 1976.

Salem. Salem Art Association. A. N. Bush Gallery. *Then and Now.* An Exhibition of work by artists represented in the Permanent Collection. August 12–September 12, 1993.

San Francisco. San Francisco Art Museum. *10th Annual Drawing and Print Exhibition.* San Francisco Art Association. February 1946.

Seattle, Washington. Seattle Art Museum. *15th Annual Exhibition of Northwest Printmakers.* April 7–March 9, 1943.

Seattle. Henry Gallery, University of Washington. *Northwest Print Exhibition.* 1958.

Seattle. Seattle Art Museum. *34th Annual Northwest Printmakers Exhibition.* 1963.

Seattle. Seattle Art Museum. *35th Annual Northwest Printmakers International Exhibition.* 1964.

Seattle. Henry Gallery, University of Washington. *Northwest Printmakers Exhibition.* 1966.

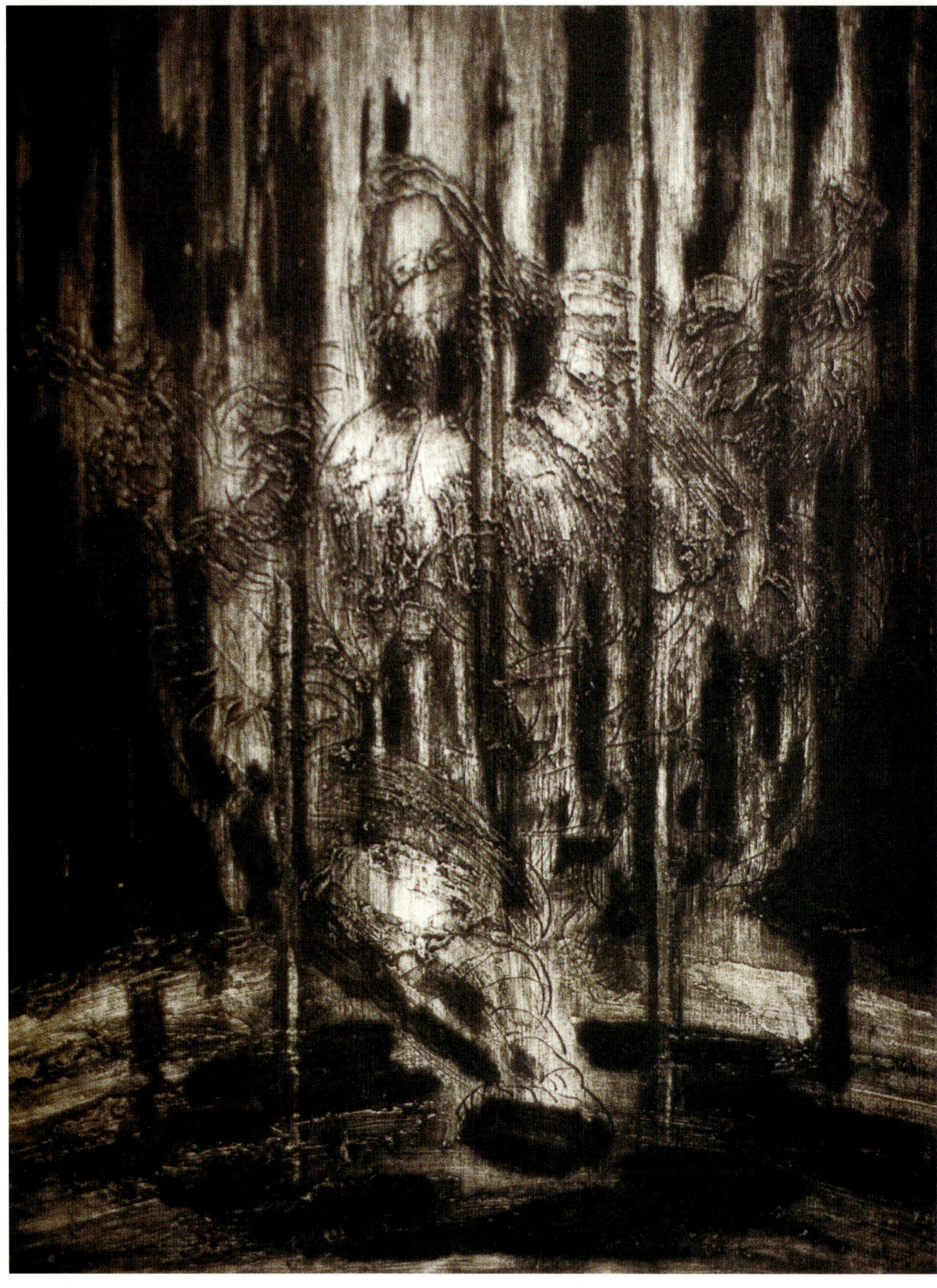

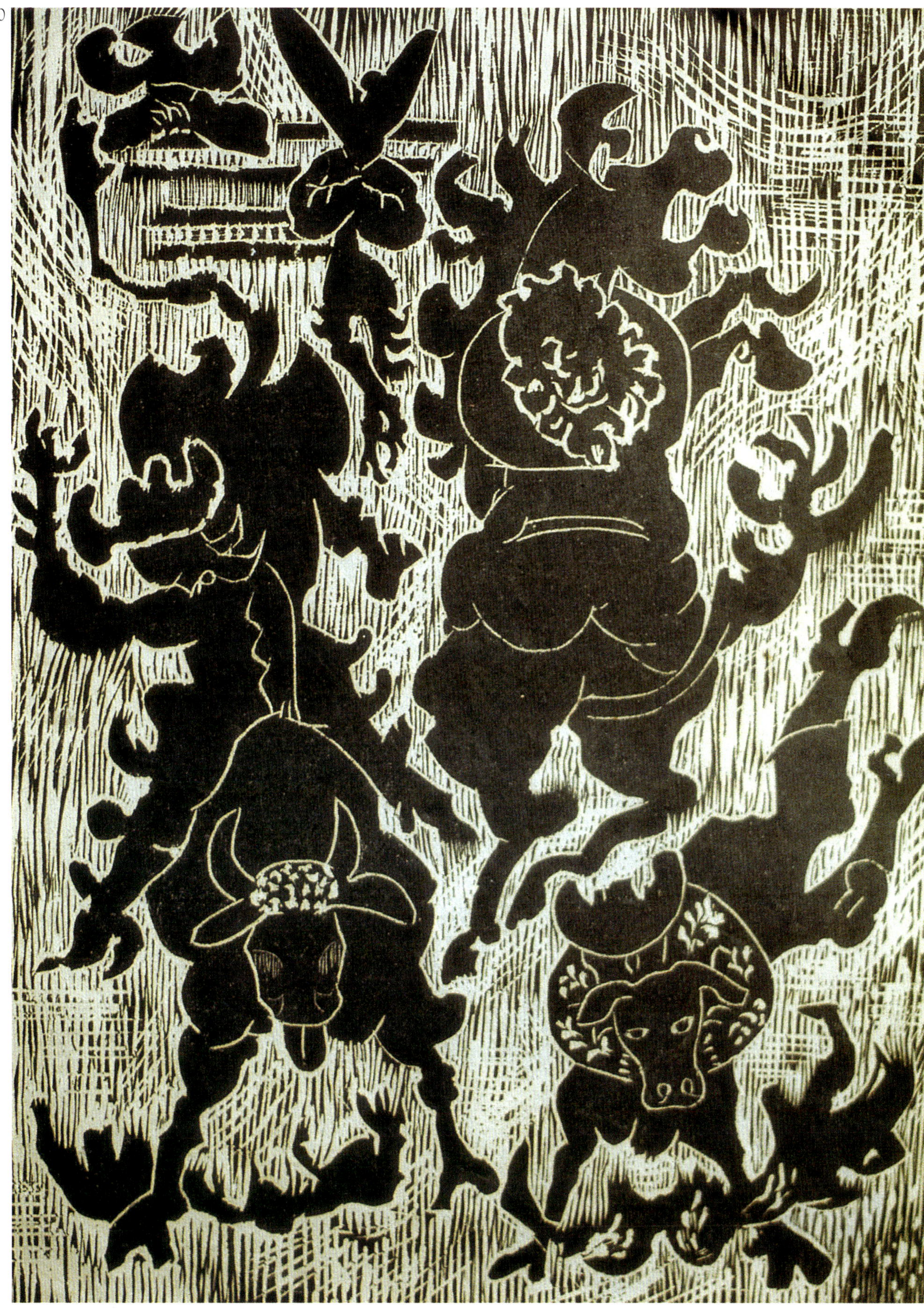

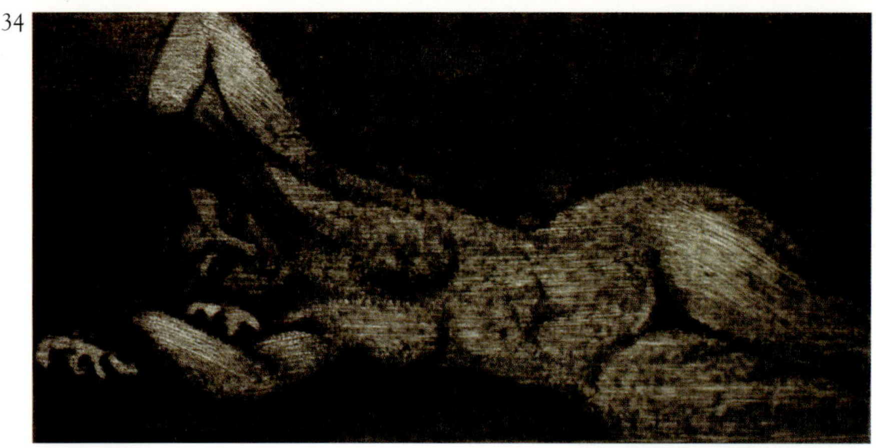

34

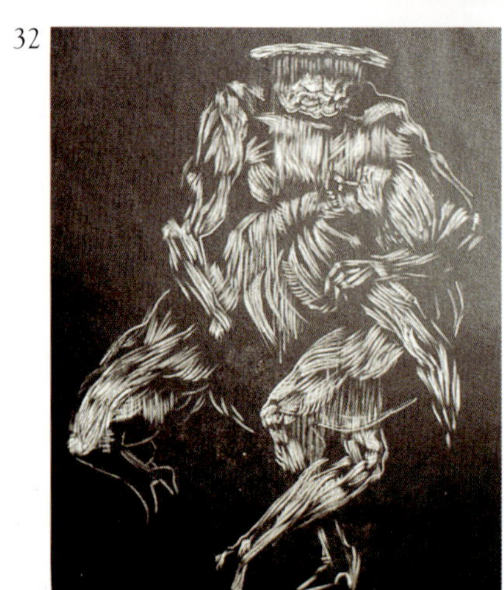

32

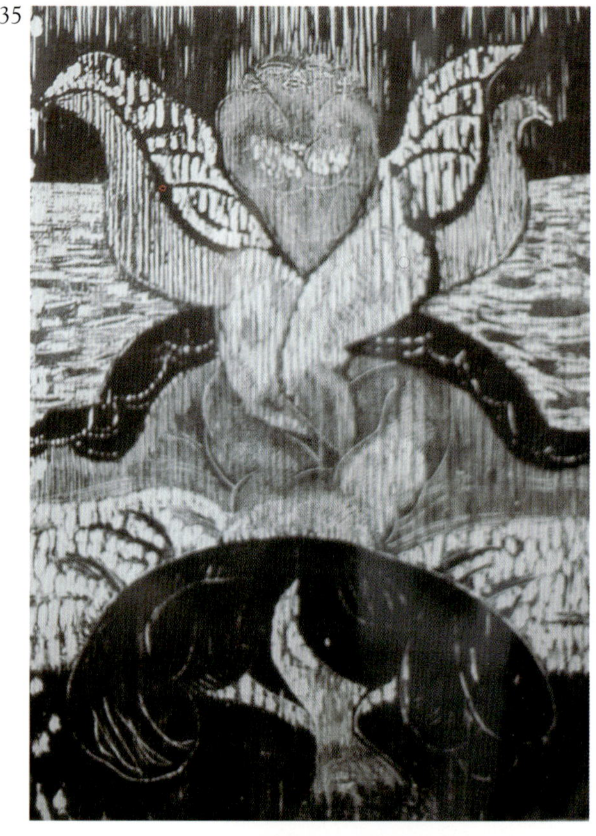

35

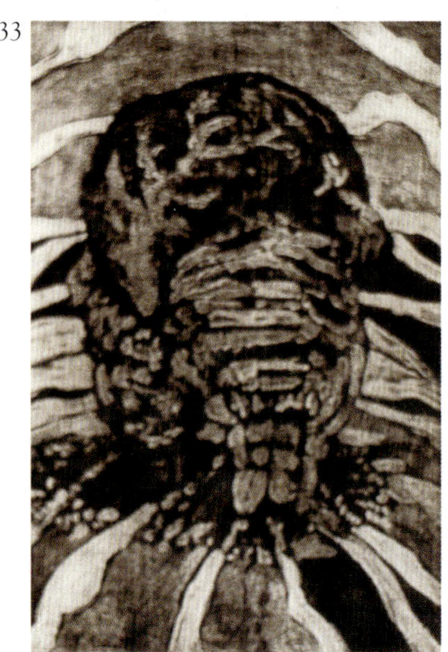

33

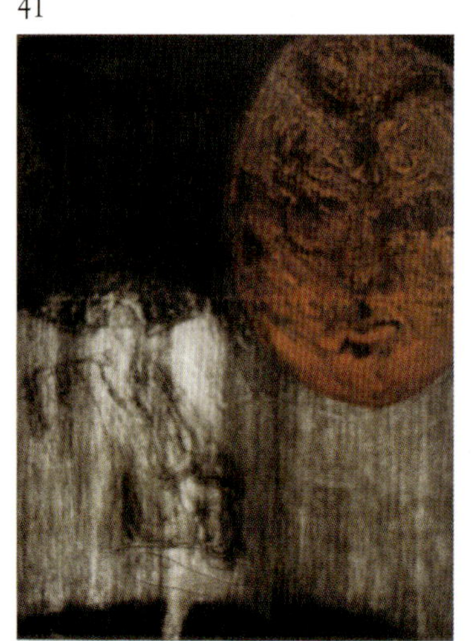

41

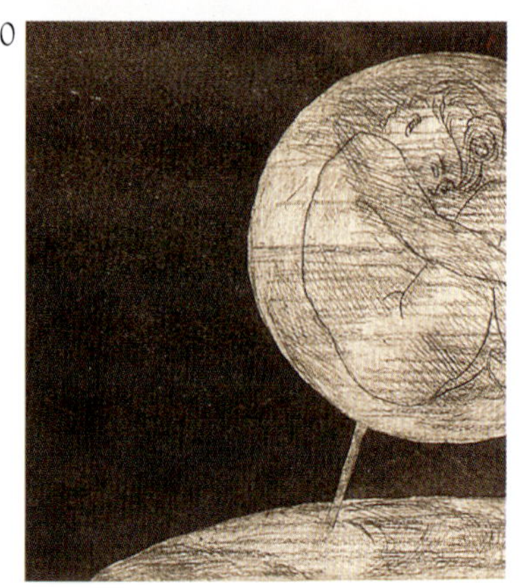

40

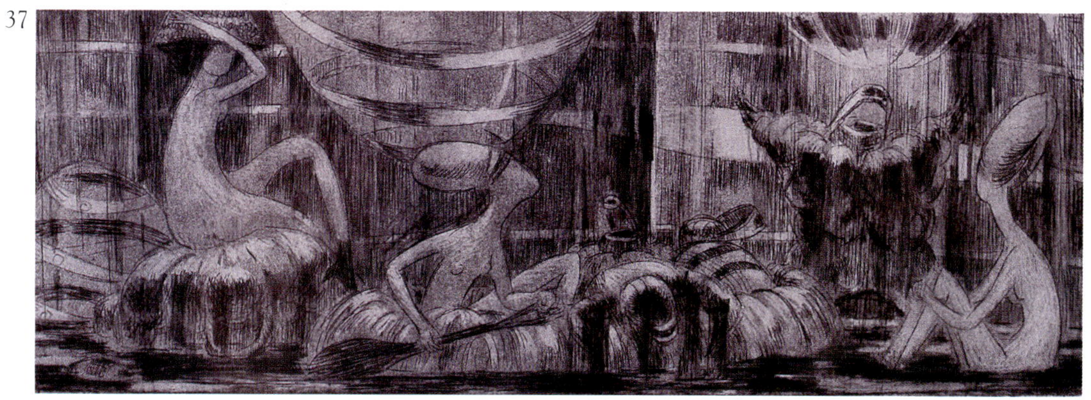

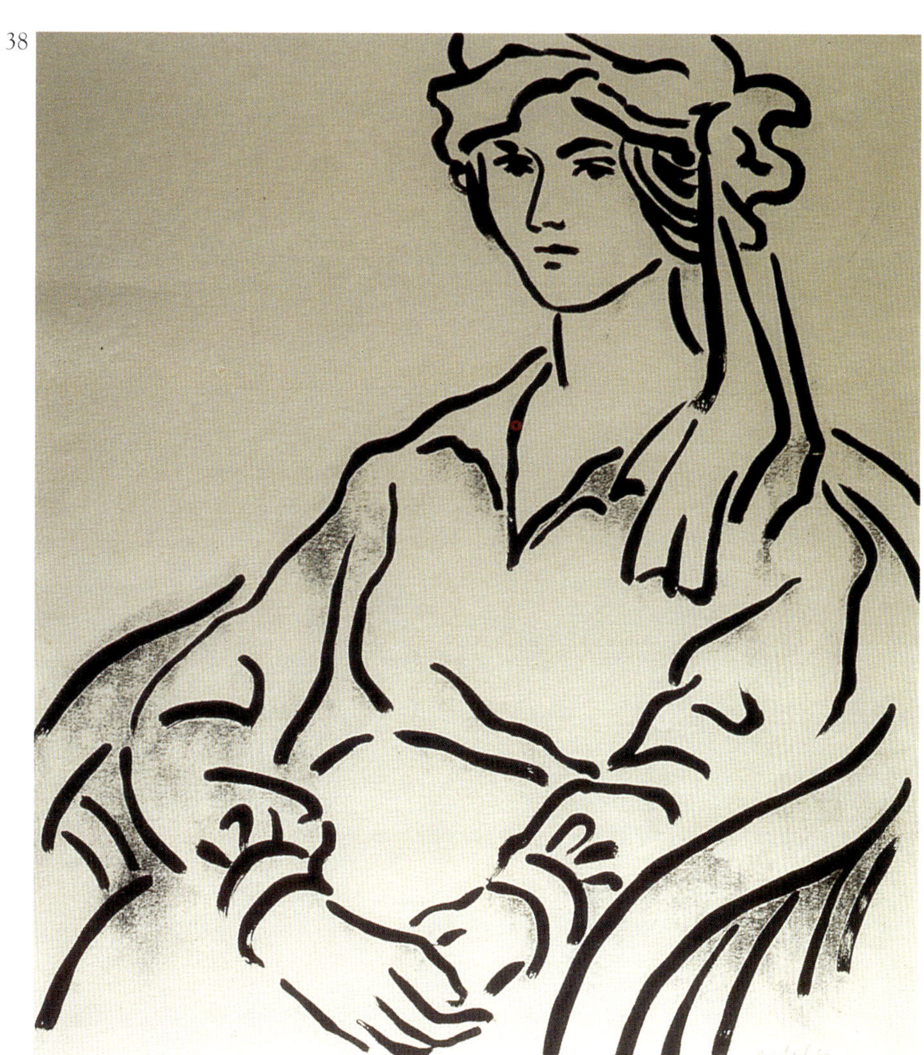

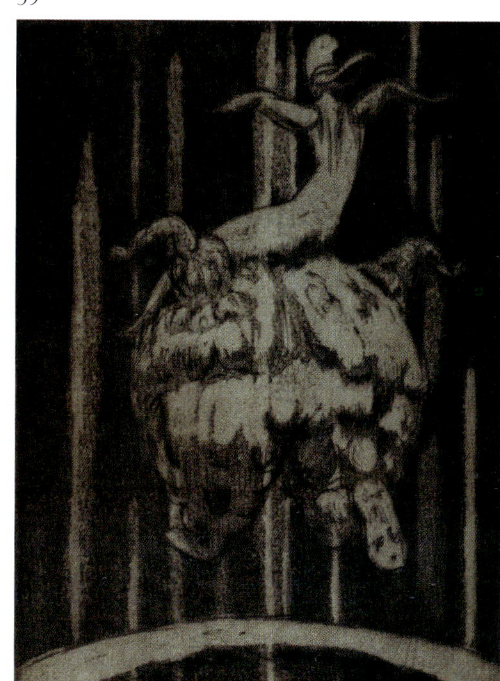

32. Wrestlers (woodengraving) 1959 10 x 8
33. The Hunter (collograph) 1960 11½ x 9
34. Reclining Nude (collograph) 1961 3¾ x 7¼
35. "Butterfly" (woodcut) 1961 16¼ x 12
36. Giant Runner (collograph) 1962
    14¾ x 11¼ (*see page 18*)
37. The Hat Game (also titled "The Game")
    (etching) 1962 4¾ x 14
38. Girl with a Scarf (serigraph) 1962 32 x 18
39. Over and Out (etching) 1963 10 x 12
40. Moon Chair (etching) 1963 5¾ x 6¾
41. Portrait of George (collograph) 1963
    11¾ x 9

42

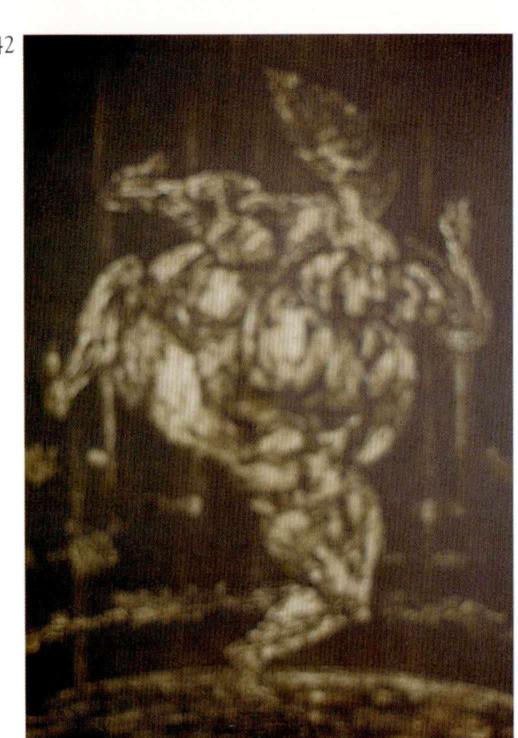

44

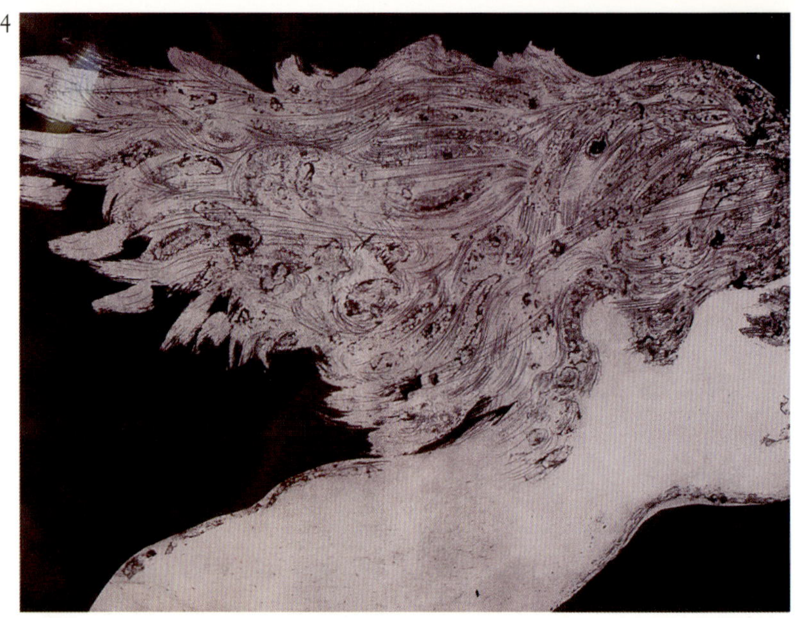

43

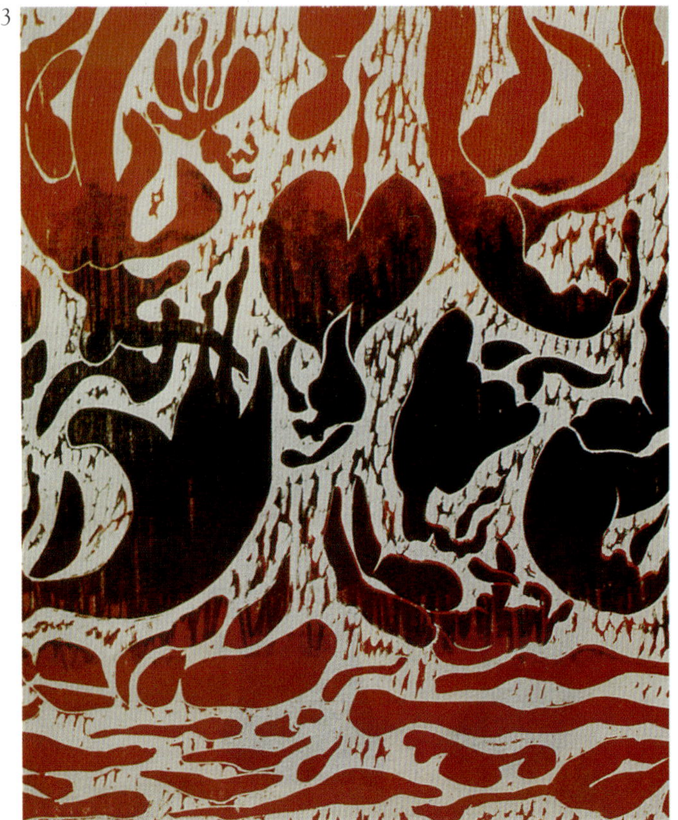

45

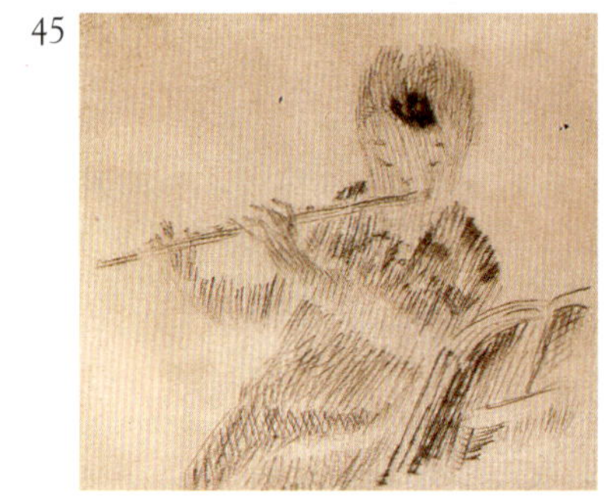

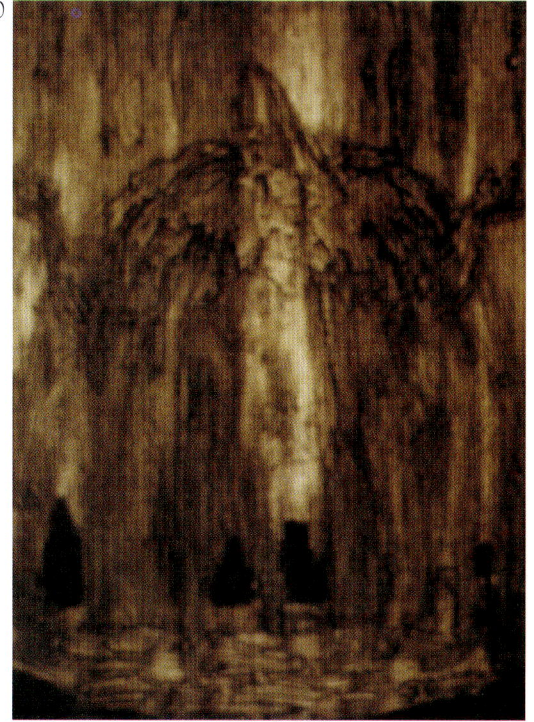

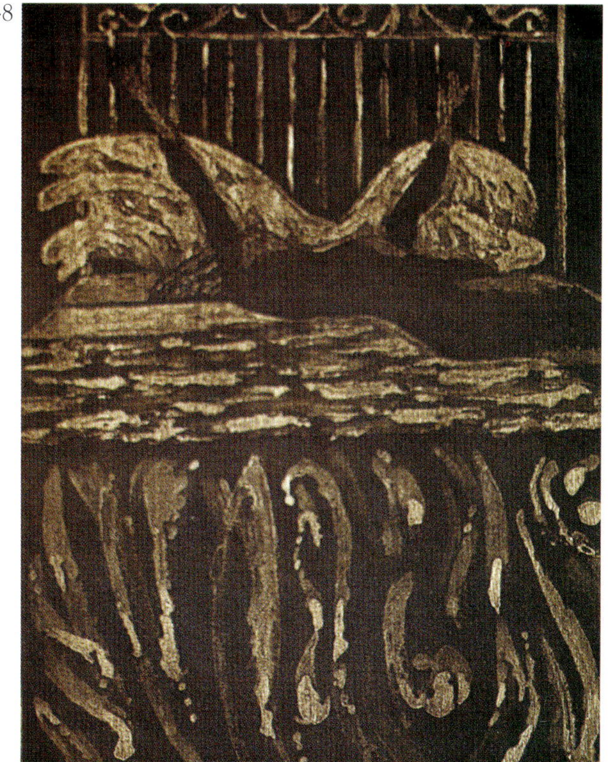

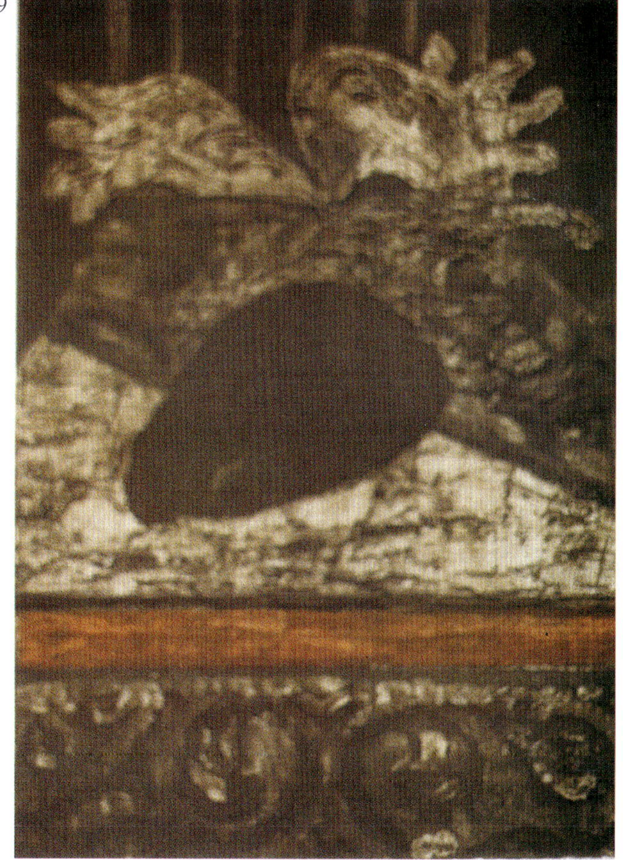

42. The Green Girl (collograph) 1963 15 x 11½
43. Fall Gently (color woodcut) 1963 13 x 12
44. Profile of a Woman (etching) 1963 12 x 15½
45. The Flute (also titled "Flutist") (etching) 1964 2 x 2⅛
46. Warm Figure (collograph) 1964 12 x 8¾ (*see page 24*)
47. Dark Struggle (also titled "Lady Wrestlers") (collograph) 1964
    15 x 12 (*see page 24*)
48. Angel of Love (collograph) 1964 15 x 11¾
49. The White Bed (collograph) 1964 13¼ x 9½
50. Rain Figure (collograph) 1964 11½ x 9

56

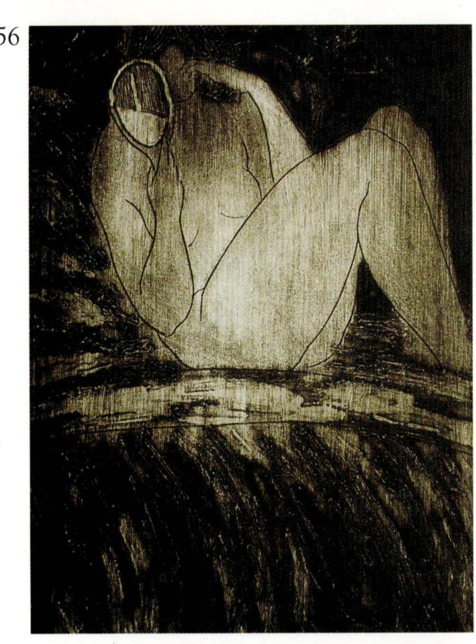

53

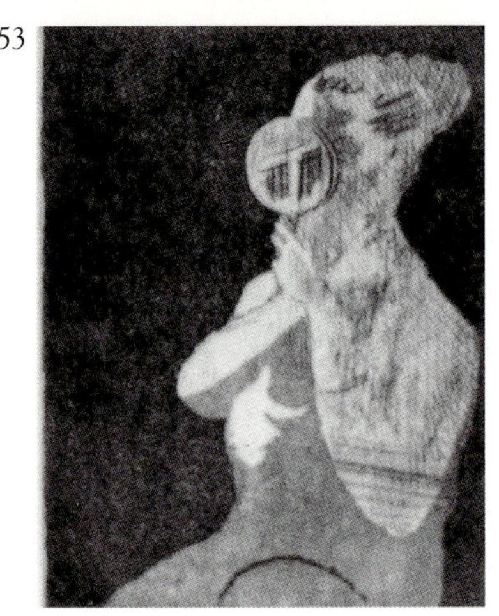

46

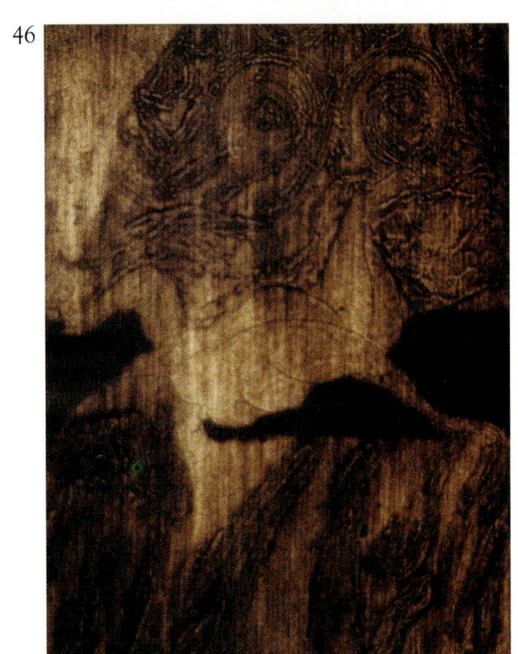

47

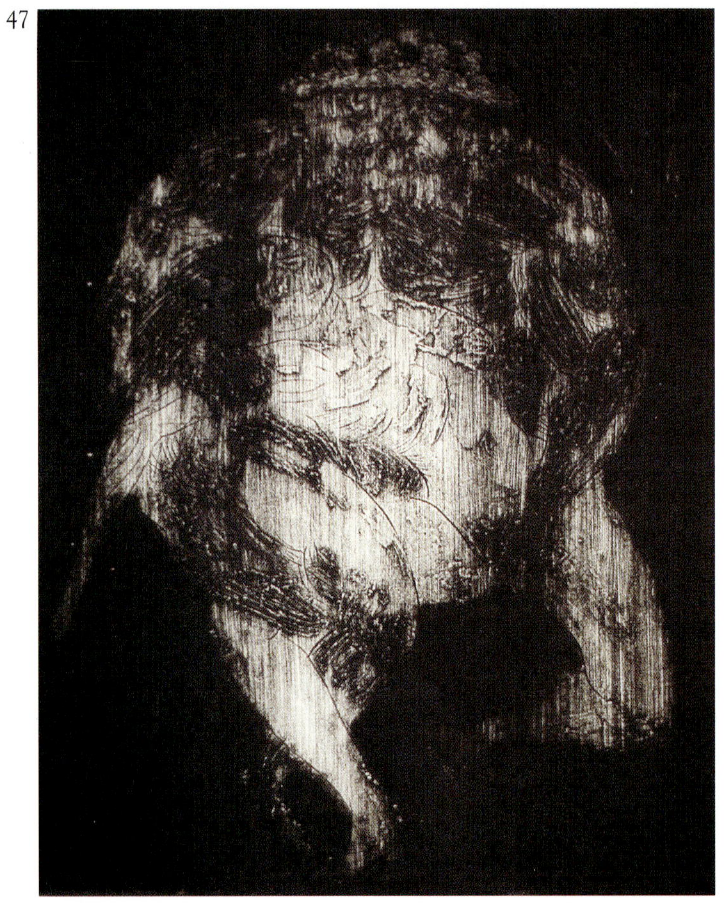

ARTICLES:

Tunturi, Ruth A'Court. "A Perfect Party." *Sunday Journal*. 30 October 1949.

Grondahl, Gretchen. "Artists Explore Various Media." *Oregonian*. 18 January 1953.

McLarty, Jack. "Fine Art: the Current Situation." *Oregon Higher Education Bulletin*. Vol. I, No. 3, Spring 1958.

Aaron, Louise. "Many Artists Help Make Fair Attractive." *Oregon Journal*. June 1959.

Fagan, Beth. "Collectors Enjoy Art." *Oregonian*. 21 January 1962.

Whelan, Pat. "17 Love Poems." *Northwest Review*, University of Oregon. Vol. 8, No. 3, Spring 1967.

"Portland Artist Jack McLarty Currently Showing Selected Paintings & Drawings at Art Center." *Corvallis Gazette-Times*, Corvallis, Oregon. January 1967.

McLarty, Jack. Statement on creating "Emerging Woman" (woodcut) to provide multiple illustrations for *Northwest Review*. Vol. 8, No. 3, Spring 1967.

Bangs, Stephen. "McLarty's Fantasies Urge Viewer to 'Follow His Dream'." *Oregon Daily Emerald*, University of Oregon, Eugene, Oregon. 26 July 1973.

Fagan, Beth. "A Treasure from 8th Century Japan." *Oregonian*. 21 January 1978.

Avila, Penny. "Love the Same in 8th Century." *Oregonian Northwest Magazine*. 1 April 1978.

Gamblin, Carol, "Museum Art School: A Story of Dedication." *Oregonian Northwest Magazine*. 8 July 1979.

Stone, Sumner, "Calligraphic Books: Wind and Pines." *Fine Print*, a Review for the Arts of the Book, Vol. V, Number II, San Francisco. April 1979.

Campbell, Mary Ann. "Leading Artists Display Prints." Medford *Mail-Tribune*. 17 February 1985.

Hayakawa, Alan. "Oregon Galleries Challenge Accepted Ways of Marketing Art." *Oregonian*. 24 March 1985.

"McLarty Opens Pacific Art Season." *Pacific Today*, Pacific University Alumni Letter, Forest Grove, Oregon. Vol. 19, No. 1, Fall 1985.

"Printmaker Kicks Off Art Season." Hillsboro *Argus*, Hillsboro, Oregon. 29 August 1985.

"Galleries Feature Northwest Artists." Eugene *Register-Guard*, Eugene, Oregon. 9 July 1986.

Allan, Lois. "A Confrontation with Devils." *Artweek*. 22 October 1988.

Whittemore, L. J. "Modest Maverick." *Oregonian*. 24 May 1991.

Hull, Roger. "Getting Around to Now." *Salem Art Association Bulletin*. August 1993.

"Alumna Shows McLarty Work." *Linfield College Alumni Newsletter*. McMinnville, Oregon. May–June 1993.

Henderson, Judy. "Review." *Ashland Daily Tidings*, Ashland, Oregon. 17 December 1994.

Ross, Terry. "Reliving McLarty's Portland." *Oregonian*. 28 July 1995.

Gragg, Randy. "City Hall Will Accessorize with Postmodern Patina." *Oregonian*. 14 February 1996.

Gragg, Randy. "'World Watcher' McLarty Looks to a Liquidation." Sunday *Oregonian*. 1 December 1996.

Gragg, Randy. "Do It Yourself History." Sunday *Oregonian*. 15 December 1996.

MISCELLANEOUS REFERENCES:

Prize-Winning Graphics Book 5. Allied Publications, Ft. Lauderdale, Florida, 1967.

Ferdinand Roten Galleries Catalog No. 9, 1967.

Ferdinand Roten Galleries & Aquarius Press Catalog, 1973.

Boffey, Peter. Personal Letter to Jack McLarty, 24 July 1973.

Lakeside Editions Catalog. Lakeside Studios, Lakeside, Michigan, 1974.

Oregon Arts News. Oregon Arts Commission, Salem, Oregon, 1985.

Gordon, Robert Ellis. "Going in with the Guerrillas." *Clinton Street Quarterly*, Vol. 7, No. 2, 1985.

Designed to Wear: Program, Poster, Tickets, T-Shirt. Oregon School of Arts & Crafts, Portland, Oregon, 1988, 1990, 1991; Tickets only: 1992.

Art Futures. Alumni and Friends of Pacific Northwest College of Art, 8 May 1993.

Gordon, Walter. Personal Letter to Jack and Barbara McLarty, 9 August 1995.

Moore, Neil J. Personal Letter to Jack and Barbara McLarty, 9 December 1995.

Witter, Janet W. Statement written for this catalog, 26 January 1996.

Schiller, Dennis. Statement written for this catalog, November 1996.

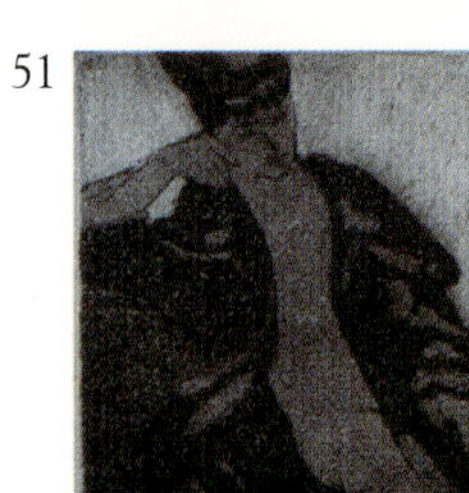

51

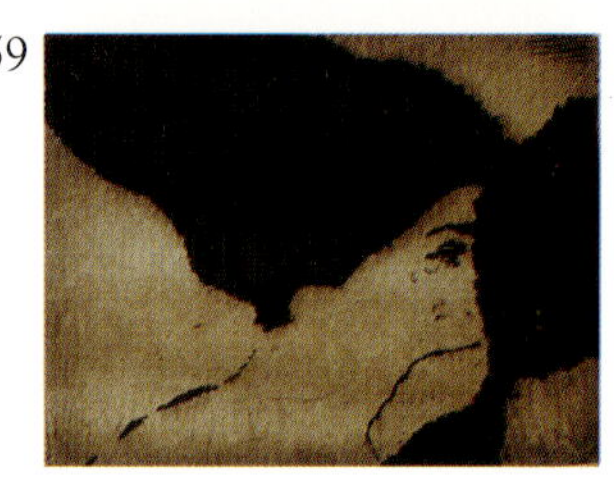

59

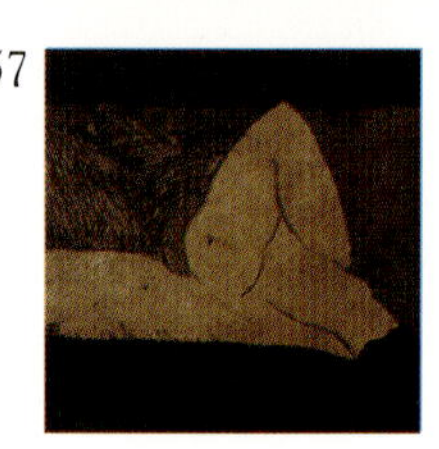

57

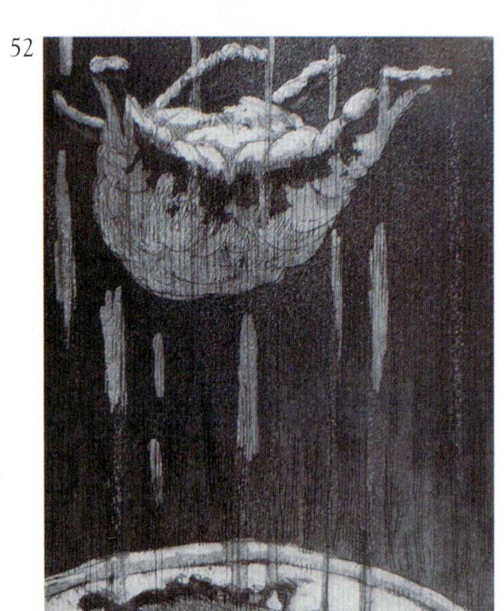

52

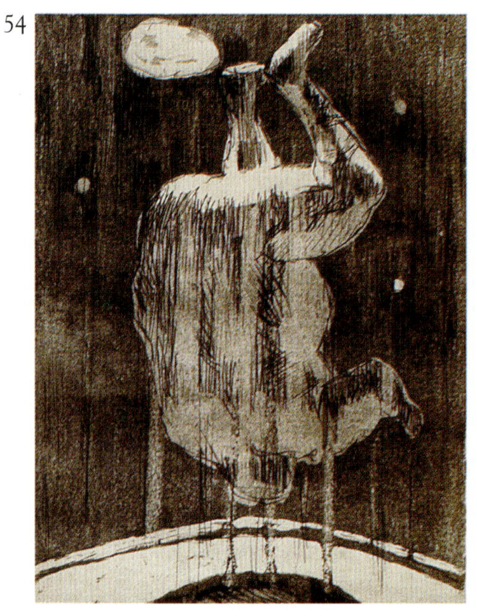

54

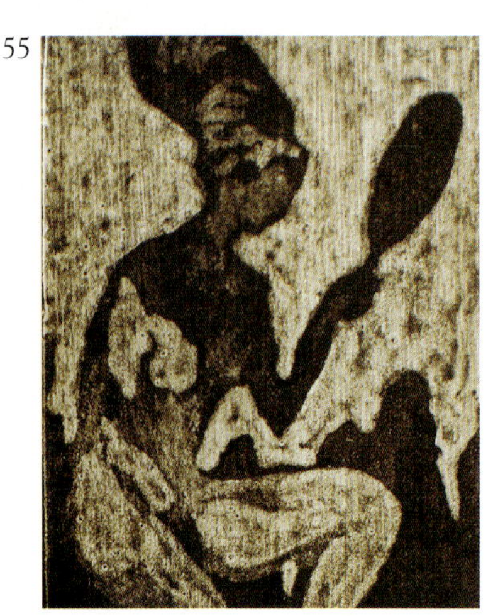

55

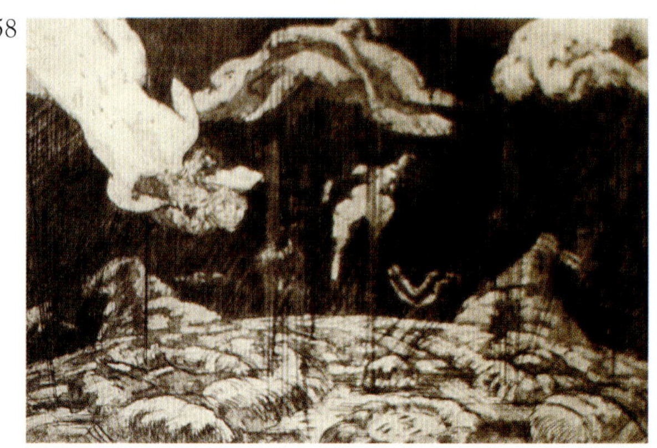

58

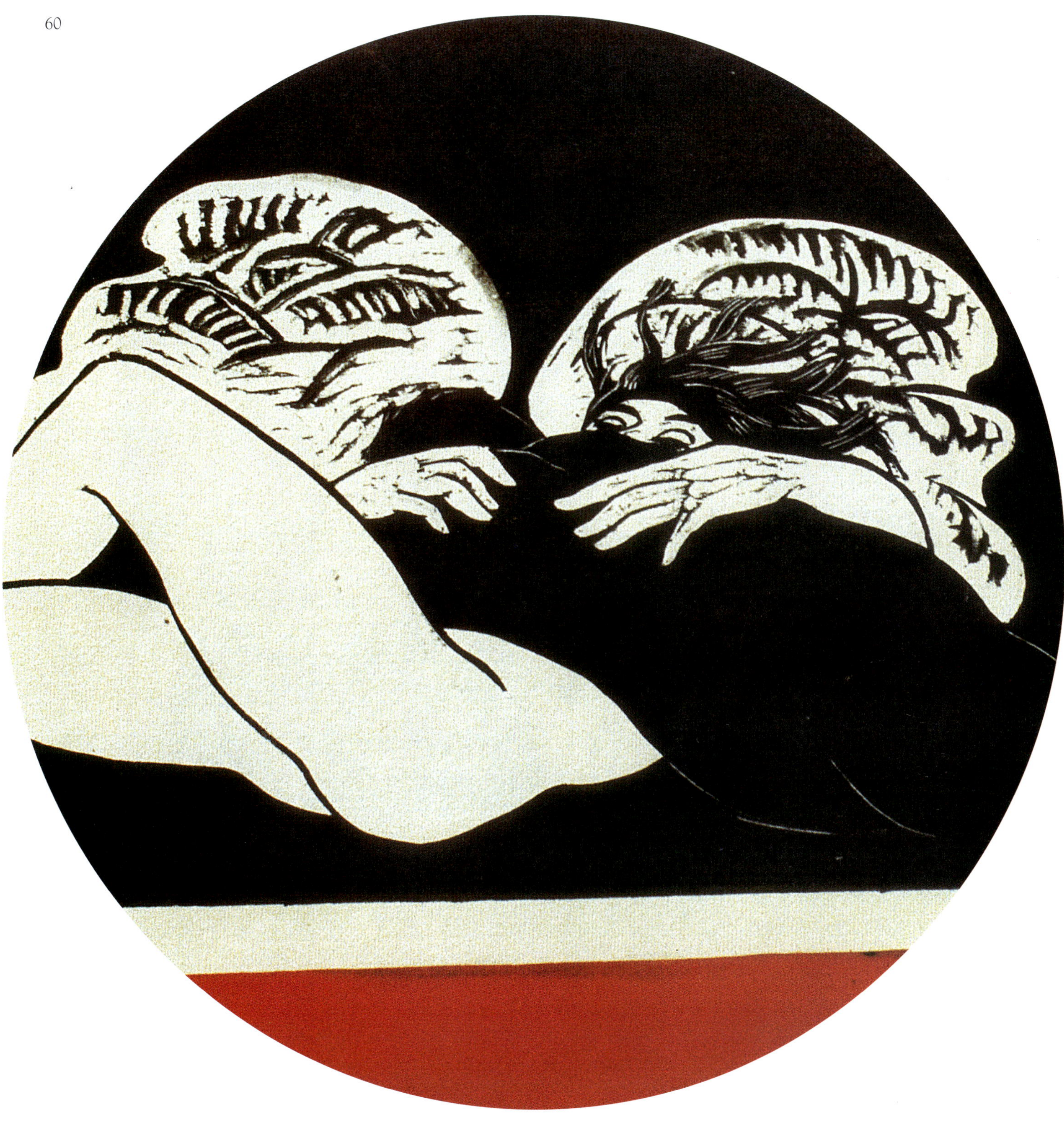

51. The Black Coat (aquatint) 1964 2 x 2
52. The Flexible Flyer (etching) 1964 5½ x 4⅛
53. Looking Glass (aquatint) 1964 5½ x 4¼ (*see page 24*)
54. Heads Up (etching) 1964 5½ x 4¼
55. Dark Mirror (collograph) 1965 4½ x 3⅛

56. The Mirror (collograph) 1965 12 x 9 (*see page 24*)
57. Venus (aquatint) 1965 2 x 2
58. Floaters (etching) 1965 5½ x 8¾
59. The Woman (aquatint) 1966 1¾ x 2¼
60. Circle of Love (color woodcut) 1966 8" circle

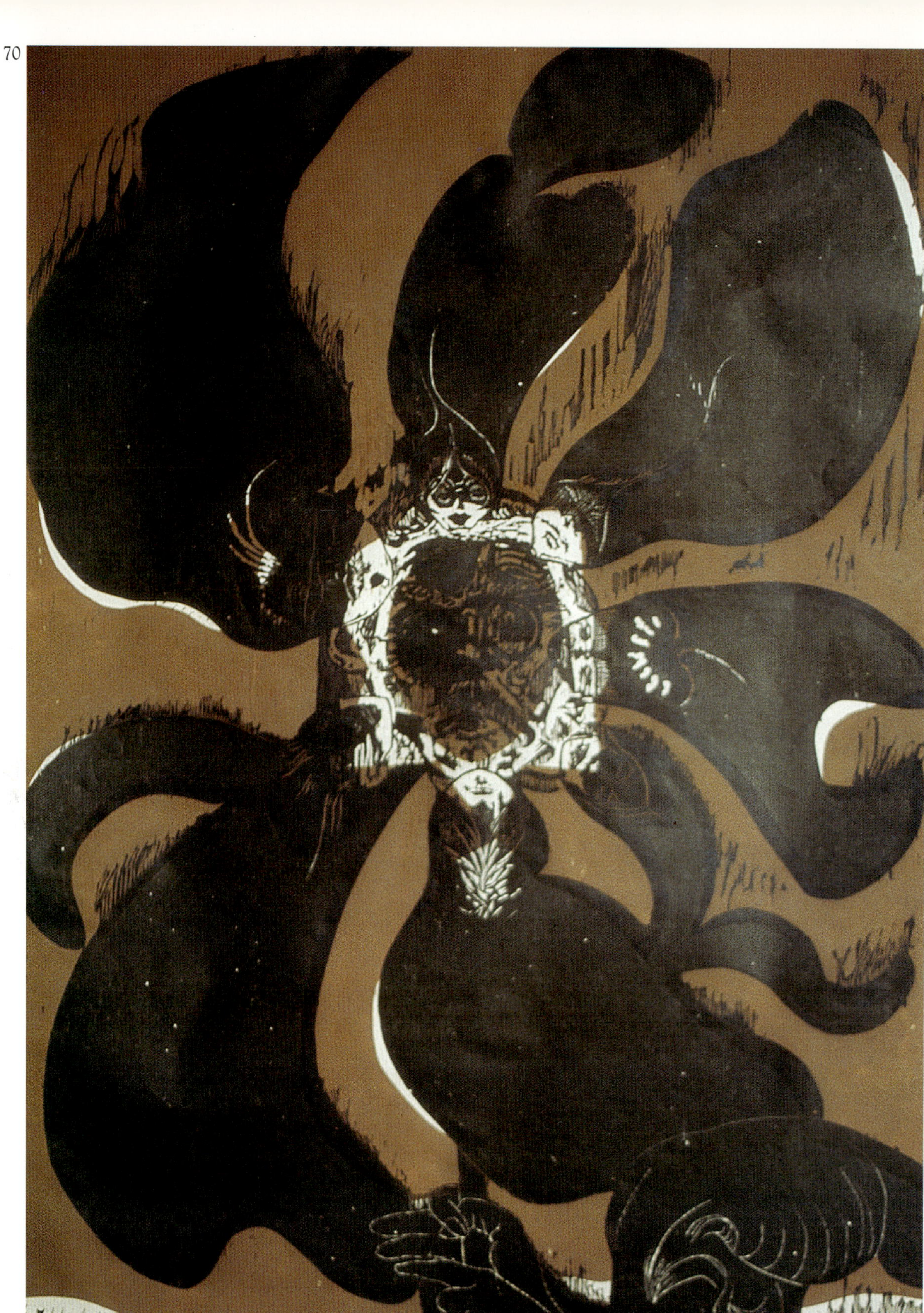

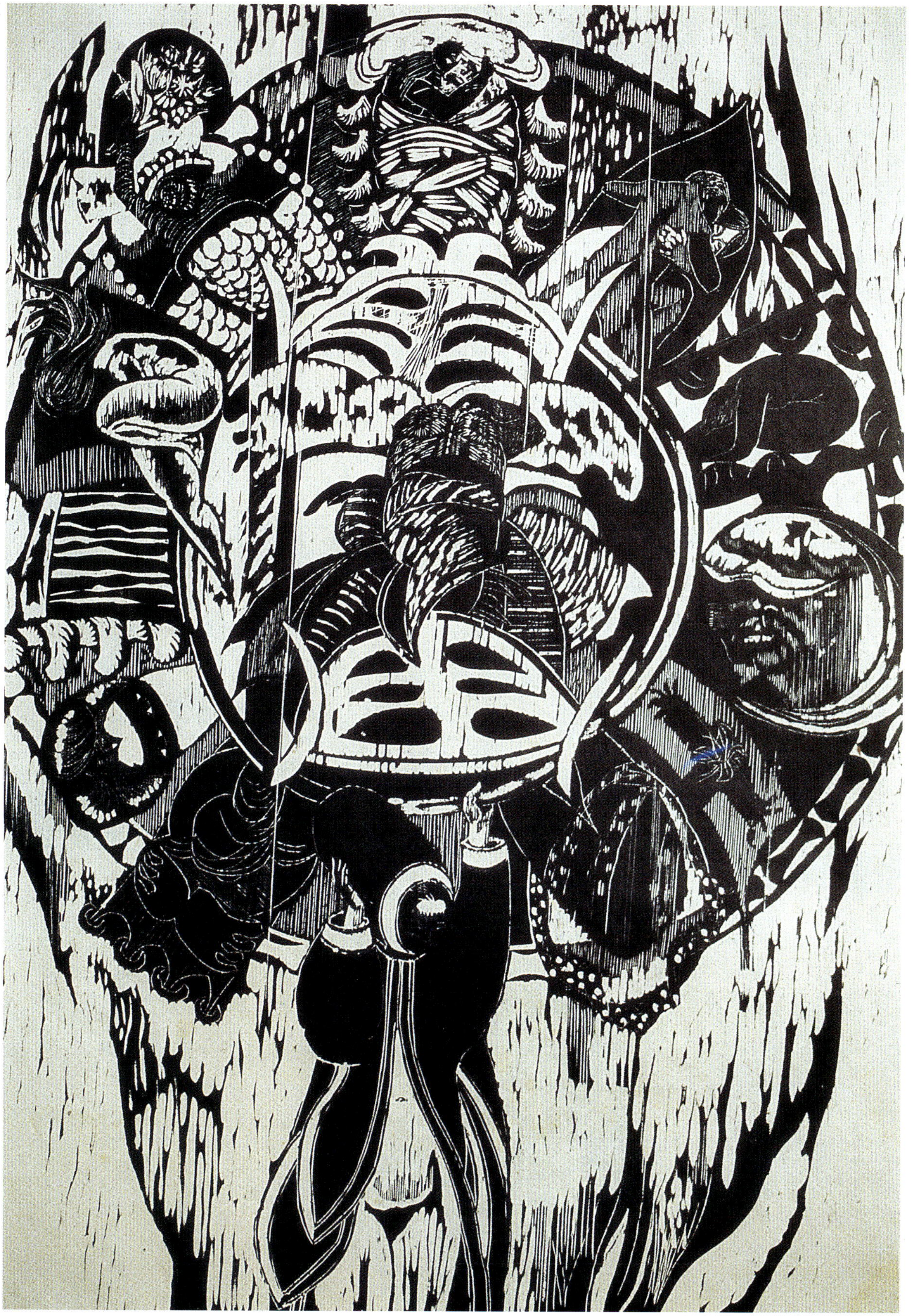

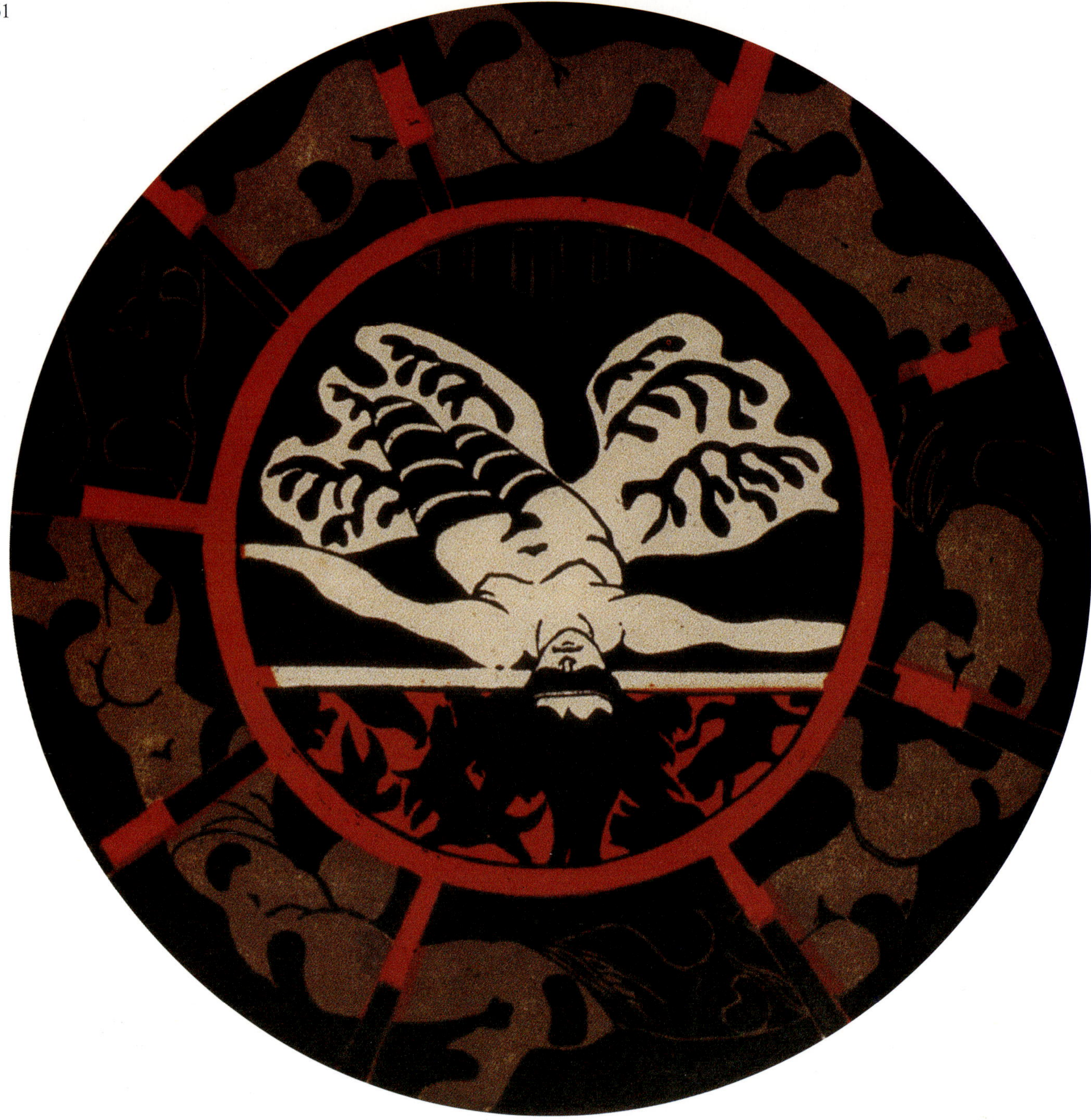

61. The Night Clock (color woodcut) 1966 12" circle
62. The Shape of Love (color woodcut from "17 Love Poems") 1966 4 x 1
63. Dark Woman (color woodcut from "17 Love Poems") 1966 3 x 4
64. Intimate Moment (color woodcut from "17 Love Poems") 1966 4 x 3
65. Wings of Love (color woodcut from "17 Love Poems") 1966 3 x 4
66. Self (also titled "J. M.") (color woodcut from "17 Love Poems") 1966 1½ x 2
67. The Wind (color woodcut from "17 Love Poems") 1966 2⅛ x 4½
68. Madame M (color woodcut from "17 Love Poems") 1966 2 x 2
69. The Siren (color woodcut from "17 Love Poems") 1966 2 x 2
70. Propeller of Night (color woodcut) 1966 30 x 21 (*see page 28*)
71. Mirror Image (woodcut) 1966 30 x 21 (*see page 29*)

"17 LOVE POEMS" was published by Image Gallery, Portland, Oregon, in September 1966 in an edition of one hundred signed, numbered copies. It contains 8 woodcuts by Jack McLarty, printed from the original blocks. Design and production were by Clyde Van Cleve. The text was printed from Bembo types on Strathmore Impress paper. The woodcuts were pulled on Okawara rice paper and the end papers were Sandstone Talisman Text.

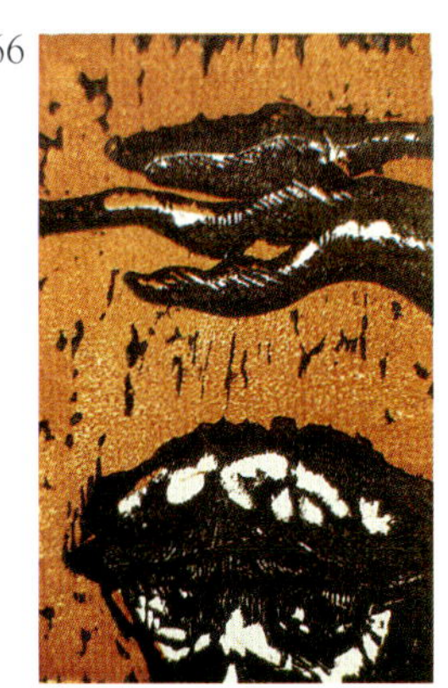

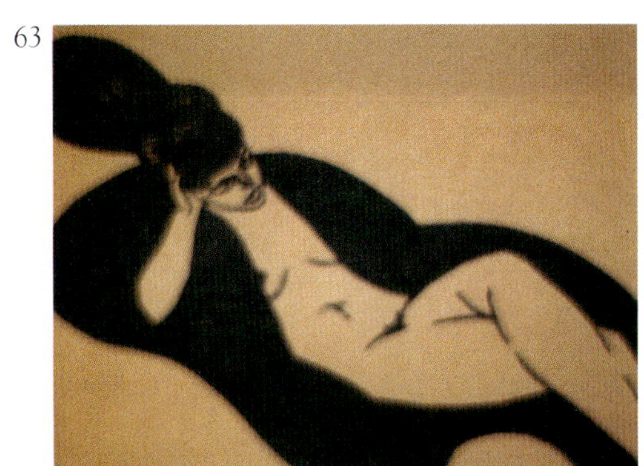

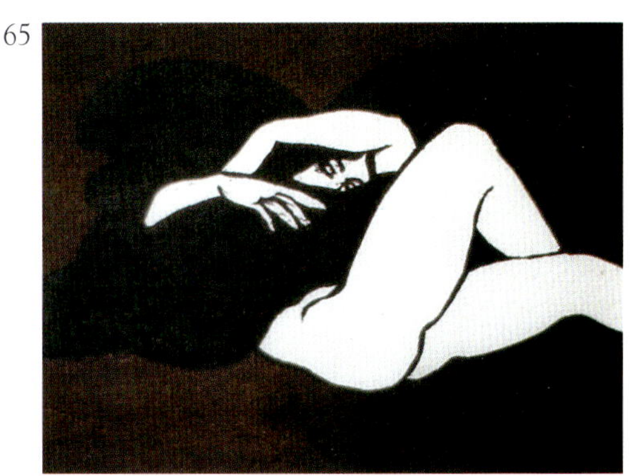

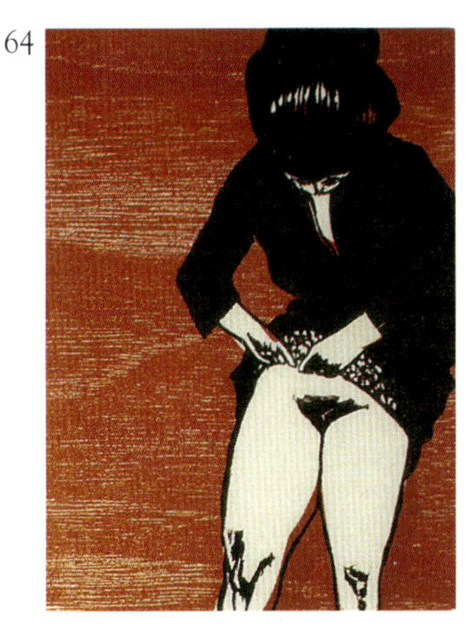

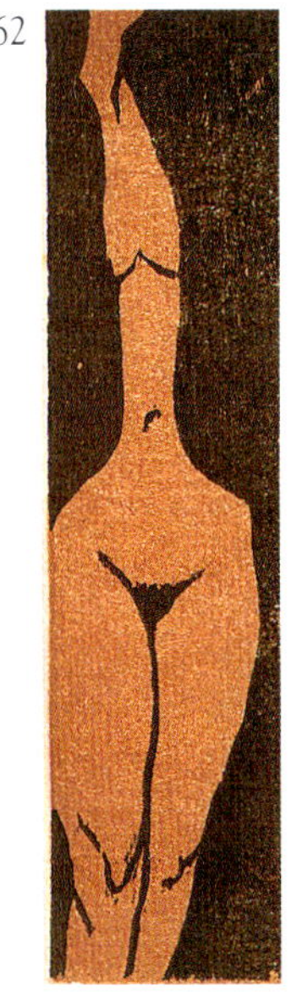

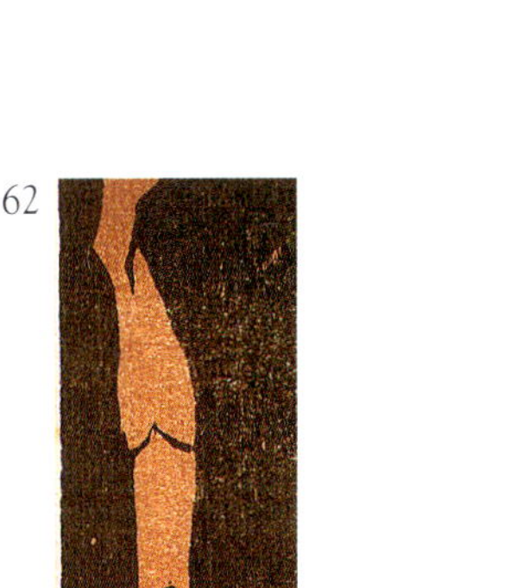

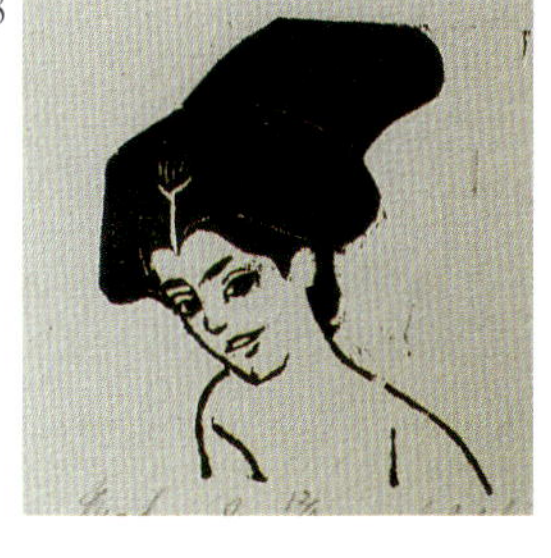

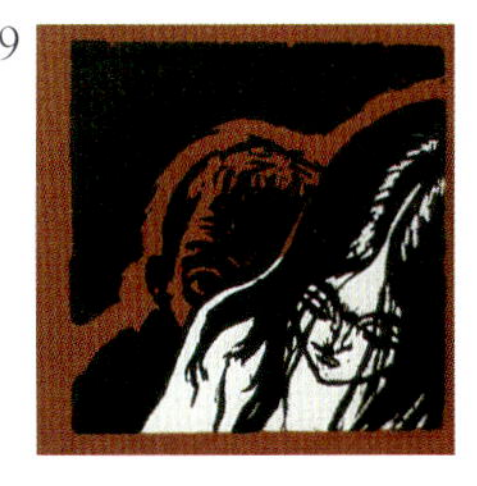

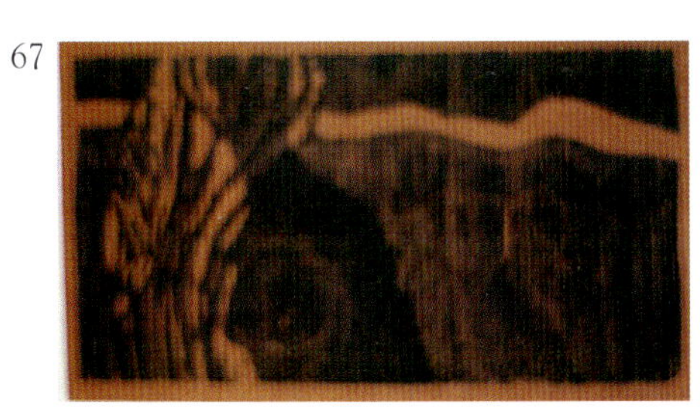

Jack McLarty and Clyde Van Cleve have joined talents in the creation of a book consisting of seventeen love poems and eight woodcuts. The book has been carefully organized to blend the two media.

Each woodcut frames a fragile and erotic picture. A sensuous lady blossoming like a vine wraps herself around a pillowy, winglike shape of black. Another lady raises her skirt, perhaps to fix a loose thread in her hem but more likely to prepare for her lover. The woodcuts are not used to illustrate the poems although the reader can easily relate them. For instance, the expression of sloe-eyed delight and independence mixed with submissiveness on the face of one lady might be said to resemble John Donne's lady in "The Bait."

The poems are set high on the page with, as Mr. Van Cleve has said, "air around the page," a device that hopefully will attract the reader's attention to them as separate graphic and artistic items.

W. H. Auden's "Lullaby," which begins with the words:

> Lay your sleeping head, my love,
> Human on my faithless arm;

is the first poem in the book and extols the foibles of love as well as its pleasures. . . . "Nude Kneeling in the Sand" by John Logan speaks of the feeling of freedom the sun and sand give when they touch:

> The girl in the sand
> colored hat
> of unfinished straw
> with its waves
> of water weaving
> in the winds of her
> yellow hair . . .

Carolyn Kizer, Theodore Roethke, Thomas Cole, Laurence Durrell, Robert Peterson and Arthur Symonds are represented poetically, complementing and being complemented by Mr. McLarty's woodcuts.

17 Love Poems is a loving tribute to the craft of bookmaking. But in the words of Dylan Thomas from the last poem in the book, "In My Craft or Sullen Art," it is also

> . . . for the lovers, their arms
> Round the griefs of ages,
> Who pay no prise or wages
> Nor heed my craft or art

Pat Whalen, *Northwest Review*, Vol. 8, No. 3, Spring 1967

Confronted with the problem of either using drawings or prints to provide illustrations for stories and poems in this issue of *Northwest Review*, I felt that one large print with a number of parts might provide the answer. This moved into a particular area that I like when the Japanese kimono came to mind. In many of the older Japanese prints, the kimono is covered with a number of images contained in circles as design on the robe. With this in mind, I evolved a theme having to do with the evolution of Woman. The idea developed in several directions, loosely held together by the kimono loosely held by the woman. Within the circles, the parts of the body—fingers, teeth, legs, lips, ears, hair and heart—are cast into somewhat biological forms. The mermaid, the black girl, the Birth of Venus, the two-faced woman and the split-face clown all make casual reference to the mythology of Woman. The man in the mirror is obviously the strong man who is behind every Great Woman (!?)

Jack McLarty, *Northwest Review*, Vol. 8, No. 3, Spring 1967

Dear Mr. McLarty,

. . . I am glad to report that the graphics which you completed in the sixties are still coming on strong. I am currently delighting in the opportunity that the Statewide Services display of your work in the EMU Gallery affords me. I can drop in at leisure on my way to or from my afternoon's work at the bookstore.

I am especially drawn to the images of women which dominate the woodcuts. . . . "Emerging Woman" manifests that pursuit of an image of woman precisely, the ultimate product of the process of cutting that block of wood comes alive as both a publicly recognizable female form and your particular . . . individual woman. . . .

There is such a complexity of attitude involved in dedicating oneself to the expression of an image of women, especially in these particular times. Personally, I respond in creative confusion to the mélange of erotica, dream imagery and idealization that permeates the woodcuts to which I keep returning. The breaking down of the barriers between the head and hair of the woman and the background townscape in "Evening Dreamer"; the almost anatomical clouds above her body as a landscape in "Love Is Black"; the inhabitation by wild animals of her hair in "Night Clock" and "Mask"; the faces we see in dreams in "Propeller of Night," our own at the center. I am amazed by the vision and the handiwork . . . that you wed your drive and method in the same images—manifesting as well as transcending your particular sex as gender and cultural identity—this achievement bespeaks a maturity of craft and person I aspire to. . . .

All of which is to say I am enjoying having so many of your works so available. They seem personal without being private, accessible without being redundant of anyone else's work except in broad historical ways. Your work sets up a commotion in my mind and won't let it stop. . . .

Perhaps I *ought* to write an organized review of the show but that's not easy. Still, there is something silly about my telling you about your work; yet as I study some of those pieces I feel that you are telling me about myself and my work. . . . A show such as yours affirms for me the paradoxical actuality of great personal communication evolving from what seems at times to be simply great personal isolation. As a writer I am concerned with communicating to readers but am also aware that there is this necessity to spend a lot of time in withdrawn concentration. Having become aware of your art in the last year makes me grateful.

Peter Boffey, Eugene, Oregon, 24 July 1973

115

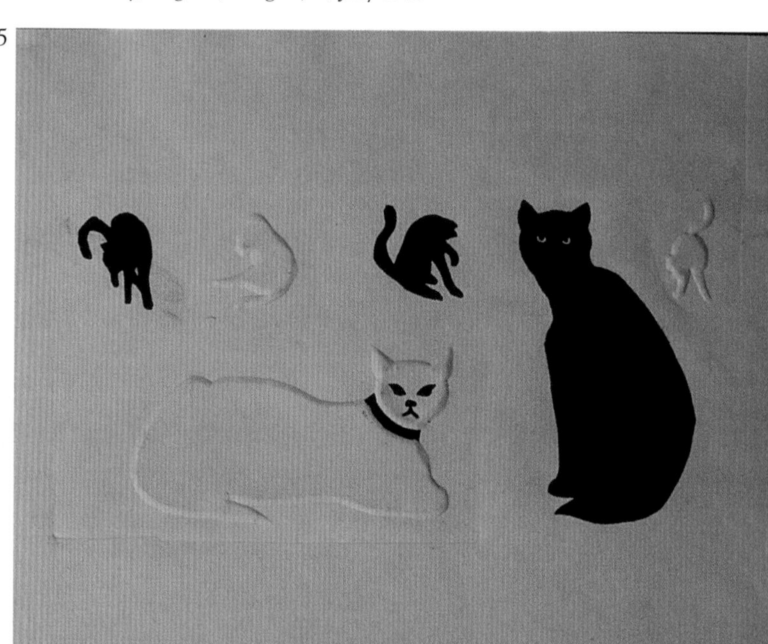

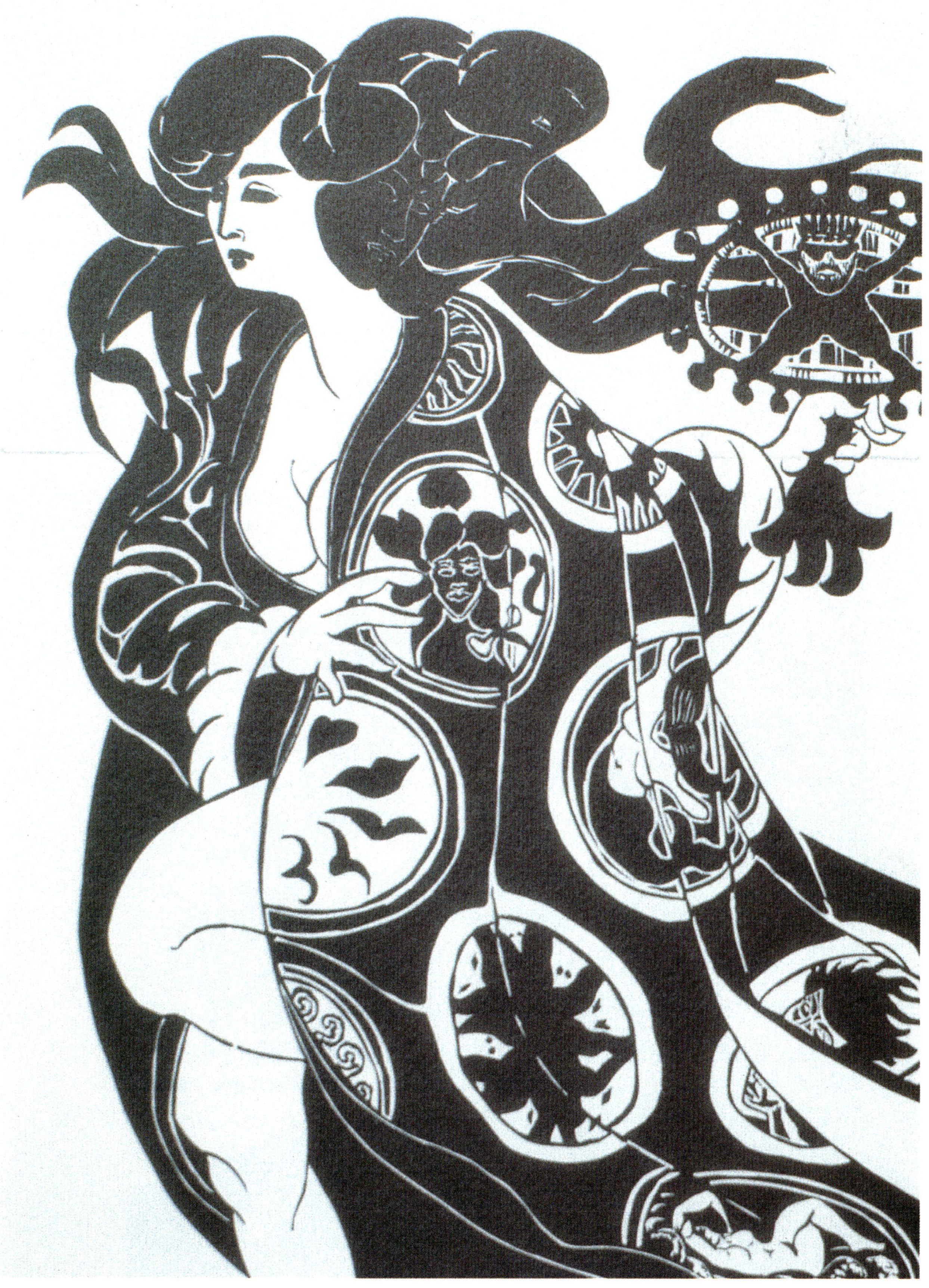

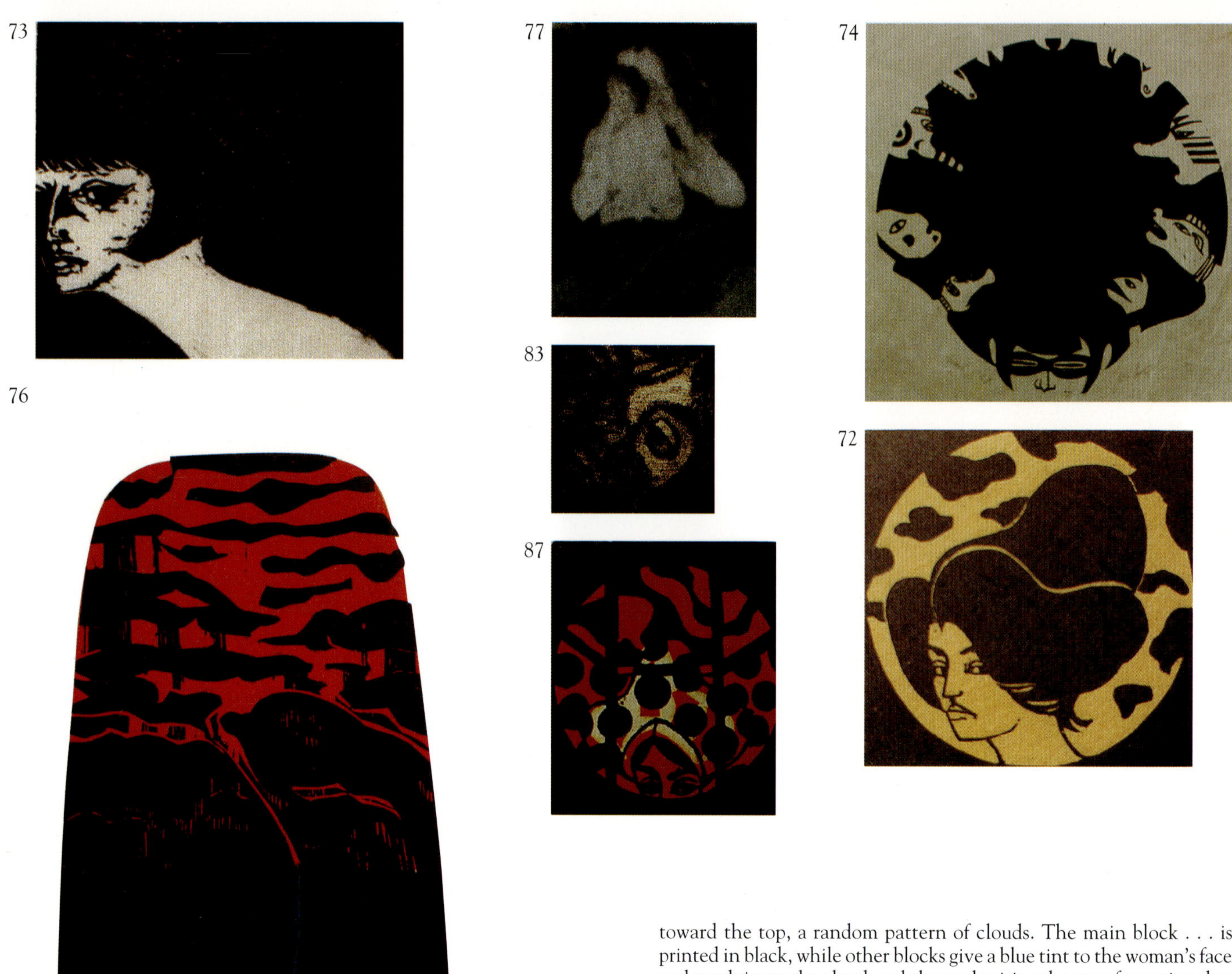

A calm reflective quality pervades the graphic work of Portland artist Jack McLarty on display in the EMU. . . . And the woodcuts, drawings, etchings and collographs that comprise the show . . . induce a sympathetic state of calm and reflection in the viewer. Each piece, even the most straightforward of the drawings of nudes, is a self-contained fantasy. . . .

. . . In the woodcut, a medium that McLarty seems particularly suited to, is "Evening Dreamer." He creates an image of the state of reflection. . . . The dark hair on a woman's head that appears in the bottom half of the print slowly breaks apart as the viewer's eyes move upward, becoming, toward the top, a random pattern of clouds. The main block . . . is printed in black, while other blocks give a blue tint to the woman's face and a red tint to the clouds, subtly emphasizing the transformation that is taking place.

. . . He often starts with something as common as a woman's hair, a flowing robe, or a curiously static motion of cars on a highway, and [then] precipitates . . . a wealth of imagery. . . .

One of the most impressive in this category is a large woodcut, "Emerging Woman." The woman of the title is shown putting on (or is it taking off?) a richly decorated oriental robe. In the disarray of her hair, the mirror she holds, and the decoration of her robe, all of which flow in and out of each other into one organic whole, McLarty has sewn more symbols of transformation and images of woman and (in the mirror, significantly) man. The complexity of this print is such that it simultaneously invites and frustrates the effort to interpret. The artist's work becomes his dream, his fantasy, and though he gives the viewer a look into his own private world, the imagery that appears can never be interpreted in any one way. . . . In its complexity, it can only be grasped intuitively.

. . . When the poet John Logan visited the University last spring, he spoke of his activity, like McLarty's, a specifically creative one, as "following the dream." . . .

Stephen Bangs, "McLarty's Fantasies Urge Viewer to 'Follow His Dreams'," *Oregon Daily Emerald*, 26 July 1973

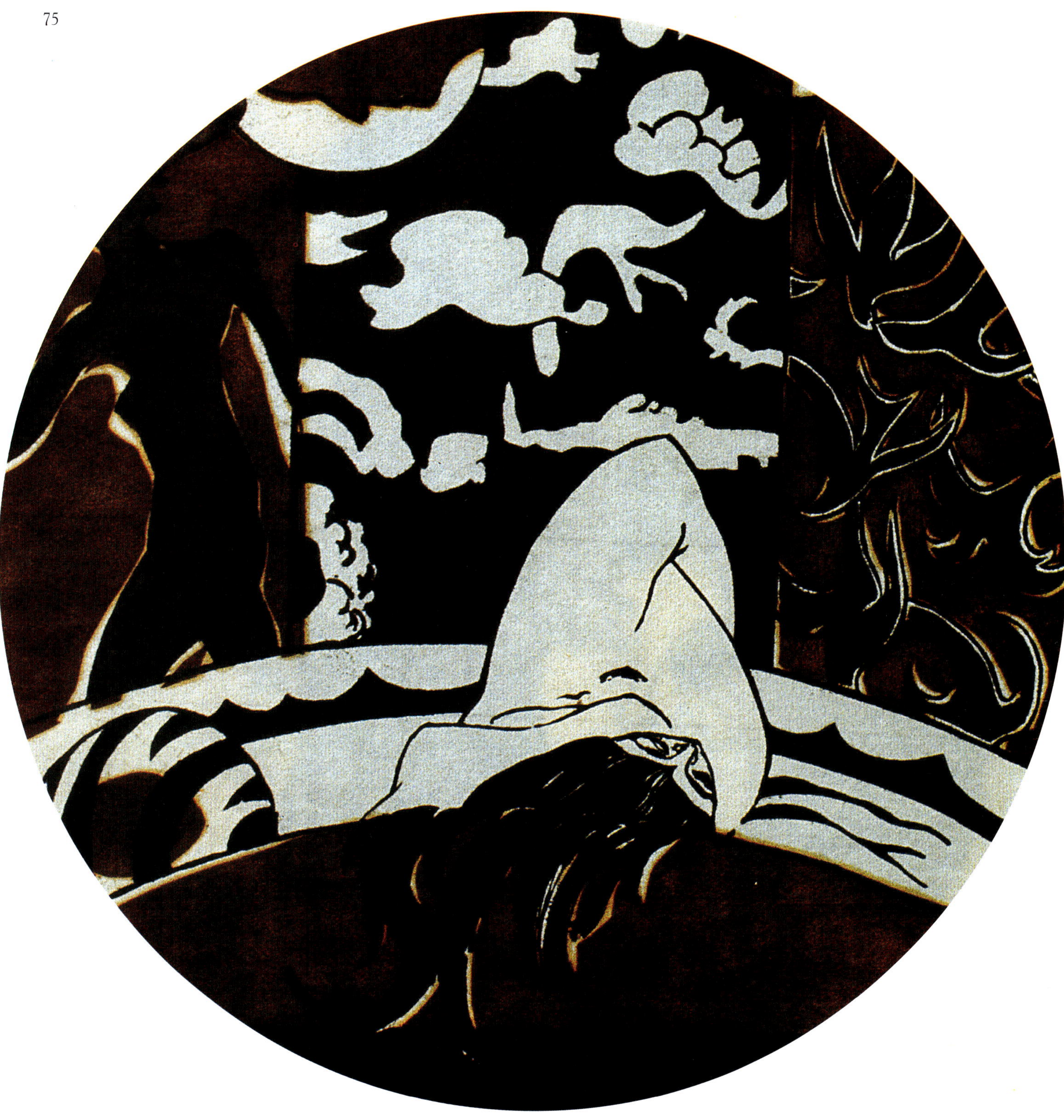

72. Clouds (linocut) 1966 3 x 4
73. Pretty Woman (woodcut) 1967 4½ x 5½
74. Troubled Mind (also titled "The Mask" and "Masked Woman")
    (woodcut) 1967 8 x 8
75. The Body of the Dreamer (color woodcut) 1967 9½" circle

76. Evening Dream (also titled "Evening Dreamer") (color woodcut)
    1967 9 x 5
77. Nude with Mirror (etching) 1967 2 x 1¾
78. Emerging Woman (woodcut) 1967 33 x 23 (*see page 33*)

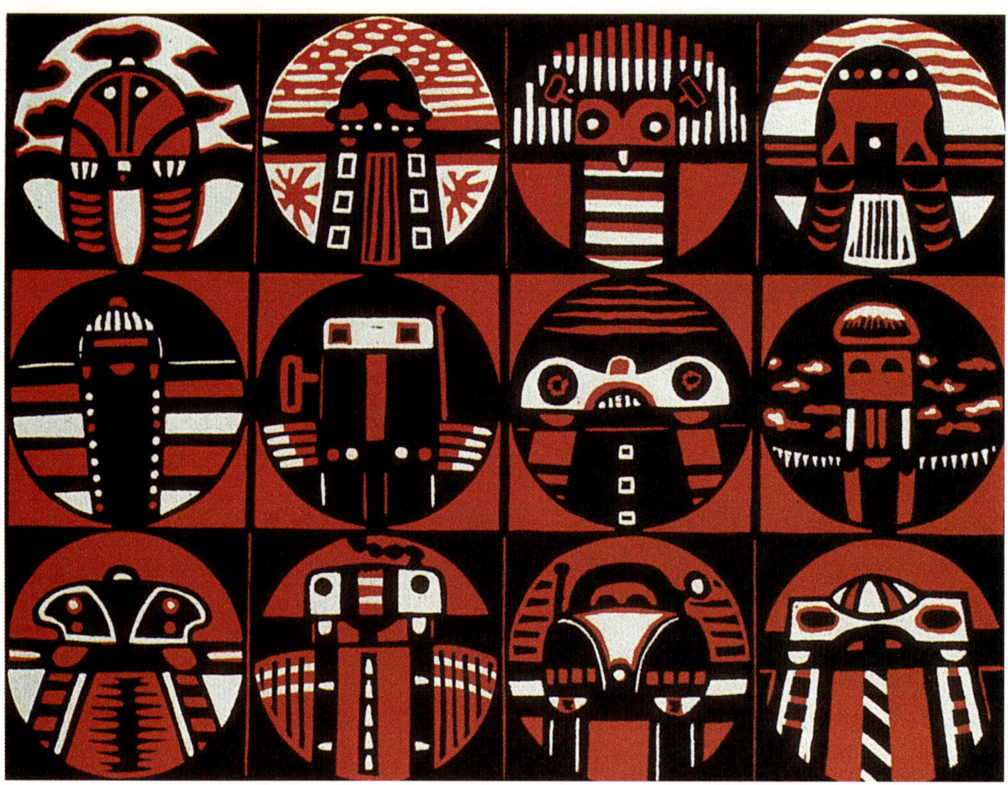

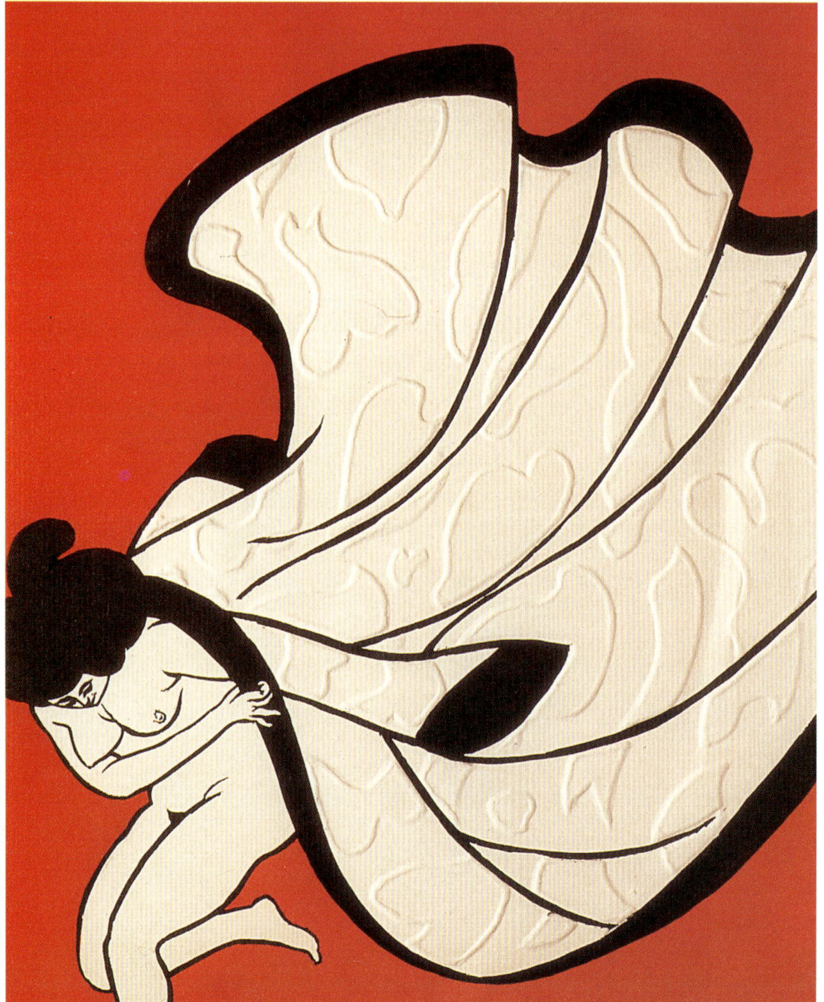

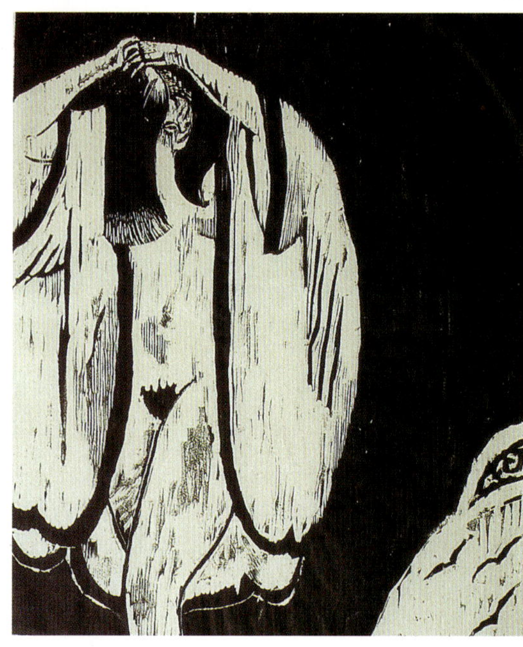

79. Ornaments of Love (woodcut) 1967 7½ x 6½
80. Secret Mind (woodcut) 1968 12¾ x 9½
81. Love is Black (woodcut) 1968 4 x 3 (*see page 41*)
82. The White Robe (woodcut) 1968 14 x 12¼
83. Close Up (etching) 1968 2 x 2 (*see page 34*)
84. The Party Pig (color woodcut) 1969 4¾ x 10
85. Half-Dark (color woodcut embossment) 1969
   6 x 4 (*see page 41*)
86. Out of the Beautiful Past (color woodcut
   embossment) 1969 16 x 13
87. Look-In (color linocut) 1969 2 x 2 (*see page 34*)
88. Road Birds (color linocut) 1970 6 x 8

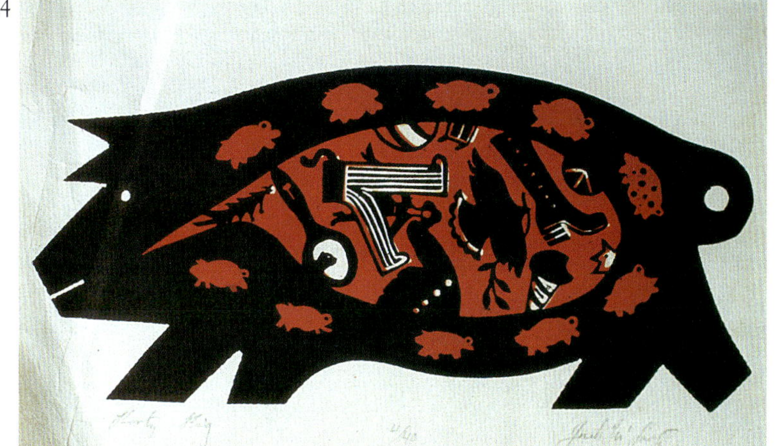

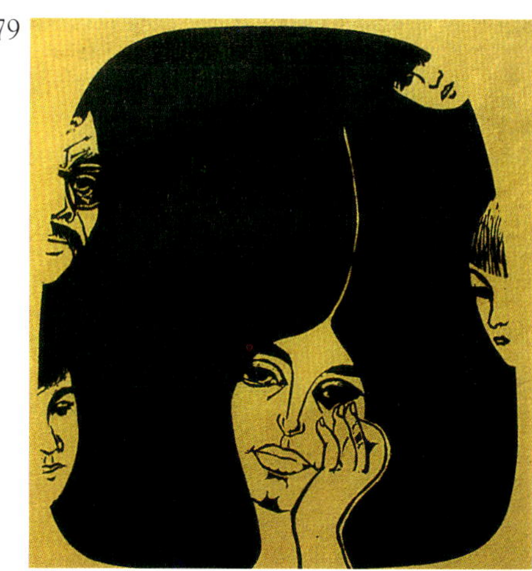

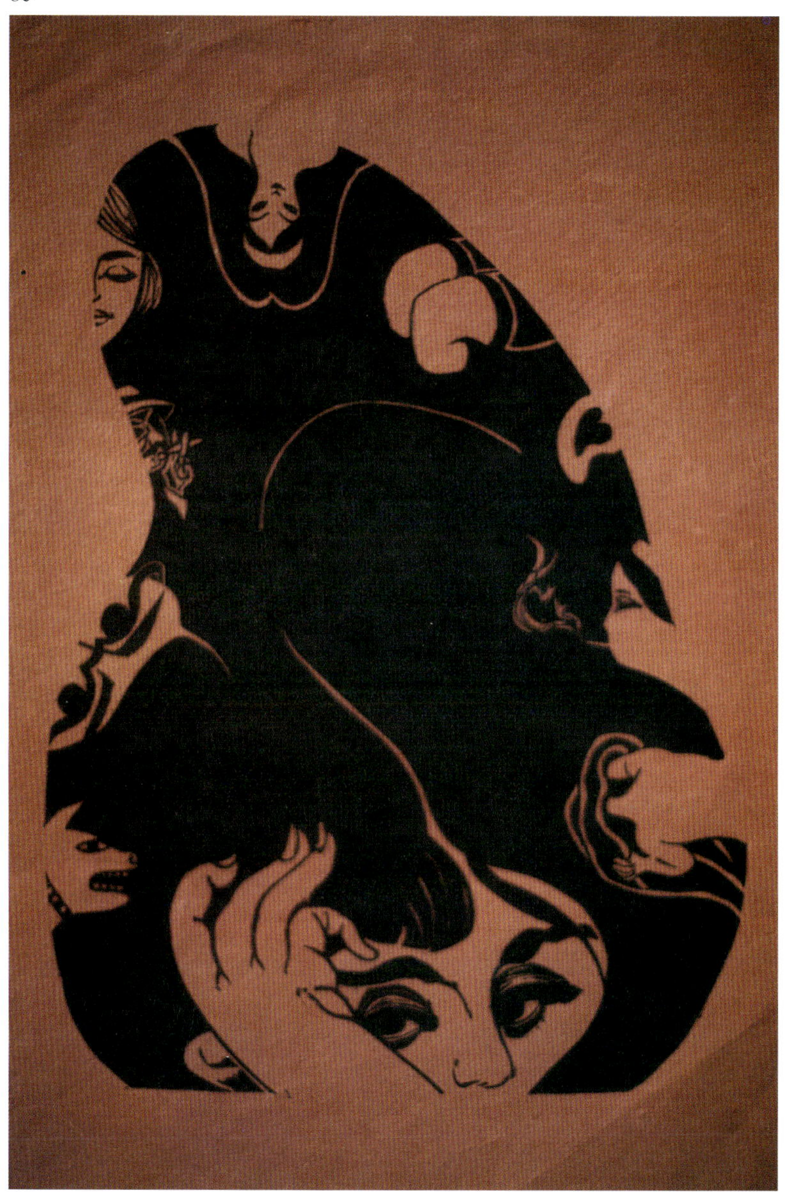

CHRONOLOGY

1939 He is studying at the Museum Art School, Portland, and his primary interest is in painting and drawing. He has not yet tried his hand at printmaking.

1941 While studying and working in New York, he executes a few linocuts.

1942 After his return to Portland, he is offered a fellowship in Lithography at the Museum School. He will print the stones for students in the night classes of William Givler. He begins to investigate the medium for himself.

1943 "City" (lithograph) is accepted for the *15th Annual Exhibition of Northwest Printmakers*, Seattle Art Museum.

1944 "Portland in '43" (lithograph) is accepted for the *Northwest Printmakers 16th International Exhibition*, Seattle Art Museum.

1946 "Winter" and "Summer" (both lithographs) are accepted for the *10th Annual Drawing & Print Exhibition*, San Francisco Museum.

"Winter" is also accepted for *American Prints Today*, a national juried show at the John Herron Art Museum, Indianapolis. Important names in this exhibition include: John Taylor Arms, Isabel Bishop, Marion Greenwood, William Gropper, Lynd Ward and Stow Wengenroth. Other Oregon printmakers picked to show: Constance Fowler, William Givler, Charles Heaney and Mary Taylor.

"The Bridge" (lithograph) is accepted for the *18th Northwest Printmakers International Exhibition*, Seattle Art Museum.

1947 He joins the staff of the Museum Art School as part-time instructor. He will teach a Saturday class for high school students and an adult class in drawing.

1948 Casting about for income to cover the unsalaried summer months, he and Louis Bunce decide to launch the Newport School of Art. They will offer outdoor painting and sketching classes on two levels. He will teach beginning students; Louis will teach the advanced class. The summer classes continue for three years and offer a fine experience for all concerned. The coastal landscape, the quality of light, and the interesting activities along the bayfront, among the fishermen and boats—all of this will have a singular affect on both painters.

1951 Working in night class with Louis Bunce, he starts to explore the medium of serigraph (silkscreen).

1952 "Old Woman with Turkeys" and "Birds in the Hedge" (both serigraphs) are accepted for *Prints by Oregon Artists 1952*, Portland Art Museum.

1953 *The Oregonian* runs a full-page feature on Oregon printmakers. He is one of those interviewed and is shown pulling an impression of "Birds in the Hedge" (serigraph).

1955 "The Shop" (woodcut) receives an Honorable Mention in the *7th Annual Oregon Print Exhibition*, Portland Art Museum.

1956 Although he is selected for *Artists of Oregon, Drawings and Prints 1956*, Portland Art Museum, he elects to show a drawing instead of a print.

1958 "Market" (aquatint) receives Honorable Mention, *Northwest Print Exhibition*, Henry Gallery, University of Washington, Seattle. This print is chosen for a special show that travels in 1959 to Spokane Museum.

"Butcher" (woodcut) and "Rodeo" (woodcut) are both accepted for the same *Northwest Printmakers Show*.

He is invited to take part in the *1st Annual Invitational for Drawings & Prints*, University of Portland.

He is currently working in woodcut, woodengraving, etching and aquatint. He has almost abandoned the serigraph medium. Now he is beginning to experiment with the collograph (Glen Alps' medium). He will produce many collographs in small editions during the next ten years.

1959 This is the year of the Oregon Centennial Exposition. He exhibits and sells a number of prints in the *Printmakers Fair*, a continuing and popular exhibition at the Exposition.

John Storrs invites him to design a play sculpture for the wood products pavillion.

Trading houses and studios with Canadian artist Donald Jarvis, he spends much of the summer in the wonderful wooded setting of West Vancouver, B.C. It proves to be a delightful summer. Don Jarvis is teaching a summer course at the Museum Art School, Portland. The Jarvis house is a marvelous change—contemporary and beautiful!

1963 He pulls a special edition of "Over and Out" for special supporters of Image Gallery, which he and Barbara are operating out of their big house at 2483 Northwest Overton. Opened in late 1961, it will showcase the work of fine Northwest artists for more than 30 years. He takes sabbatical leave from the Museum Art School and, in the summer, makes his first trip to Europe with Barbara. She returns to re-open the Image for the fall. He stays in Paris and spends several months printmaking in the studio/workshop of Paul Franck, a Belgian printmaker. He produces several beautiful plates and Franck pulls proofs for him. Unfortunately, no editions are ever possible because he discovers he cannot duplicate the technical elements with which he worked in Franck's workshop.

"Fall Gently" (color woodcut) is accepted for the *34th Annual Northwest Printmakers Show*, Seattle Art Museum.

"Butterfly" (woodcut) is shown in *Pacific Northwest Heritage, the Haseltine Collection*, University of Oregon Museum, Eugene.

1964 "The Game" (etching) is accepted for the *35th Printmakers International*, Seattle Art Museum.

"The Black Coat" (aquatint) is accepted for the *1st International Miniature Print Exhibition*, Pratt Graphic Art Center, New York. It will be shown in New York and circulate with the show nationwide in 1965. It is shown at Image Gallery 1965 in the Pratt circulating show.

1965 "Fall Gently" is selected for the Salishan Collection.

"Pretty Woman" is included in the *1st Printmakers in Oregon Invitational*, organized by Ron Tore Janson, director of Maude Kerns Art Center, Eugene. It is shown in Eugene, at Image Gallery, at Linfield College, and at Salishan Lodge.

1966 "Circle of Love" wins a Purchase Award, *Northwest Printmakers Show*, Henry Gallery, Seattle.

Image Gallery publishes "17 Love Poems" in an edition of 100. Designed and handbound by Clyde Van Cleve, it contains 8 original color woodcuts by McLarty.

"The Woman" (aquatint) is accepted for the *2nd International Miniature Print Exhibition*, Pratt Graphic Art Center, New York. The exhibition travels nationwide after a showing in New York. It is shown at the Image Gallery December 1966.

1967 "Emerging Woman" (woodcut) is commissioned for the *Northwest Review*, University of Oregon, spring issue. It will be used for the frontispiece and for a series of separate illustrations throughout the magazine. His drawing of Bernard Malamud is also a feature of this issue. Ferdinand Roten Galleries, Baltimore, commissions a special edition of "Emerging Woman" and of "Circle of Love." Corvallis Arts Center presents a one-man show of his paintings and prints.

"Circle of Love" is chosen for reproduction in "Prize Winning Graphics" Book #5, Allied Publications, Ft. Lauderdale, Fla.

He is included in *Northwest Printmakers International*, Henry Gallery, Seattle.

1968 He begins a long, productive association with John Wilson, Lakeside Studios, Michigan. They will buy many of his prints and show a great many more. They will circulate both his drawings and his prints, arranging shows at colleges and art centers. In addition, Lakeside is sending out a traveling show of books with original prints, in which he has a special interest.

He sells a selection of his prints to Ruth Green, The Little Gallery, Raleigh, N.C., and to her friends, the de Cinques, who have a gallery in Miramar, Florida.

University of Missouri presents a one-man show of his drawings and prints, arranged by John Wilson of Lakeside.

1969 Washburne University, Topeka, presents a one-man show of his drawings and prints.

The Little Gallery hangs a one-man show of his prints.

He is invited to show in the *9th Pacific Northwest Annual*, Erb Memorial Student Union, University of Oregon.

He shows selected drawings, paintings and prints at Riverdale School, Portland.

1970 "Out of the Beautiful Past" (embossment color woodcut) is purchased by Kalamazoo Art Museum for the Permanent Collection.

He attends a special workshop on Japanese woodblock techniques at Oregon State University, Corvallis, with Junichiro Sekino.

He contributes two prints to *Spectrum '70*, a benefit for the Building Fund, Portland Art Association: "The White Sea" and "Emerging Woman."

1971 He presents the Opening Exhibition at the new Jewish Community Center.

"New Orleans Street Band" (color woodcut) is commissioned by Abe Tahir of Tahir Gallery, New Orleans.

He sells a number of small, color woodcuts from "17 Love Poems" to editions de la Tortue, Paris.

He shows in the *6th Annual Printmakers in Oregon Invitational*, Bush Barn Gallery, Salem, Oregon.

1972 Statewide Services, University of Oregon Museum, will circulate a one-man show of his drawings and prints in its *Oregon Artist Series*. It will travel for two years and be shown at: Erb Memorial Student Union, Eugene; Umpqua Community College, Roseburg; Rogue Valley Art Association, Medford; Mt. Hood Community College, Gresham; Linn-Benton Community College, Lebanon; The Dalles Art Club.

Image Gallery publishes "To His Coy Mistress" (Andrew Marvell). It contains four original woodcuts by McLarty.

Ferdinand Roten Galleries purchase partial editions of two prints from the book: "Stocking Dance" and "Lady with a Cat."

The Eye Corporation, Chicago, buys partial editions of two woodcuts: "Jackie" and "Contour."

1973 Statewide Services continues to circulate his show of drawings and prints.

Lakeside Studios is organizing a special traveling show of books with original prints, including "To His Coy Mistress."

Copies of the book are sold to: University of Oregon Library; Institute of Contemporary Art, Boston; the Library of Congress.

1974 "Japanese Red" (color woodcut) is pulled by Niel Borch Jensen, Lakeside Studios. Half of the edition of 60 goes to the Artist; half goes to Lakeside Editions. It will be reproduced in their catalog. It is distributed to: the Smithsonian Institution, the Library of Congress, the British Museum, and twenty-two museum and college/university collections.

1975 Ferdinand Roten Galleries commission editions of four color woodcuts: "The Shape of Life," "Loren Eiseley," "Double Mirror," and "Reclining Figure."

He holds a one-man show of paintings and prints at Hillsboro Public Library.

Three works are accepted for *Oregon Printmakers*, Portland Art Museum: "Figured Robe," "Jazz Shadows," and "Mexican Dogs."

1976 Portland Art Museum organizes and circulates in Multnomah County a study exhibition, *The Process of Woodcut & Woodengraving*. Seven of his woodcuts and woodengravings are featured in the show.

"Red Passage" is selected for *Art for People with More Taste than Money*, a traveling show organized by Oregon Arts Commission to showcase the work of 34 Oregon printmakers. A handsome poster accompanies the exhibition and reproduces work of each artist.

He gives three prints to the collection of Portland Community College: two are early lithographs of the city; the third is "Evening Dream."

1977 Image Gallery publishes "Wind and Pines," translations from the ancient Japanese. Certain members of Art Advocates serve as sponsors underwriting the cost of publication. It is a special handbound volume with eight embossed woodcuts by McLarty. Clyde Van Cleve is the designer. William Elliott and Noah Brannen are co-translators. It is chosen for the annual Book Show of the American Institute of Graphic Arts, New York, and AIGA adds the book to the Rare Book and Manuscript Library of Columbia University.

He holds a show of prints at Keller Gallery, Salem, exhibiting with Brian Johnstone, potter.

He participates in *First Edition Prints*, a traveling exhibition organized by Oregon Arts Commission. It will travel for two years and be shown at: Copper Village Museum, Montana; Southern Oregon State College; Montana State College; Silverbow Arts Chateau, Montana; Everett Public Library, Washington; Mt. Hood Community College; Eastern Oregon State College; Clark County Library, Las Vegas; Lower Columbia College, Washington; Clackamas School District; Seattle Public Library; J. K. Ralston Museum, Montana; Spokane Falls Community College; Toppenish City Museum, Washington.

1978 "Printmaker," an award-winning documentary film, is produced by Manson Kennedy and George Johanson. It covers the work of seven Oregon printmakers, including McLarty.

He attends a two-week workshop at the Kala Institute, Berkeley, studying and working with Akira Kurosaki, internationally known Japanese printmaker. McLarty is shifting to Japanese techniques and tools as he produces color woodcuts. (All of the work so done is indicated as "hanga" in the catalog text.)

International Communication Agency, Washington, D.C., purchases six copies of "Wind and Pines" for prestige book shows representing the U.S. in Belgrade, New Delhi and Leipzig.

"Red Passage" is purchased by the Oregon Arts Commission for the collection of Southern Oregon State College, Ashland.

He is invited as Guest Printmaker and Instructor in Woodengraving, University of Oregon Department of Art, spring term.

1980 He gives two collographs and three woodcuts to the collection of Southwestern Oregon Community College: "Giant Runner," "Angel of Love," "Fall Gently," "The White Robe," and "Ornaments of Love." Participates in *Five Prints by Five Fine Printmakers*, McMinnville Association of the Arts.

1981 He takes early retirement from the Museum Art School (now Pacific Northwest College of Art), after more than 30 years of teaching. He will concentrate on his own work in painting and printmaking and do some traveling.

1982 "Some Dogs in the Fountain" (woodcut) receives a Purchase Award in *Northwest Prints '82*, the inaugural exhibition of the Northwest Print Council, Portland Art Museum. He is a founding member of NWPC. The purchase is added to the Gilkey Collection.

"Descent of Man" (color woodcut) is his contribution to a three-man Print Project funded by members of Art Advocates. The other participants are Lyle Matoush and Art Hansen.

He creates a woodcut design for a poster for a concert by Pete Seeger, a musician he has long admired.

He teaches a special workshop on Japanese woodblock techniques with Akira Kurosaki. They are guest instructors at PNCA.

He and Barbara take a small trailer down to Central Mexico for the winter. He works with Ralph Gray at Estudio Patzcuaro and has a productive and wonderful period.

1983 After returning from Mexico, where he produced linocuts and reduction linocuts, he turns again to woodengraving and color woodcut (hanga).

1984 He pulls a special edition of 40 of "Storms and Dreams" (woodengraving) for the 75th Anniversary Print Portfolio, a benefit for Pacific Northwest College of Art.

"Adios Amor" (color linocut) is chosen for a *Northwest Print Council Invitational*, The Alaska Show, Anchorage Community College, a branch of University of Alaska.

1985 Invited to hold a one-man show in the governor's office, State Capitol, Salem. He exhibits paintings as well as these prints: "Aqua Figured Robe" (color woodcut); "Some Dogs in the Fountain" (woodcut); "Changing Colors" (color woodcut); "Adios Amor" (linocut); "Swimmers in a Dark River" (linocut); "Free Fall" (linocut).

Cawein Gallery, Pacific University, presents a retrospective of his prints plus some recent paintings.

"The Devil Lives Under Ocumicho" (color linocut) is selected for *Western States Print Invitational*, Portland Art Museum. It is listed as "Viva Mexico," a title he used for it at first.

"Butterfly Dogs" (color linocut) is chosen by the Salem Public Library Foundation for the collection of the library, Salem, Oregon.

"Red Passage" (color linocut) is shown in the *Sapporo-Portland Print Exhibition*, sponsored by Northwest Print Council at Portland State University.

Pacific Northwest College of Art offers a series of special events: *New Horizons in Printmaking*. One event is a workshop he conducts with Elaine Chandler and Dennis Cunningham.

Clinton Street Quarterly runs "Going in with the Guerrillas" by Robert Ellis Gordon, for which McLarty creates linocut illustrations.

He marks the 24th year of Image Gallery with an original color woodcut poster.

His prints are shown at Northwest Print Council exhibitions at: North Central Washington Museum, Wenatchee; University of Oregon Museum, Eugene; the Wentz Gallery, Pacific Northwest College of Art.

1986 Maude Kerns Art Center, Eugene, presents a comprehensive retrospective of his drawings, paintings, and prints.

He creates a cover design and woodcuts to illustrate "Encounters with the White Train" by Andy Robinson. It is issued in a limited edition of 500.

He participates in the *Northwest Print Council Biennial*, Memorial Union, Oregon State University, Corvallis.

He creates a cover design and woodcut illustrations for "Song of the Ponderosa," a volume of poetry by his long-time friend, Russell Roberts, of Pacific University.

1987 Image Gallery hangs a five-person print exhibition with: Bill Colby, William Givler, Art Hansen, Mery Lynn McCorkle and Jack McLarty. He shows "36 Basic Cat Positions" (color woodcut).

1988 *Forty Oregon Printmakers*, sponsored by Northwest Print Council and Oregon Arts Commission, is shown at Image Gallery. A handsome color catalog accompanies the exhibit and "The Devil Lives Under Ocumicho" (color linocut) is reproduced.

He designs the first of three woodcut/posters for *Designed to Wear*, the annual high-fashion show of wearable art at Oregon School of Arts & Crafts (OSAC).

1989 He contributes several prints to the Permanent Collection of Pacific University, Forest Grove, including "Red Passage" (color linocut).

During the winter he and Barbara return to Central Mexico, taking the trailer down for three months.

1990 "Flower Vendor" (color woodcut) is reproduced in "The Art of Printmaking," a handbook for print collectors published by the Northwest Print Council.

He creates a second woodcut/poster for *Designed to Wear*, the fashion show at Oregon School of Arts & Crafts.

High point of the year is publication of *"The Book of Color,"* a stunning handbound book for which he creates eight color woodcuts. Production costs are underwritten by sponsors who are members of Art Advocates, Inc. Nancy N. Ramsay is designer, and Ash Creek Press does the production. It is a beautiful book in a small edition of 60.

1991 Image Gallery presents a show of his prints covering the years 1974–90.

He designs the third woodcut/poster for the annual fashion show at Oregon School of Arts & Crafts.

Bypass surgery in the fall will limit his activities, but not for long. His recovery goes very well. Now all those years of playing table tennis stand him in good stead! He gives a copy of "Wind & Pines" and impressions of "Adios Amor" and "Dogs in the Fountain" to the University of New Mexico Museum.

1992 He begins work on a series of large woodcuts. He will handcolor them instead of using the press. It is much less stressful yet very satisfying. It puts them in the class of monotypes, of course.

"The Devil Lives Under Ocumicho" (color linocut) is chosen for the cover and utilized for illustrations throughout "Left Bank," Summer Issue, Vol. No. 2. This publication is from Blue Heron Press, Hillsboro, Oregon. The theme of this issue is extinction.

1993 He participates in an invitational, *West Coast Edition Printmakers*, Claudia Chapline Gallery, Stinson Beach, California.

He shows with Northwest Print Council at L.A. Society of Printmakers, Woodland Hills, California.

He contributes to *101 Prints*, a major benefit for Friends of the Gilkey Center and the Northwest Print Council, Portland Art Museum.

He contributes to *Art Futures*, a benefit for Pacific Northwest College of Art.

Linfield College (Renshaw Gallery) mounts a major exhibition of his work, the collection of Mayo Rae Rolph Roy. The show covers 50 years and includes drawings, paintings, prints and books with original art. The prints shown are: "Cat Cap," "Double Mirror," "Powell's," "Some Dogs in the Fountain," and "Giant Catfish" from "Wind & Pines."

Metropolitan Arts Commission adds "Powell's" (woodcut) to the *Visual Chronicle of Portland.*

1994   "The Doll Collector" (hand-colored woodcut) is shown with Northwest Print Council members at Bellevue Art Museum, Bellevue, Washington.

"The Sugar Angel" (color woodcut) is chosen for the Associate Members' Portfolio by the Northwest Print Council.

Three of his prints are included in the *Northwest Print Council Invitational*, University of Hawaii, Hilo: "Las Vegas," "Some Dogs in the Fountain," and "The Devil Lives Under Ocumicho."

He is invited to serve on the advisory panel for the *Visual Chronicle of Portland* by the Metropolitan Arts Commission.

Graven Images Gallery, Ashland, offers a one-man show of his prints.

1995   Sovereign Gallery, Portland, holds a special exhibition of his work of the forties. Included are the early lithographs as well as a number of his recent hand-colored woodcuts.

Sponsors/patrons for the McLarty 50-year painting catalog, "World Watcher," receive an impression of a special edition woodcut of "Powell's" pulled for the Artist by Atelier Mars, Portland.

His one-man shows include: Paintings & Prints, Art Space, Bay City, Oregon; Recent Pastels & Prints plus Paintings, Cawein Gallery, Pacific University, Forest Grove, Oregon.

1996   He is given a special commission for a mural in woodcut for City Hall, Portland, which is undergoing major renovation.

Sovereign Gallery, Portland, offers a stunning show of his *Paintings, Drawings & Prints of the Fifties.*

McLartys' Choice offers an exhibition of all his recent work in printmaking.

Lois Allan selects three works for her "Northwest Printmakers," an important volume to be issued in 1997. They are: "The Left Hand of God," "The Devil Lives Under Ocumicho," and "Wall City."

81
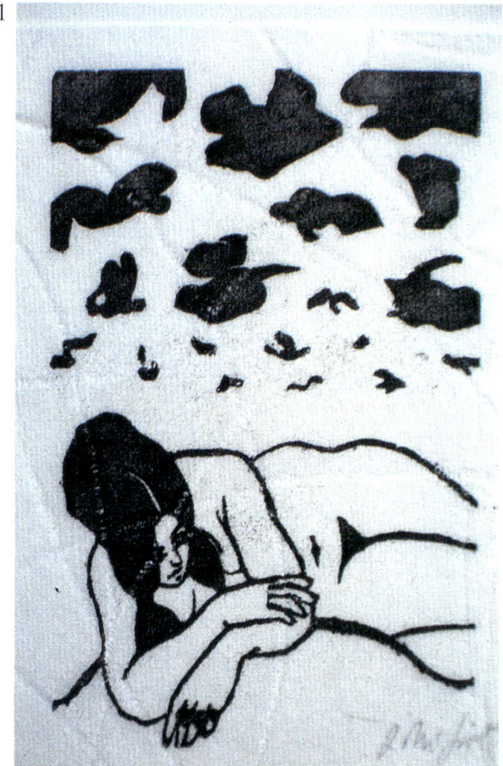

85
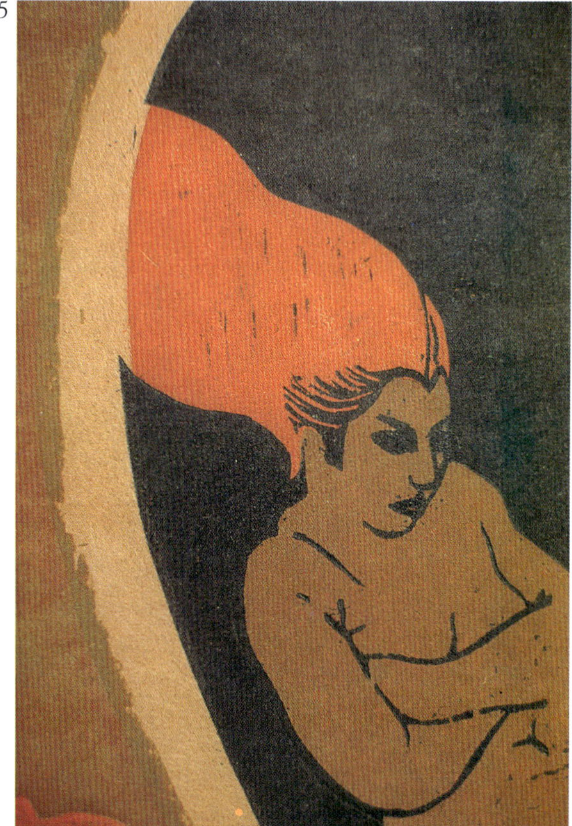

115A
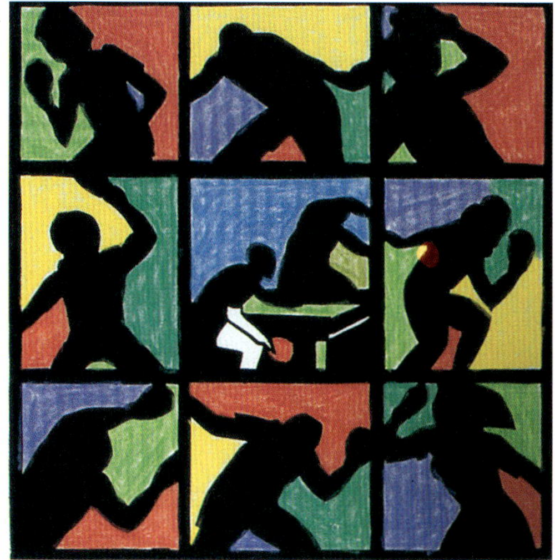

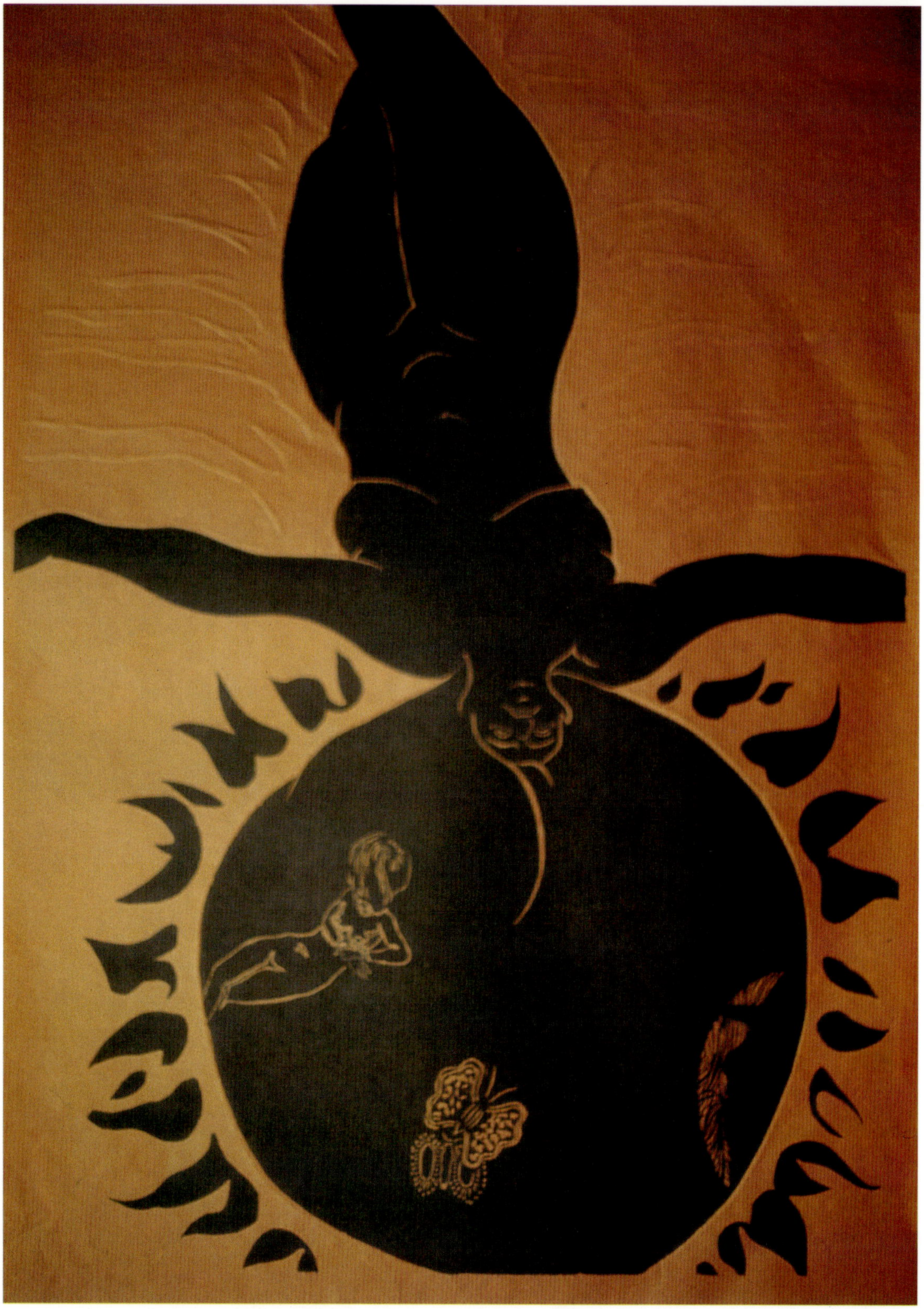

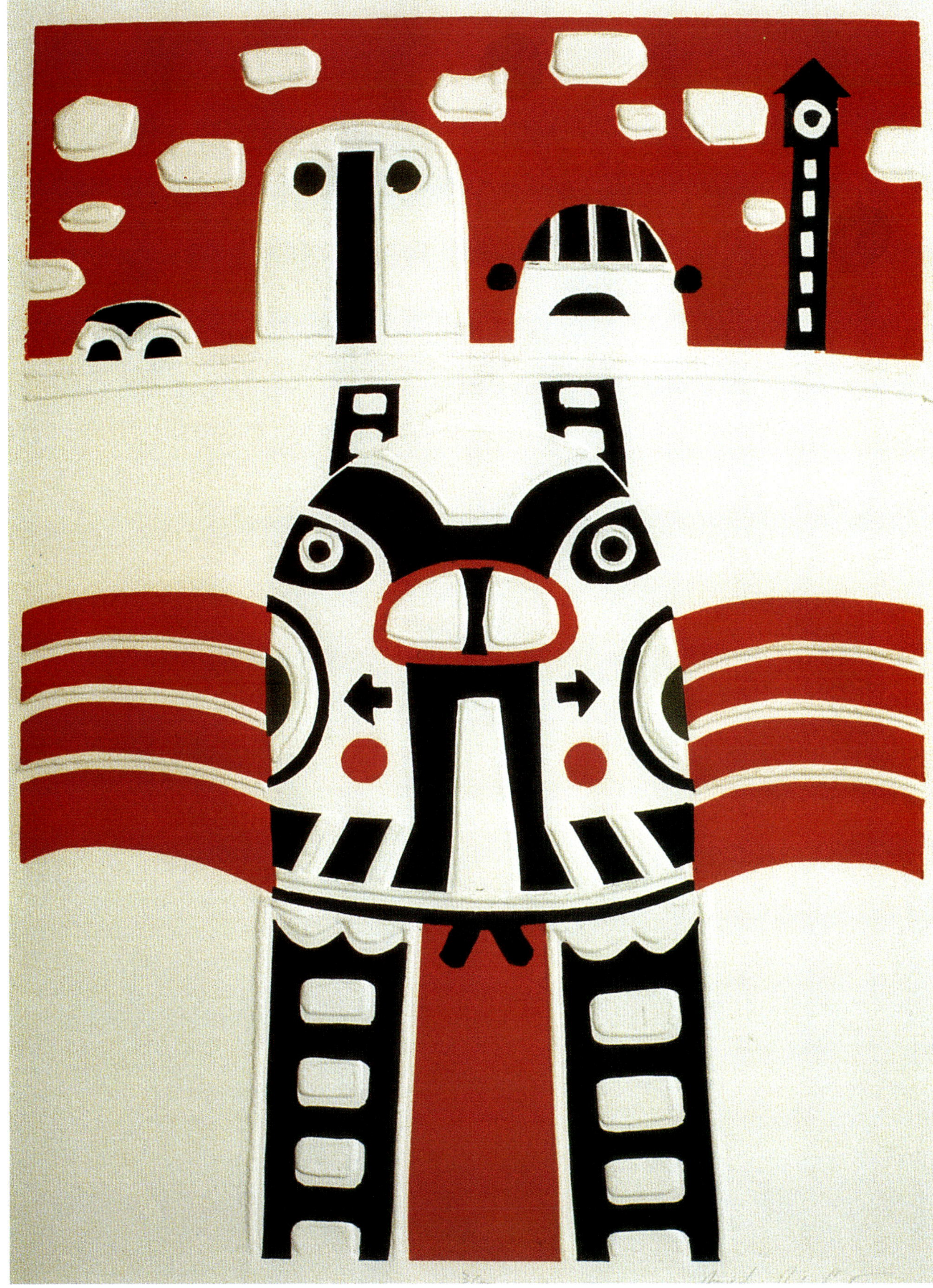

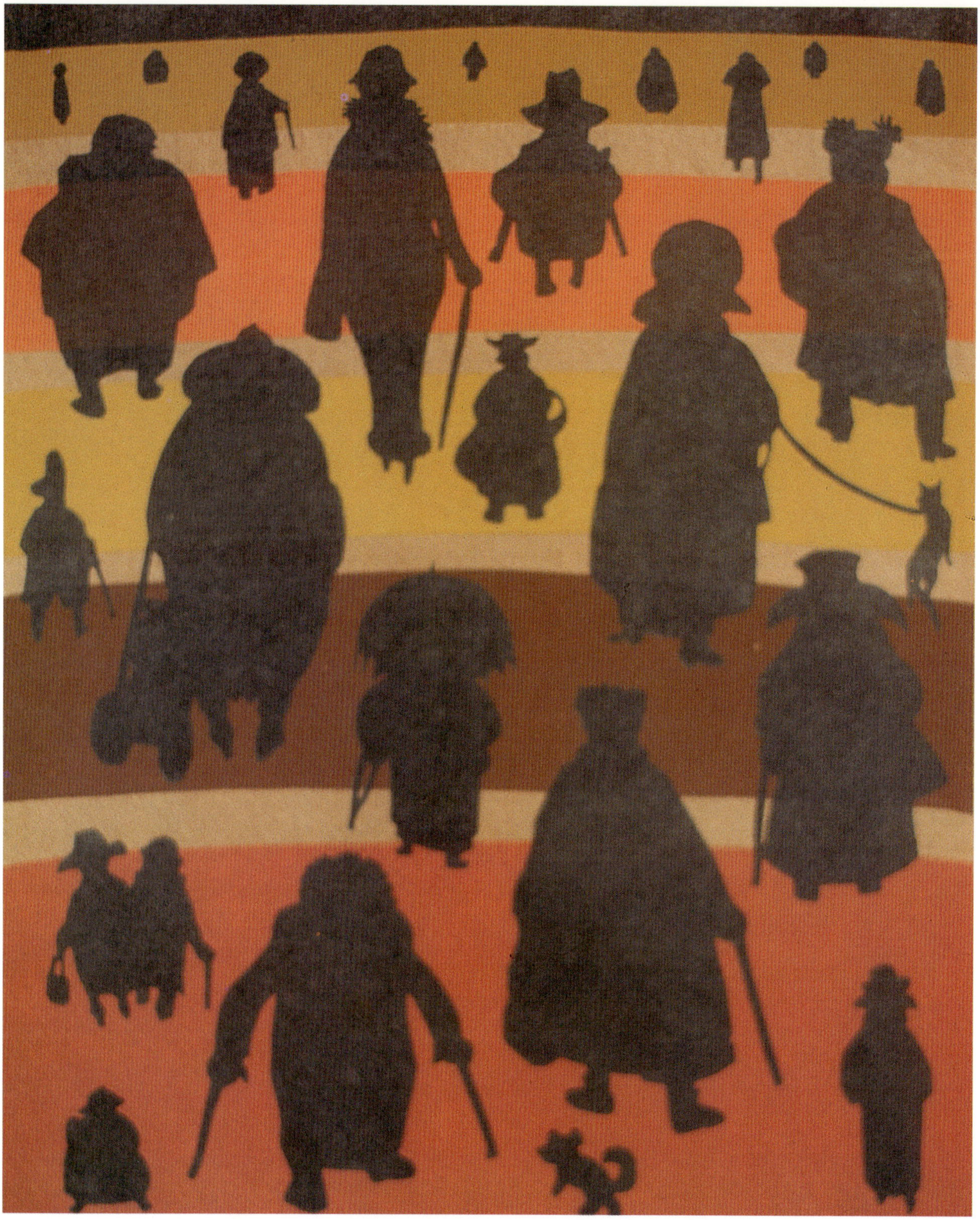

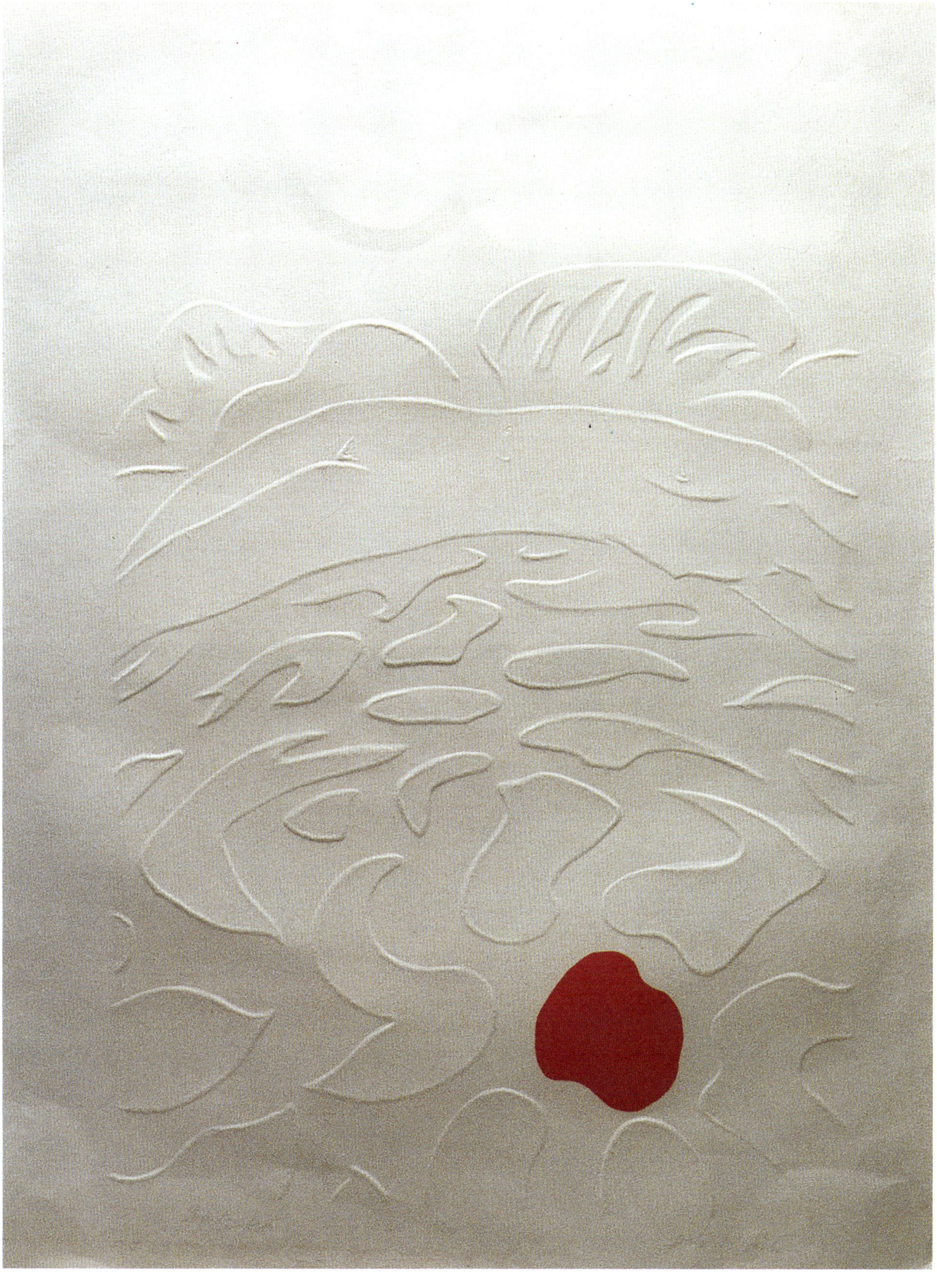

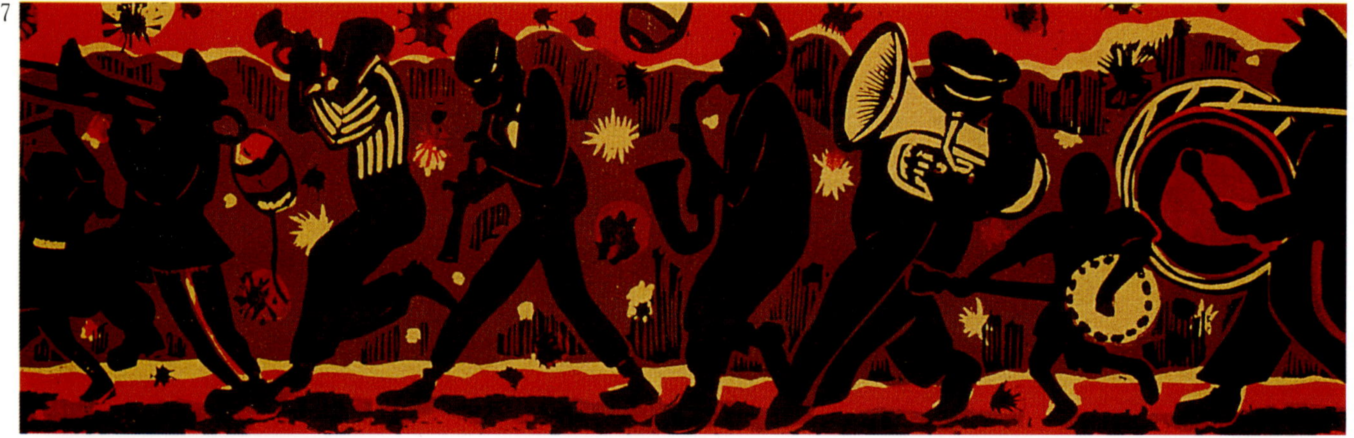

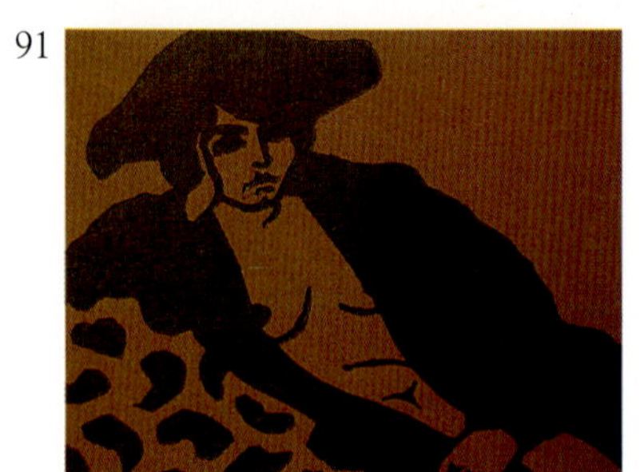

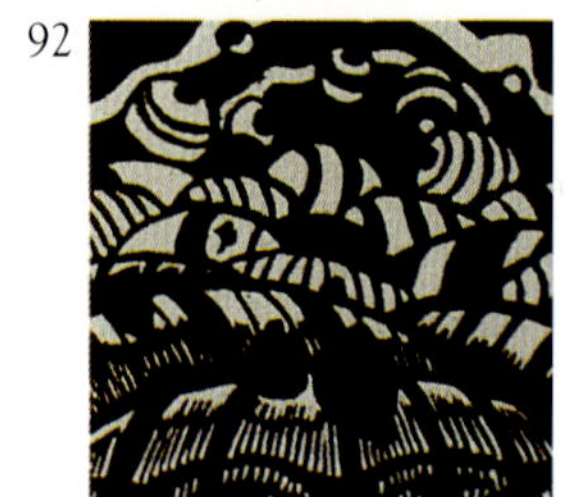

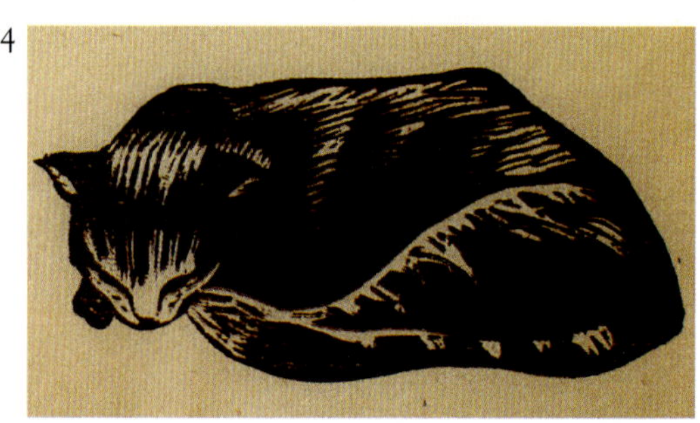

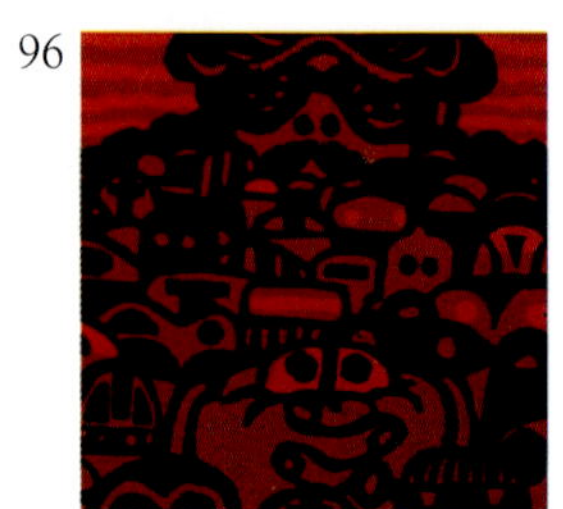

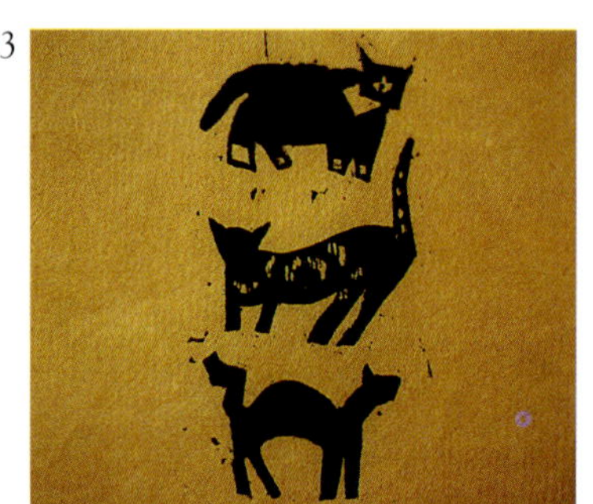

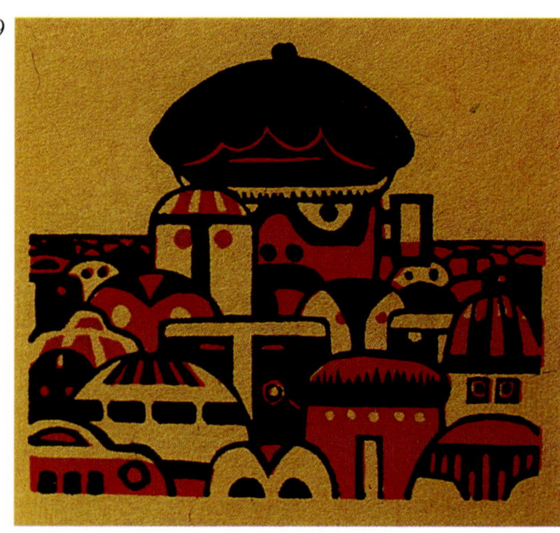

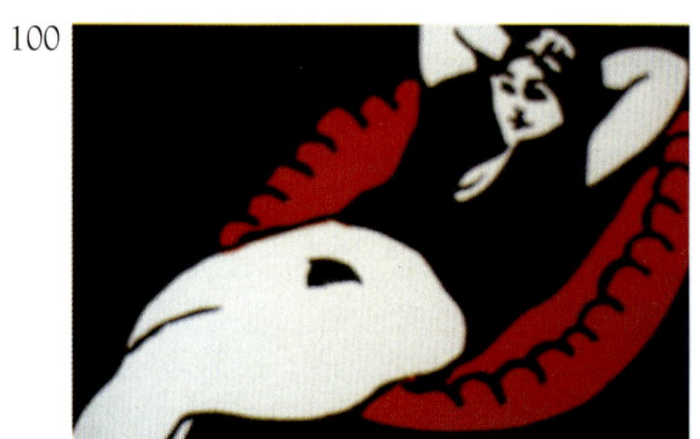

89. The Dark Sun (color woodcut embossment) 1970 30 x 21 (*see page 42*)

90. The White Sea (embossment) 1970 20 x 14 (*see page 45*)

91. Black & Tan (also titled "Black & Brown") (linocut) 1970 3 x 4

92. Head Space (linocut) 1970 2 x 2

93. Three Cats (linocut) c. 1970 3½ x 2

94. Catty (linocut) 1970 1½ x 3¼

95. The Chief (color woodcut embossment) 1971 16 x 12 (*see page 43*)

96. Auto-Portrait (color linocut) 1971 2 x 2

97. New Orleans Street Band (color woodcut) 1971 4½ x 14

98. Mardi Gras (color linocut) 1972 8 x 10

99. My Followers (color woodcut) 1972 2⅝ x 3

100. Jackie (color woodcut) 1972 4 x 6

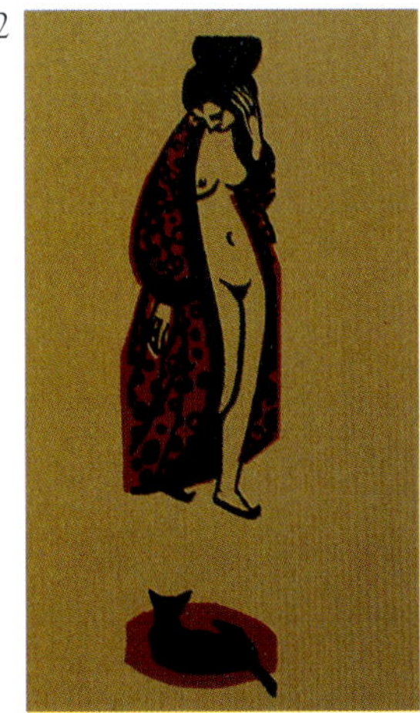

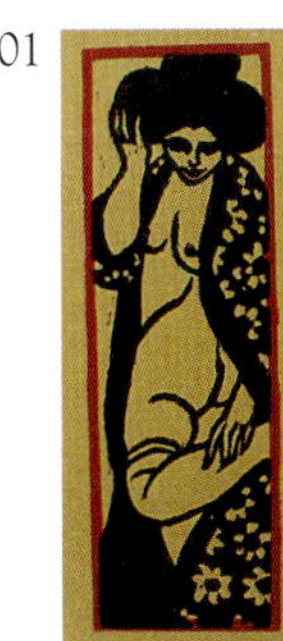

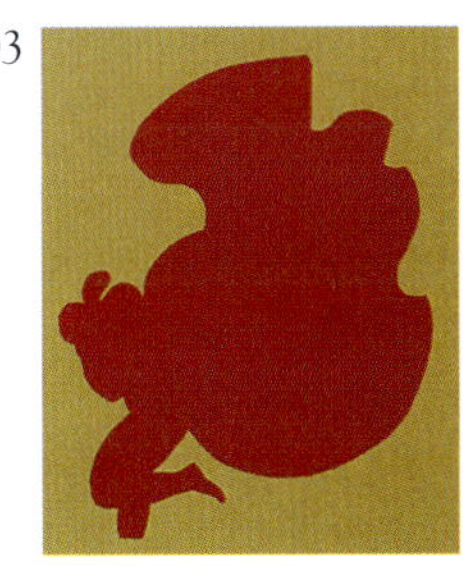

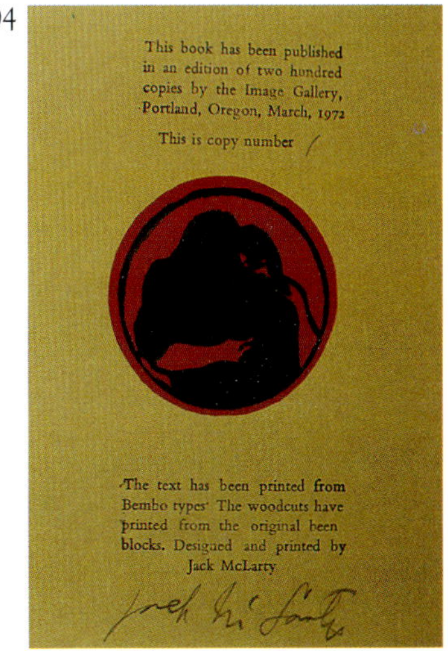

"TO HIS COY MISTRESS" was published by Image Gallery in March 1972 in an edition of two hundred copies. Each copy is signed and numbered on the colophon by the Artist and each contains four color woodcuts by Jack McLarty, printed from the original blocks. The text was printed from Bembo types at the Museum Art School, Portland, by the Artist.

101. Stocking Dance (color woodcut from "To His Coy Mistress")
1972 3½ x 1
102. Lady with a Cat (color woodcut from "To His Coy Mistress")
1972 4 x 1
103. Frontispiece for "To His Coy Mistress" (color woodcut) 1972
3½ x 3
104. Tail Piece for "To His Coy Mistress" (color woodcut) 1972
2" circle

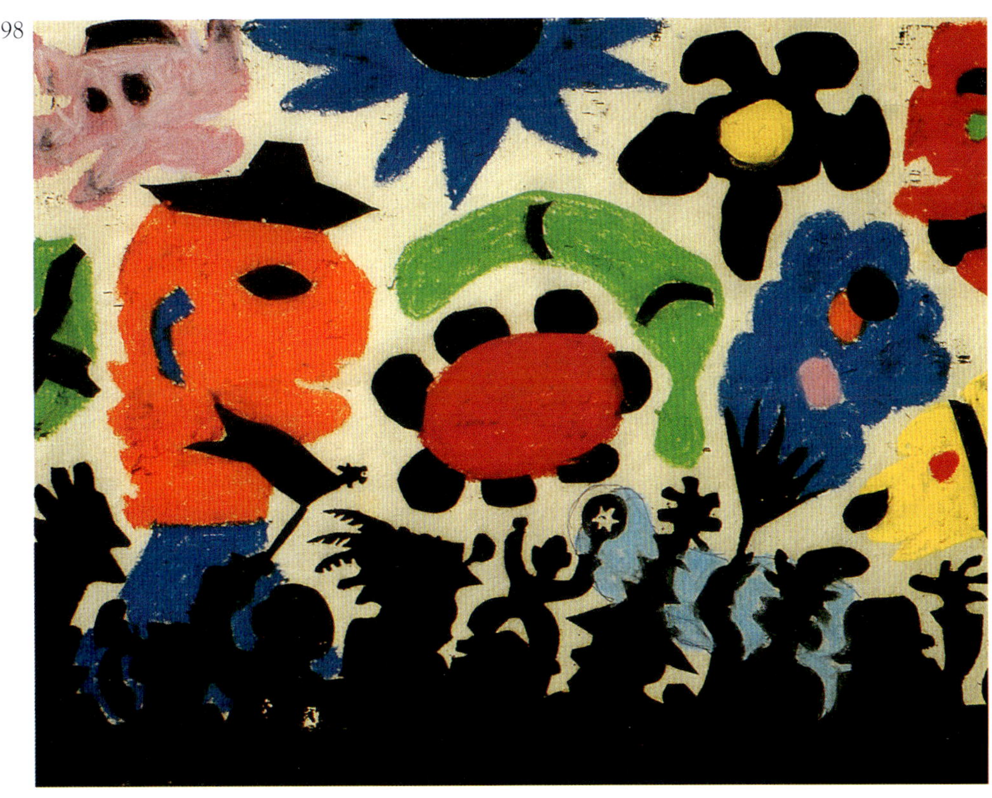

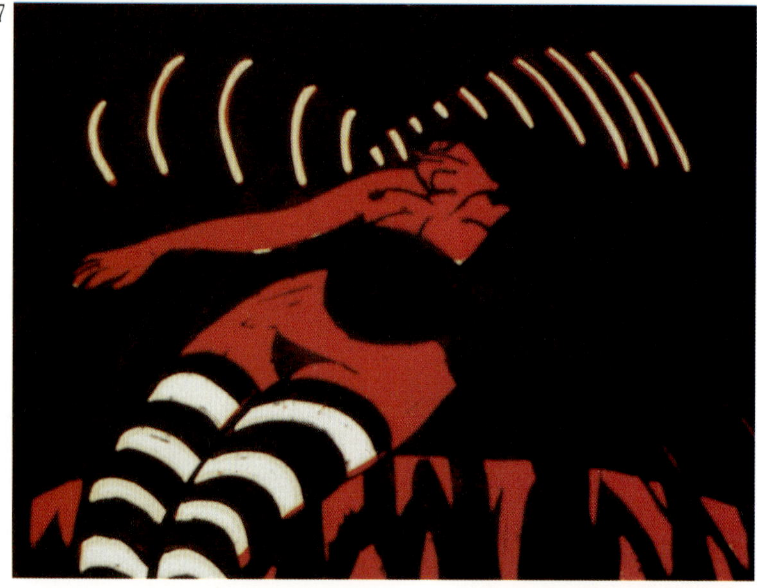

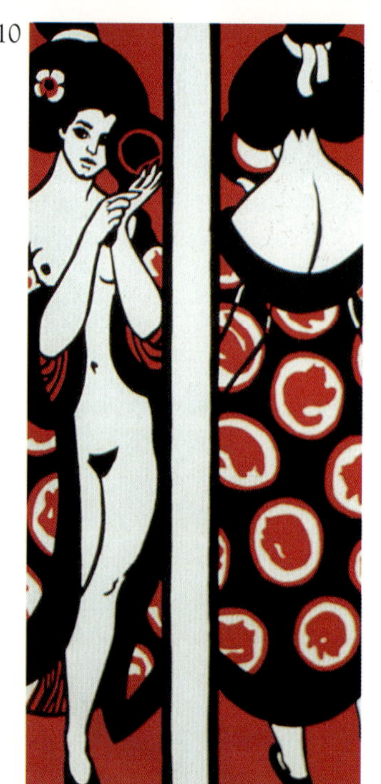

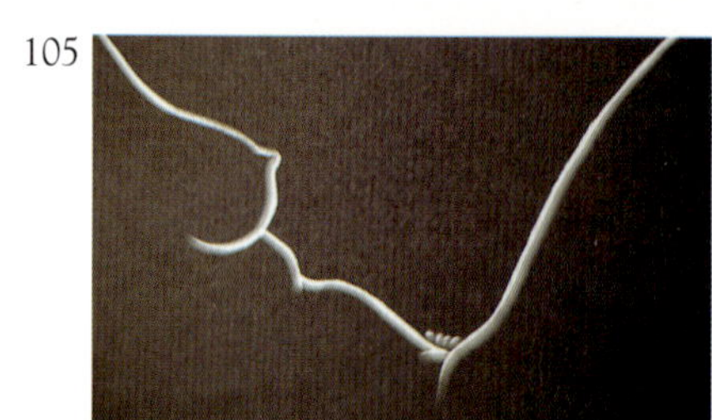

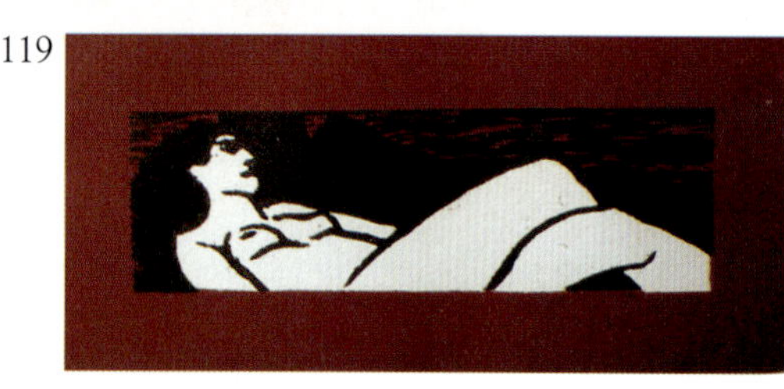
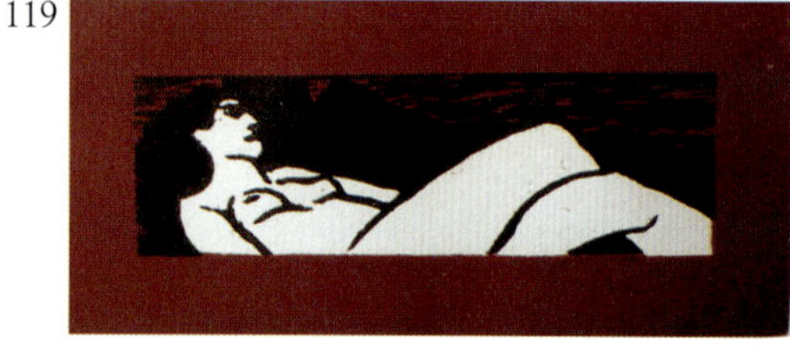

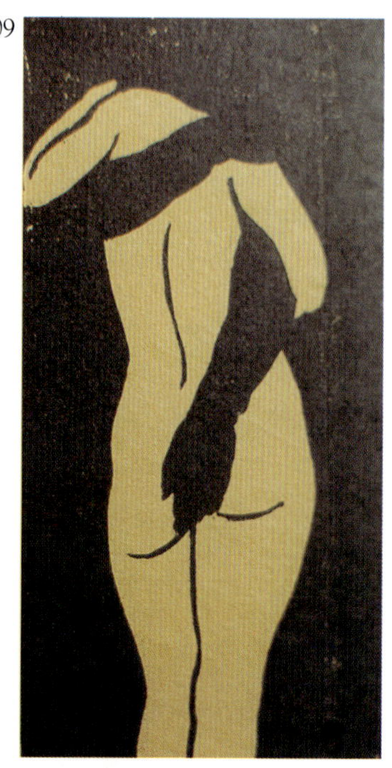

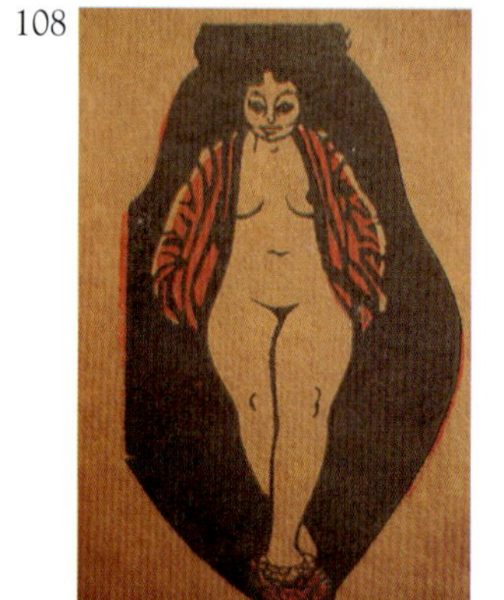

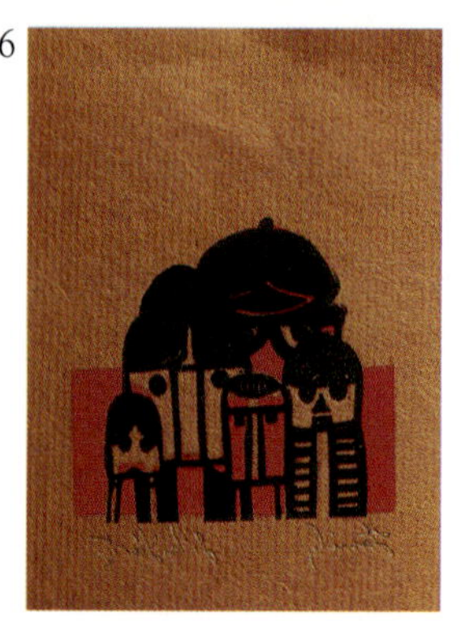

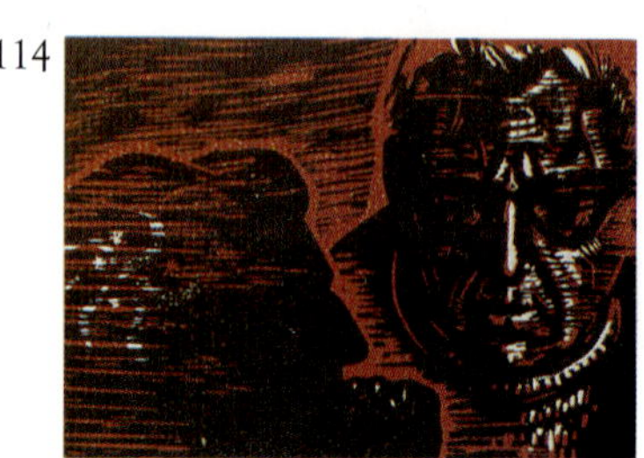

105. Contour (woodcut) 1972 4 x 5
106. The Family (color woodcut) 1972 2 x 2
107. The Striped Stockings (linocut) 1972 6 x 8
108. Caroline (also titled "Carey") (color woodcut) 1973 5 x 3
109. The Embrace (woodcut) 1973 4¾ x 2½
110. Double Mirror (color woodcut) 1973 21 x 10
111. The Shape of Life (color woodcut) 1973 10½ x 8¼ (*see page 44*)
112. Late Travelers (color linocut) 1974 9 x 12

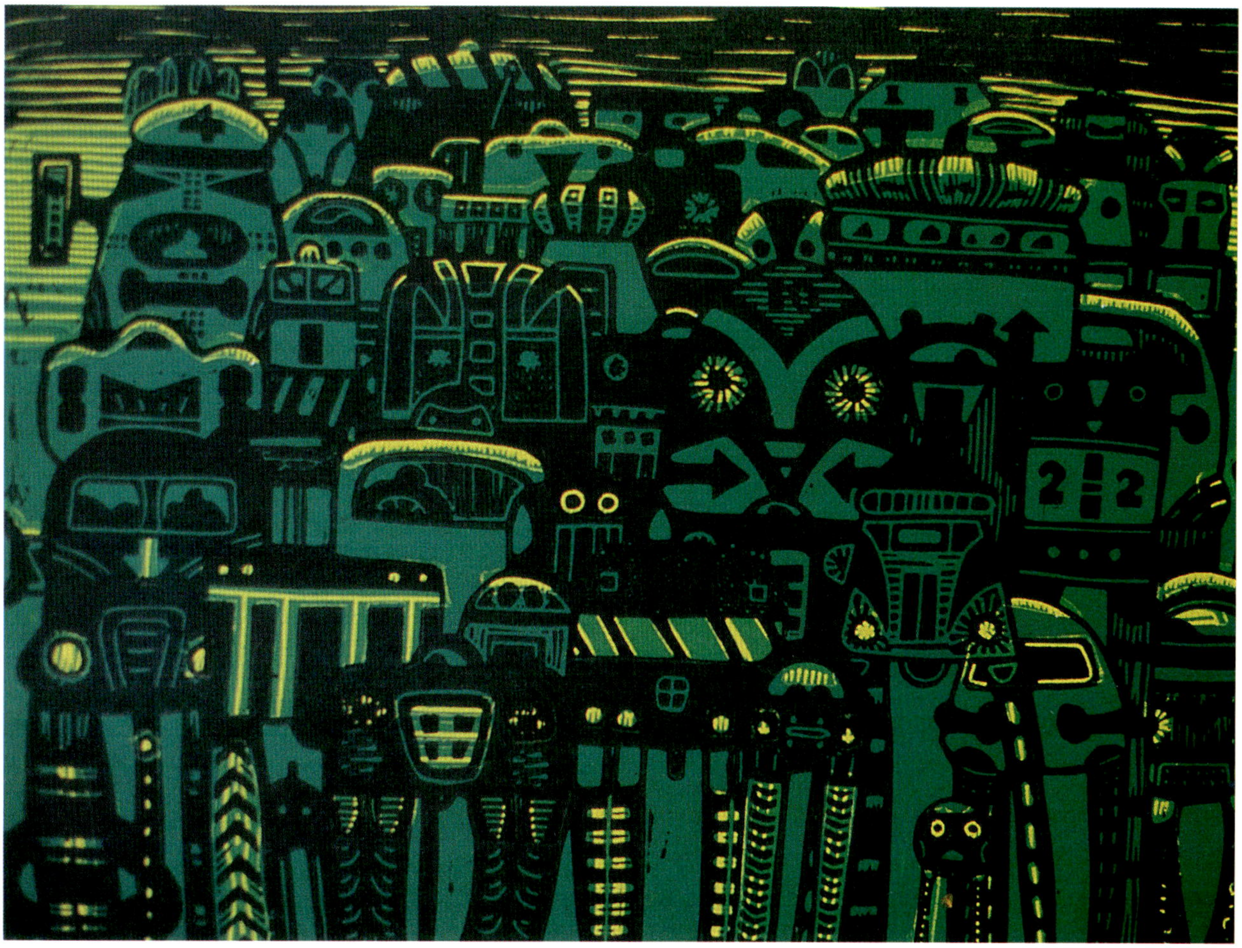

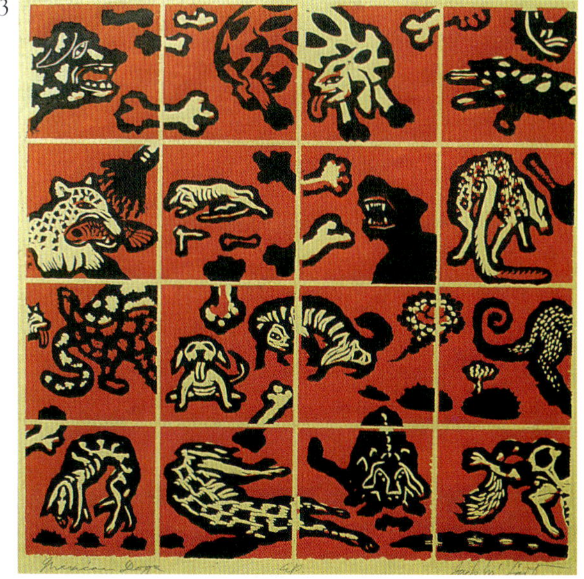

123

Dear Jack and Barbara,

. . . When I study and enjoy Jack's [work] I feel that I am being invited to look at the world I live in rather than the private world I might wish to create for escape. In my view, Jack has kept in contact with that social world we all live in . . . and we are responsible for what we make of this only world we have.

I appreciated the photo of the stained glass window in Newport at Sacred Heart Church. That was the last piece of work I was involved with before coming to Aloha. I know Walter was proud of that work. He used to bring friends to the chapel to see it.

The years go quickly by. I can still remember the first time I ever visited your gallery on N.W. Overton and found some wonderful Eskimo sculpture. And then, the many works of folkart from Mexico . . . you have brought to Portland have been a great gift to the people here. . . .

I just wanted to say thank you for the many ways you have increased my appreciation and love of art. . . .

Neil J. Moore, Aloha, Oregon, 9 December 1995

PRINTS IN THIS CATALOG:

1. Noel 1941
linocut 5 x 3
Sent as a Christmas card from NY December 1941
Very limited edition

2. Self 1942
lithograph 7¾ x 5
edition: 10
Shown: Image Gallery 1973; Cawein Gallery 1985; Maude Kerns
Art Center 1986

3. Painter 1942
lithograph 8½ x 6
edition: 10
Collection: Gilkey Center, Portland Art Museum, gift of the
Artist 1996

3A. Christmas Umbrellas 1943
lithograph 7 x 3¼
Sent as a Christmas card
Limited edition

4. Pinball City (also titled "City") 1943
lithograph 9½ x 16
edition: 12
Collections: Portland Community College, gift of the Artist
1976; Gilkey Center, Portland Art Museum, gift of the Artist
1996
Shown: *15th Annual Exhibition of Northwest Printmakers*, Seattle
Art Museum 1943; Image Gallery 1973; Cawein Gallery 1985;
McLartys' Choice 1995

5. Summer (also titled "Portland '43" and "Woman with Umbrella")
1944
lithograph 12 x 9¼
edition: 17
Collections: Portland Community College, gift of the Artist
1976; Gilkey Center, Portland Art Museum, gift of the Artist
1996
Shown: *10th Annual Drawing & Print Exhibition*, San Francisco
Art Museum 1946; Image Gallery 1973 & 1985; Cawein Gallery
1985

6. Street Corner 1944
lithograph 13¾ x 10
edition: 15
Collection: Gilkey Center, Portland Art Museum, gift of the
Artist 1996

7. Street 1944
lithograph 9 x 12
edition: 10
Collections: Gilkey Center, Portland Art Museum, gift of the
Artist 1996; Wallace K. Huntington
Shown: *16th Northwest Printmakers International Exhibition*, Seattle Art Museum 1946; Image Gallery 1973; Graven Images
Gallery 1994

8. Winter (also titled "Night City") 1945
lithograph 8½ x 13
edition: 10
Collections: Jean & Milan Stoyanov; Roger P. Hull; Gilkey Center, Portland Art Museum, gift of the Artist 1996
Shown: *10th Annual Drawing & Print Exhibition*, San Francisco
Art Museum 1946; *American Prints Today*, John Herron Art Museum, Indianapolis 1946; Image Gallery 1973 & 1985; McLartys'
Choice 1994

9. Betty 1945
lithograph 12 x 9
edition: 10
Collection: Gilkey Center, Portland Art Museum, gift of the
Artist 1996

9A. Christmas Umbrellas 1945
linocut 6 x 4
Sent as a Christmas card
Limited edition

10. The Bridge 1946
lithograph 14¾ x 10
edition: 15
Shown: *18th Northwest Printmakers International Exhibition*, Seattle Art Museum 1946; Image Gallery 1973 & 1985; Cawein
Gallery 1985; McLartys' Choice 1994; Graven Images Gallery
1994

11. Old Woman 1946
lithograph 17 x 10
edition: 15
Collections: Greta Morley; Gilkey Center, Portland Art Museum,
gift of Harrison Taylor 1989; George & Phyllis Johanson
Shown: Image Gallery 1973 & 1985; Cawein Gallery 1985

12. Birth Announcement: Polly Harrison McLarty May 1949
linocut 4 x 3
Limited edition

13. Polly with a Book 1950
linocut 2½ x 2¾
Sent as a Christmas card December 1950
Limited edition

14. Rose Parade Rider (also titled "Festival Rider") 1951
serigraph 16½ x 5¾
edition: 15
Collection: George & Phyllis Johanson
Shown: Kharouba Gallery 1953; *Printmakers' Fair*, Oregon Centennial Exposition 1959; Image Gallery 1973; Sovereign Gallery
1996

15. Old Woman with Turkeys (earlier titled "Turkeys" and "Old
Woman") 1951
serigraph 15½ x 7¾
edition: 15
Collections: George & Phyllis Johanson; Byrl Shellhart
Shown: *Prints by Oregon Artists 1952*, Portland Art Museum;
Kharouba Gallery 1953; *Printmakers' Fair*, Oregon Centennial
Exposition 1959; Image Gallery 1963 & 1973; Sovereign Gallery
1996

16. Birds in the Hedge (originally titled "The Hedge") 1952
serigraph 9¾ x 16
edition: 10
Shown: *Prints by Oregon Artists 1952*, Portland Art Museum;
Kharouba Gallery 1953; *Printmakers' Fair*, Oregon Centennial
Exposition 1959; Image Gallery 1963 & 1973; Sovereign Gallery
1996

17. Merry-Go-Round (Oaks Park) 1953
woodcut 9¼ x 18½
edition: 8
Collections: Willotta H. Asbjornsen; Greta Morley; Peter Melrose
Shown: *Printmakers' Fair*, Oregon Centennial Exposition 1959;
Image Gallery 1963 & 1973; Lakeside Studios Traveling Shows
1968–75; Cawein Gallery 1985; Sovereign Gallery 1996

18. Birth Announcement: Hugh Jensen McLarty June 1953
    linocut 2 x 2
    Limited edition

19. Birth Announcement: Charles Malcolm McLarty March 1955
    linocut 2 x 1½
    Limited edition

20. The Shop (also titled "The Butcher") 1955
    woodcut 12 x 9¼
    edition: 5
    Award: Honorable Mention, *7th Annual Oregon Print Exhibition*,
    Portland Art Museum 1955
    Shown also: *1958 Northwest Print Exhibition*, Henry Gallery, Seattle (a selection from the show traveled to Spokane Museum 1959); Image Gallery 1963 & 1973; Lakeside Studios Traveling Shows 1968–75; Cawein Gallery 1985; Graven Images Gallery 1994; Sovereign Gallery 1996

21. King of the River 1956
    etching 6⅜ x 4⅜
    edition: 5
    Collection: Michael Foster
    Shown: Image Gallery 1963 & 1973; Sovereign Gallery 1996

22. Beef 1956
    woodcut 18 x 3
    edition: 10
    Collection: Michael Kavanaugh
    Shown: Image Gallery 1963; Sovereign Gallery 1996

23. Rodeo Princess 1956
    woodcut 12¾ x 3½
    edition: 10
    Shown: Image Gallery 1963; Sovereign Gallery 1996

24. Merry-Go-Round #2 1956
    woodcut 20¼ x 3½
    edition: 10

25. Barbara 1956
    drypoint 7 x 5
    edition: 8
    Shown: Image Gallery 1963; Sovereign Gallery 1996

26. The Birds 1956
    linocut 6 x 9
    Sent as a Christmas card December 1956
    Limited edition

27. Persephone 1957
    aquatint 15 x 8¾
    edition: 5
    Shown: Image Gallery 1963; Sovereign Gallery 1996

28. The Market (originally titled "Butcher Shop") 1957
    aquatint 9 x 11½
    edition: 10
    Award: Honorable Mention, *1958 Northwest Print Exhibition*, Henry Gallery, Seattle (it went to Spokane Museum 1959 with a selection from the show)
    Collection: Kathleen McCuistion
    Shown also: Image Gallery 1963

29. Butchers' Ball 1957
    aquatint 9 x 14¾
    edition: 5
    Not Shown

30. Rodeo 1958
    woodcut 16 x 12
    edition: 15
    Collection: Gilkey Center, Portland Art Museum, gift of Dora Oake 1982
    Shown: *1958 Northwest Print Exhibition*, Henry Gallery, Seattle; *Printmakers' Fair*, Oregon Centennial Exposition 1959; Image Gallery 1963, 1973 & 1985; Carlin Galleries 1967; Lakeside Studios Traveling Shows 1968–75; Sovereign Gallery 1996

31. Hughie 1958
    color woodcut 7¾ x 6
    edition: 6
    Collection: Michael Foster
    Shown: Image Gallery 1963 & 1973; Cawein Gallery 1985; Sovereign Gallery 1996

32. Wrestlers 1959
    woodengraving 10 x 8
    edition: 5
    Shown: Image Gallery 1963 & 1973

33. The Hunter 1960
    collograph 11½ x 9
    edition: 10
    Shown: *Oregon Artist Series*, a circulating show of McLarty drawings and prints, organized by Statewide Services, University of Oregon Museum. The exhibition traveled during 1972–73 to: Erb Memorial Student Union, Eugene; The Dalles Art Club; Mt. Hood Community College, Gresham; Linn-Benton Community College, Lebanon; Umpqua Community College, Roseburg; Rogue Valley Art Center, Medford
    Shown also: Image Gallery 1973 & 1985; Cawein Gallery 1985

34. Reclining Nude 1961
    collograph 3¾ x 7¼
    edition: 10
    Collection: Bruce Wildrick
    Shown: Image Gallery 1962 & 1973; Lakeside Studios Traveling Shows 1968–75

35. "Butterfly" 1961
    woodcut 16¼ x 12
    Special edition of 15 pulled for supporting patrons of Image Gallery
    Collections: Virginia Haseltine Collection of Northwest Art, University of Oregon Museum; Lillie H. Lauha; Hilda & Moshe Lenske
    Shown: Image Gallery 1962 & 1973; *Pacific Northwest Art, the Haseltine Collection*, University of Oregon Museum 1963; Corvallis Arts Center 1967; *Oregon Artist Series*, Statewide Services Circulating Show 1972–73 (See #33); Maude Kerns Art Center 1986

36. Giant Runner 1962
    collograph 14¾ x 11¼
    edition: 5
    Collection: Southwestern Oregon Community College, gift of the Artist 1978
    Shown: Carlin Galleries, Ft. Worth 1967; Image Gallery 1973 & 1985; Maude Kerns Art Center, Eugene 1986

37. The Hat Game (also titled "The Game") 1962
etching 4¾ x 14
edition: 10
Collection: Bob & Beverly Shoemaker
Shown: *Northwest Printmakers 35th International Exhibition*, Seattle Art Museum 1964; Image Gallery 1962 & 1973; *4th Pacific Northwest Art Annual*, Erb Memorial Student Union, Eugene 1964; *Oregon Artist Series*, Statewide Services 1972–73 (See #33); Cawein Gallery 1985

38. Girl with a Scarf 1962
serigraph 32 x 18
edition: 20
Collection: Mrs. Gus J. Solomon; Ray & Ruth Matthews
Shown: Image Gallery 1963

39. Over and Out 1963
etching 10 x 12
Special edition of 20 pulled for supporting patrons of Image Gallery
Collections: Win & Madeleine Liepe; Virginia Haseltine Collection of Northwest Art; Clyde & Jane Van Cleve
Shown: Image Gallery 1963 & 1973; *4th Pacific Northwest Art Annual*, Erb Memorial Student Union, Eugene 1964; *Oregon Artist Series*, Statewide Services 1972–73 (See #33); Cawein Gallery 1985; Maude Kerns Art Center 1986

40. Moon Chair 1963
etching 5¾ x 6¾
edition: 5
Shown: Image Gallery 1963 & 1973

41. Portrait of George 1963
collograph 11¾ x 9
edition: 8
Shown: Image Gallery 1963 & 1973; *Oregon Artist Series*, Statewide Services 1972–73 (See #33)

42. The Green Girl 1963
collograph 15 x 11½
edition: 5
Shown: Image Gallery 1963 & 1973

43. Fall Gently 1963
color woodcut 13 x 12
edition: 10
Collections: Salishan Lodge; Southwestern Oregon Community College, gift of the Artist 1978; Evelyn Gordon
Shown: *Northwest Printmakers Exhibition*, Seattle 1963; Image Gallery 1963 & 1973; Carlin Galleries, Ft. Worth 1967

44. Profile of a Woman 1963
etching 12 x 15½
edition: 3
Executed in the workshop of Paul Franck, Paris
Collection: Marian Lee & Henry S. Mears, Jr.
Shown: Image Gallery 1964

45. The Flute (also titled "Flutist") 1964
etching 2 x 2⅛
edition: 5
Collections: Hugh & Lisbeth McLarty; Bill & Barbara Lewis; Virginia Haseltine Collection of Northwest Art
Shown: Image Gallery 1964

46. Warm Figure 1964
collograph 12 x 8¾
edition: 10
Shown: Image Gallery 1964 & 1973; Corvallis Arts Center 1967; Cawein Gallery 1985

47. Dark Struggle (also titled "Lady Wrestlers") 1964
collograph 15 x 12
edition: 5
Collections: Byrl Shellhart; Lillie H. Lauha
Shown: Image Gallery 1964 & 1973; *Oregon Artist Series*, Statewide Services 1972–73 (See #33); Cawein Gallery 1985

48. Angel of Love 196
collograph 15 x 11¾
editions: 6 & 10
There were two versions. We show version No. 1, which is in the Collection of Southwestern Oregon Community College, gift of the Artist 1978. No. 2 was shown: Image Gallery 1964 & 1973; *Oregon Artist Series*, Statewide Services 1972–73 (See #33)

49. The White Bed 1964
collograph 13¼ x 9½
edition: 10
Collection: Jim & Maury Haseltine
Shown: Image Gallery 1964 & 1973; Boise Art Gallery 1967; *Oregon Artist Series*, Statewide Services 1972–73 (See #33)

50. Rain Figure 1964
collograph 11½ x 9
edition: 10
Collection: Greta Morley
Shown: Image Gallery 1964 & 1973; Carlin Galleries 1967

51. The Black Coat 1964
aquatint 2 x 2
edition: 12, 2nd edition pulled 1965
Collections: Virginia Haseltine Collection of Northwest Art; Marian Lee & Henry S. Mears, Jr.; Edward & Judy Peck; Delores Gardner; Laura L. Chaivoe; Rene McCullough; Sally Kibbee; William Cumming
Shown: *1st International Miniature Print Exhibition*, Pratt Graphic Art Center, N.Y. The show circulated nationwide 1964–65. Shown also: Image Gallery 1964 & 1973

52. The Flexible Flyer 1964
etching 5½ x 4⅛
edition: 10
Collection: Jim & Maury Haseltine
Shown: Image Gallery 1964 & 1973; *4th Pacific Northwest Art Annual*, Erb Memorial Student Union, Eugene 1964; Boise Art Gallery 1967; Carlin Galleries 1967; *Oregon Artist Series*, Statewide Services Circulating Show 1972–73 (See #33); Maude Kerns Art Center 1986

53. Looking Glass 1964
aquatint 5½ x 4¼
edition: 10
Shown: Carlin Galleries 1967; Image Gallery 1964 & 1973

54. Heads Up 1964
etching 5½ x 4¼
edition: 10
Collection: Karen Wasser
Shown: Image Gallery 1964 & 1973

55. Dark Mirror 1965
collograph 4½ x 3⅛
edition: 7
Collections: Bob & Beverly Shoemaker; David E. Lindenberger
Shown: Image Gallery 1965 & 1973; Lakeside Studios Traveling Shows 1968–75

56. The Mirror 1965
collograph 12 x 9
edition: 10
Shown: Image Gallery 1965

57. Venus 1965
aquatint 2 x 2
edition: 8
Collection: David E. Lindenberger
Shown: Image Gallery 1965 & 1973; Lakeside Studios Traveling
Shows 1968–75

58. Floaters 1965
etching 5½ x 8¾
edition: 10
Collection: Virginia Haseltine Collection of Northwest Art
Shown: Image Gallery 1965 & 1973; *Oregon Artist Series*; Statewide Services Circulating Show 1972–73 (See #33)

59. The Woman 1966
aquatint 1¾ x 2¼
edition: 15
Shown: *2nd International Miniature Print Exhibition*, Pratt Graphic Art Center, N.Y. The show circulated nationwide 1966–67
Shown also: Image Gallery 1966 & 1973; The Little Gallery, Raleigh, N.C. 1968; *Oregon Artist Series*, Statewide Services Circulating Show 1972–73 (See #33)

60. Circle of Love 1966
color woodcut 8" circle
editions: 15 on white; 10 on yellow moriki
Special edition of 25 commissioned by Ferdinand Roten Galleries, Baltimore 1967
Awards: Purchase Award, *Northwest Printmakers Exhibition*, Henry Gallery, Seattle 1966; chosen for reproduction Book #5, "Prize Winning Graphics," Allied Publications, Ft. Lauderdale, Fla. 1967
Collections: Henry Gallery, University of Washington; University of Missouri, Columbia; State University of New York, Brockport
Shown: *2nd Annual Printmakers in Oregon Invitational*, organized by Ron Tore Janson, Maude Kerns Art Center, and circulated to: Brigham Young University, Salt Lake City; Yellowstone Art Center, Billings; Salishan Lodge, Gleneden, Oregon
Shown also: Image Gallery 1966 & 1973; The Little Gallery, Raleigh, N.C. 1968; Lakeside Studios Traveling Shows 1968–75; *Oregon Artist Series*, Statewide Services 1972–73 (See #33); Cawein Gallery 1985

61. The Night Clock 1966
color woodcut 12" circle
edition: 50
Collection: David E. Lindenberger
Shown: Image Gallery 1967 & 1973; Lakeside Studios Traveling Shows 1972–73 (See #33)

62. The Shape of Love 1966
color woodcut from "17 Love Poems" 4 x 1
edition: 20
Shown: Image Gallery 1966 & 1973; The Little Gallery 1967; Lakeside Studios Traveling Shows 1968–75

63. Dark Woman 1966
color woodcut from "17 Love Poems" 3 x 4
edition: 20
Shown: Image Gallery 1966 & 1973; The Little Gallery 1967; Lakeside Studios Traveling Shows 1968–75

64. Intimate Moment 1966
color woodcut from "17 Love Poems" 4 x 3
edition: 20
Collection: Stephen Leflar
Shown: Image Gallery 1966 & 1973; The Little Gallery 1967; Lakeside Studios Traveling shows 1968–75

65. Wings of Love 1966
color woodcut from "17 Love Poems" 3 x 4
edition: 20
Shown: Image Gallery 1966 & 1973; Lakeside Studios Traveling Shows 1968–75; *Oregon Artist Series*, Statewide Services 1972–73 (See #33); The Little Gallery 1973

66. Self (also titled "J. M.") 1966
color woodcut from "17 Love Poems" 1½ x 2
edition: 20
Shown: Image Gallery 1966 & 1973; Lakeside Studios Traveling Shows 1968–75; *Oregon Artist Series*, Statewide Services 1972–73 (See #33); The Little Gallery 1973

67. The Wind 1966
color woodcut from "17 Love Poems" 2⅛ x 4½
edition: 20
Collection: Princeton University Library
Shown: Image Gallery 1966 & 1973; The Little Gallery 1968; Lakeside Studios Traveling Shows 1968–75

68. Madame M 1966
color woodcut from "17 Love Poems" 2 x 2
edition: 30
Shown: Image Gallery 1966 & 1973; The Little Gallery 1968; Lakeside Studios Traveling Shows 1968–75

69. The Siren 1966
color woodcut from "17 Love Poems" 2 x 2
edition: 20
Shown: Image Gallery 1966 & 1973; Lakeside Studios Traveling Shows 1968–75

70. Propeller of Night 1966
color woodcut 30 x 21
edition: 15
Collections: Salem Art Association, gift of the Artist; First Interstate Bank; Mary T. Winch; Phyllis Bottomly; William F. Yee
Shown: Image Gallery 1966 & 1973; *2nd Annual Printmakers in Oregon Invitational*, organized by Ron Tore Janson, Maude Kerns Art Center, Eugene (See #60); Lakeside Studios Traveling Shows 1968–75; *Oregon Artist Series*, Statewide Services Circulating Show 1972–73 (See #33); Cawein Gallery 1985; Art Space 1995

71. Mirror Image 1966
woodcut 30 x 21
edition: 8
Collection: Nancy J. Snow
Shown: Image Gallery 1967 & 1973; Corvallis Arts Center 1967; Lakeside Studios Traveling Shows 1968–75; *Oregon Artist Series*, Statewide Services Circulating Show 1972–73 (See #33); Cawein Gallery 1985

72. Clouds 1966
linocut 3 x 4
sent as a Christmas card December 1966
Limited edition
Collection: Clyde & Jane Van Cleve
Shown: Lakeside Studios Traveling Shows 1968–75

73. Pretty Woman 1967
woodcut 4½ x 5½
edition: 11
Shown: Image Gallery 1967 & 1973; Salishan Lodge 1967; Lakeside Studios Traveling Shows 1968–75

74. Troubled Mind (also titled "The Mask" and "Masked Woman") 1967
woodcut 8 x 8
edition: 10
Collection: Kathryn Longstreth-Brown
Shown: Image Gallery 1967 & 1973; *Oregon Artist Series*, Statewide Services Circulating Show 1972–73 (See #33)

75. The Body of the Dreamer 1967
color woodcut 9½" circle
editions: 50 on yellow moriki; 50 on red moriki
Collections: Gilkey Center, Portland Art Museum, gift of Harrison Taylor 1989; Lynda & Michael Falkenstein
Shown: Image Gallery 1967 & 1973; The Little Gallery 1968; Lakeside Studios Traveling Shows 1968–75; *9th Pacific Northwest Art Annual*, an invitational, Erb Memorial Student Union, Eugene 1969; *Oregon Artist Series* Statewide Services Circulating Show 1972–73 (See #33)

76. Evening Dream (also titled "Evening Dreamer") 1967
color woodcut 9 x 5
edition: 20
Collections: Deborah L. Martin; Portland Community College, gift of the Artist 1976; Virginia Haseltine Collection of Northwest Art
Shown: Image Gallery 1967, 1973 & 1985; *Oregon Artist Series*, Statewide Services Circulating Show 1972–73 (See #33); The Little Gallery 1973

77. Nude with Mirror 1967
etching 2 x 1¾
edition: 10
Shown: Image Gallery 1967 & 1973

78. Emerging Woman 1967
woodcut 33 x 23
editions: 35 on white; 25 on yellow moriki
Special edition of 25 commissioned by Ferdinand Roten Galleries 1967
Originally conceived for and commissioned by *Northwest Review* at University of Oregon for Spring Issue 1967
Collections: Gilkey Collection, Portland Art Museum; Bucknell University; Huntington Public Library, Huntington, N.Y.; Virginia Haseltine Collection of Northwest Art; Antonio Diez; Laille & Leon Gabinet; Neva Williamson; Willotta H. Asbjornsen; Arlene & Noah Krall; Laura McLarty & Keith Thompson; Martin Bloom; Ginger Walter
Selected for: *The Process of Woodcut & Woodengraving*, a traveling educational exhibition organized and circulated in Multnomah County by Portland Art Museum 1976
Shown: Image Gallery 1967 & 1973; Portland Art Museum 1967; The Little Gallery 1967; University of Oregon Museum 1968; Lakeside Studios Traveling Shows 1968–75; *Oregon Artist Series*, Statewide Services Circulating Show 1972–73 (See #33)

79. Ornaments of Love 1967
woodcut 7½ x 6½
edition: 50
Special edition of 35 pulled for supporting patrons of Image Gallery and titled "Beardsley's Mother"
Collections: Mary & John Uchiyama; Lillie H. Lauha
Shown: Image Gallery 1967 & 1973; Lakeside Studios Traveling Shows 1968–75; Oregon Artist Series, Statewide Services Circulating Show 1972–73 (See #33)

80. Secret Mind 1968
woodcut 12¾ x 9½
edition: 40
Collections: Bob Childerhose & Marje Trim; Thomas & Meredith Dement; Bill & Barbara Lewis; Virginia Haseltine Collection of Northwest Art; Byrl Shellhart; Arthur & Margaret Wasser
Shown: Image Gallery 1968 & 1973; Lakeside Studios Traveling Shows 1968–75; *9th Pacific Northwest Art Annual*, an invitational, Erb Memorial Student Union, Eugene 1969; *Oregon Artist Series*, Statewide Services Circulating Show 1972–73 (See #33)

81. Love is Black 1968
woodcut 4 x 3
edition: 50
Collection: David E. Lindenberger
Shown: Image Gallery 1968 & 1973; Lakeside Studios Traveling Shows 1968–75; *Oregon Artist Series*, Statewide Services Circulating Show 1972–73 (See #33); The Little Gallery 1973

82. The White Robe 1968
woodcut 14 x 12¼
edition: 5
Collections: Southwestern Oregon Community College, gift of the Artist 1978; Bill & Barbara Lewis
Shown: Image Gallery 1968 & 1973; The Little Gallery 1968; Southwestern Oregon Community College 1980

83. Close Up 1968
etching 2 x 2
No edition pulled
Not Shown

84. The Party Pig 1969
color woodcut 4¾ x 10
edition: 40
Collections: Eloise J. McGraw; Sylvia Sheppard; Anne Lever
Shown: Image Gallery 1969 & 1973

85. Half-Dark 1969
color woodcut embossment 6 x 4
edition: 50
Collections: David E. Lindenberger; Ray & Ruth Matthews
Shown: Image Gallery 1969 & 1973; Lakeside Studios Traveling Shows 1968–75; *6th Annual Printmakers in Oregon Invitational*, Bush Barn Gallery, Salem 1971

86. Out of the Beautiful Past 1969
color woodcut embossment 16 x 13
edition: 50
Purchased for the Permanent Collection, Kalamazoo Art Museum 1970
Collections: Blanche & Milo Wold; Ray & Ruth Matthews
Shown: Image Gallery 1969 & 1973; Lakeside Studios Traveling Shows 1968–75; Renshaw Gallery 1971; Oregon Artist Series, Statewide Services Circulating Show 1972–73 (See #33); Cawein Gallery 1985

87. Look-In 1969
color linocut 2 x 2
edition: 40
Collection: Carol & Wayne Bridges
Shown: Image Gallery 1969 & 1973; Lakeside Studios Traveling
Shows 1968–75; *6th Annual Printmakers in Oregon Invitational*,
Bush Barn Gallery 1971; The Little Gallery 1973

88. Road Birds 1970
color linocut 6 x 8
edition: 50
Collections: George & Phyllis Johanson; Bill Rhoades & Coralee
Popp
Shown: Image Gallery 1972, 1973 & 1985; *Oregon Artist Series*,
Statewide Services Circulating Show 1972–73 (See #33); Tahir
Galleries 1973; Cawein Gallery 1985

89. The Dark Sun 1970
color woodcut embossment 30 x 21
edition: 12
Shown: Image Gallery 1970; Lakeside Studios Traveling Shows
1968–75; *Oregon Artist Series*, Statewide Services Circulating
Show 1972–73 (See #33)

90. The White Sea 1970
embossment 20 x 14
edition: 15
Collection: Bob & Martha Warnock
Shown: Image Gallery 1970 & 1973; *Spectrum '70*, Portland Art
Museum

91. Black & Tan (also titled "Black & Brown") 1970
linocut 3 x 4
edition: 100
Collections: Thomas & Meredith Dement; David E. Lindenberger
Shown: Image Gallery 1970

92. Head Space 1970
linocut 2 x 2
No edition pulled
Not Shown

93. Three Cats c. 1970
linocut 3½ x 2
Limited edition
Sent as a Christmas card

94. Catty 1970
linocut 1½ x 3¼
edition: 20
Shown: Image Gallery 1970; The Little Gallery 1973

95. The Chief 1971
color woodcut embossment 16 x 12
edition: 15
Shown: Image Gallery 1972 & 1973; *Oregon Artist Series*, Statewide Services 1972–73 (See #33); Cawein Gallery 1985; Maude
Kerns Art Center 1986

96. Auto-Portrait 1971
color linocut 2 x 2
edition: 15
Shown: Image Gallery 1972 & 1973; *Oregon Artist Series*, Statewide Services 1972–73 (See #33)

97. New Orleans Street Band 1971
color woodcut 4½ x 14
edition: 60
Commissioned by Abe Tahir, Director of Tahir Galleries, New
Orleans 1971
Collections: University of Mississippi, gift of Abe Tahir; Elinor
Shank
Shown: Tahir Galleries 1971; Image Gallery 1972 & 1973; Cawein Gallery 1985

98. Mardi Gras 1972
color linocut 8 x 10
edition: 5
Shown: Image Gallery 1973; Tahir Galleries 1973

99. My Followers 1972
color woodcut 2⅝ x 3
edition: 25
Shown: *Oregon Artist Series*, Statewide Services 1972–73 (See
#33); Image Gallery 1974

100. Jackie 1972
color woodcut 4 x 6
edition: 50
Half the edition purchased by the Eye Corporation, Chicago 1972
Shown: The Little Gallery 1973; Image Gallery 1974

101. Stocking Dance 1972
color woodcut from "To His Coy Mistress" 3½ x 1
edition: 100
Ferdinand Roten Galleries purchased part of the edition 1972
Shown: Image Gallery 1972; The Little Gallery 1973

102. Lady with a Cat 1972
color woodcut from "To His Coy Mistress" 4 x 1
edition: 100
Ferdinand Roten Galleries purchased part of the edition 1972
Collection: University of Oregon Museum, gift of Francis B.
Gesley 1979
Shown: Image Gallery 1972; The Little Gallery 1973

103. Frontispiece for "To His Coy Mistress" 1972
color woodcut 3½ x 3

104. Tail Piece for "To His Coy Mistress" 1972
color woodcut 2" circle

105. Contour 1972
woodcut 4 x 5
edition: 75
One-third of the edition purchased by the Eye Corporation, Chicago 1972
Selected for: *The Process of Woodcut & Woodengraving*, a traveling
educational exhibition organized and circulated in Multnomah
County by Portland Art Museum 1976
Shown: The Little Gallery 1973; Image Gallery 1974

106. The Family 1972
color woodcut 2 x 2
edition: 40
Shown: Image Gallery 1972 & 1991; The Little Gallery 1973

107. The Striped Stockings 1972
linocut 6 x 8
No edition pulled
Not Shown

108. Caroline (also titled "Carey") 1973
color woodcut 5 x 3
edition: 15
Shown: Image Gallery 1974

109. The Embrace 1973
woodcut 4¾ x 2½
edition: 50
Collection: Private Collection in Oregon
Shown: Image Gallery 1973

110. Double Mirror 1973
color woodcut 21 x 10
Special edition of 25 pulled for members of Art Advocates, Inc., who were project sponsors for McLarty for a year's work 1972–73
Special edition of 60 commissioned by Ferdinand Roten Galleries 1975
Collections: Lillie H. Lauha; Grace McDonald; Mayo Rae Rolph Roy; Simone Smith; Lynda & Michael Falkenstein
Shown: Image Gallery 1973; The Little Gallery 1973; Renshaw Gallery, Linfield College 1993

111. The Shape of Life 1973
color woodcut 10½ x 8¼
edition: 25
Collection: Hilda & Moshe Lenske
Special edition of 60 commissioned by Ferdinand Roten Galleries 1975
Shown: The Little Gallery 1973; Image Gallery 1973; Tahir Galleries, New Orleans 1973

112. Late Travelers 1974
color linocut 9 x 12
edition: 40
Shown: Image Gallery 1974 & 1991; Art Space 1995

113. Japanese Red 1974
color woodcut 22½ x 15
Commissioned by Lakeside Editions and pulled by Niel Borch Jensen at Lakeside Studios 1974
editions: 30 plus 10 proofs to the Artist; 19 and 10 proofs to Lakeside Editions. Block was effaced
The Lakeside impressions were distributed as follows: Benoit College; Bowdoin College; the British Museum; California Palace of the Legion of Honor; Davidson College; Dayton Art Institute; Drury College; Indiana State University; Kalamazoo Institute of Art; Kohler Art Center; the Library of Congress; Mesa Community College; Michigan State University; Nasson College; Museum of Fine Arts, Springfield, Mass.; Ringling Museum; Rockford College; the Smithsonian Institution; Southern Illinois University; University of Georgia; University of Maine; University of Nebraska; University of North Carolina; University of Utah; Wittenberg University.
Other Collections: Gilkey Center, Portland Art Museum; Marjorie Abramovitz & Marshall Goldberg; Gordon & Loise Hunter; Jon & Marian Granby
Shown: Image Gallery 1974, 1986 & 1991; Keller Gallery, Salem 1977

114. Loren Eiseley 1974
color woodcut 3 x 4
edition: 10
Special edition of 50 commissioned by Ferdinand Roten Galleries 1975
Collection: Loren D. Eiseley, gift of the Artist
Shown: Image Gallery 1974, 1986 & 1991

115. Black and White Cats 1974
woodcut embossment 6½ x 10½
edition: 50
Special edition of 30 commissioned by Portland Art Association to be offered to 25-year members
Collection: Carol & Wayne Bridges
Selected for: *The Process of Woodcut and Woodengraving*, a traveling educational exhibition organized and circulated in Multnomah County by Portland Art Museum 1976
Shown: Image Gallery 1974, 1986 & 1991; McMinnville Association of the Arts 1976; Art Space 1995

115A. Table Tennis Match c. 1975
color woodcut 11 x 11
No edition pulled, proofs only
Collections: Charles & Hiromi McLarty; Mayo Rae Rolph Roy
The basic design was used for a t-shirt commissioned by the Paddle Palace, Portland 1995

116. Figured Robe 1975 (Later edition "Aqua Figured Robe" not embossed)
color woodcut embossment 12 x 9
edition: 10; later edition: 20
Collections: Nell & William Givler; Barbara & Bill Lewis; J. Michael Deeney
Shown: *Oregon Printmakers 1975*, Portland Art Museum; Image Gallery 1975 & 1986; the Governor's Invitational Show 1985; Cawein Gallery 1985; Maude Kerns Art Center 1986

117. Lovers 1975
woodcut 3 x 3
Created for the cover of "You Wouldn't Know Us," poems by James Fleming 1975
Limited edition
Shown: Image Gallery 1975

118. Kat 1975
woodengraving 2 x 2
edition: 40
Shown: Image Gallery 1974; Art Space 1995

119. Reclining Figure 1975
color woodcut 2¼ x 5
edition: 25
Collection: Harry & Hanne Greaver
Special edition of 75 commissioned by Ferdinand Roten Galleries 1975
Shown: Image Gallery 1975

120. "August 1968" (also titled "The Ogre") 1975
woodengraving 3 x 2¾
edition: 25
Selected for: *The Process of Woodcut and Woodengraving*, a traveling educational exhibition organized and circulated in Multnomah County by Portland Art Museum 1976
Collection: Wilma Nelson
Shown: Image Gallery 1976, 1986 & 1991

121. The Heart of John Donne 1975 (Shown on the front cover)
color woodcut 21¾ x 14¾
edition: 20
Collections: Jane Huston Rawlins; Neva Williamson
Shown: Image Gallery 1975; Cawein Gallery 1985; Sovereign Gallery 1995

122. Jazz Shadows 1975
    woodcut 10 x 7
    edition: 50
    A partial edition purchased by Ferdinand Roten Galleries 1977
    Shown: *Oregon Printmakers 1975*, Portland Art Museum; Image
    Gallery 1975, 1986 & 1991

123. Mexican Dogs 1975
    color woodcut 12 x 12
    edition: 40
    Collection: Oregon Humane Society, gift of David E. Linden-
    berger honoring Daniel Lindenberger
    Shown: *Oregon Printmakers 1975*, Portland Art Museum; Image
    Gallery 1975, 1986 & 1991

124. The Return 1975
    woodengraving 4 x 3
    edition: 10
    Collection: Carol & Wayne Bridges
    Shown: Image Gallery 1975 & 1991

125. Red Passage 1976
    color linocut 15 x 23
    edition: 40
    Collections: Pacific University, gift of the Artist 1985; Southern
    Oregon State College, presented by the Oregon Arts Commis-
    sion 1977; Neil J. Moore; Elaine & George Chandler; Thomas &
    Meredith Dement
    Chosen for: *Art for People with More Taste than Money*, a traveling
    show sponsored by Oregon Arts Commission. Work by 34 Oregon
    printmakers was included, documented on a handsome large-scale
    poster
    Shown: Image Gallery 1976 & 1991; *Sapporo-Portland Print Exhi-
    bition*, sponsored jointly by the Northwest Print Council and Port-
    land State University 1984; the Governor's Invitational Show
    1985; Rogue Gallery 1985; Cawein Gallery 1985; Maude Kerns
    Art Center 1986; Art Space 1995

126. Thirty-six Basic Cat Positions 1976
    color woodcut 21½ x 14½
    edition: 40
    Collections: Eloise J. McGraw; Tom Hardy; Jon & Marian
    Granby; Oregon Humane Society, gift of David E. Lindenberger
    honoring Daniel Lindenberger
    Shown: Image Gallery 1976, 1987 & 1991; Cawein Gallery 1985;
    Graven Image Gallery 1994

127. Wedding Announcement for Joe McDonald 1976
    woodengraving 3 x 1½
    Limited edition
    Shown: Image Gallery 1976 & 1986

128. La India 1976
    woodengraving 2½ x 1¾
    edition: 10
    Collection: Angela Cappelli
    Shown: Image Gallery 1976 & 1986

129. W. H. Auden 1976
    woodengraving 1¾ x 1
    edition: 15
    Selected for: *The Process of Woodcut & Woodengraving*, a traveling
    educational exhibition organized and circulated in Multnomah
    County by Portland Art Museum 1976
    Shown: Image Gallery 1976, 1986 & 1991

130. The Wind 1977
    color woodcut embossment 10 x 21
    Special edition of 35 pulled just for members of Art Advocates,
    Inc. who sponsored publication of "Wind and Pines"
    Collections: Maribeth Collins; Mayo Rae Rolph Roy; Lillie H.
    Lauha; Evelyn Gordon; J. Michael Deeney
    Shown: Image Gallery 1977 & 1991; Renshaw Gallery 1993;
    Graven Images Gallery 1994

131. Ohisa 1977
    embossment from "Wind and Pines" 9 x 9
    Special edition: 33
    Collections: Evelyn Gordon; Dennis Strayer
    Shown: Image Gallery 1977 & 1991

131A. Sand Dollar 1977
    embossment from "Wind and Pines" 9 x 9
    Special edition: 20
    Collections: Jon & Marian Granby; Margaret Dement
    Shown: Image Gallery 1977 & 1991

132. Sign of the Butterfly 1977
    embossment from "Wind and Pines" 9 x 16
    Special edition: 29
    Collections: Dan & Fern Momyer; Judy Henderson
    Shown: Image Gallery 1977 & 1991

133. The Octopus 1977
    embossment from "Wind and Pines" 9 x 16
    Special edition: 15
    Collections: Jill & Stuart Asbjornsen; Kelton Walston; Kathleen
    McCuistion; Martin Bloom; Dick & Jeannette Lever
    Shown: Image Gallery 1977 & 1991

134. The Giant Catfish 1977
    embossment from "Wind and Pines" 9 x 16
    Special edition: 28
    Collections: Muriel K. Oliver; Ed & Sandy Martin; Ginger Walter
    Shown: Image Gallery 1977 & 1991; Renshaw Gallery 1993

135. Clouds 1977
    embossment from "Wind and Pines" 9 x 16
    Special edition: 80
    Collections: Grace McDonald; Roger Saydack & Elaine Bernat
    Shown: Image Gallery 1977 & 1991

136. Cover for the Special edition of "Wind and Pines" presented to
    Sponsors 1977
    woodcut 9 x 9
    limited edition: 35

137. Trees 1978
    hanga (color woodcut) 10 x 10
    edition: 15
    Shown: Image Gallery 1978, 1986 & 1991

138. The Lovers 1978
    hanga (color woodcut) 6½ x 4½
    edition: 15
    Shown: Image Gallery 1978, 1986 & 1991

139. Japanese Moment 1978
    hanga (color woodcut) 5⅞ x 5⅞
    edition: 15
    Shown: Image Gallery 1978

140. Playboys 1978
hanga (color woodcut) 4 x 5½
edition: 20
Collection: Jim & Maury Haseltine
Shown: Image Gallery 1978 & 1991; Cawein Gallery 1985;
Rogue Gallery 1985

141. Playboys #2 1978
hanga (color woodcut) 5 x 9⅝
edition: 10
Collection: Elaine & George Chandler
Shown: Image Gallery 1978

142. Xmas Greeting with Cars 1978
linocut 5 x 7
Sent as a Christmas card December 1978
Limited edition

143. Dream Wars 1978
color woodcut 11½" circle
editions: 40 on white; 10 on other colors
Collections: Eloise J. McGraw; Neil J. Moore; Peter Melrose; John
& JoAnne Booth
Shown: Image Gallery 1978 & 1986; Graven Images Gallery 1994

144. Butterfly Dogs 1978
color linocut 12 x 12
edition: 40
Collections: Salem Public Library; Eleanor Milne
Shown: Image Gallery 1978, 1986 & 1991; Rogue Gallery 1985

145. Butterfly Dogs 1978
color linocut 12 x 12
Limited edition on black
Shown: Image Gallery 1978

146. Book Plate for Evelyn Childerhose 1978
woodengraving 3½ x 2½
Limited edition
Shown: Image Gallery 1982

147. Traffic Patterns 1978
hanga (color woodcut) 8 x 12
edition: 20
Collection: Doris C. Carlsen
Shown: Image Gallery 1978 & 1991; McLartys' Choice 1995

148. AutoArk c. 1979
linocut 3 x 4
edition: 12
Shown: McLartys' Choice 1996

149. Las Vegas 1979
woodcut 16 x 22
edition: 20
Later impressions were hand-colored
Collections: J. Michael Deeney; Bob & Martha Warnock
Shown: Image Gallery 1980 & 1991; Cawein Gallery 1985; the
Gallery at the Airport, Eugene 1994; *Northwest Print Council In-
vitational*, University of Hawaii, Hilo 1994; Art Space 1995

150. The Poison Tree 1979
color woodcut 4 x 4
edition: 15
Shown: Image Gallery 1980 & 1991

151. The Roman Room c. 1979
color woodcut 3 x 3
edition: 10
Collections: David E. Lindenberger; Tom Henning; Private Collection in Oregon; Karen Wasser
Shown: McLartys' Choice 1996

152. Man with a Cane c. 1979
color woodcut 3 x 2
edition: 10
Shown: McLartys' Choice 1996

153. Changing Colors 1979
hanga (color woodcut) 12 x 12
edition: 15
Shown: Image Gallery 1979, 1986 & 1991; the Governor's Invitational Show 1985; Cawein Gallery 1985; Graven Images
Gallery 1994

154. The Gift of Peace 1979
hanga (color woodcut) 11 x 7
Special edition of 10 pulled to benefit the Peace Institute
Shown: Image Gallery 1979

155. Some Dogs in the Fountain 1979
woodcut 16 x 24
edition: 40
Collections: Gilkey Center, Portland Art Museum; University of
New Mexico Museum, gift of the Artist 1991; John & JoAnne
Booth; Nick & Judy Chaivoe; Thomas & Meredith Dement;
Michael Foster; Jane & James L. Hansen; George & Phyllis Jo-
hanson; Paige Lambert; Martha Pfanschmidt; Bill Rhoades &
Coralee Popp; Jan & John Stahl
Purchase Award: *Northwest Prints 1982*, the inaugural show of the
Northwest Print Council, Portland Art Museum
Shown: Image Gallery 1980, 1986 & 1991; Cawein Gallery 1985;
Rogue Gallery 1985; the Governor's Invitational Show 1985;
Maude Kerns Art Center 1986; Renshaw Gallery 1993; *North-
west Print Council Invitational*, University of Hawaii, Hilo 1994;
Graven Images Gallery 1994

156. Freeway Life Forms 1979
color linocut 12 x 18
edition: 10
Collection: Bob & Martha Warnock
Shown: Image Gallery 1980, 1986 & 1991

157. Kahneeta 1980
color linocut 10 x 8
edition: 10
Shown: Image Gallery 1980, 1986 & 1991

158. Cat Dancing 1980
color woodcut 13½ x 12¾
edition: 40
Collections: Angela Cappelli; Peg Bracken Ohman; Bob & Patti
Burke; Robert Dozono; Lynda & Michael Falkenstein; Walline
Fuller; Karen & Harry Groth; Lawrence Monical; Kelton Wal-
ston; Anne Lever
Shown: Image Gallery 1980, 1986 & 1991; Graven Images
Gallery 1994; McLartys' Choice 1996

159. World Man (also titled "Giant") 1980
hanga (color woodcut) 8¼ x 6½
edition: 20
Shown: Image Gallery 1980, 1986 & 1991

160. Cat Cap 1980
hanga (color woodcut) 4 x 5½
edition: 20
Collections: Angela Cappelli; Laura McLarty & Keith Thompson; Jim & Maury Haseltine; Mayo Rae Rolph Roy; Kathleen McCuistion
Shown: Image Gallery 1980 & 1986; Rogue Gallery 1985; Cawein Gallery 1985; Maude Kerns Art Center 1986; Renshaw Gallery 1993; Art Space 1995

161. Dumpling 1980
woodcut 5 x 5½
edition: 40
Collections: Angela Cappelli; Lynda & Michael Falkenstein; Laura McLarty & Keith Thompson; Ginger Walter
Shown: Image Gallery 1980 & 1991; Graven Images Gallery 1994; Art Space 1995

162. Wedding Announcement: Hugh McLarty & Lisbeth Vanderlinden July 1980
woodengraving 3 x 1¾
Limited edition
Shown: Image Gallery 1982 & 1991

163. Hotel Grand 1980
woodengraving 4 x 4
edition: 12
Shown: Image Gallery 1980, 1986 & 1991

164. Night Rooms 1980
woodengraving 5 x 5
edition: 40
Shown: Image Gallery 1980, 1986 & 1991

165. The Giant Tree 1980
woodengraving 7 x 5
edition: 12
Collection: Cleo Kielbowitz
Shown: Image Gallery 1980, 1986 & 1991

166. Trees 1980
woodengraving 2 x 8
edition: 12
Shown: Image Gallery 1980, 1986 & 1991

167. Death and HK 1980
woodengraving 3¾ x 3½
edition: 6
Collection: Wilma Nelson
Shown: Image Gallery 1980

168. Jennifer 1980
woodengraving 2 x 1¾
edition: 20
Collection: Walline Fuller
Shown: Image Gallery 1980

169. Sea Siren 1980
woodengraving 4" circle
No edition pulled
Not Shown

170. St. Francis in Japan 1981
hanga (color woodcut) 10¼ x 7⅜
edition: 15
Collections: Elinor Shank; Cleo Kielbowitz
Shown: Image Gallery 1981, 1986 & 1991

171. The City (also titled "Fire") 1981
lino-engraving 3 x 3
Collection: John Saling
Shown: Image Gallery 1981, 1986 & 1991

172. Wedding Announcement: Laura Marguerite McLarty 1981
woodengraving 3 x 1
Limited edition
Shown: Image Gallery 1982 & 1991

173. Giant Back with Running Man c. 1981
woodengraving 2 x 2
No edition pulled
Not Shown

174. LaVerne 1981
woodengraving 1¼ x 1
edition: 20
Collection: University of Oregon Museum, gift of the Artist 1987
Shown: Image Gallery 1982

175. Wedding Announcement: Karen Chaivoe & Rob Holladay 1981
woodengraving 3 x 2¼
No edition pulled
Not Shown

176. Poster for Pete Seeger Concert 1982
serigraph 11 x 11
Limited edition
Shown: Image Gallery 1982 & 1985

177. The Pool, Kahneeta 1982
hanga (color woodcut) 10 x 11¾
edition: 10
Collection: Kimberly J. Beach
Shown: Image Gallery 1982, 1986 & 1991; Maude Kerns Art Center 1986

178. War Games 1982
hanga (color woodcut) 8½ x 8½
edition: 40
Collection: Cornelia Cerf
Shown: Image Gallery 1982, 1986 & 1991; Cawein Gallery 1985; Maude Kerns Art Center 1986; Rogue Gallery 1985; Art Space 1995

179. Artist and Models 1982
linocut 5 x 7
edition: 20
Shown: Image Gallery 1982, 1986 & 1991

180. The Descent of Man 1982
hanga (color woodcut) 15 x 11½
Created for a 3-man print project sponsored by members of Art Advocates, Inc. Printmakers who each contributed one print: McLarty, Matoush, Hansen.
Special edition for Project Sponsors: 20
Collections: Gilkey Center, Portland Art Museum, gift of Art Advocates in memory of Evelyn Childerhose; Virginia Haseltine Collection of Northwest Art; Pacific University, gift of the Artist; Portland Community College, gift of Art Advocates; Cornelia Cerf; Ginger Walter
Shown: Image Gallery 1982, 1986 & 1991; Cawein Gallery 1985

181. Small Volcanoes 1982
hanga (color woodcut) 6½ x 6½
edition: 20
Collections: Elaine & George Chandler; Laura McLarty & Keith Thompson
Shown: Image Gallery 1982, 1986 & 1991; Moku Hanga Traveling Exhibition 1997

182. The Family 1983
hanga (color woodcut) 10 x 7
edition: 5
Shown: Image Gallery 1983 & 1986

183. Adios Amor 1983
color linocut 11½ x 18
edition: 30
Collections: University of New Mexico Museum, gift of the Artist 1991; Southeast Multicultural Center, Portland, gift of the Artist 1995; Bob & Martha Warnock; Arthur & Margaret Wasser; Martin Bloom
Shown: Image Gallery 1983, 1986 & 1991; the Governor's Invitational Show 1985; *The Alaska Show, Northwest Print Council Invitational*, Anchorage Community College of the University of Alaska 1984; Maude Kerns Art Center 1986; Graven Images Gallery 1994; Art Space 1995

184. Free Fall 1983
color linocut 16 x 16
edition: 15
Collections: Sarah Mahler; Bob & Martha Warnock
Shown: Image Gallery 1983, 1986 & 1991; the Governor's Invitational Show 1985; Cawein Gallery 1985; Rogue Gallery 1985; Maude Kerns Art Center 1986; Graven Images Gallery 1994; Art Space 1995

185. Swimmers in a Dark River 1983
color linocut 16 x 16
edition: 18
Collections: Win & Madeleine Liepe; Lyle & Jime Matoush
Shown: Image Gallery 1983, 1986 & 1991; the Governor's Invitational Show 1985

186. Bienvenidos a Mexico 1983
linocut 10 x 8
edition: 15
Shown: Image Gallery 1983, 1986 & 1991; Graven Images Gallery 1994

187. Storms and Dreams 1984
woodengraving 11 x 13
Special edition of 40 pulled for 75th Anniversary Portfolio of PNCA 1984
Collection: Virginia Haseltine Collection of Northwest Art
Shown: Image Gallery 1984, 1986 & 1991; Art Space 1995

188. Ottos 1984
color linocut 9 x 12
edition: 50
Collections: John & JoAnne Booth; J. Michael Deeney
Shown: Image Gallery 1984 & 1991

189. Butterfly Robe 1984
color woodcut 20 x 13¾
edition: 50
Collection: Private Collection in Oregon
Shown: Image Gallery 1984, 1987 & 1991

190. The Doll Collector 1984
hand-colored woodcut 20¾ x 15¾
edition: 20
Collections: Manuel Izquierdo; Kathryn Longstreth-Brown; Bill Rhoades & Coralee Popp
Shown: Image Gallery 1985; *Northwest Print Council Circulating Show*, Bellevue Art Museum 1994; Graven Images Gallery 1994; Art Space 1995; McLartys' Choice 1996; Graystone Gallery 1996

191. The Cat Problem 1984
lino-engraving 8 x 6
edition: 40
Shown: Image Gallery 1987, 1988 & 1991; McLartys' Choice 1996

192. Image Gallery Poster 1985
color woodcut 19 x 12¾
edition: 50
To mark the 24th year of Barbara & Jack McLarty's Image Gallery
Collections: Hugh & Lisbeth McLarty; Roger Saydack & Elaine Bernat; Kathleen McCuistion
Shown: Image Gallery 1985, 1986 & 1991; Maude Kerns Art Center 1986; Renshaw Gallery 1993

193. The Guardian 1985
woodcut 15¾ x 13
No edition pulled; proofs only
Collections: Carol & Seymour Haber; Pinegar/McPherson
Shown: Image Gallery 1985

194. "Willis" — Bookplate for Carol & Seymour Haber 1985
woodcut 3 x 2
Limited edition
Not Shown

195. The Cage 1985
linocut created to illustrate a story in *Clinton Street Quarterly* 15½ x 5¼
Limited edition
Shown: Image Gallery 1986 & 1988

196. The Devil Lives Under Ocumicho (earlier title "Viva Mexico") 1985
color linocut 22½ x 17
edition: 40
Collections: Bob & Patti Burke; John & Marjorie Butler; George & Phyllis Johanson; Bill Rhoades & Coralee Popp; Bob & Martha Warnock
Selected for cover and illustrations: *Left Bank No. 2*, Spring Issue 1992 on "Extinction"
Chosen for: "Forty Oregon Printmakers," a catalog of limited edition, award-winning prints, published jointly by Oregon Arts Commission and Northwest Print Council 1988
To be included: "Northwest Printmakers" by Lois Allan 1997
Shown: *Western States Print Invitational*, Portland Art Museum 1985; Image Gallery 1988 & 1991; *West Coast Edition Printmakers*, Claudia Chapline Gallery, Stinson Beach, Ca. 1994; *Northwest Print Council Invitational*, University of Hawaii, Hilo 1994; Graven Images Gallery 1994; McLartys' Choice 1996

197. "Newt" 1986
woodcut 2 x 2
No edition pulled
Not Shown

198. "The Song of the Ponderosa" 1986
woodcut for cover of a volume of poems by Russell Roberts 4 x 4
Limited edition
Shown: Image Gallery 1986 & 1991

199. "Encounters with the White Train" 1986
8 linocuts all approximately 5 x 4 including cover.
All illustrate the book by Andy Robinson
Limited edition of 500 of which 50 contained an original linocut
and were signed by Author and Artist
Shown: Image Gallery 1986 & 1991

200. Noah 1988
woodcut 19 x 14
edition: 50
Collections: Thomas & Meredith Dement; Simone Smith
Shown: Image Gallery 1986 (proofs prior to edition); Graven Images Gallery 1994; Art Space 1995

201. Designed to Wear #1 1988
color woodcut 20 x 14½
edition: 40
Collection: Evelyn Gordon
Created for the annual fashion show of wearable art, Oregon School of Arts & Crafts, Portland
Shown: OSAC 1988; Image Gallery 1988 & 1991; Graven Images Gallery 1994

202. Wedding Announcement: Dick Shoemaker 1988
linocut 3¾ x 2½
Limited edition
Not Shown

203. Birth Announcement: Katherine Spencer McLarty August 1988
linocut 3 x 2
Limited edition
Shown: Image Gallery 1988 & 1991

204. Posada Ajijic 1989
hand-colored woodcut 18 x 12
edition: 40
Collection: William Gordon
Shown: Image Gallery 1989, 1991; Graven Images Gallery 1994; Art Space 1995; McLartys' Choice 1995; Sovereign Gallery 1995; Cawein Gallery 1995

205. Paper Flower Vendor 1989
hand-colored woodcut 19 x 11
edition: 20
Collection: Byrl Shellhart
Selected for: "The Art of Printmaking" published by Northwest Print Council 1990
Shown: Image Gallery 1989 & 1991; Graven Images Gallery 1994; Art Space 1995; McLartys' Choice 1995; Sovereign Gallery 1995

206. Designed to Wear #2 1990
color woodcut 20 x 14
edition: 40
Created for the annual fashion show of Oregon School of Arts & Crafts
Shown: OSAC 1990; Image Gallery 1990 & 1991; Graven Images Gallery 1994; McLartys' Choice 1996

207. Bonnard and Vuillard 1990
color woodcuts from the series of 8 portraits of artists included in "The Book of Color" of which we show 5
A small edition pulled of *Bonnard* for Sponsors of the book, members of Art Advocates
Collection: Lynda & Michael Falkenstein
Shown: Image Gallery 1990 & 1991; McLartys' Choice 1996

208. Gauguin 1990
color woodcut from "The Book of Color" 8 x 8
No edition pulled
Shown: (See entry on Bonnard and Vuillard)

209. Delacroix 1990
color woodcut from "The Book of Color" 8 x 8
No edition pulled
Shown: (See entry on Bonnard and Vuillard)

210. Whistler 1990
color woodcut from "The Book of Color" 8 x 8
No edition pulled
Shown: (See entry on Bonnard and Vuillard)

The following portraits are not shown in this catalog:
Matisse
Chagall
Van Gogh

211. Easels of Famous Artists 1990
color woodcut 6½ x 15
Created in connection with "The Book of Color"
edition: 10
Collection: Laura McLarty & Keith Thompson
Shown: Image Gallery 1990 & 1991; McLartys' Choice 1996

212. Cat-Man-Do 1990
linocut 10 x 8
edition: 10
Collections: Michael Foster; George & Phyllis Johanson
Shown: Sovereign Gallery 1995; McLartys' Choice 1996

213. Designed to Wear #3 1991
color woodcut 14 x 6
edition: 40
Created for the annual fashion show of wearable art, Oregon School of Arts & Crafts
Collection: Caroline & Kaspar Locher
Shown: OSAC 1991; Image Gallery 1991; Graven Images Gallery 1994; Cawein Gallery 1995

214. The Striped Robe 1991
color woodcut 10½ x 14½
edition: 10
Shown: Image Gallery 1991

215. Designed to Wear #4 (also titled "The Moth") 1992
color woodcut 14 x 7
Created for the Oregon School of Arts & Crafts, the design was used for fashion show tickets ONLY. This ended the series he did for OSAC
edition: 40
Shown: McLartys' Choice 1995

216. The Sugar Angel 1992
color woodcut 11 x 9
edition: 20
Later impressions were hand-colored. We show the original edition. Commissioned by Northwest Print Council for the Associate Members' portfolio 1994
Collection: Mary Taylor Barrier
Shown: Graven Images Gallery 1994; Art Space 1995; Cawein Gallery 1995; Sovereign Gallery 1995; McLartys' Choice 1996

217. Wedding Announcement: Charles McLarty/Hiromi Watanabe
1992
woodcut 5 x 1⅛
Reproduced in McClain's Catalog for 1993
No edition pulled, proofs only
Collection: Debby & Sam Morrow
Not Shown

218. Walter and the Boys 1993
woodcut 17¼ x 11½
Some impressions were hand-colored
edition: 12
Contributed to the Architectural Foundation Award Dinner honoring Dr. Francis J. Newton 1995
Collections: Margaret & Walter Gordon; Wilma Nelson
Shown: McLartys' Choice 1993; Art Space 1995; Cawein Gallery 1995

219. Powell's 1993
woodcut 18 x 24
Special edition of 40 only pulled by Atelier Mars, Portland, for the Sponsors of *Worldwatcher: Jack McLarty*, a 50-year catalog of his paintings published by McLartys' Choice 1995
Purchased for the *Visual Chronicle of Portland* by the Metropolitan Arts Commission 1993
Collections: Carol & Wayne Bridges; Elaine & George Chandler; Maribeth Collins; Kathleen McCuistion; Hugh & Lisbeth McLarty; the New York Public Library, gift of the Artist 1997; Muriel Oliver; Tom Prochaska; Jack & Janet Witter; Judith Wyss; William F. Yee
Shown: Renshaw Gallery 1993; Sovereign Gallery 1995; McLartys' Choice 1996

220. Dance of the One-Armed Bandit 1993
hand-colored woodcut 15 x 12
edition: 15
Collections: Dan & Fern Momyer; Dick & Jeannette Lever
Shown: McLartys' Choice 1993 & 1996; *101 Prints*, a major benefit for Friends of the Gilkey Center and Northwest Print Council 1993; Graven Images Gallery 1994; Cawein Gallery 1995; Sovereign Gallery 1995

221. Baby Game 1994
hand-colored woodcut 15½ x 12
edition: 10
Collection: Neil J. Moore
Shown: the Gallery at the Airport, Eugene 1994; Cawein Gallery 1995; Art Space 1995; McLartys' Choice 1996

222. Dream Rider 1994
hand-colored woodcut 15¾ x 12
edition: 10
Collection: Laura McLarty & Keith Thompson
Shown: Art Space 1995; McLartys' Choice 1996

223. Janesbonnets 1995
woodengraving created to illustrate a poem by Casey Bush 2⅜ x 3¾
No edition pulled
Not Shown

224. Mexican Tapestry 1995
woodcut 15 x 21
edition: 15
Collection: Mary Taylor Barrier
Shown: Cawein Gallery 1995; McLartys' Choice 1996

225. Mexico 1995
woodcut 9¾ x 29½
edition: 15
Collection: Mary Taylor Barrier
Shown: Cawein Gallery 1995; McLartys' Choice 1996

226. The Love Knot 1996
woodengraving 3 x 2
edition: 100
Collection: Marte Lamb & Michael Parsons
Not Shown

227. The Hand of God 1996
woodcut 4 x 4
edition: 40
Collection: Thomas & Meredith Dement
Shown: McLartys' Choice 1996

228. The Left Hand of God 1996
woodcut 16 x 16
edition: 40
Collection: Arthur & Margaret Wasser
Shown: McLartys' Choice 1996
To be included: "Northwest Printmakers" by Lois Allan 1997

229. The Wall City 1996
woodcut 16 x 20
edition: 40
Collection: Chris Robinson
Shown: McLartys' Choice 1996; *Social Justice*, a juried show at Mt. Hood Community College 1996
To be included: "Northwest Printmakers" by Lois Allan 1997

230. The Rain Beast 1996
hand-colored woodcut 12 x 9
edition: 15
Collections: Rodney Keyser; Mary Taylor Barrier
Shown: McLartys' Choice 1996

231. The Owl Dance 1996
woodcut 10 x 8
edition: 10
Shown: McLartys' Choice 1996

232. Gordon and Vivian 1996
color woodcut 18 x 14
edition: 50
Created for the Founders' Portfolio, Northwest Print Council 1996–97
Collections: Gilkey Collection, Portland Art Museum, gift of the Artist 1996; the New York Public Library, gift of the Artist 1997; Allen Tooke

233. C. S. Price 1996
woodcut 18 x 14
No edition pulled
Not Shown
Collection: Allen Tooke

234. Charles Heaney 1996
woodcut 18 x 14
No edition pulled
Not Shown
Collection: Allen Tooke

235. George Johanson 1996
woodcut 18 x 14
No edition pulled
Not Shown
Collections: Allen Tooke; George & Phyllis Johanson

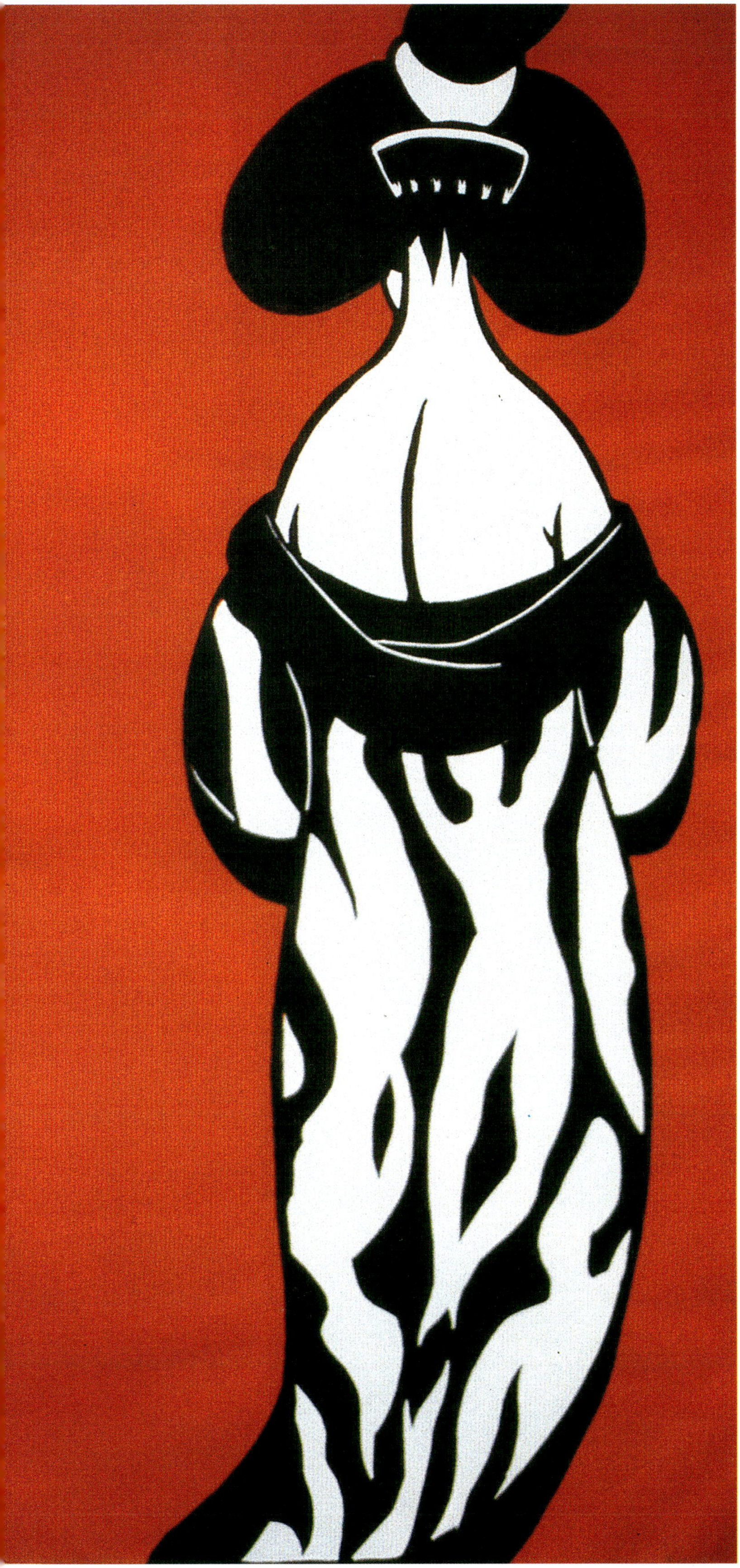

236. A. C. and Arthur Runquist 1996
woodcut 18 x 14
No edition pulled
Not Shown
Collection: Allen Tooke

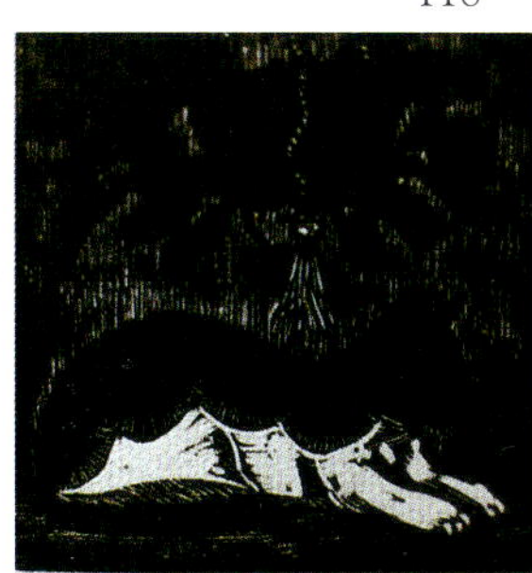

237. Bill Givler 1996
woodcut 18 x 14
No edition pulled
Not Shown
Collection: Allen Tooke

238. Charles Voorhies 1996
woodcut 18 x 14
No edition pulled
Not Shown
Collection: Allen Tooke

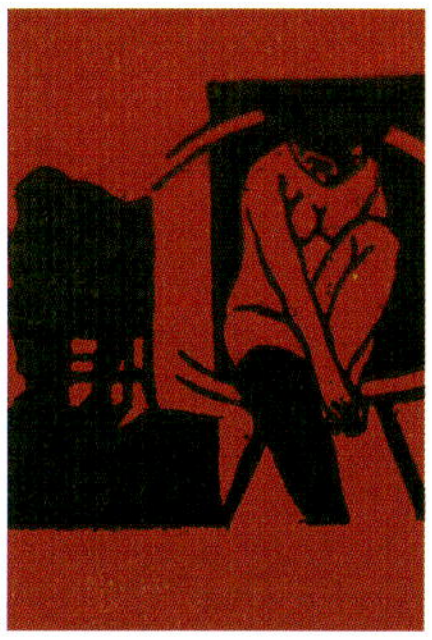

239. Jack and Barbara McLarty 1996
woodcut 18 x 14
No edition pulled
Not Shown
Collection: Allen Tooke

240. Underworld 1996
woodengraving 5 x 8
No edition pulled
Not Shown

117

241. Strange Travels 1996
woodengraving 3 x 2
Created for but not used on cover of a book of poetry by
Laura McLarty & David LaSalle published Bucknell University 1994
No edition pulled
Not Shown

242. The Pond 1996
woodengraving 11 x 9
No edition pulled
Not Shown

243. A Walk Through the Woods 1996
color woodcut 14 x 18
No edition pulled
Not Shown

244. Detail of McLarty Woodcut Mural designed for City Hall, Portland
Projected for completion/installation 1997–1998

245 through 256 portray enlarged details of some important prints. They are found on pages 129 through 135.

113. Japanese Red (color woodcut) 1974 22½ x 15
114. Loren Eiseley (color woodcut) 1974 3 x 4 (*see page 48*)
115. Black and White Cats (woodcut embossment) 1974
6½ x 10½ (*see page 32*)
115A. Table Tennis Match (color woodcut) c. 1975 11 x 11
(*see page 41*)
116. Figured Robe (color woodcut embossment) 1975 12 x 9
(*see page 67*)
117. Lovers (woodcut) 1975 3 x 3
118. Kat (woodengraving) 1975 2 x 2
119. Reclining Figure (color woodcut) 1975 2¼ x 5
(*see page 48*)

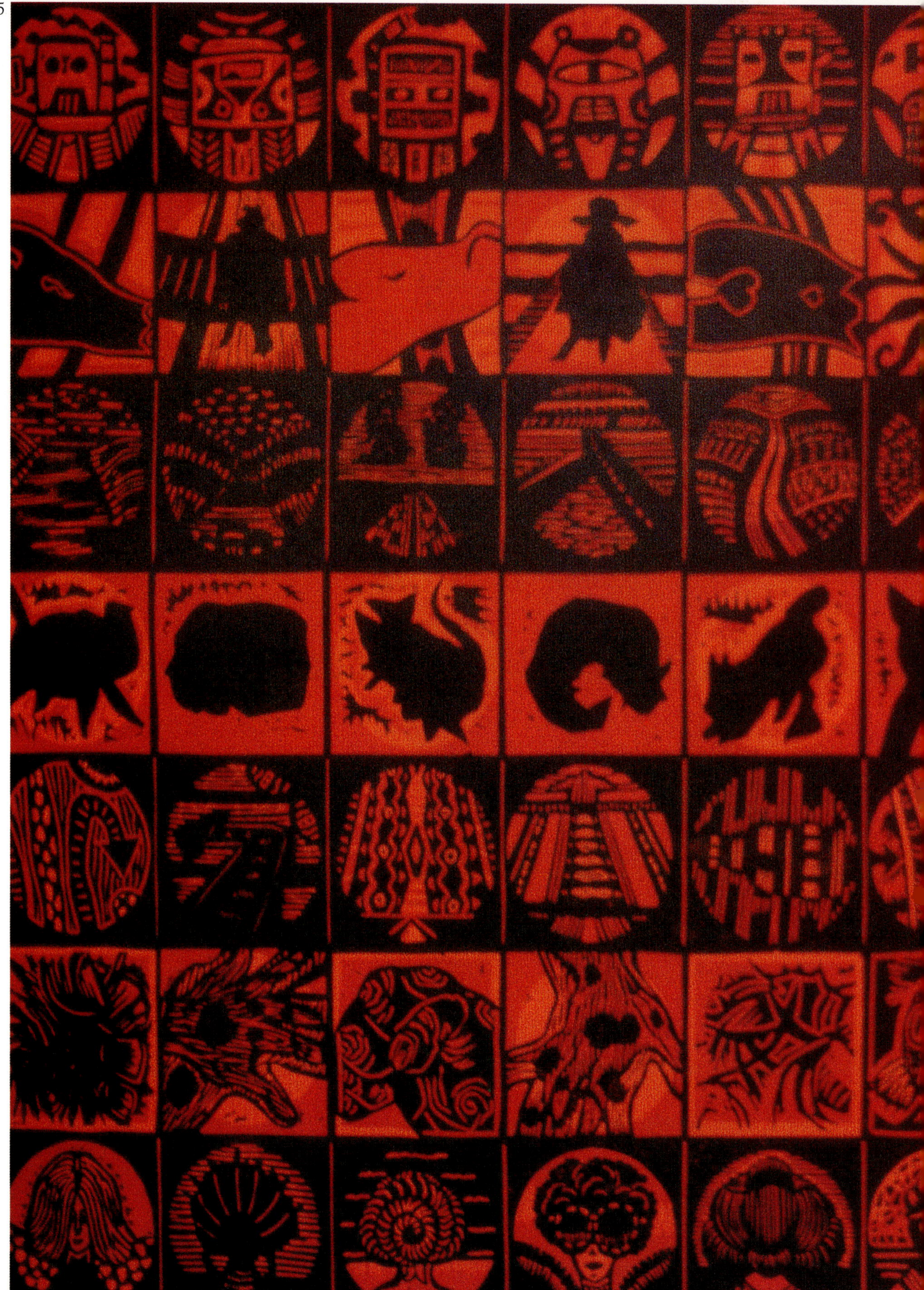

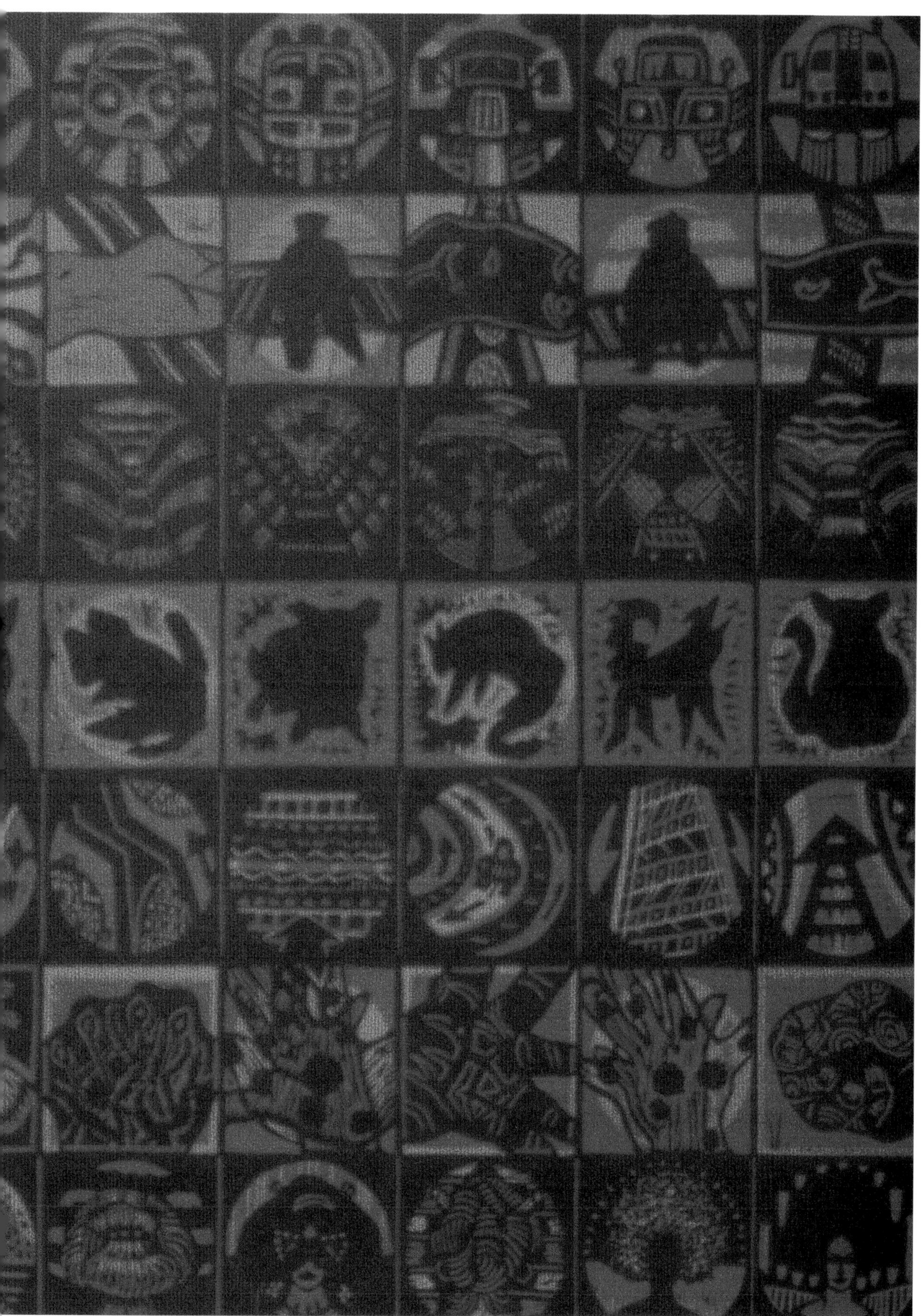

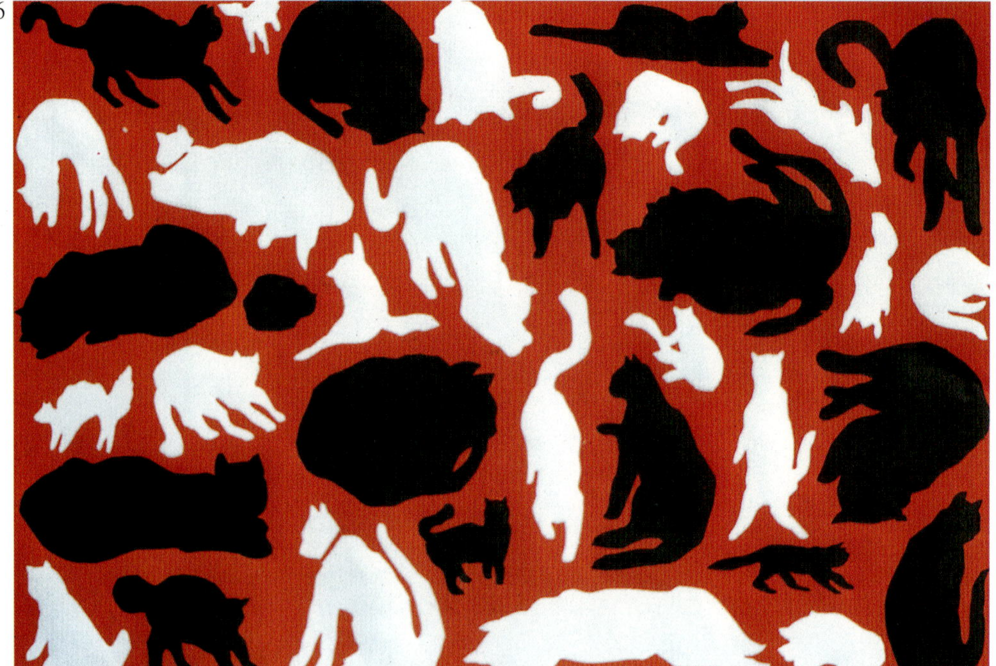

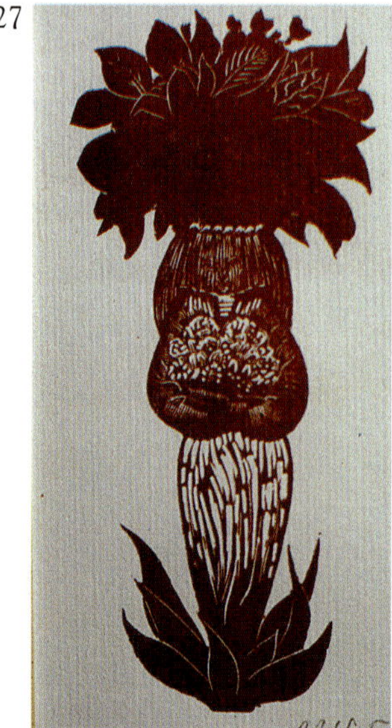

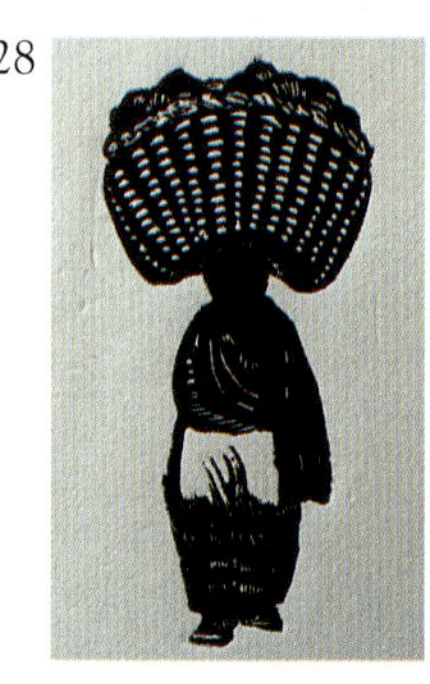

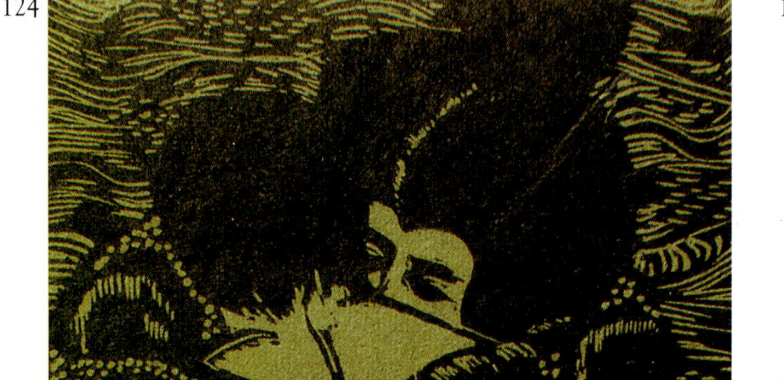

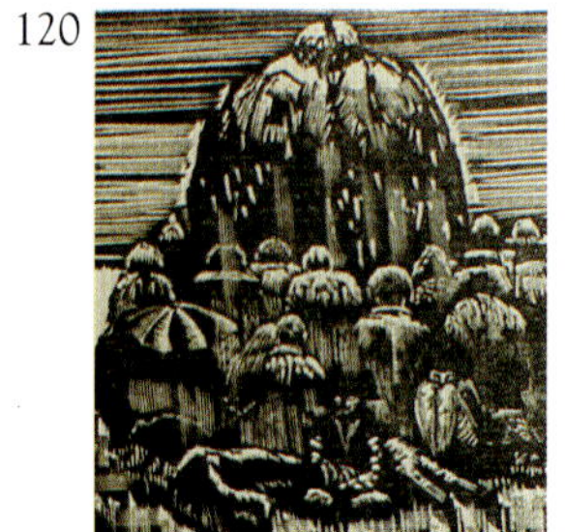

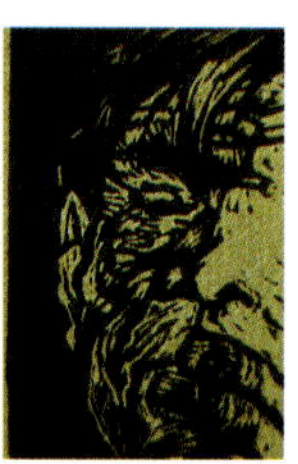

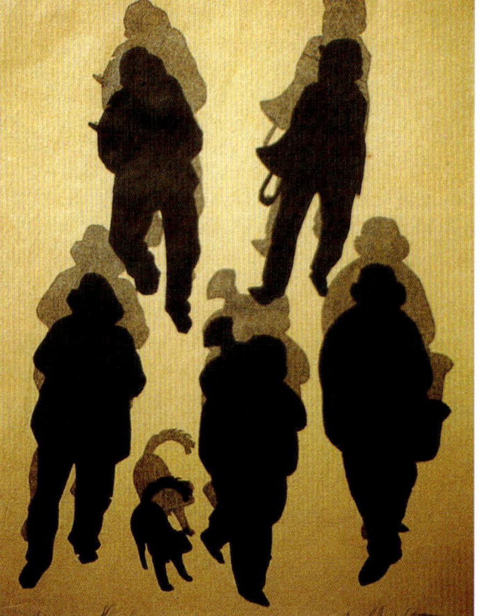

120. "August 1968" (also titled "The Ogre") (woodengraving) 1975
3 x 2¾
121. The Heart of John Donne (color woodcut) 1975 (Shown on the
front cover) 21¾ x 14¾
122. Jazz Shadows (woodcut) 1975 10 x 7
123. Mexican Dogs (color woodcut) 1975 12 x 12 (*see page 49*)
124. The Return (woodengraving) 1975 4 x 3

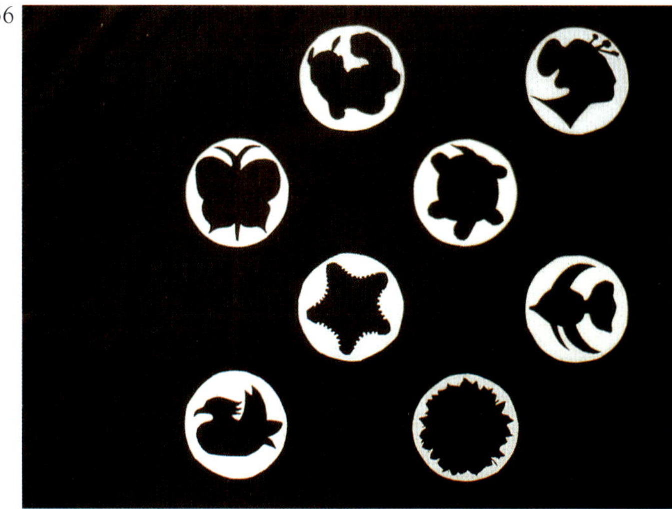

136

131A

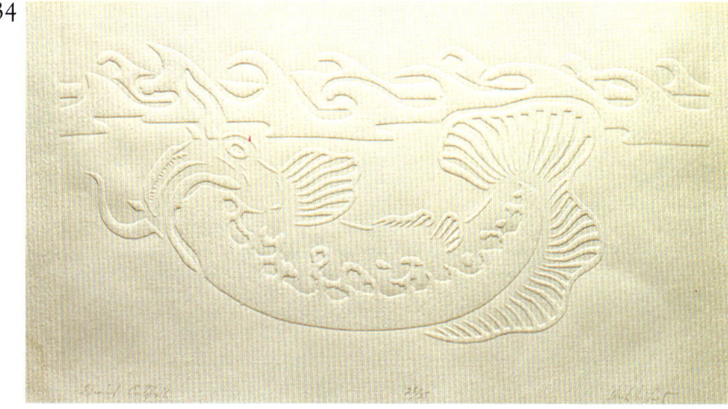

134

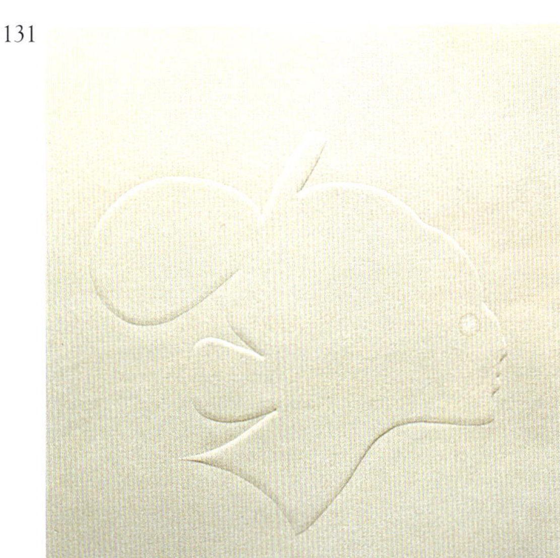

131

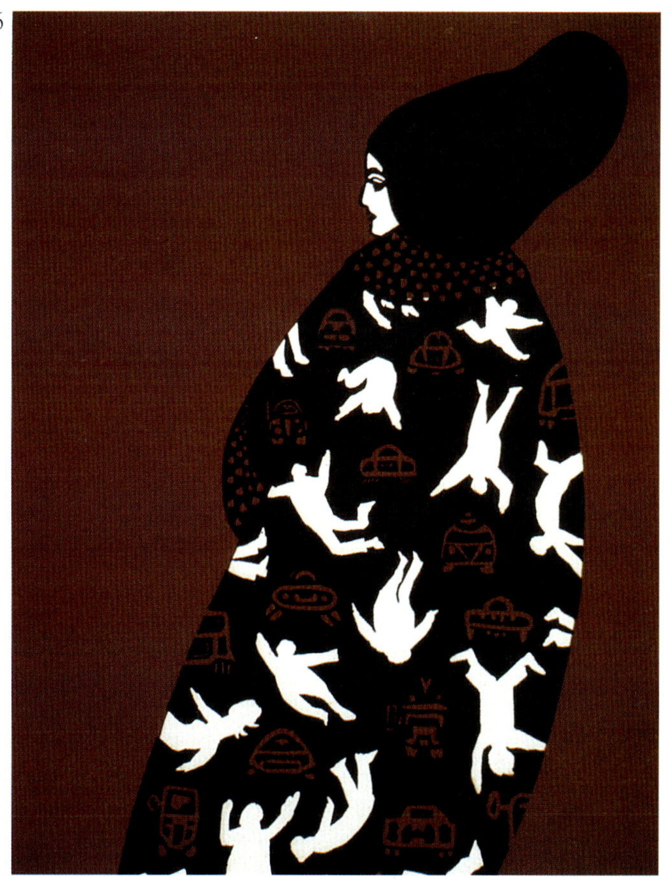

116

125. Red Passage (color linocut) 1976 15 x 23 (*see pages 64-65*)
126. Thirty-six Basic Cat Positions (color woodcut) 1976 21½ x 14½
127. Wedding Announcement for Joe McDonald (woodengraving) 1976 3 x 1½
128. La India (woodengraving) 1976 2½ x 1¾
129. W. H. Auden (woodengraving) 1976 1¾ x 1
130. The Wind (color woodcut embossment) 1977 10 x 21
131. Ohisa (embossment from "Wind and Pines") 1977 9 x 9
131A. Sand Dollar (embossment from "Wind and Pines") 1977 9 x 9
132. Sign of the Butterfly (embossment from "Wind and Pines") 1977 9 x 16
133. The Octopus (embossment from "Wind and Pines") 1977 9 x 16
134. The Giant Catfish (embossment from "Wind and Pines") 1977 9 x 16
135. Clouds (embossment from "Wind and Pines") 1977 9 x 16
136. Cover for the Special edition of "Wind and Pines" presented to Sponsors (woodcut) 1977 9 x 9
137. Trees (hanga) 1978 10 x 10

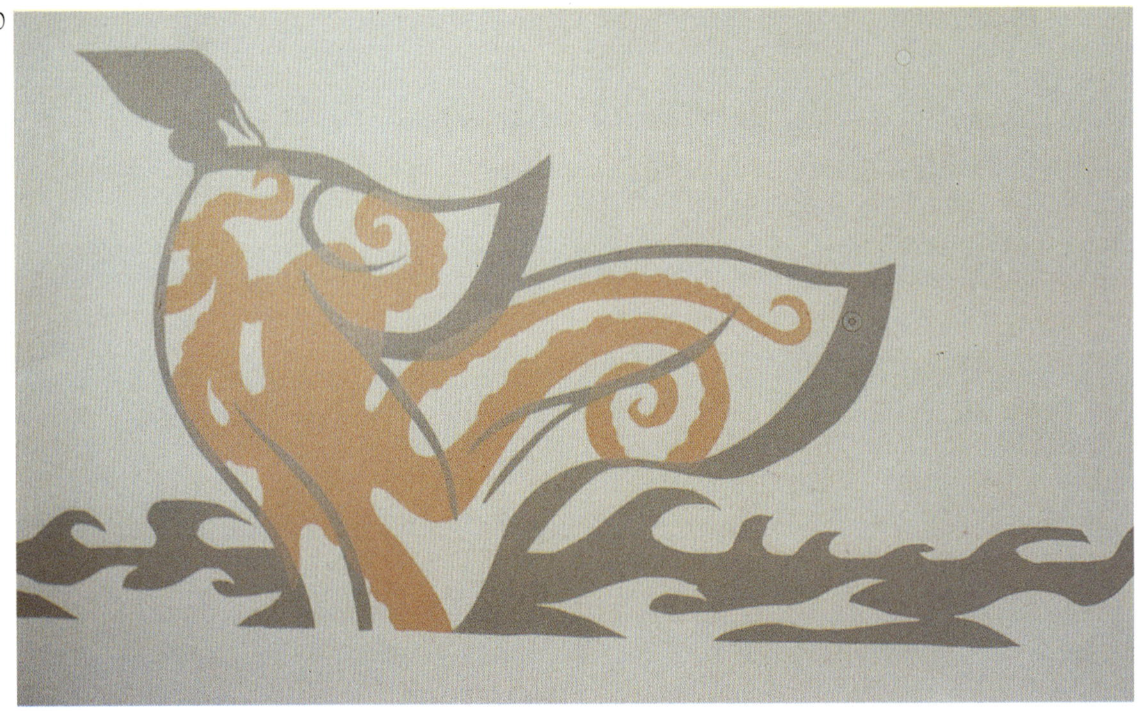

WIND AND PINES, translations from the Ancient Japanese was published by Image Gallery in February 1977 in a special edition of thirty-five (with one unbound woodcut) and a regular edition of two hundred and fifty signed, numbered copies. Co-translators were William I. Elliott and Noah S. Brannen. It was designed and printed by Clyde Van Cleve, and it contains eight embossed woodcuts by Jack McLarty. The foreword was written by Virginia Haseltine.

Edward Johnson wrote, ". . . if our work and our additions help in the proper presentation of the words, if our making of the thing is good, if in fact, we write well—then even the poets—the makers—may thank us."

This is precisely what has happened in *Wind and Pines*. . . . The cooperation between translator, artist, and designer/calligrapher/printer has been very successful in this book. The text, design, lettering, and illustrations achieve an artistic unity which is admirable.

The calligraphy is a very clear and even humanist miniscule hand. The writing is well-mannered and unpretentious, and does not interfere with the relationship between reader and text. This is the most prominent feature of the best humanist manuscripts and Van Cleve has followed their example beautifully.

The illustrations are not properly illustrations of the text, but more in the spirit of illuminations. The quiet elegance of the embossing process combined with traditional images . . . captures the flavor of the poems.

A simplicity of presentation with a richness of character is found in the poems, the calligraphy, the illustrations, and also the design of the book. . . . The layout of the book is asymmetric and simple. . . .

Sumner Stone, *Fine Print*, Vol. 5, No. 2, April 1979, San Francisco

. . . In recent years there has been a steady growth of interest in the art of the handmade book and in collaborative processes for them.

It was through Portland printmaker and collector William Givler that McLarty said he really learned to appreciate the art of the handmade book—and the collaborations with Ambroise Vollard, French publisher and art dealer, produced earlier in this century with such artists as Matisse, Maillol, Bonnard and Picasso. . . . McLarty said that Vollard had really recovered an earlier tradition of handmade books with original art, with which contemporary artists in various disciplines are once again concerned.

"In something like this," said McLarty, who was the "sparkplug" for *Wind and Pines*, "you really have to make your own opportunities."

. . . Someone put him in touch with Elliott (William) who began to provide him with Japanese poetry. "I went through a lot of poems that didn't produce images for me before he showed me these Fudoki poems. They immediately produced images for me. They fit in with my interest in mythology of all kinds and they fell into something I had wanted to do for a long time—a white book." . . .

He wanted a very low relief—just enough to be clearly visible to a person holding the book. Heavier relief would not only have made the book clumsily thick on pages which have a folded edge; it would have been inappropriate to the content of the poems. . . .

McLarty said that everything that Van Cleve did—poem spacing on the pages, weight he gave the script and all other design factors—were critical to the result. . . .

Beth Fagan, "A Treasury from 8th Century Japan," *Northwest Magazine, The Oregonian*, 21 January 1978

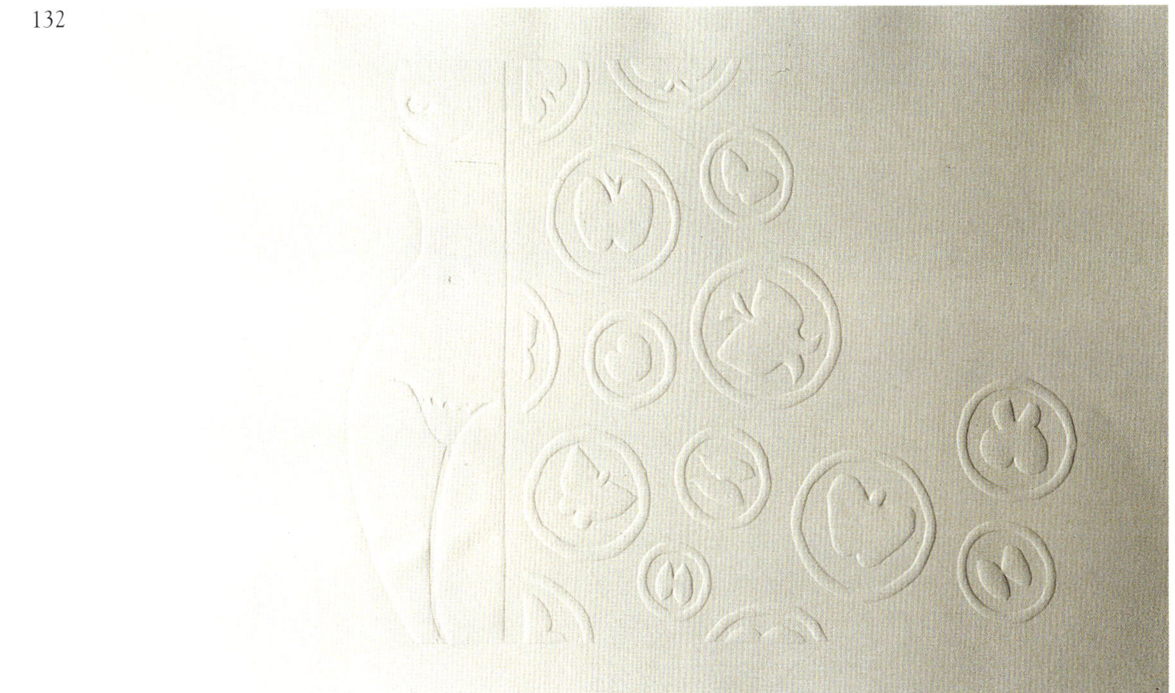

132

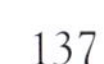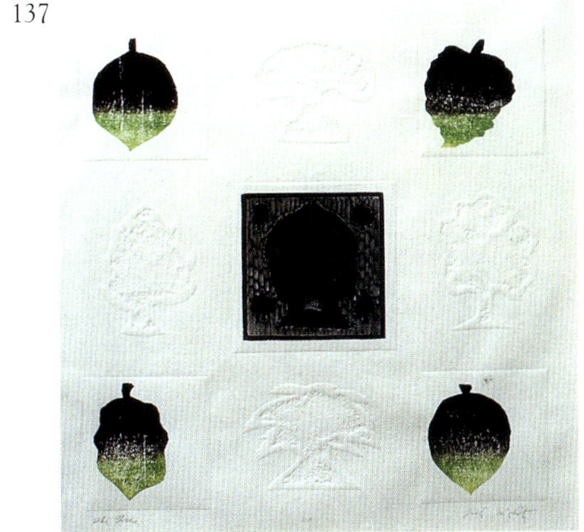

137

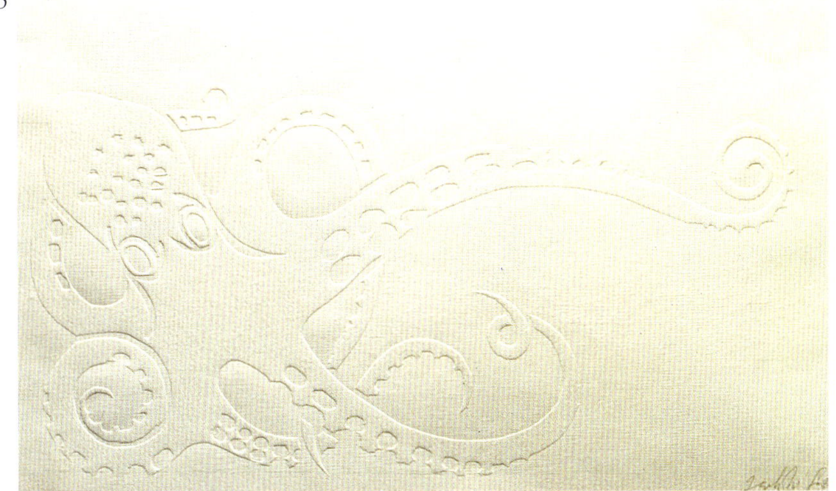

133

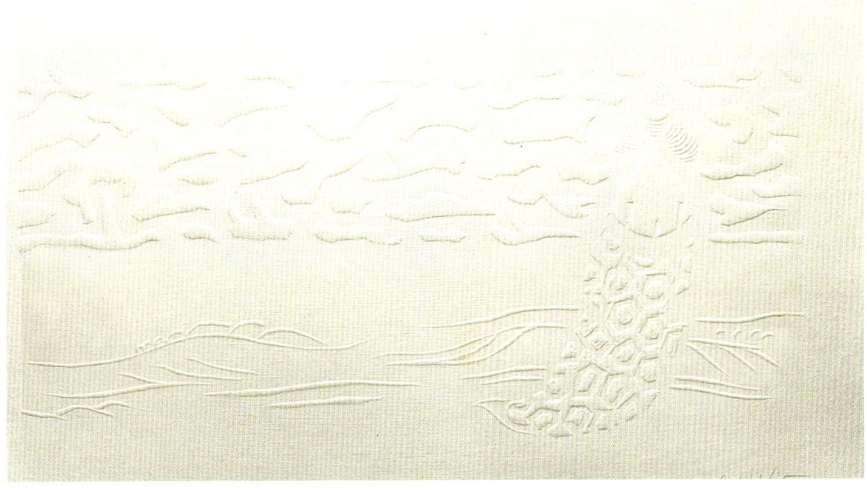

135

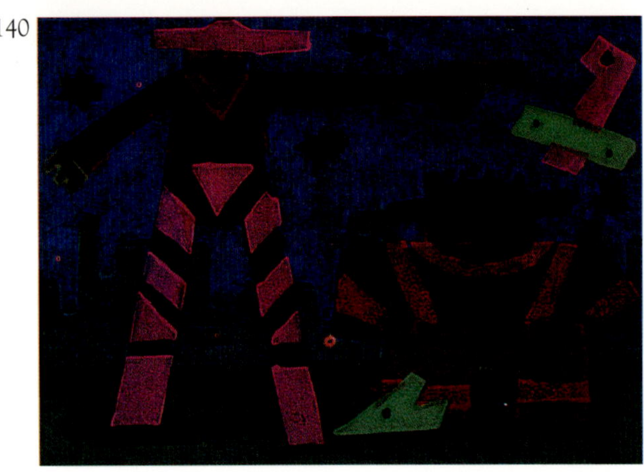

140

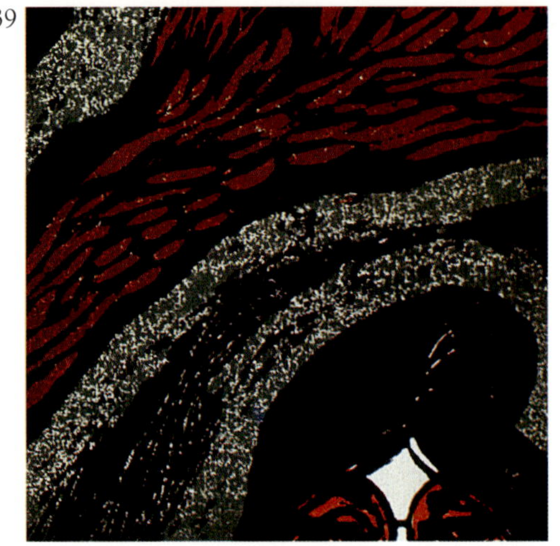

139

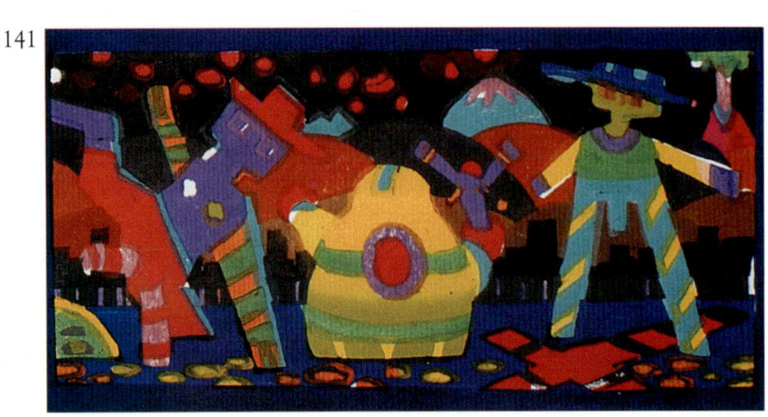

141

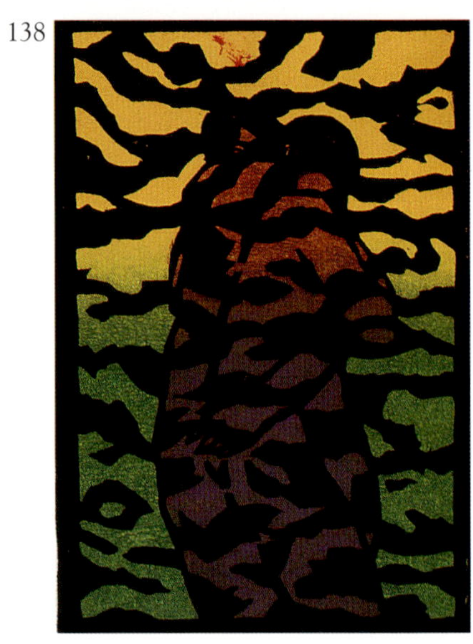

138

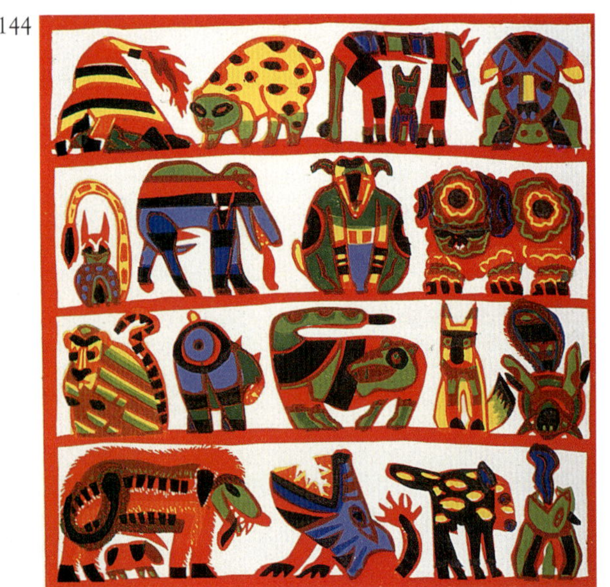

144

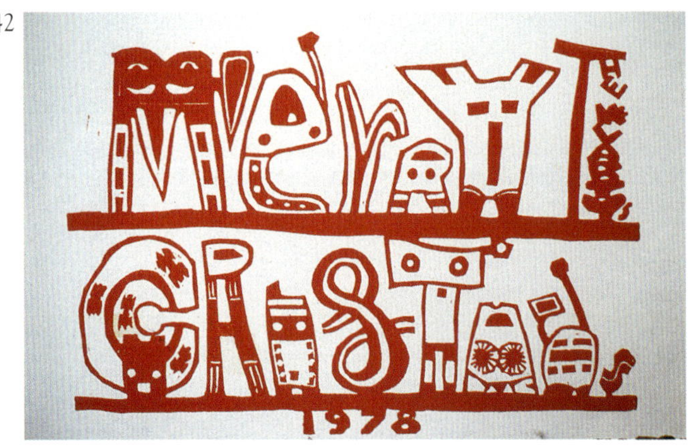

142

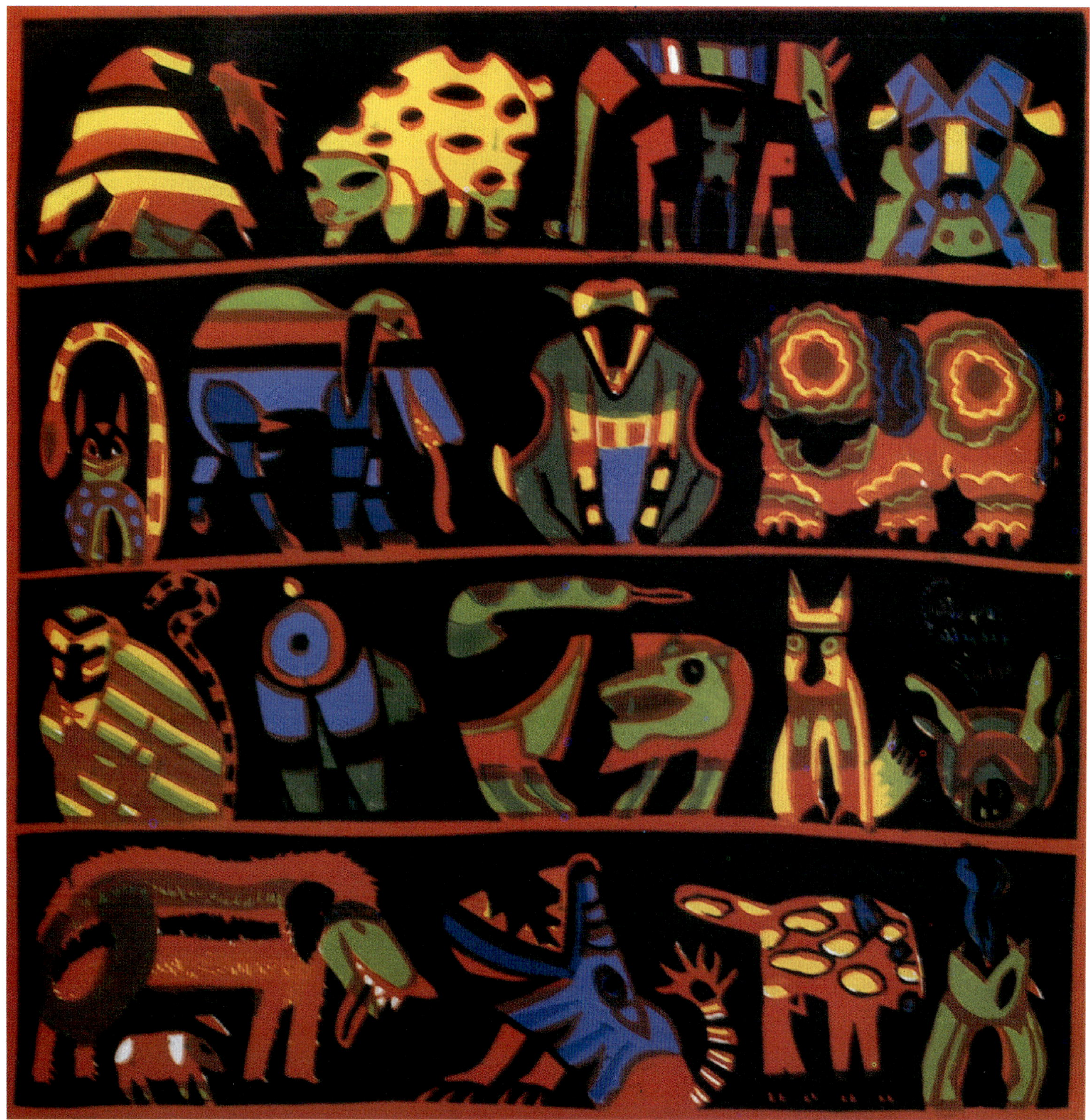

138. The Lovers (hanga) 1978 6½ x 4½
139. Japanese Moment (hanga) 1978 5⅞ x 5⅞
140. Playboys (hanga) 1978 4 x 5½
141. Playboys #2 (hanga) 1978 5 x 9⅝

142. Xmas Greeting with Cars (linocut) 1978 5 x 7
143. Dream Wars (color woodcut) 1978 11½" circle (*see page 75*)
144. Butterfly Dogs (color linocut) 1978 12 x 12
145. Butterfly Dogs (color linocut) 1978 12 x 12

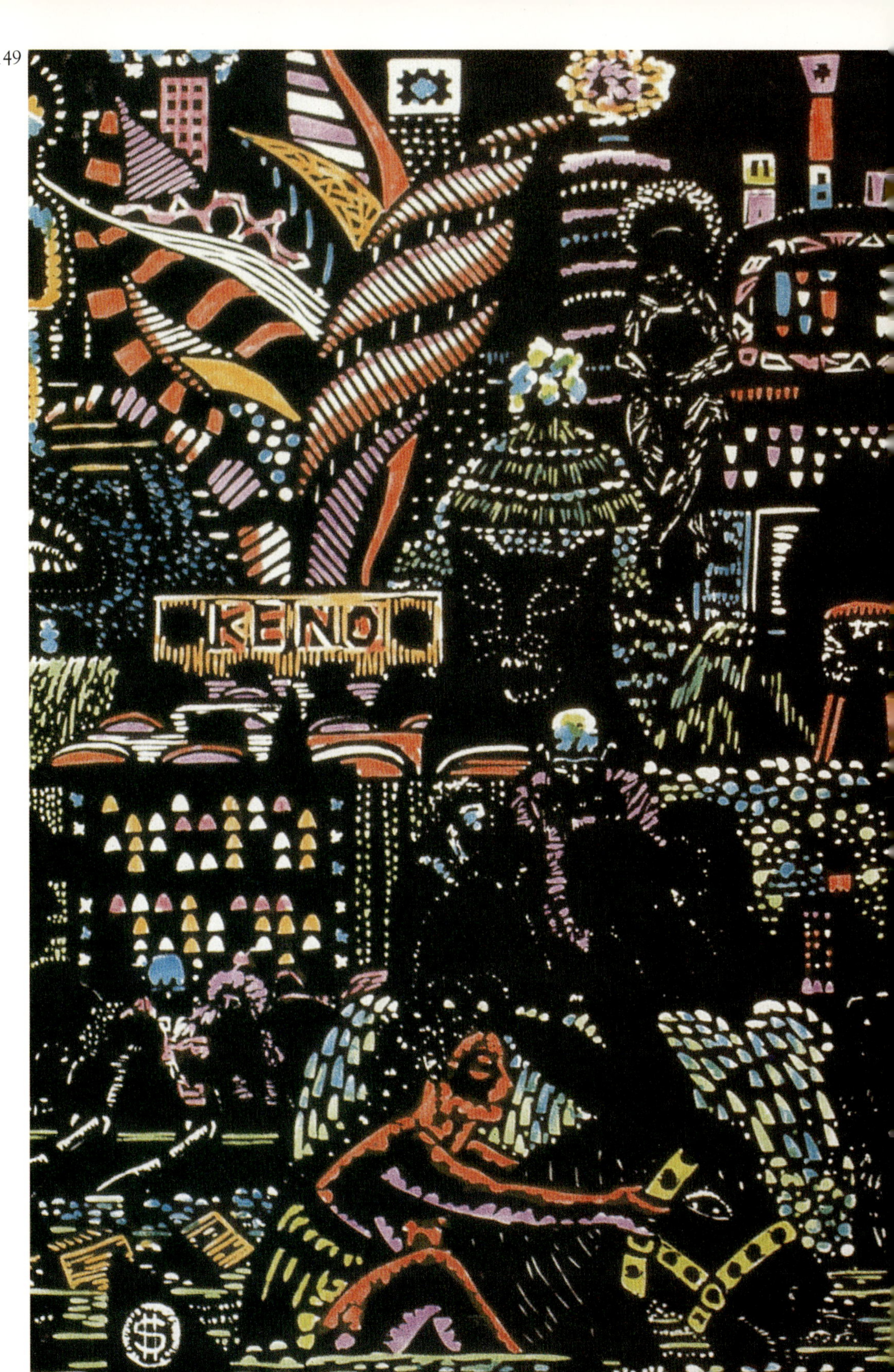
KENO

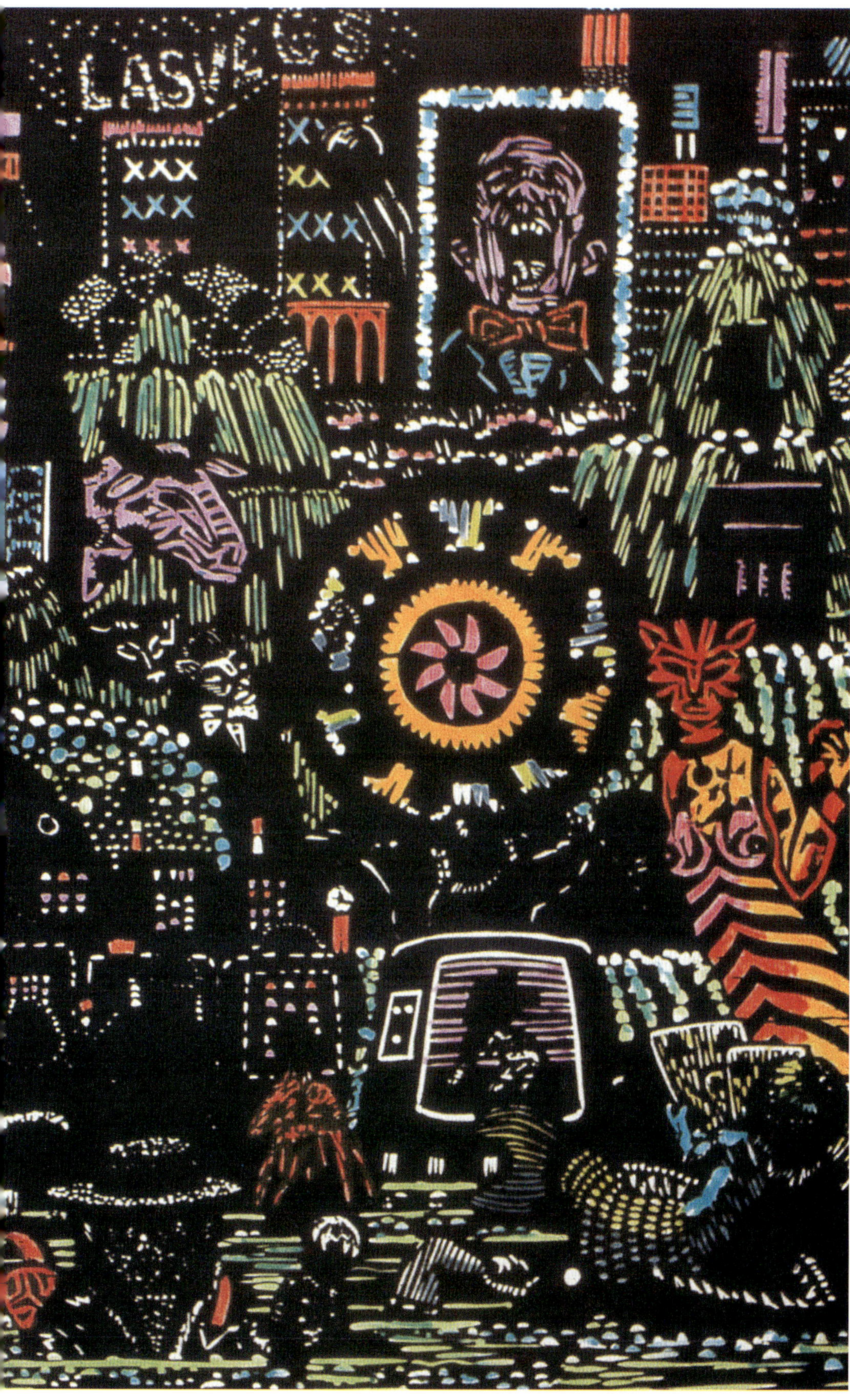

LAS VEGAS

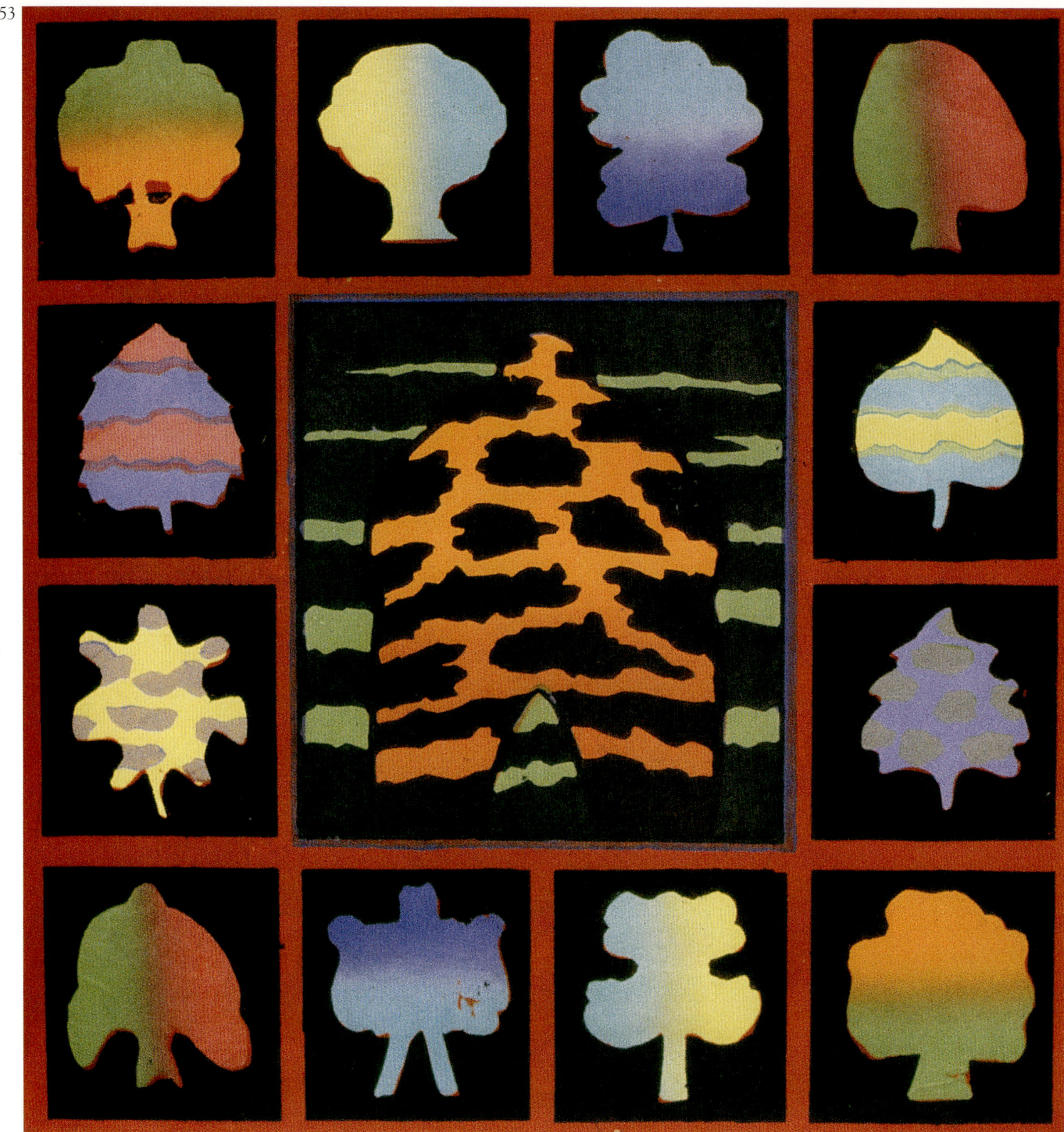

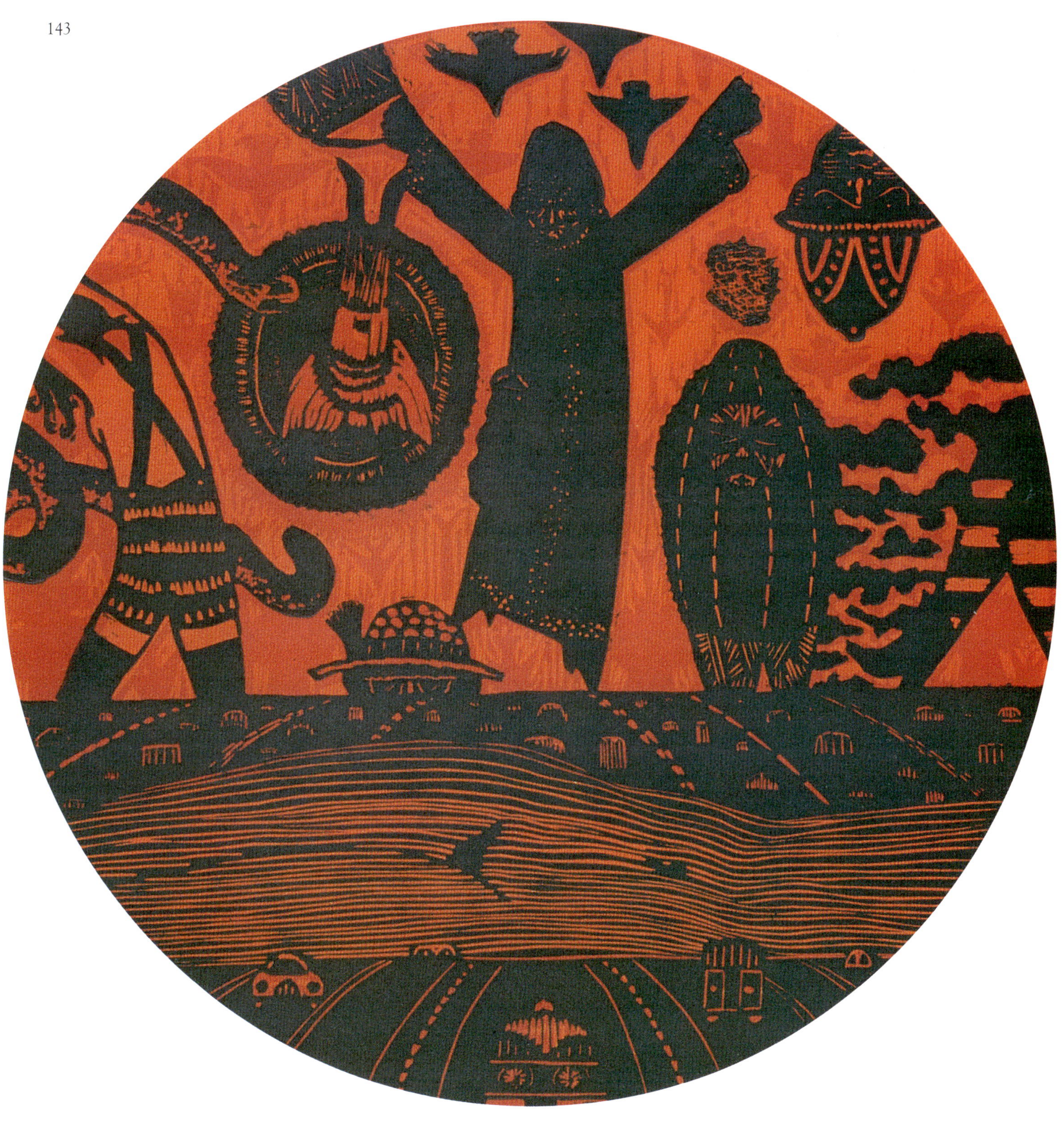

147

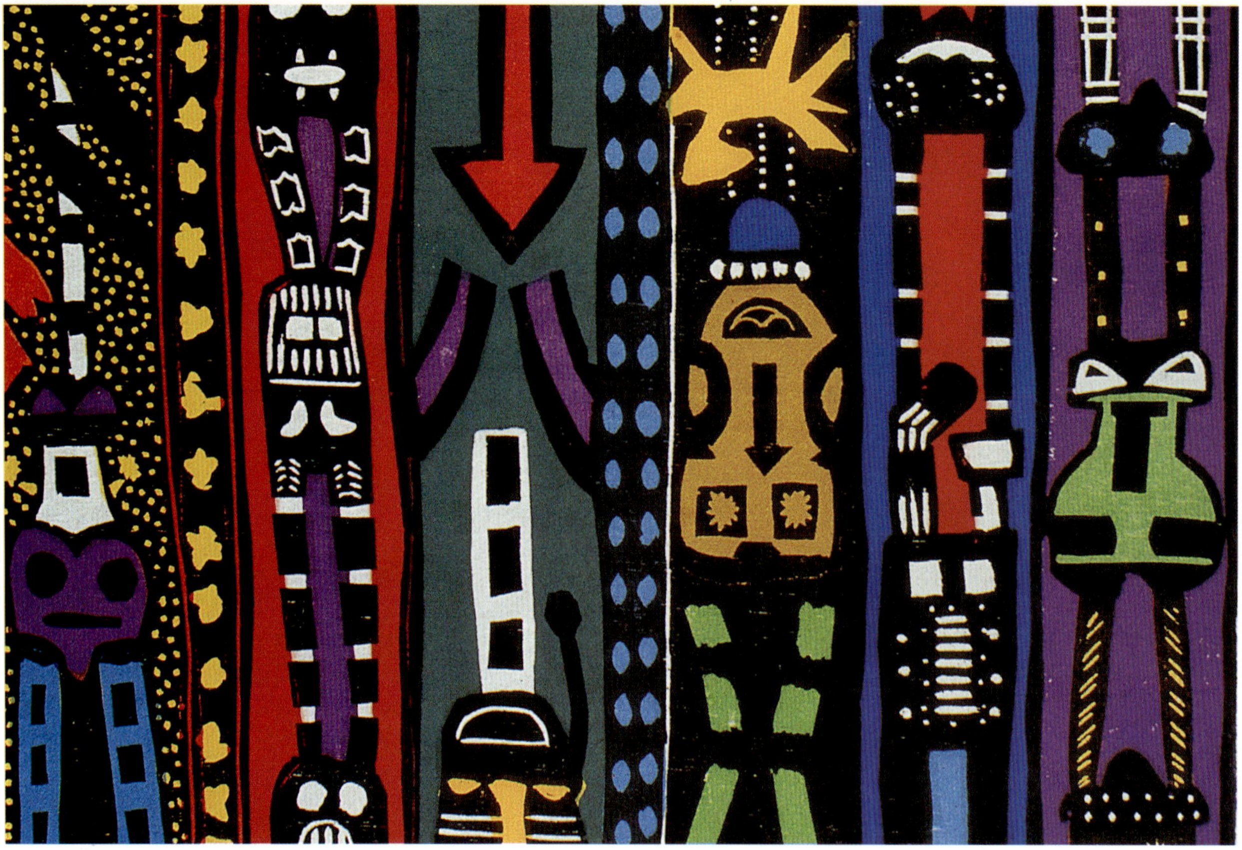

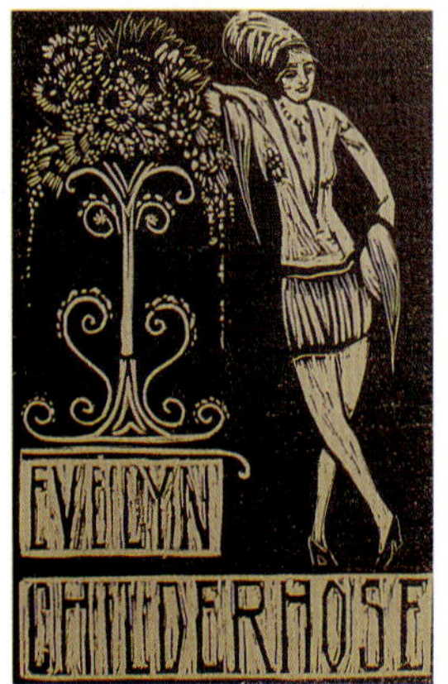
146

148

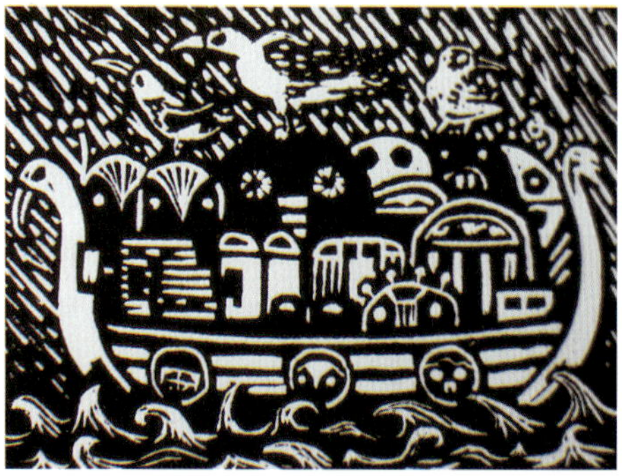

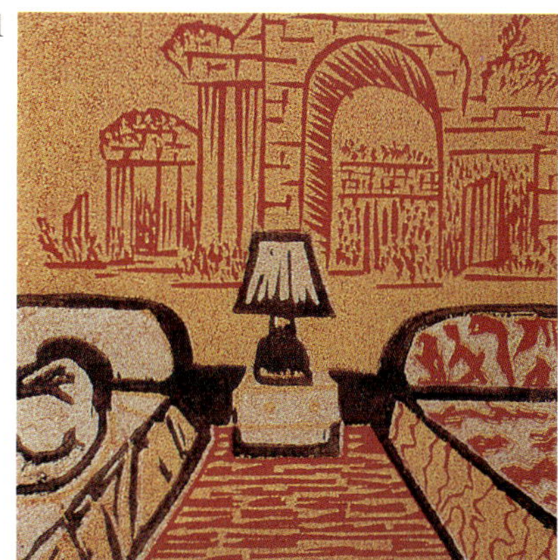

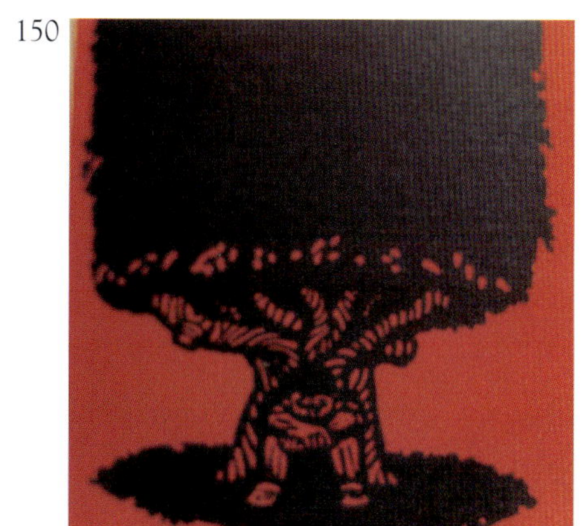

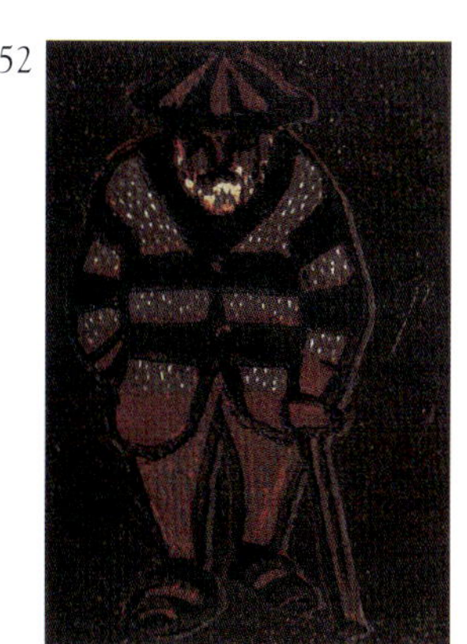

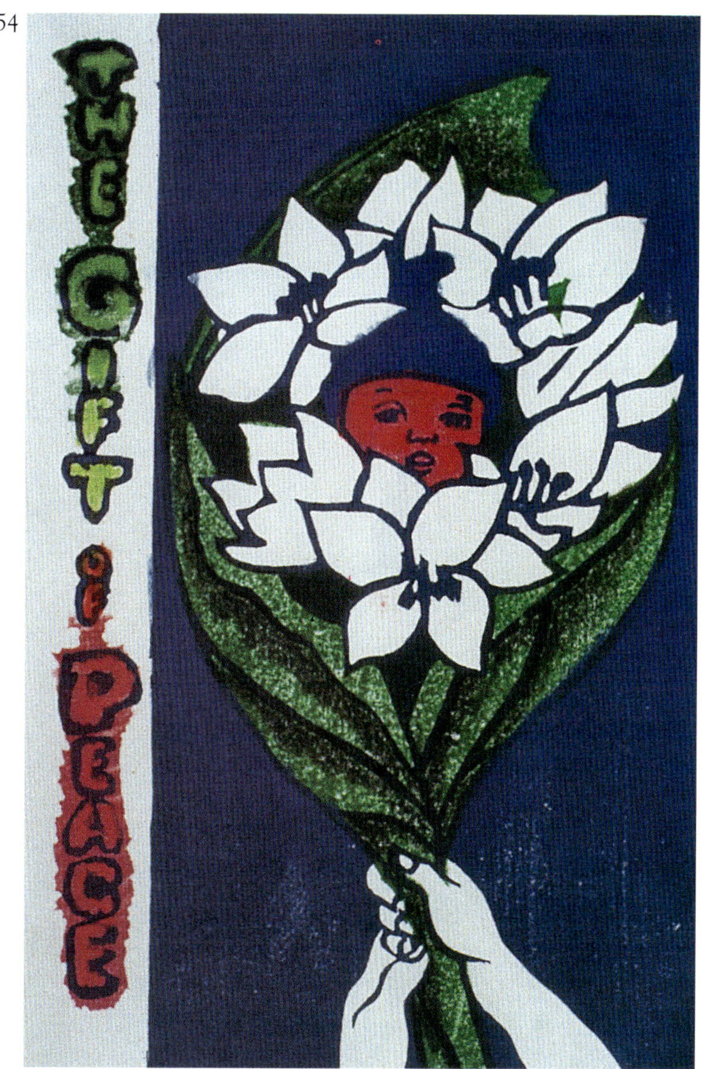

146. Book Plate for Evelyn Childerhose (woodengraving) 1978
  3½ x 2½
147. Traffic Patterns (hanga) 1978 8 x 12
148. AutoArk (linocut) c. 1979 3 x 4
149. Las Vegas (woodcut) 1979 16 x 22 (*see pages 72-73*)
150. The Poison Tree (color woodcut) 1979 4 x 4
151. The Roman Room (color woodcut) c. 1979 3 x 3
152. Man with a Cane (color woodcut) c. 1979 3 x 2
153. Changing Colors (hanga) 1979 12 x 12 (*see page 74*)
154. The Gift of Peace (hanga) 1979 11 x 7

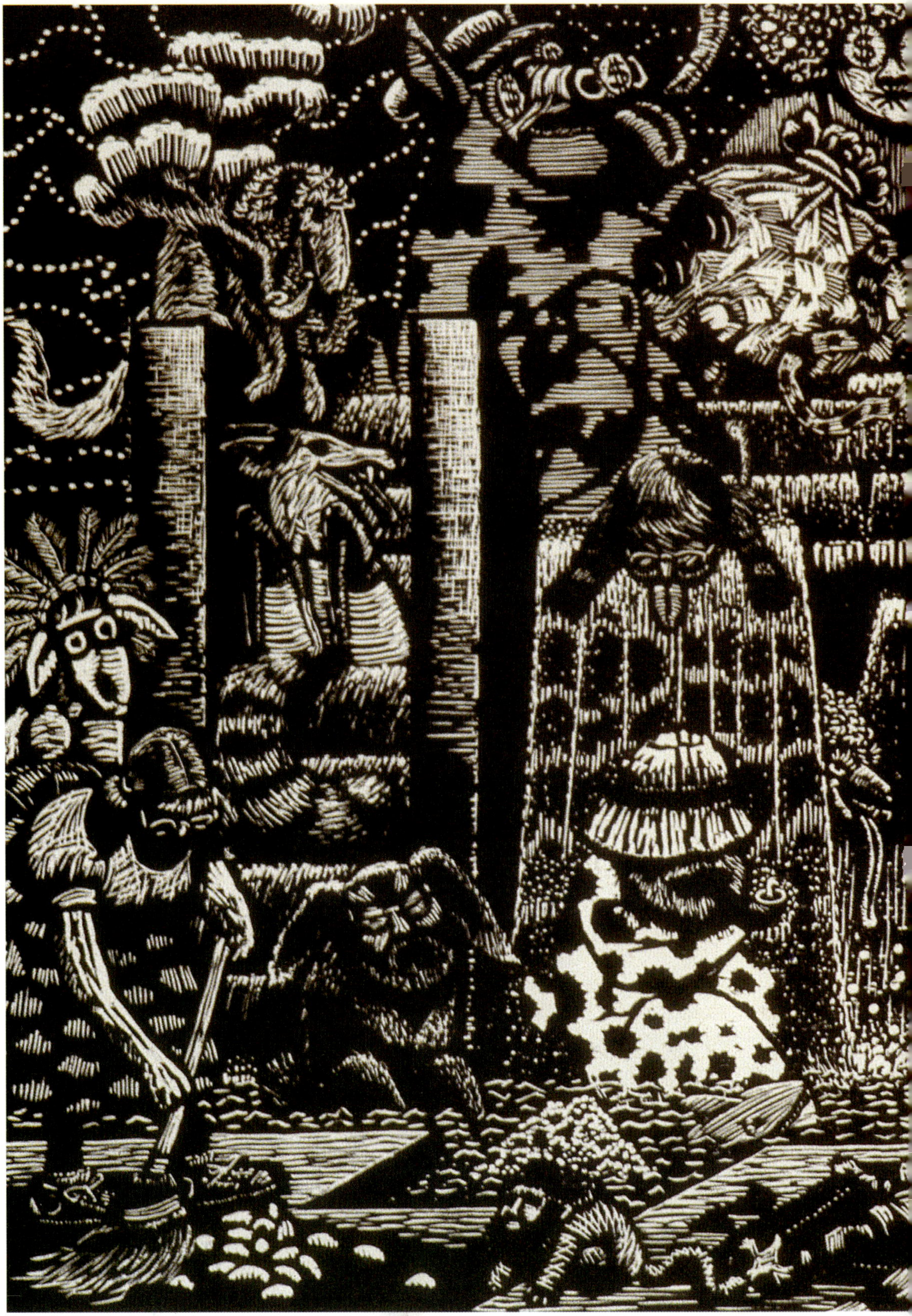

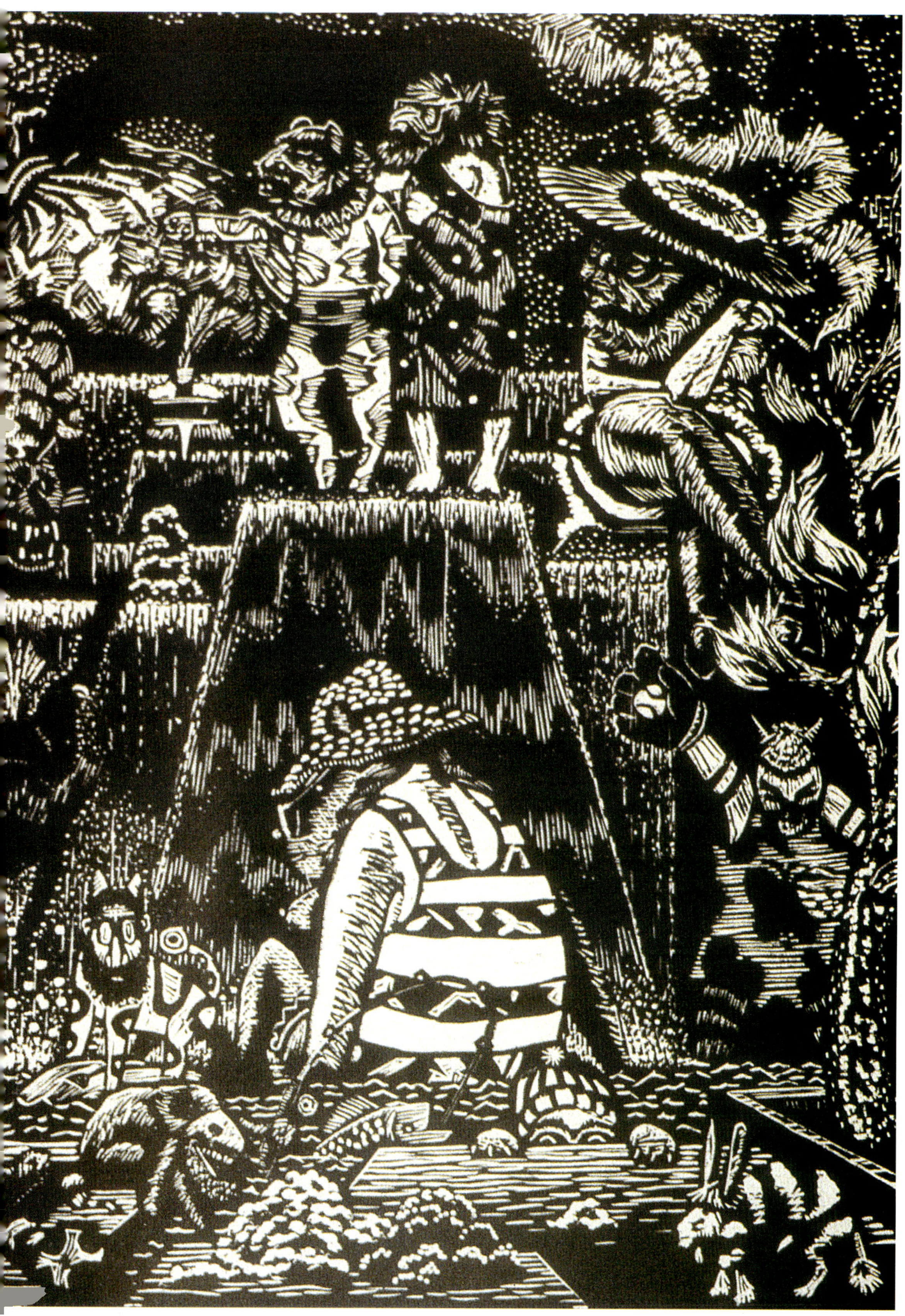

156

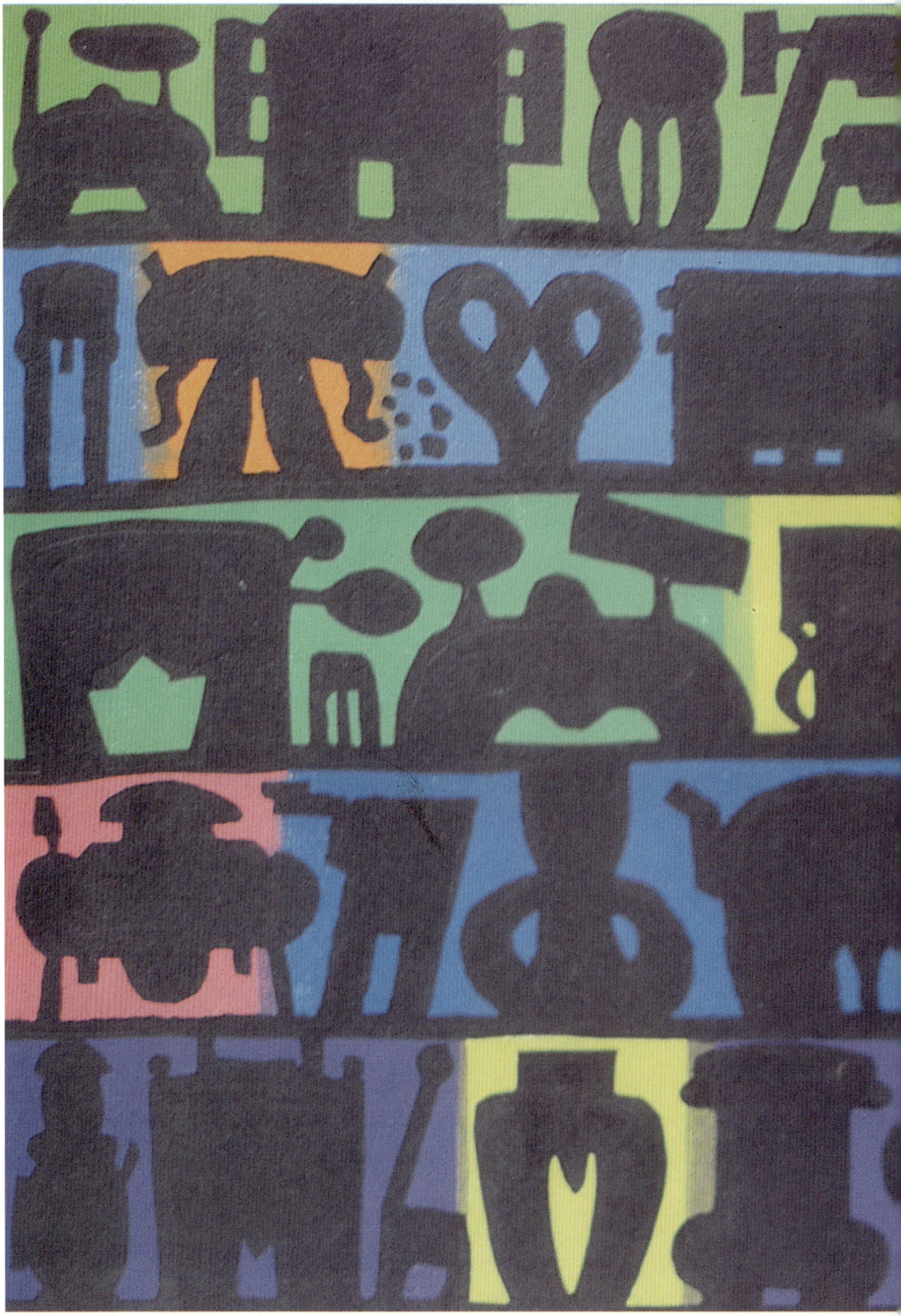

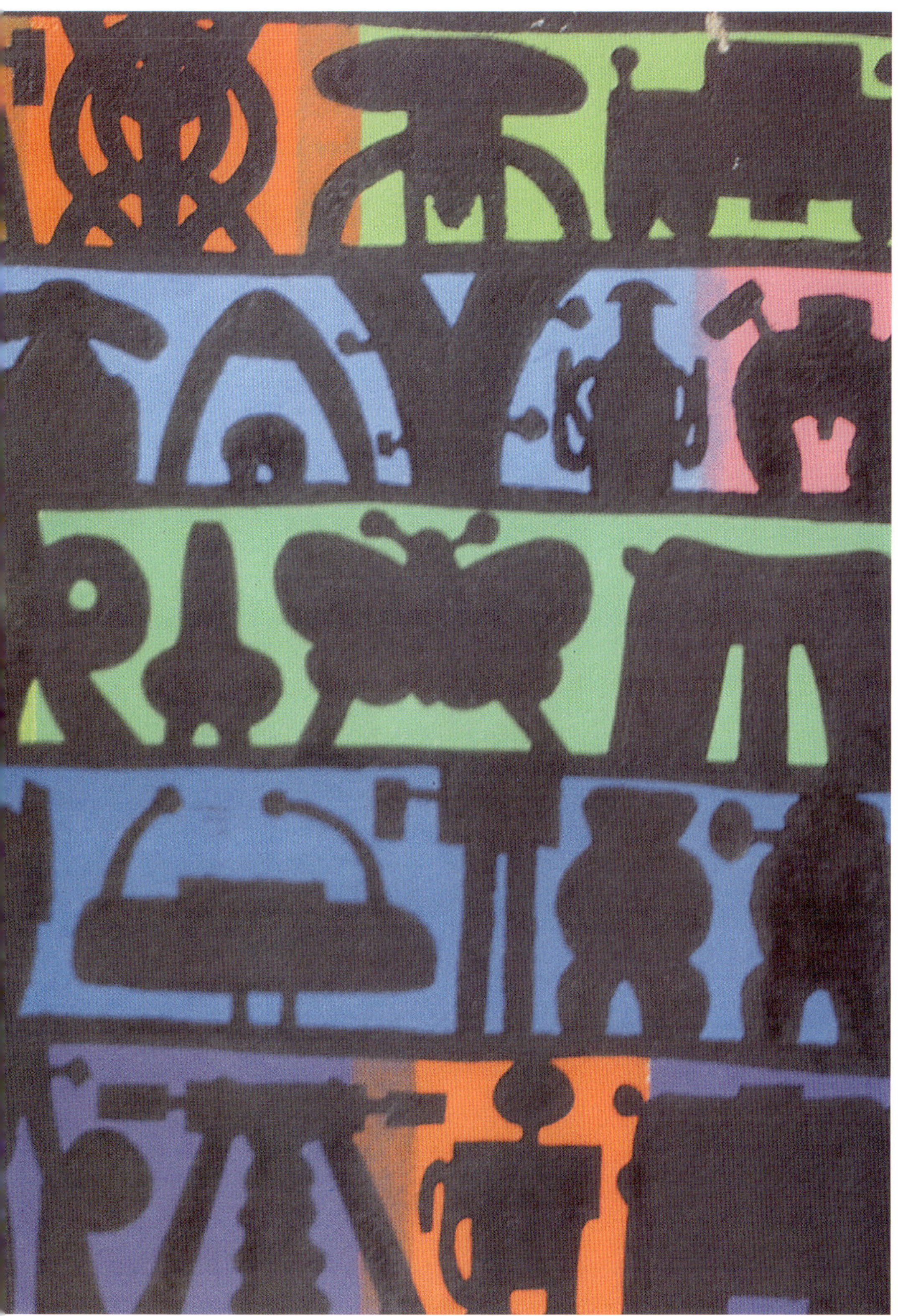

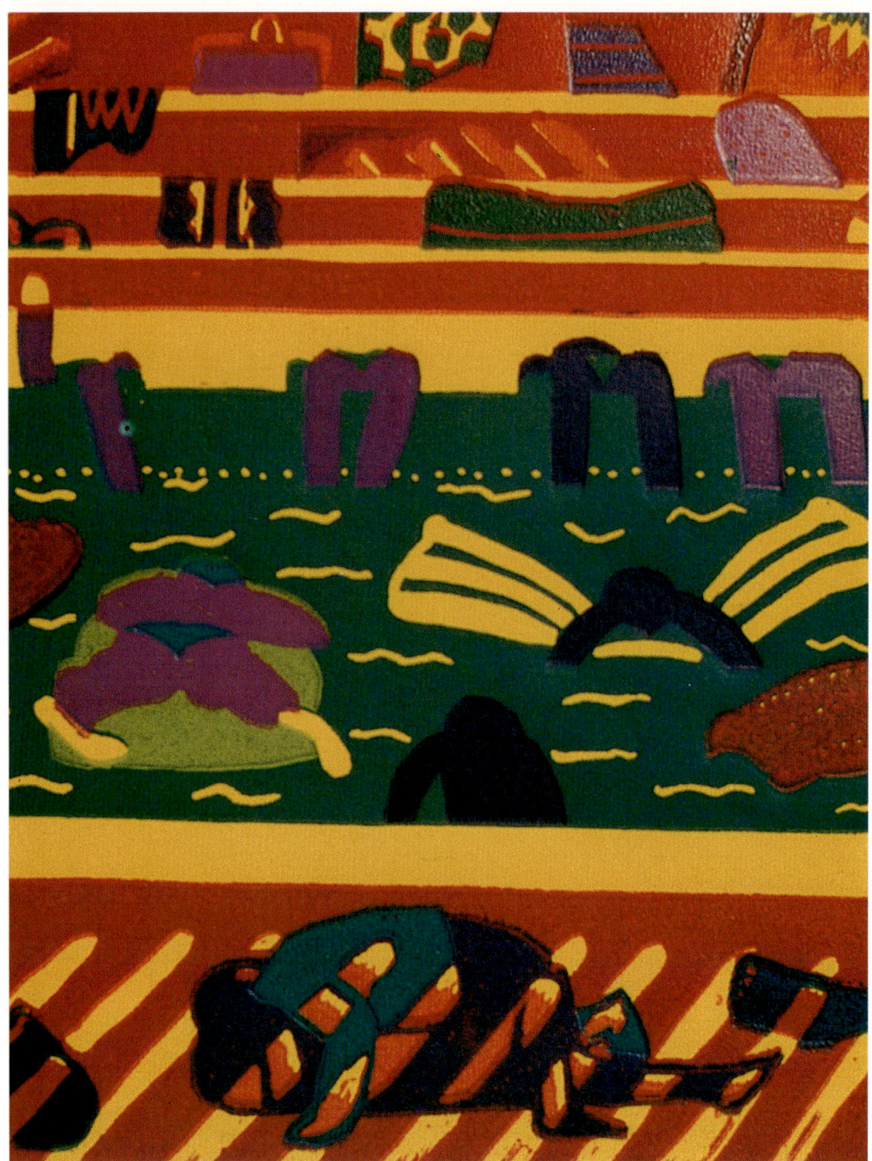

155. Some Dogs in the Fountain (woodcut) 1979 16 x 24
    (*see pages 78-79*)
156. Freeway Life Forms (color linocut) 1979 12 x 18
    (*see pages 80-81*)
157. Kahneeta (color linocut) 1980 10 x 8
158. Cat Dancing (color woodcut) 1980 13½ x 12¾
159. World Man (also titled "Giant") (hanga) 1980 8¼ x 6½
    (*see page 84*)
160. Cat Cap (hanga) 1980 4 x 5½ (*see page 84*)

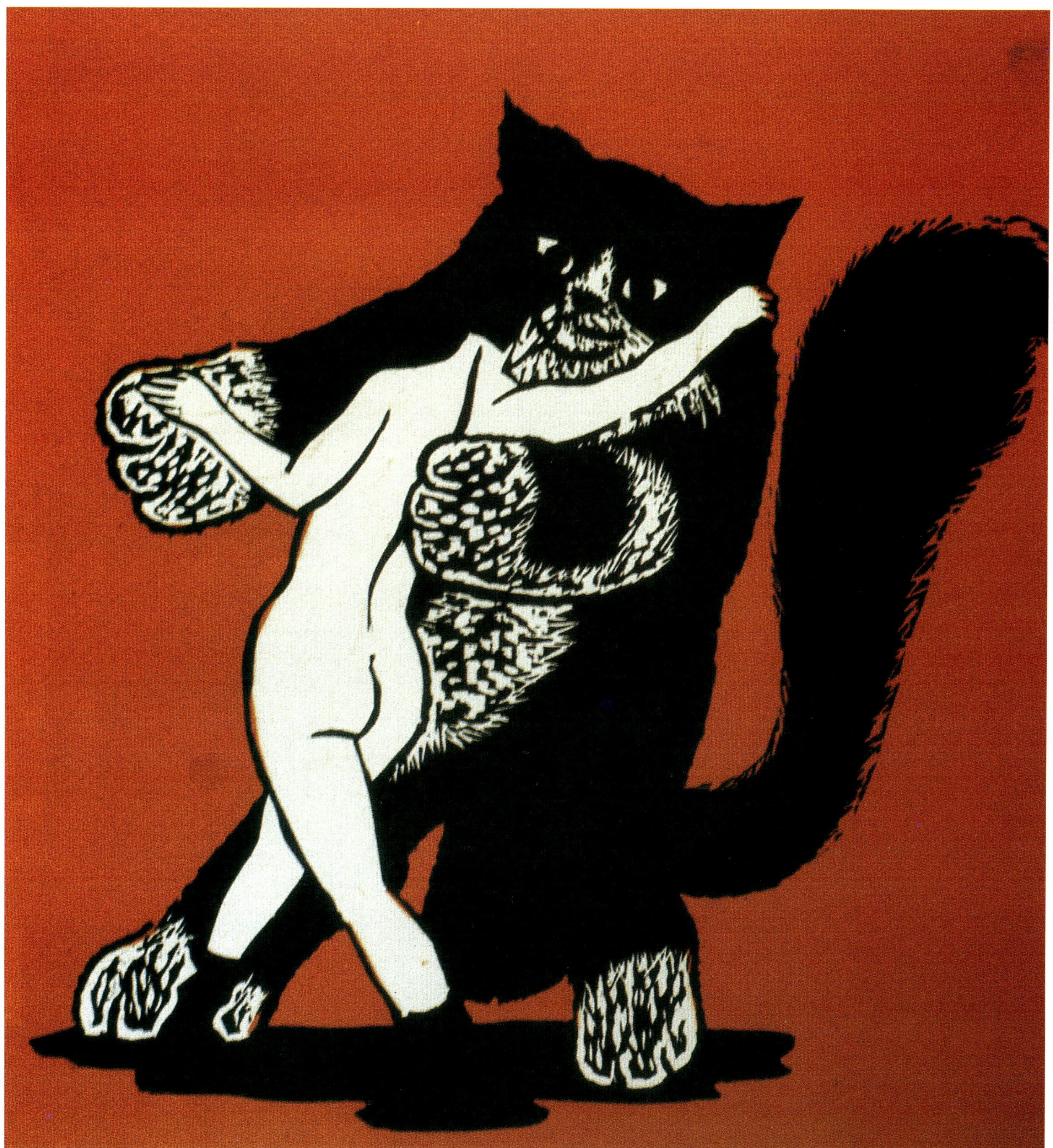

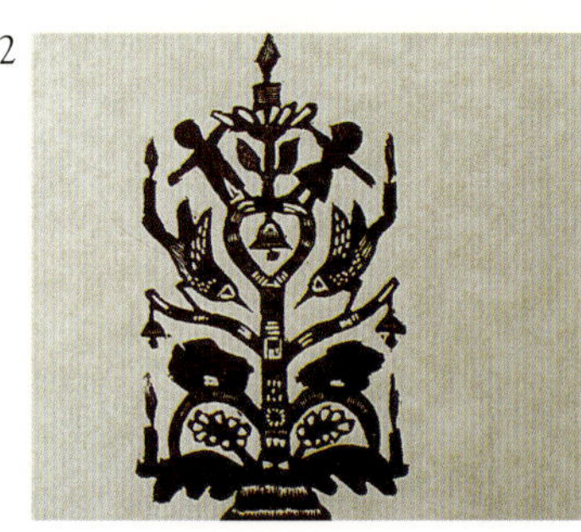

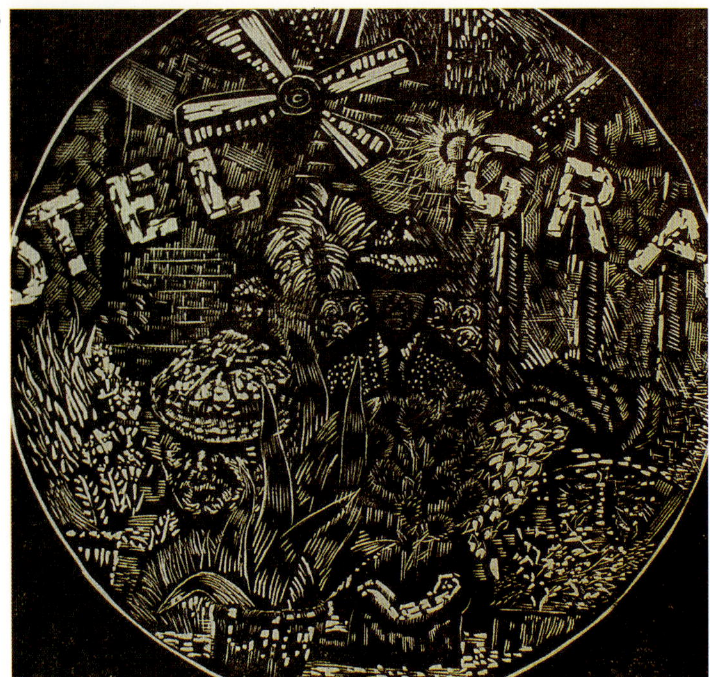

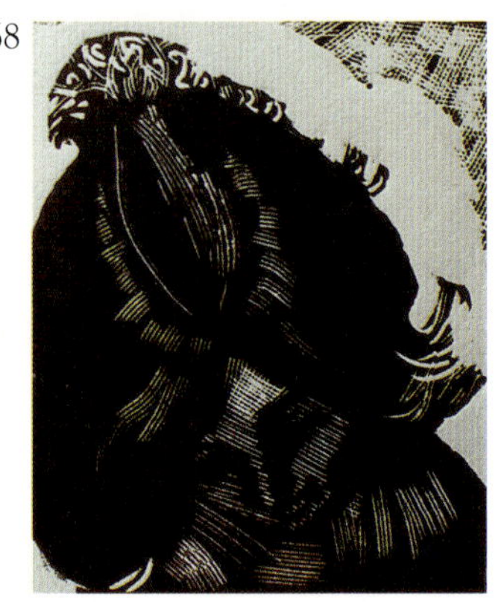

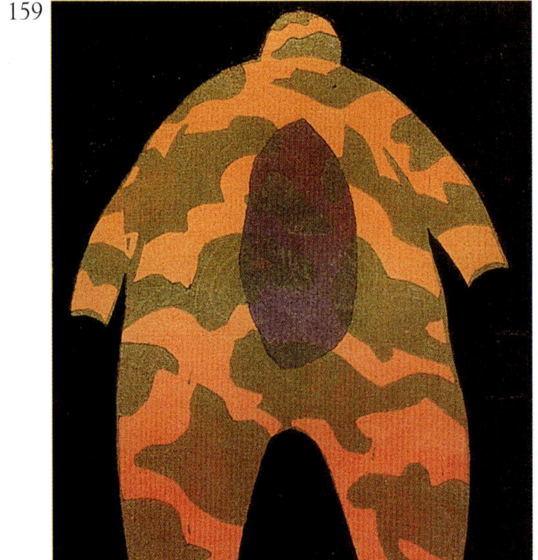

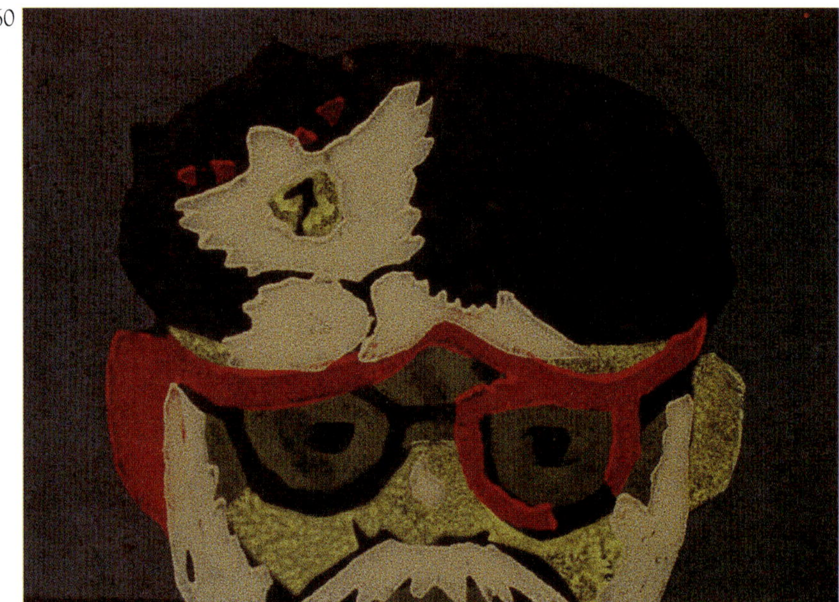

161. Dumpling (woodcut) 1980 5 x 5½
162. Wedding Announcement: Hugh McLarty & Lisbeth
     Vanderlinden (woodengraving) July 1980 3 x 1¾
163. Hotel Grand (woodengraving) 1980 4 x 4
164. Night Rooms (woodengraving) 1980 5 x 5
165. The Giant Tree (woodengraving) 1980 7 x 5
166. Trees (woodengraving) 1980 2 x 8
167. Death and HK (woodengraving) 1980 3¾ x 3½
168. Jennifer (woodengraving) 1980 2 x 1¾
169. Sea Siren (woodengraving) 1980 4" circle

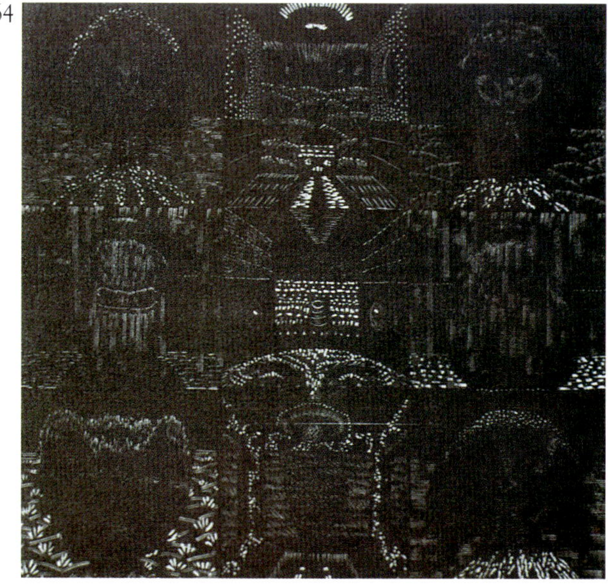

164

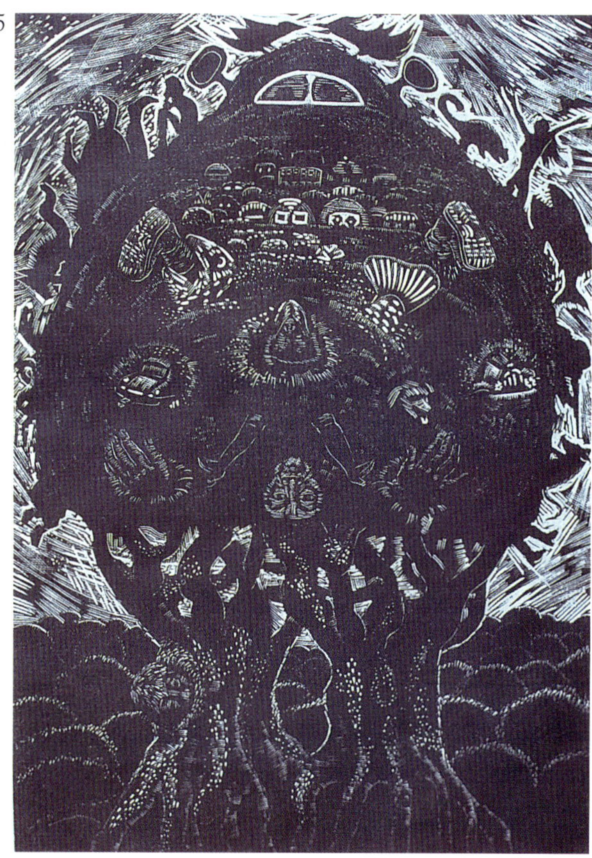

165

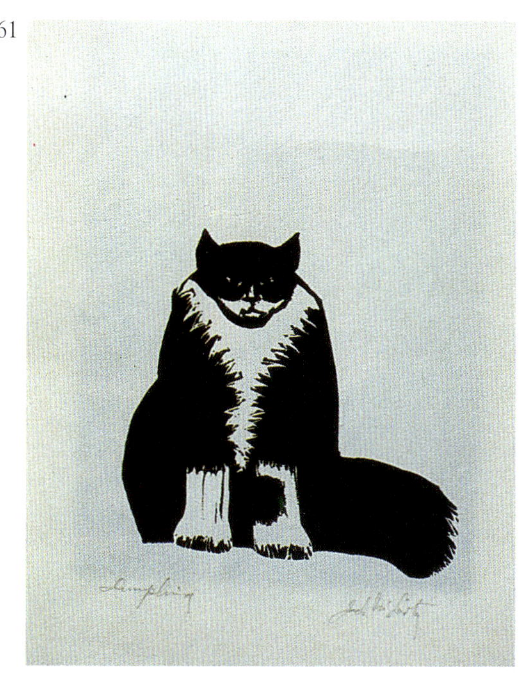

161

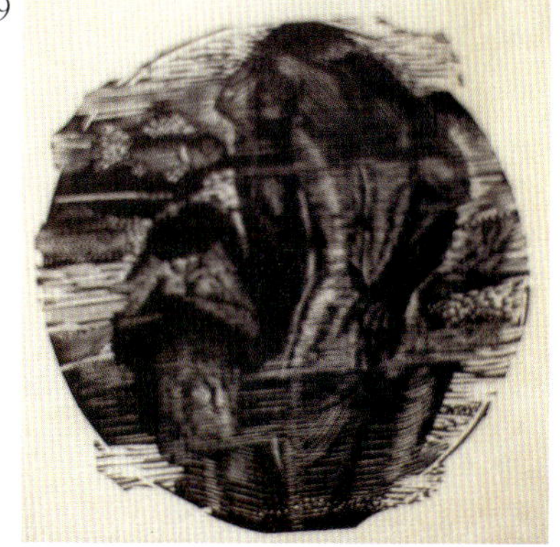

169

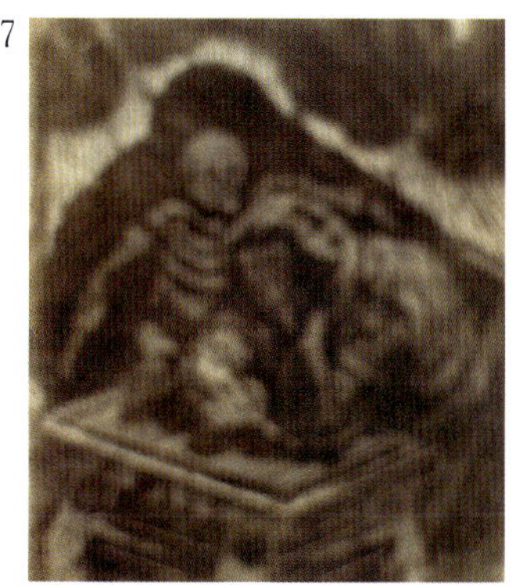

167

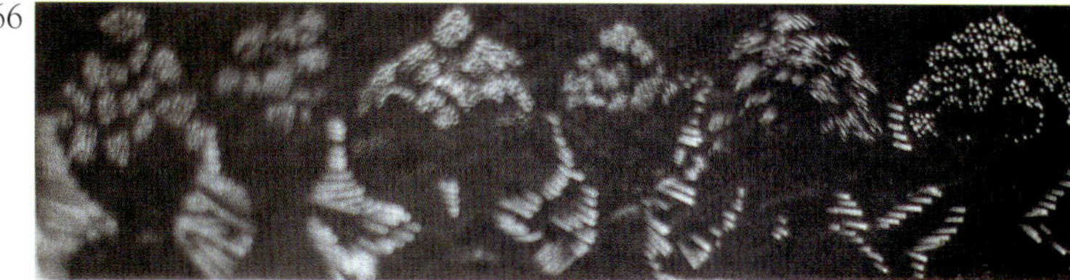

166

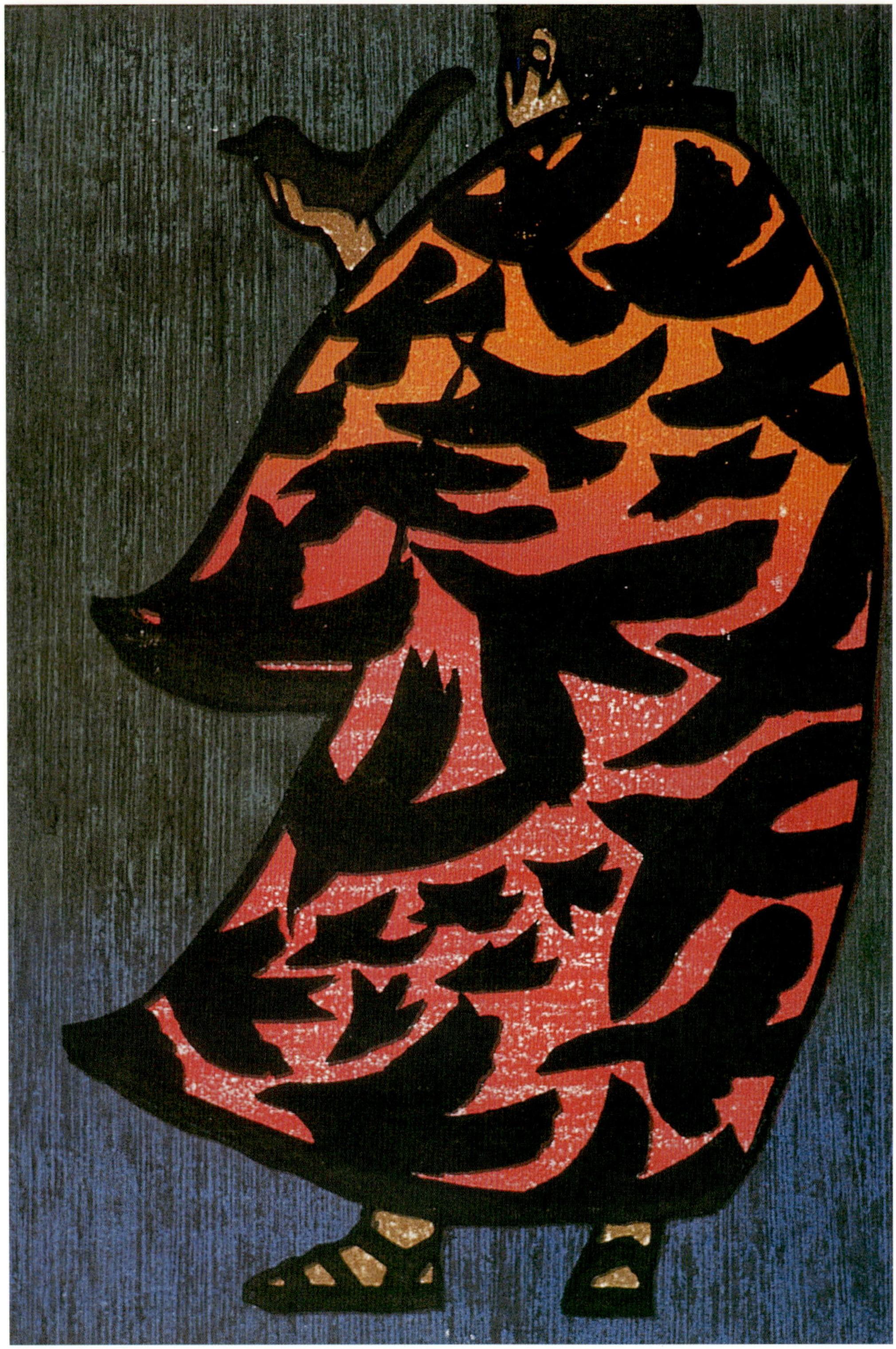

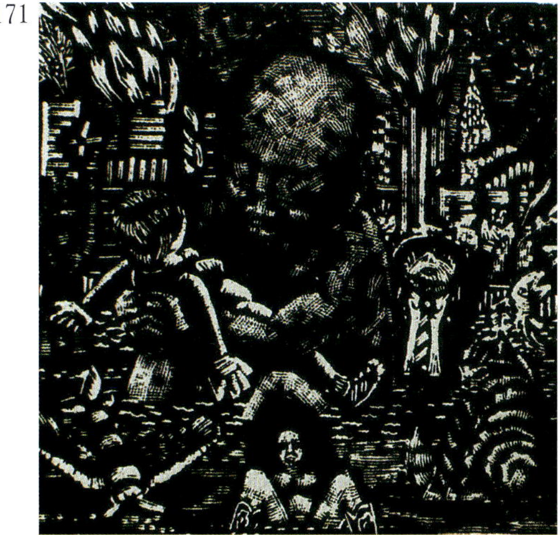

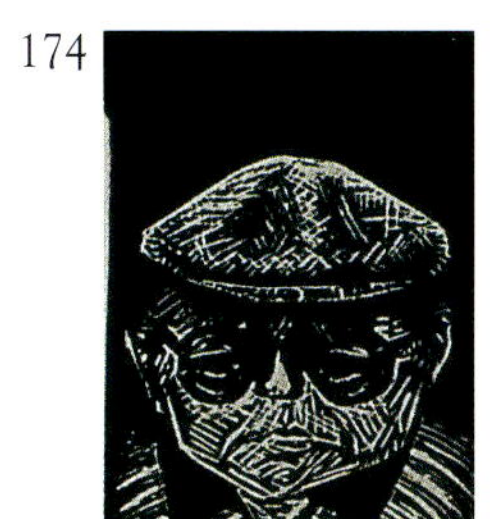

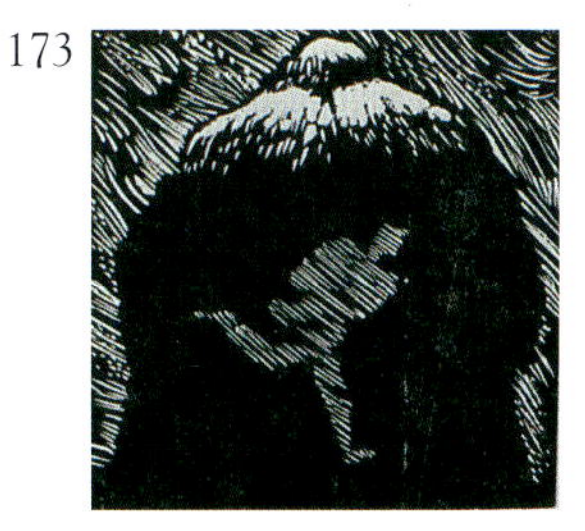

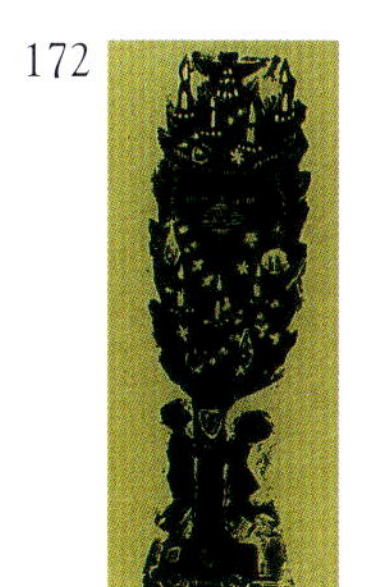

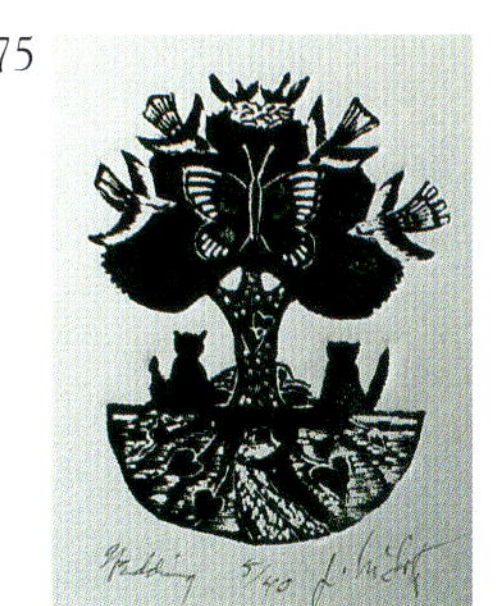

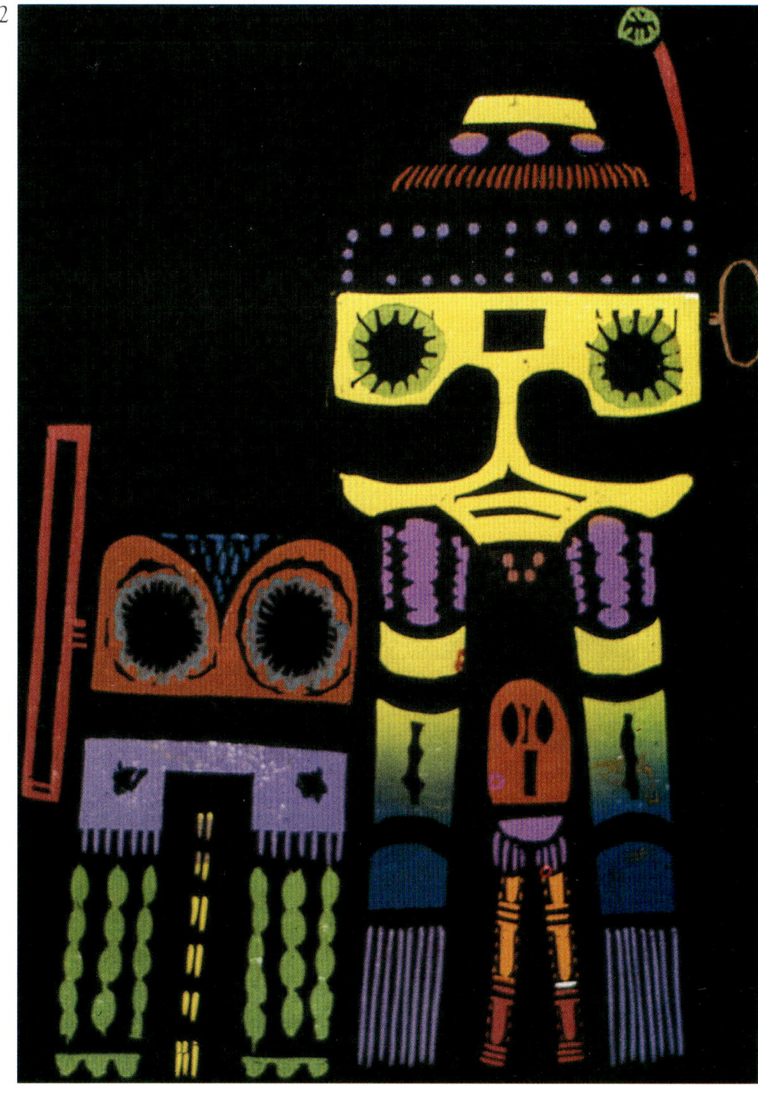

170. St. Francis in Japan (hanga) 1981 10¼ x 7⅜
171. The City (also titled "Fire") (lino-engraving) 1981 3 x 3
172. Wedding Announcement: Laura Marguerite McLarty
     (woodengraving) 1981 3 x 1
173. Giant Back with Running Man (woodengraving) c. 1981 2 x 2
174. LaVerne (woodengraving) 1981 1¼ x 1
175. Wedding Announcement: Karen Chaivoe & Rob Holladay
     (woodengraving) 1981 3 x 2¼

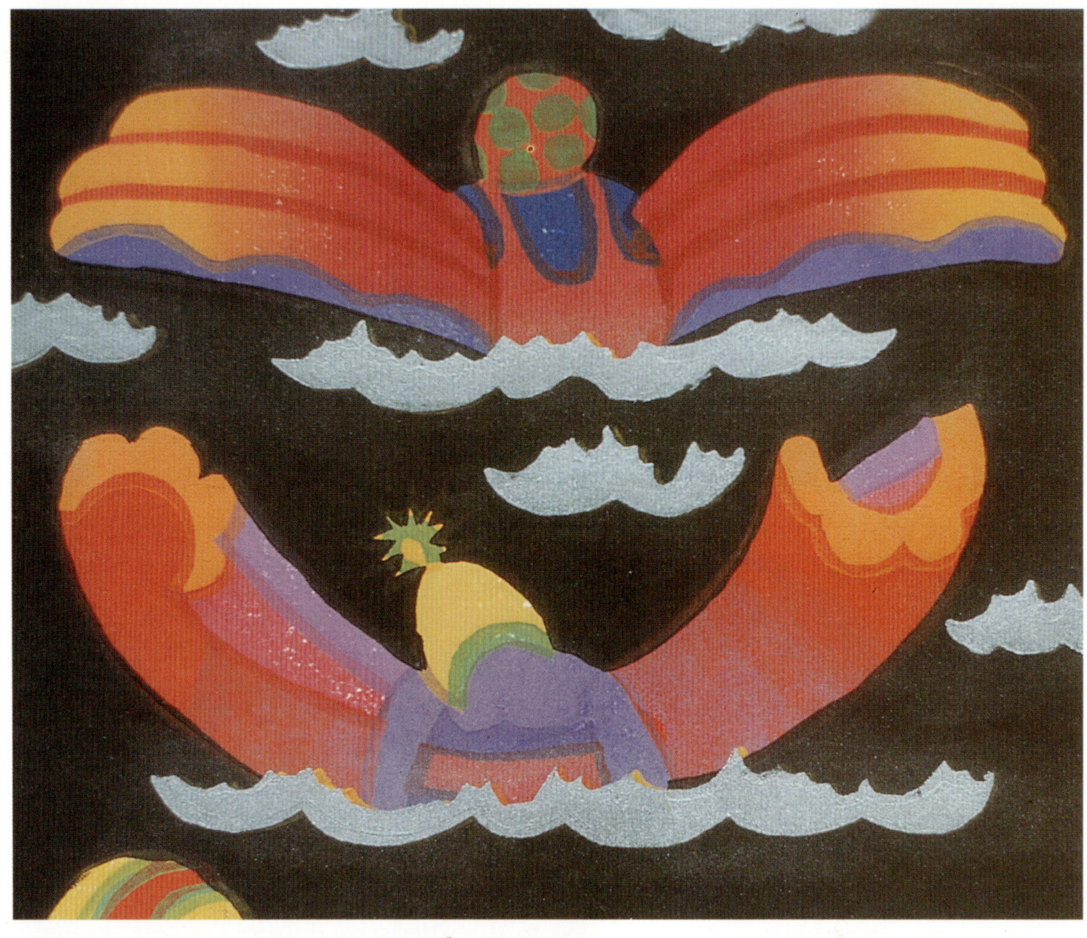

177

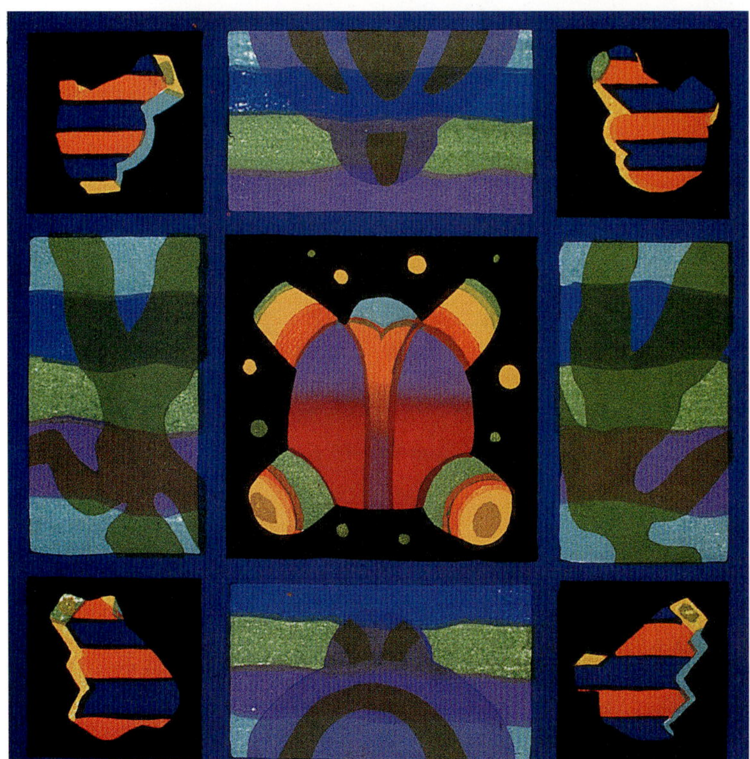

178

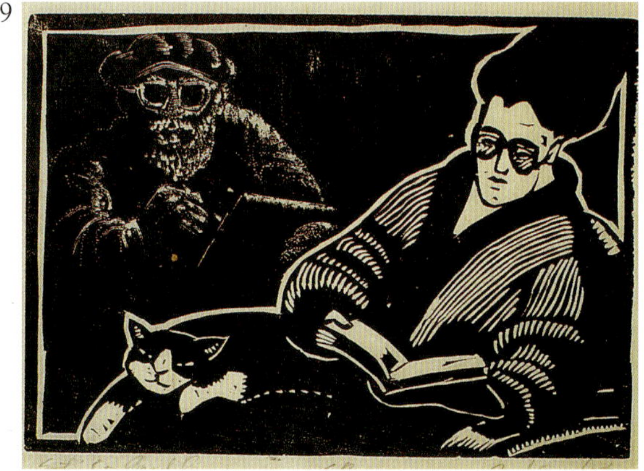

179

176. Poster for Pete Seeger Concert (serigraph) 1982
11 x 11 (*see page 90*)
177. The Pool, Kahneeta (hanga) 1982 10 x 11¾
178. War Games (hanga) 1982 8½ x 8½
179. Artist and Models (linocut) 1982 5 x 7
180. The Descent of Man (hanga) 1982 15 x 11½

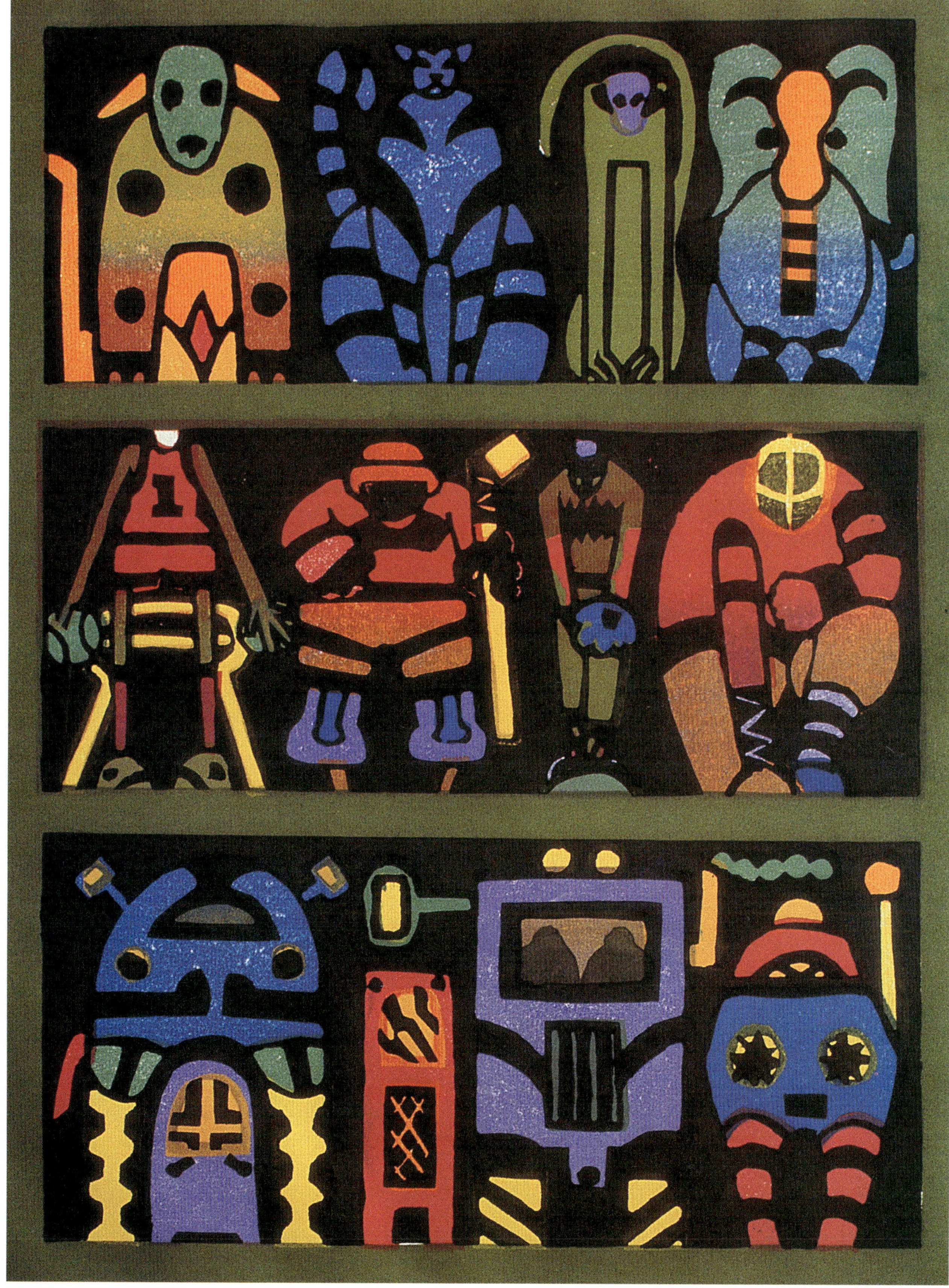

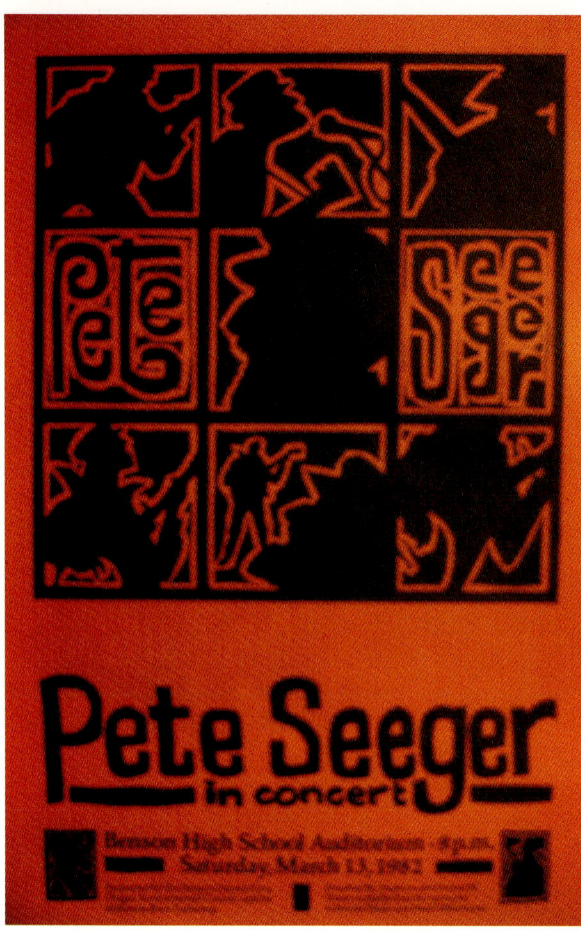

181. Small Volcanoes (hanga) 1982 6½ x 6½
182. The Family (hanga) 1983 10 x 7 (*see page 87*)
183. Adios Amor (color linocut) 1983 11½ x 18
184. Free Fall (color linocut) 1983 16 x 16 (*see page 92*)
185. Swimmers in a Dark River (color linocut) 1983 16 x 16
     (*see page 93*)

181

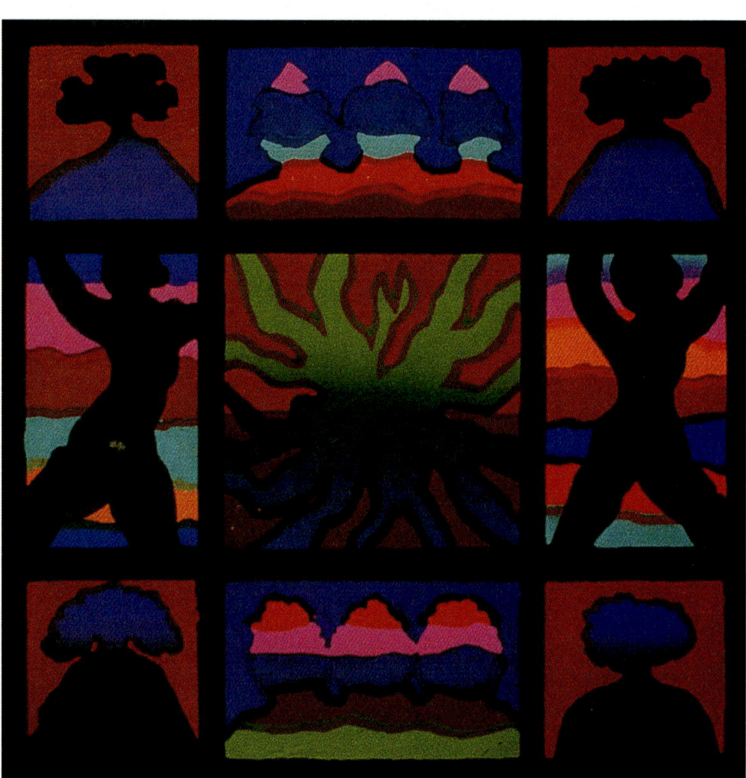

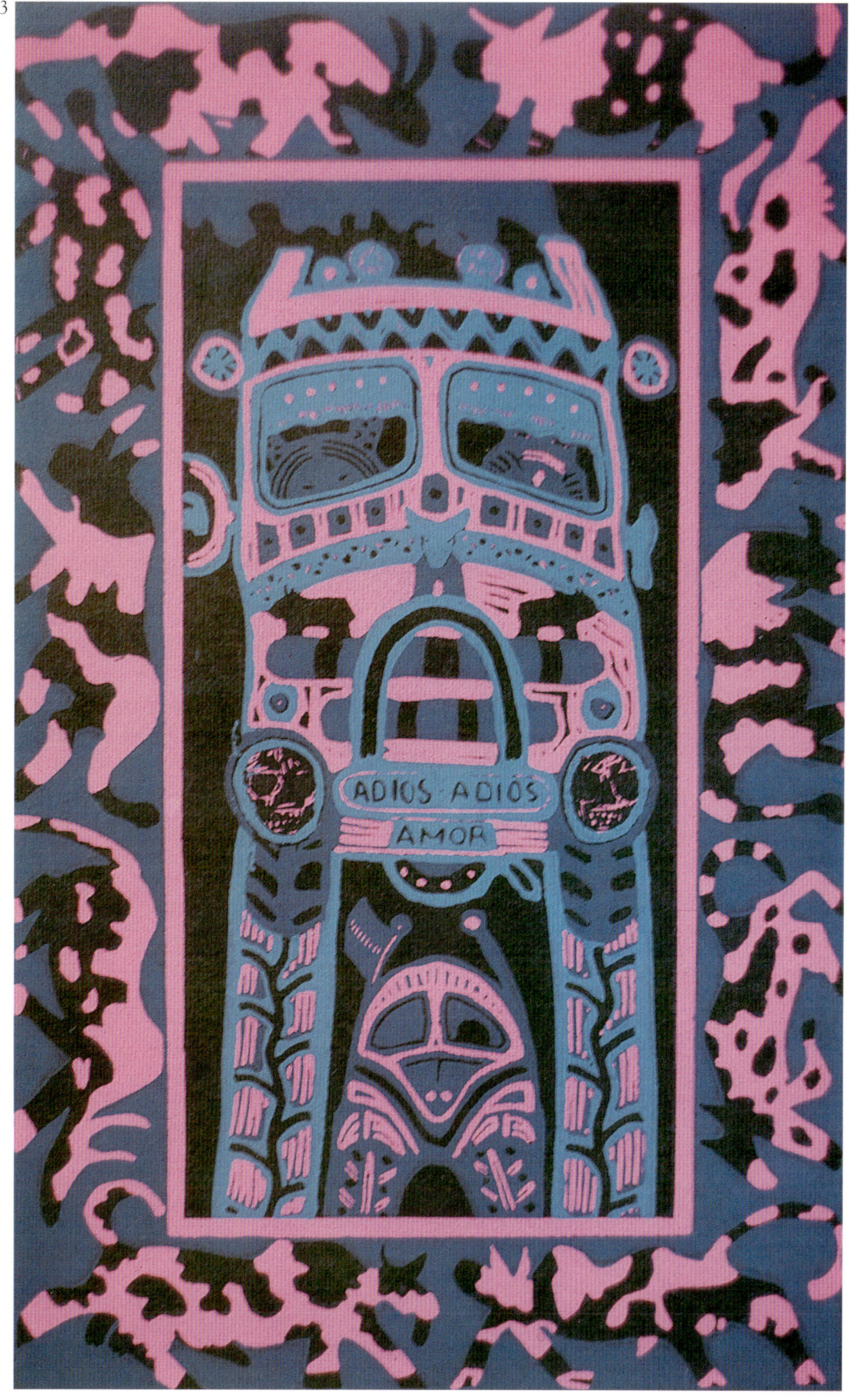
ADIOS ADIOS
AMOR

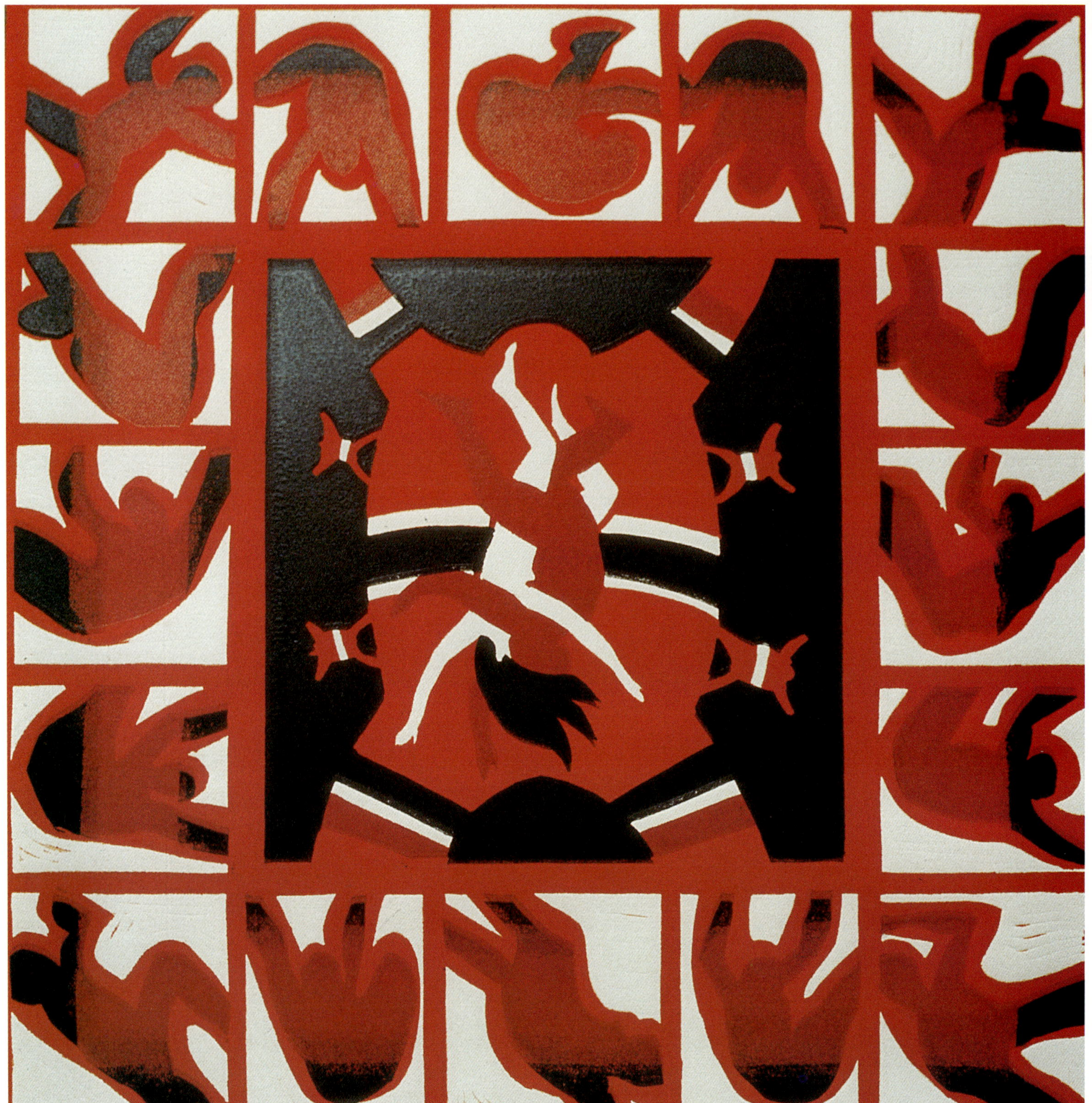

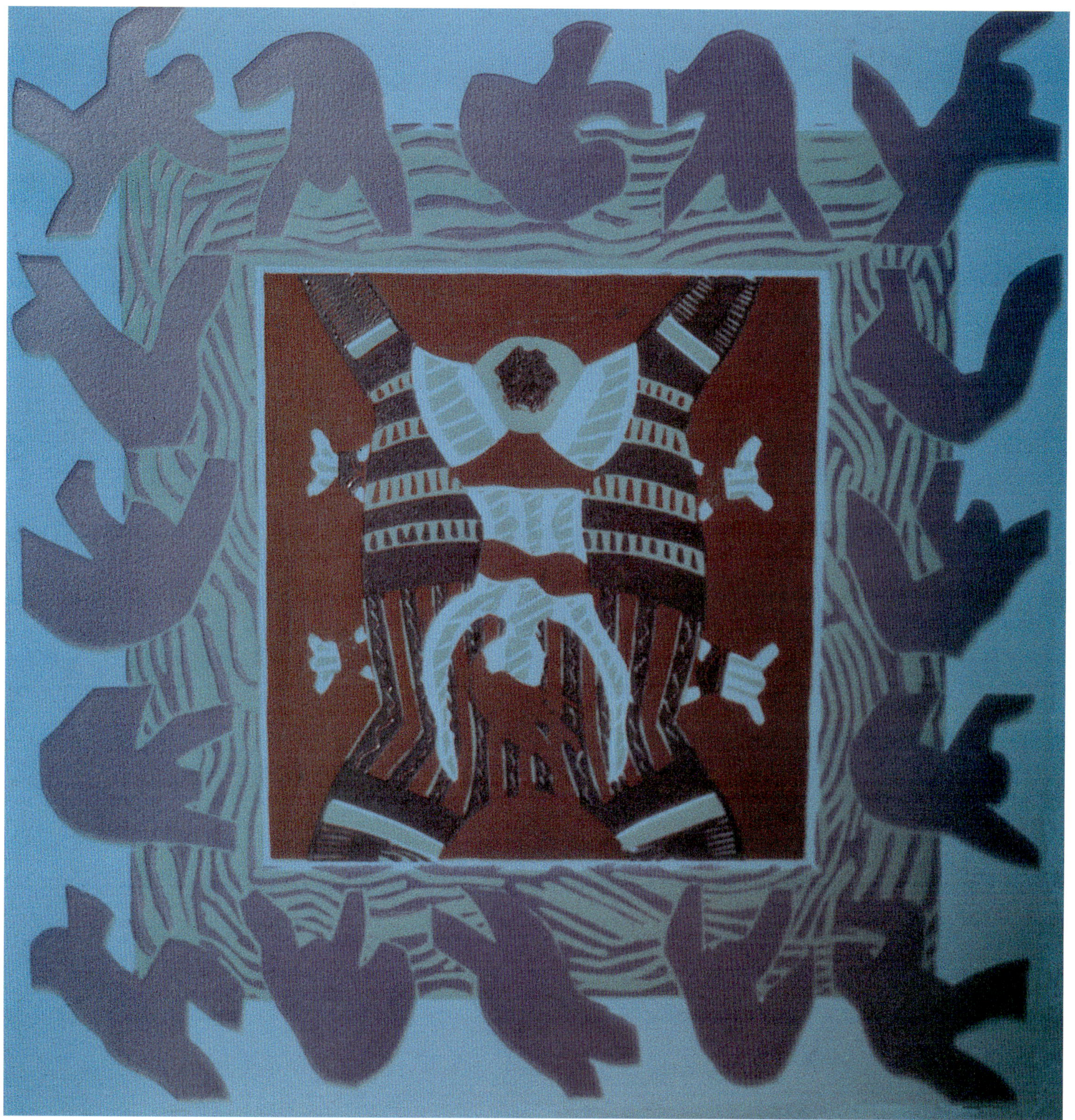

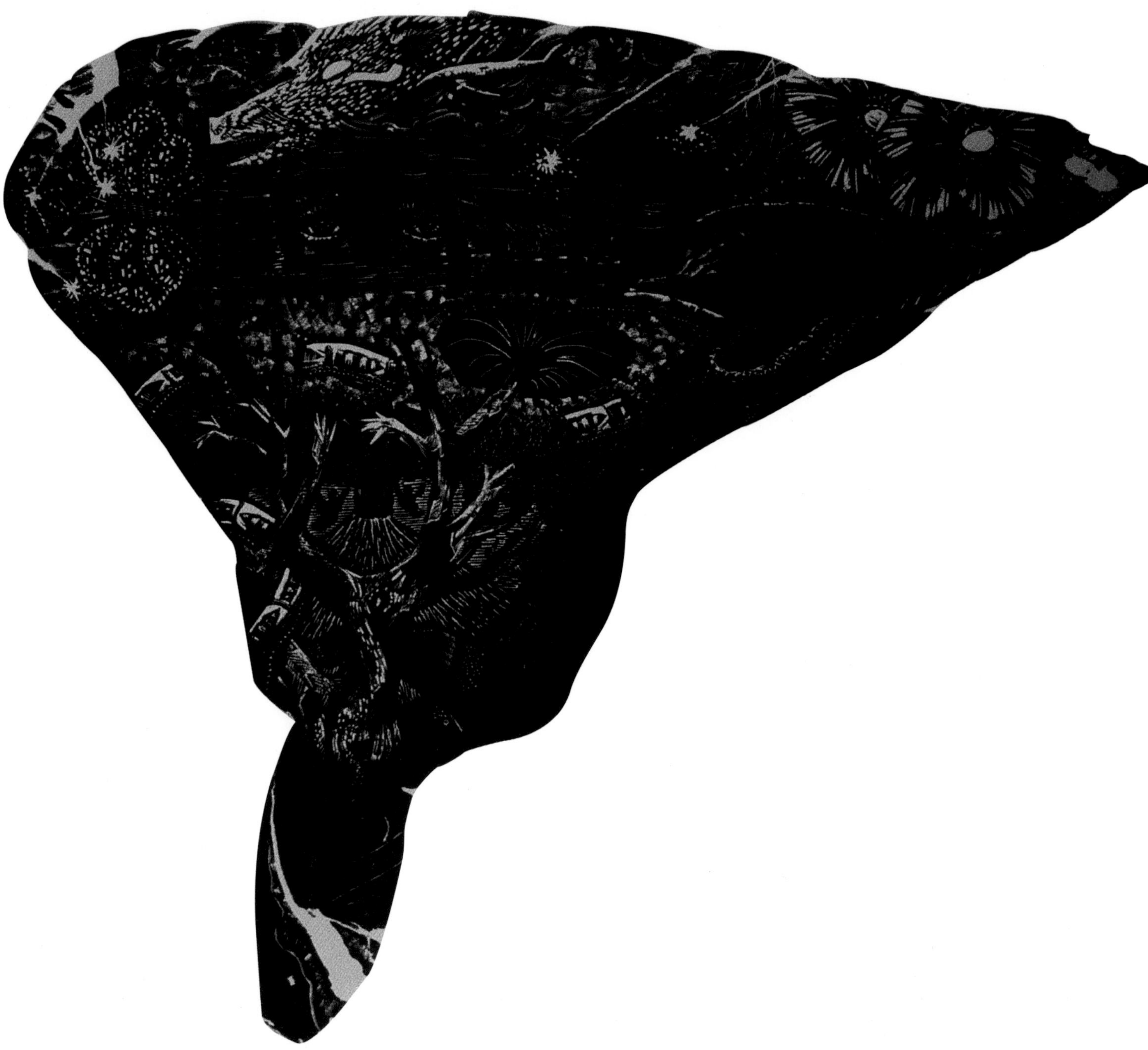

186. Bienvenidos a Mexico (linocut) 1983 10 x 8
187. Storms and Dreams (woodengraving) 1984 11 x 13
188. Ottos (color linocut) 1984 9 x 12 (*see page* 96)
189. Butterfly Robe (color woodcut) 1984 20 x 13¾ (*see page* 97)
190. The Doll Collector (hand-colored woodcut) 1984 20¾ x 15¾
    (*see page* 98)
191. The Cat Problem (lino-engraving) 1984 8 x 6 (*see page* 99)

MADRE DE DIOS
NO REBASE

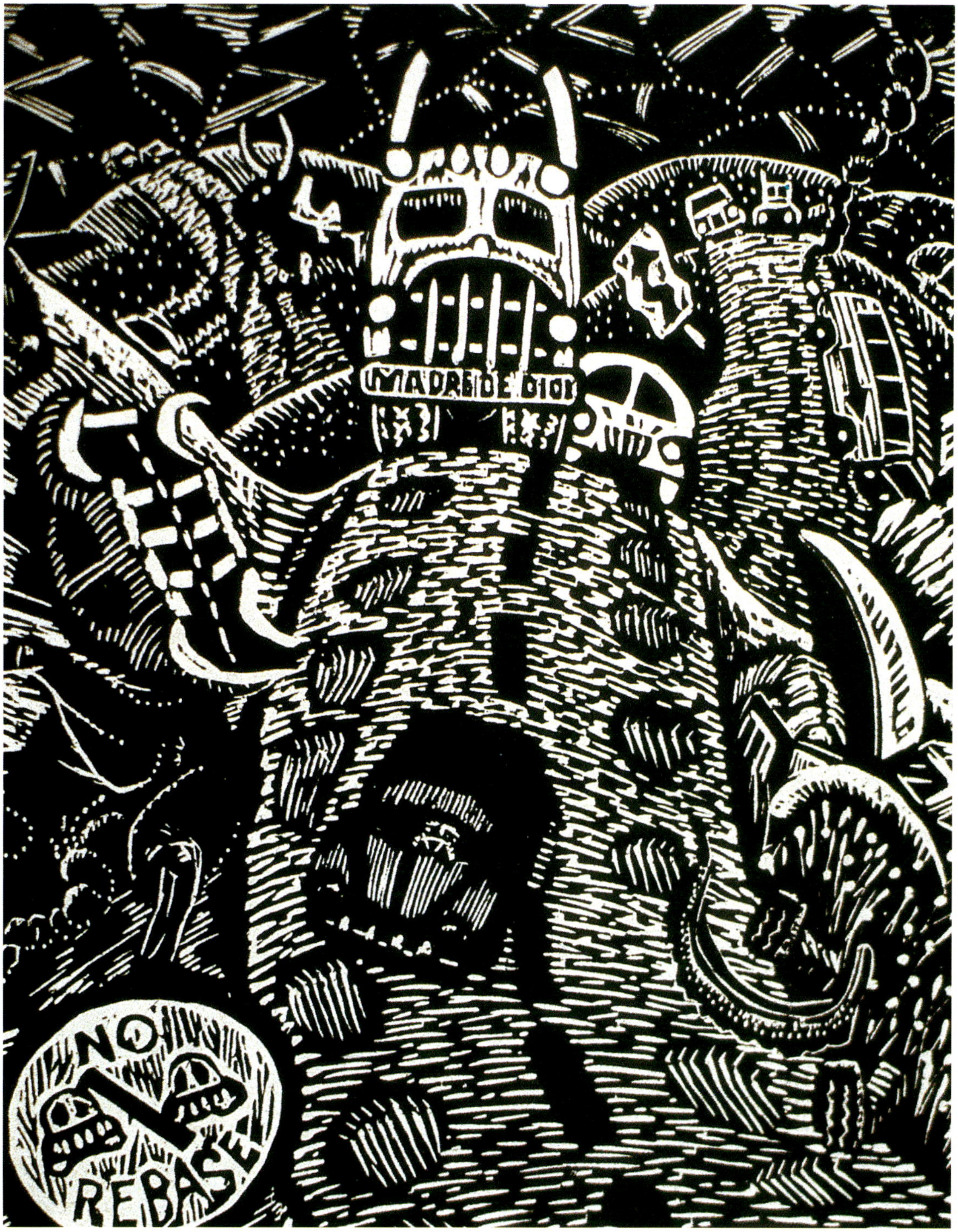

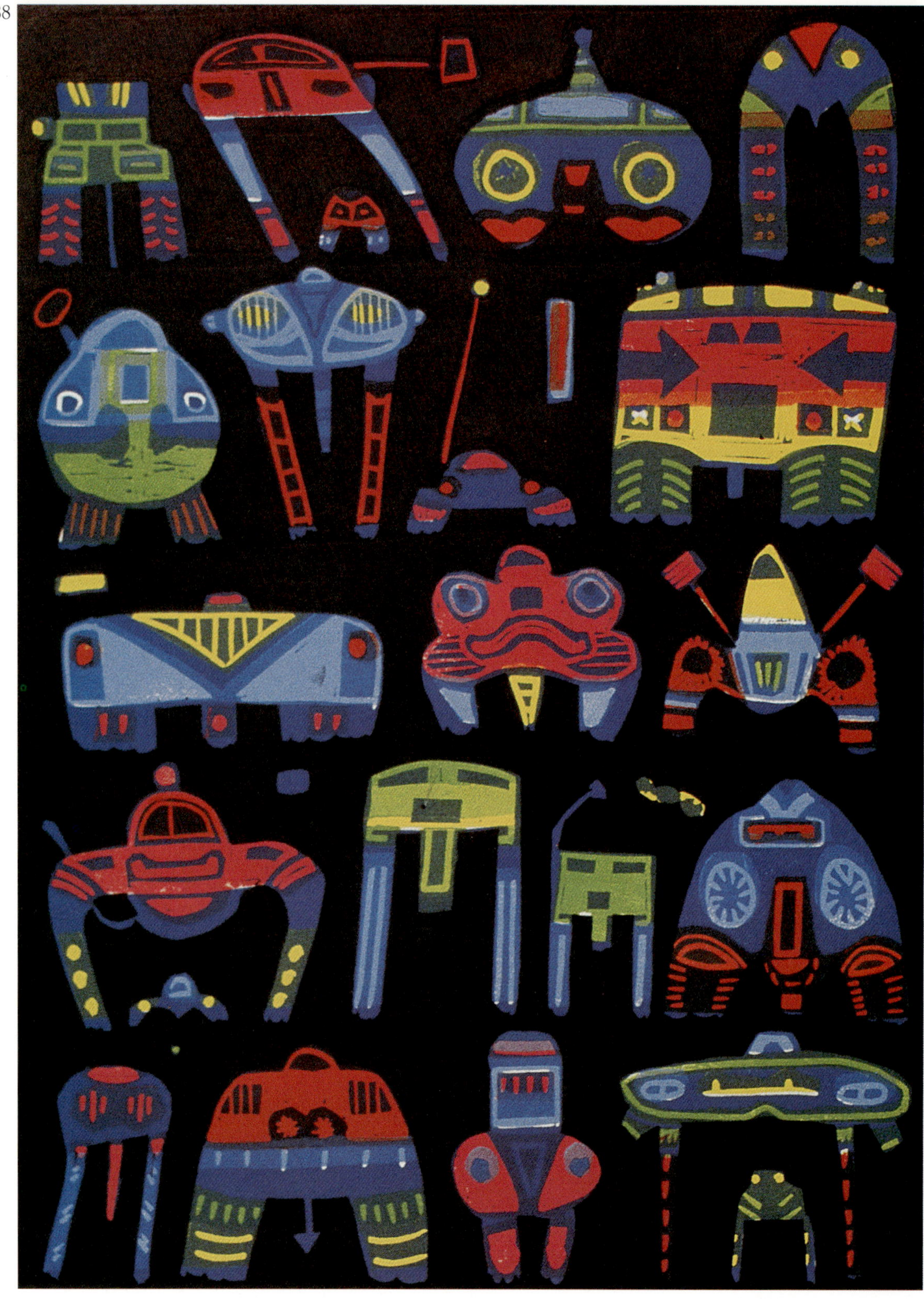

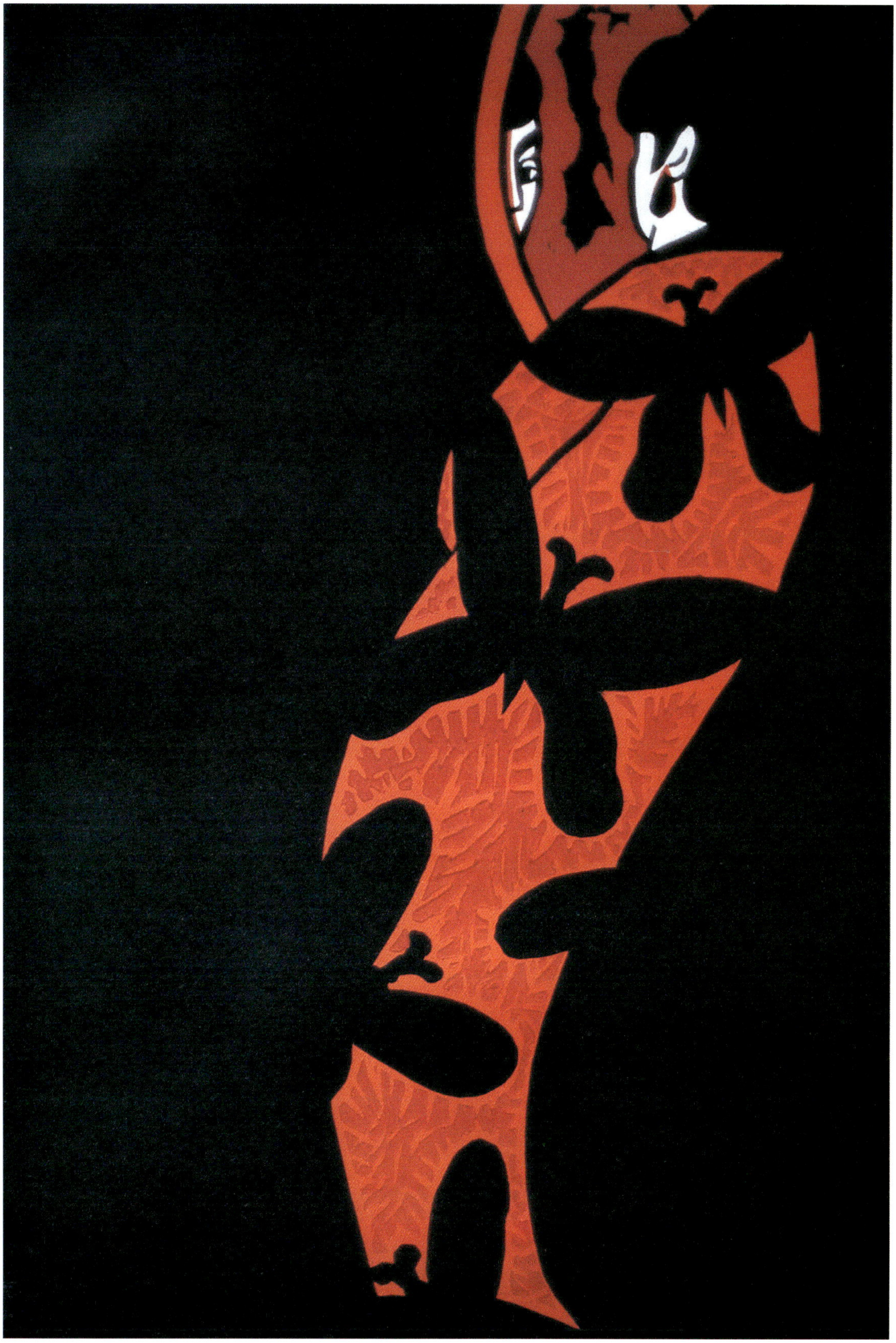

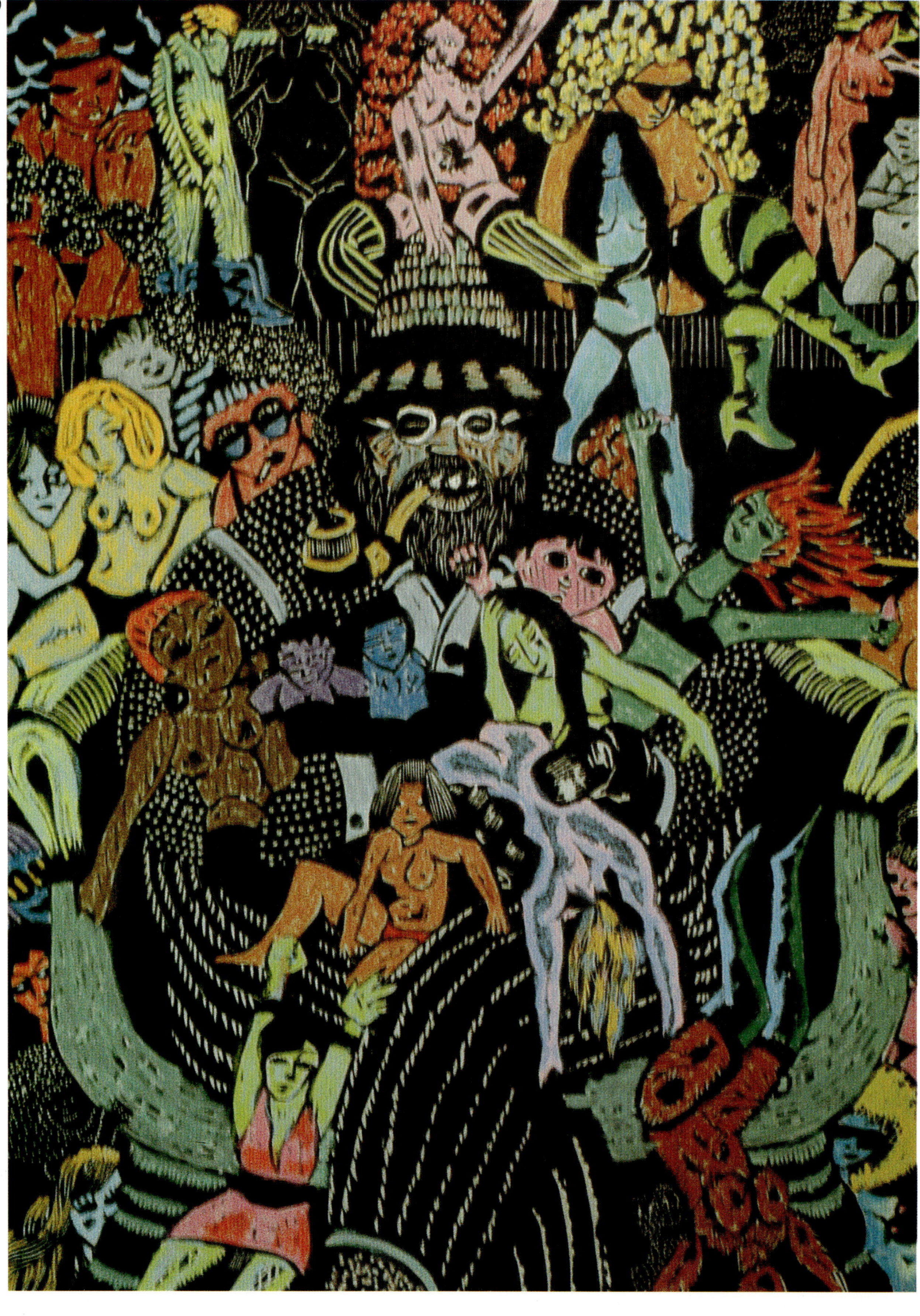

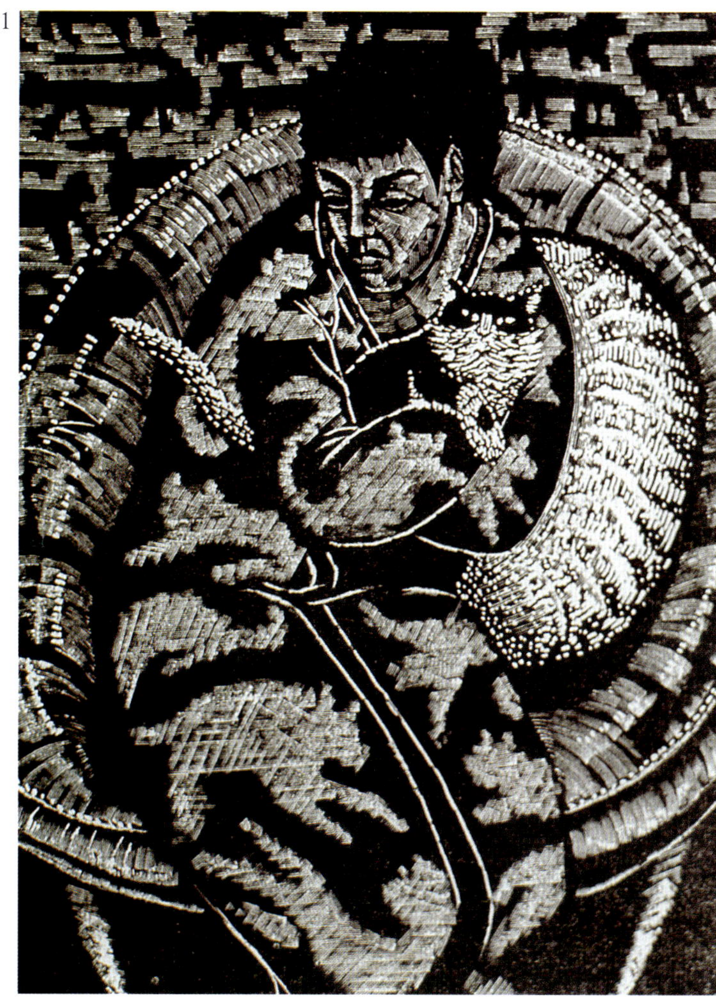

Art gives good thoughts and allows you to see your Self. It gives inner access to the Self or Soul. It develops the imagination, the most important thing for creativity. It stimulates thinking and lifts us above the small Self to discover our uniqueness. It focuses on the truth. It develops the intuitive mind to join with the rational mind. It expands our awareness and raises our consciousness. It allows us to connect with our Self, our Divinity.

The Artist enables us to experience this through his work. He is a unique master in the exhibition of thought. He is the only one who can create art. He takes the inner universe and the outer universe and joins them together in an inexplicable, magical way.

Dennis Schiller, Portland, Oregon, November 1996

My close acquaintance with Dennis has greatly increased my awareness of the way in which he absorbs art and is nourished and inspired by it. I have concluded that he would have fit admirably into the world of Bernard of Clairvaux in the 12th century.

He taught his followers how to look at a religious work of art. He urged the observer to cast his eyes over every inch and fraction of an inch of an object, crawling over it more slowly than a snail would, in order to comprehend the full meaning and the ultimate beauty.

Jack McLarty, 31 December 1996

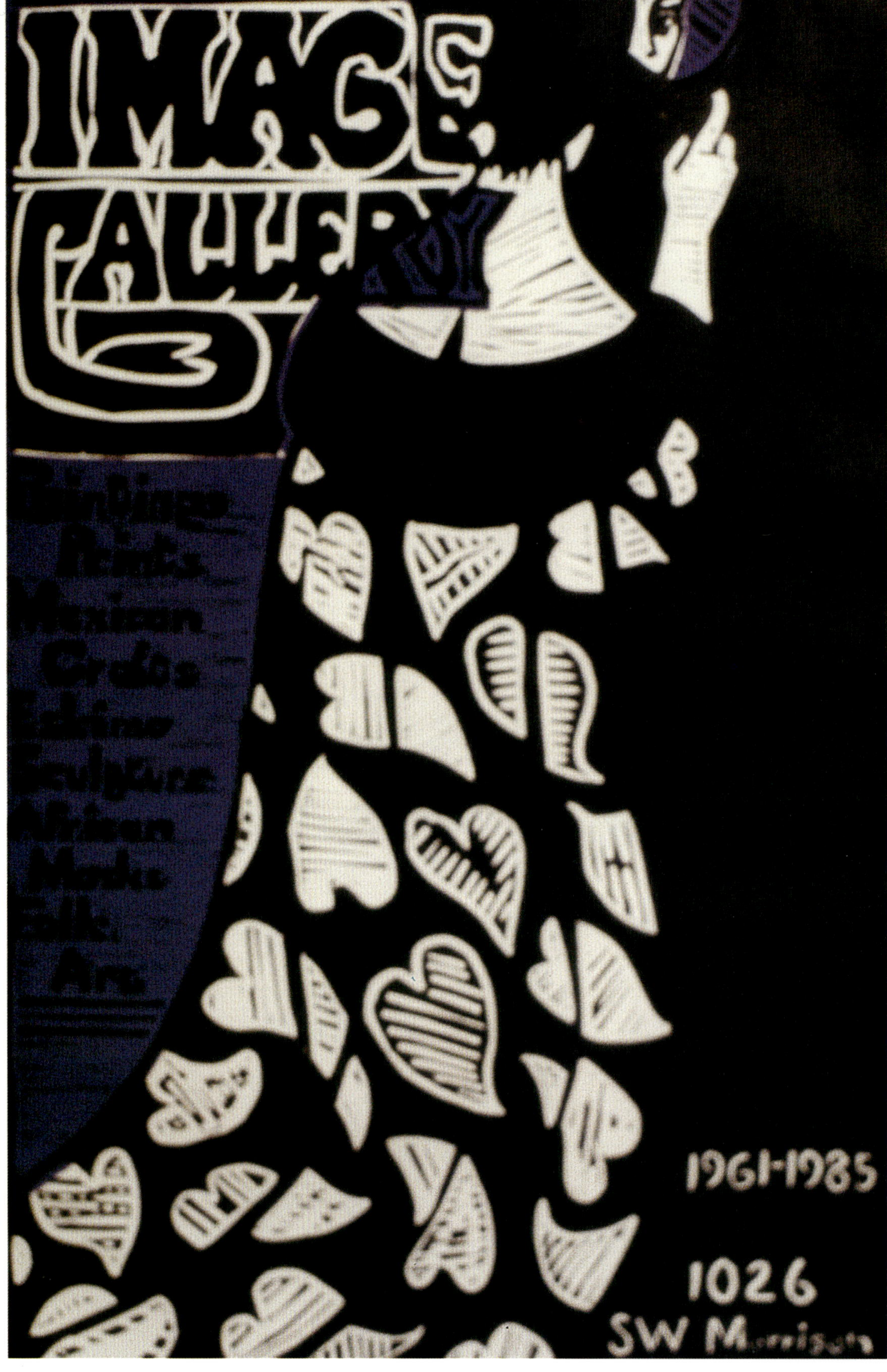
IMAGE
GALLERY
Paintings
Prints
Mexican
Codes
Sculpture
Mexican
Folk
Art
1961-1985
1026
SW Morrison

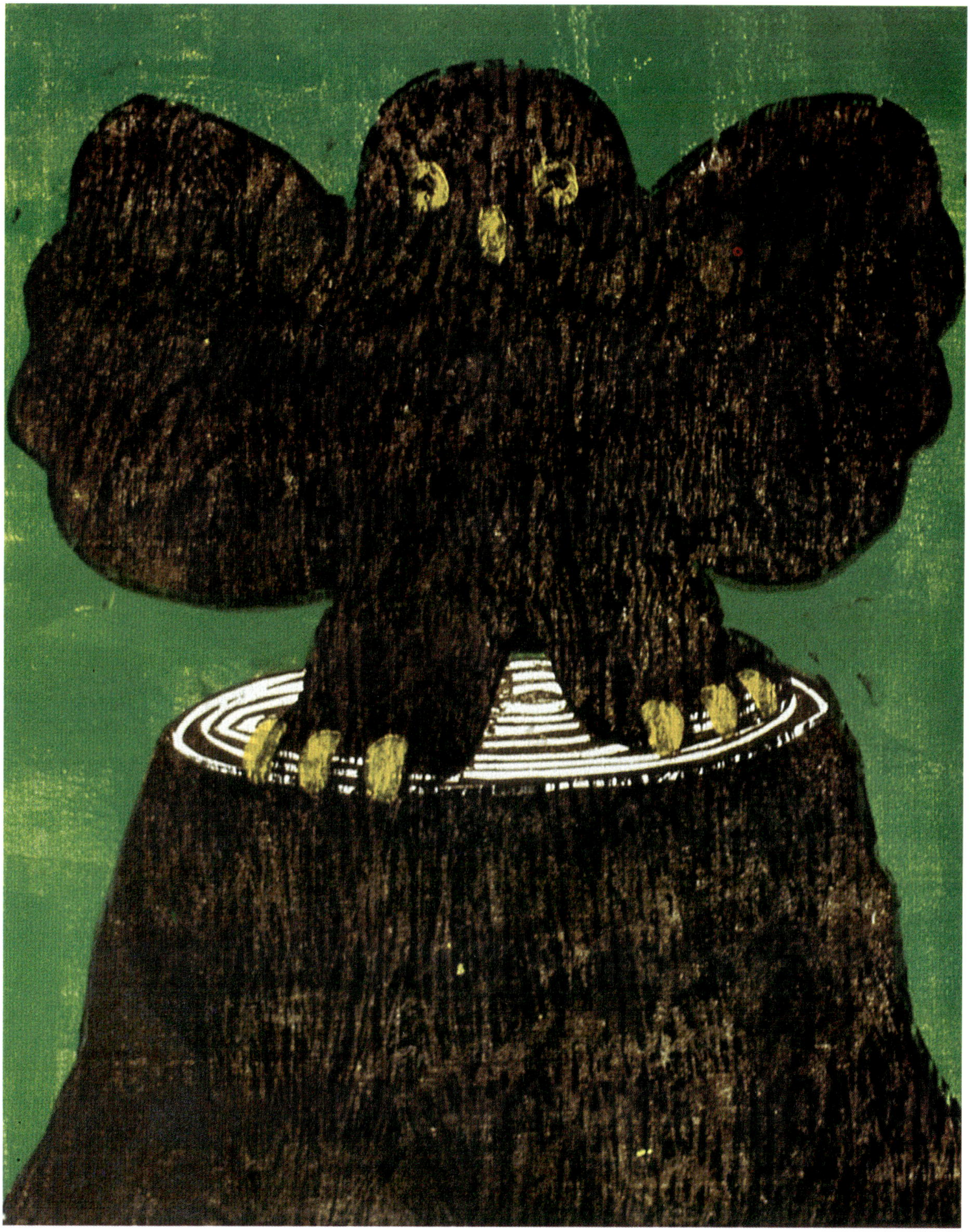

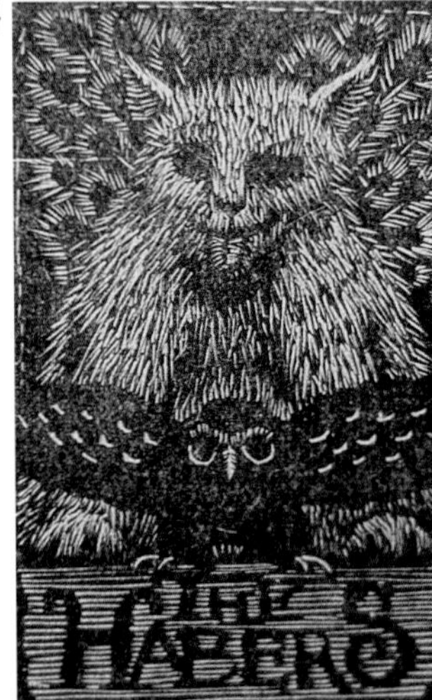

How does an artist's work remain fresh and exciting after 50 years of continuous involvement in printmaking? Jack McLarty's answer is to consciously begin his day eagerly re-seeing the world—throwing aside clichés and going with his own responses.

This printmaker has pursued his quest by learning traditional Japanese woodcut techniques from a master Japanese printmaker. He has produced beautiful embossed images as part of a handmade, handbound book of Japanese poetry. He has traveled to Mexico and absorbed techniques and imagery culminating in his own view of that fascinating culture. . . .

As a part of this mini-retrospective at Graven Images Gallery, you will see works dating from the 1940s to the current day. Each piece not only represents his clarity of sight but details a man's journey through and appreciation of his surroundings. Quality work by an eminent Oregon artist.

Judy Henderson, *Ashland Daily Tidings,* 16–23 December 1994

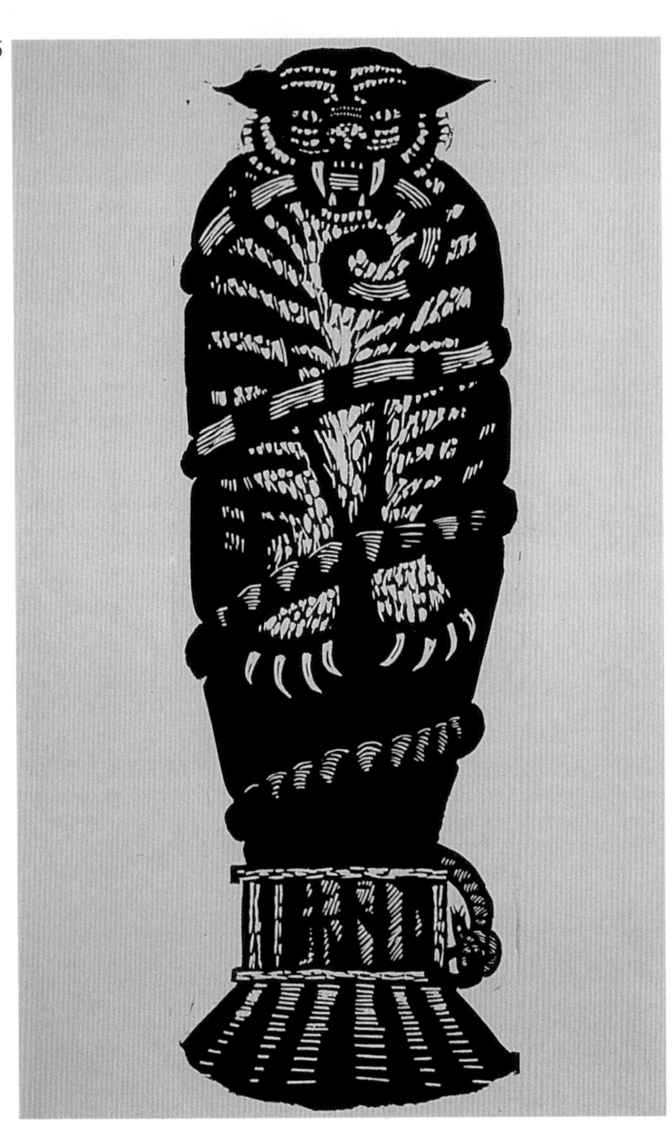

192. Image Gallery Poster (color woodcut) 1985 19 x 12¾ (*see page 100*)

193. The Guardian (woodcut) 1985 15¾ x 13 (*see page 101*)

194. "Willis" — Bookplate for Carol & Seymour Haber (woodcut) 1985 3 x 2

195. The Cage (linocut created to illustrate a story in *Clinton Street Quarterly*) 1985 15½ x 5¼

196. The Devil Lives Under Ocumicho (earlier title "Viva Mexico") (color linocut) 1985 22½ x 17

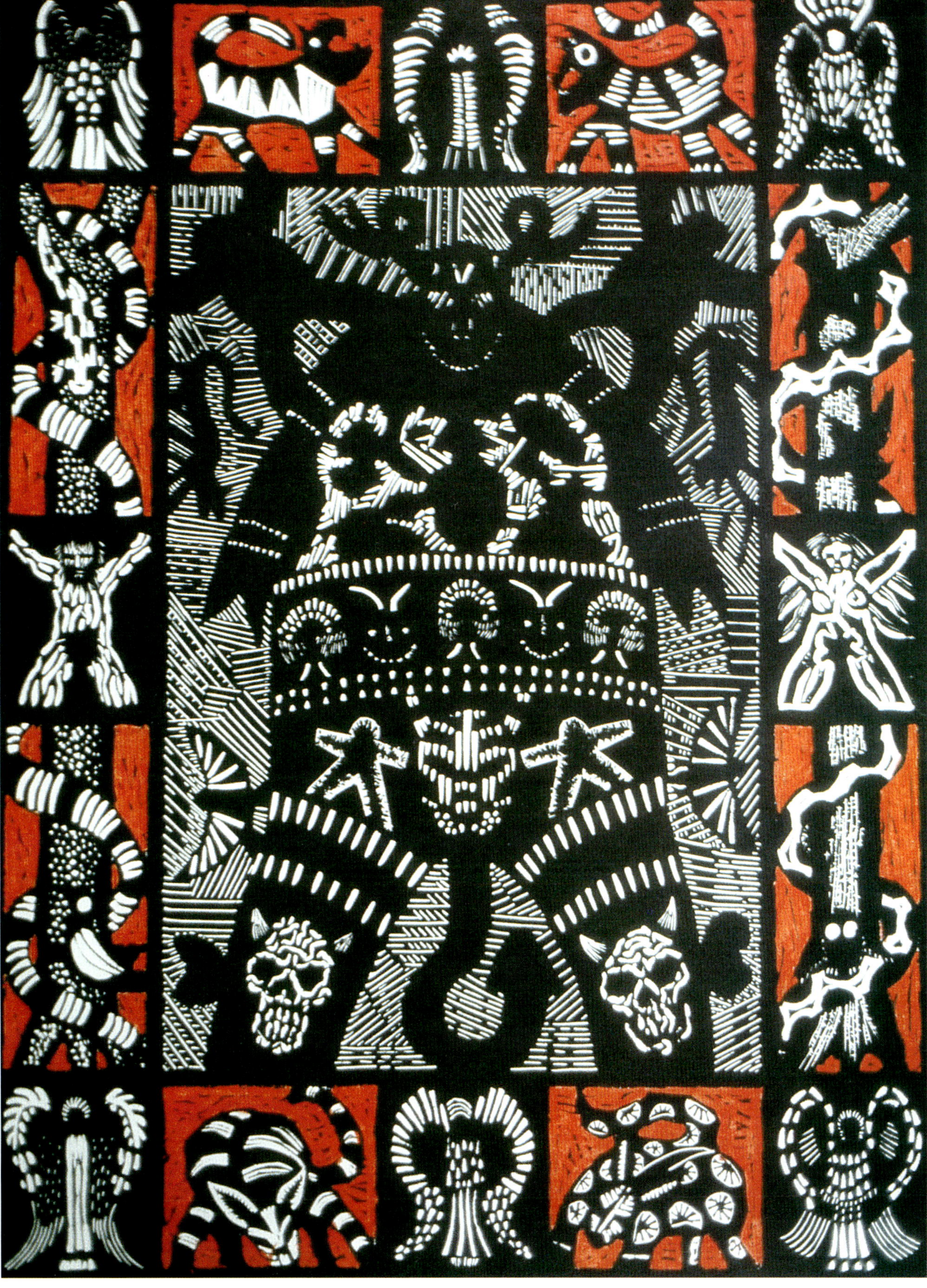

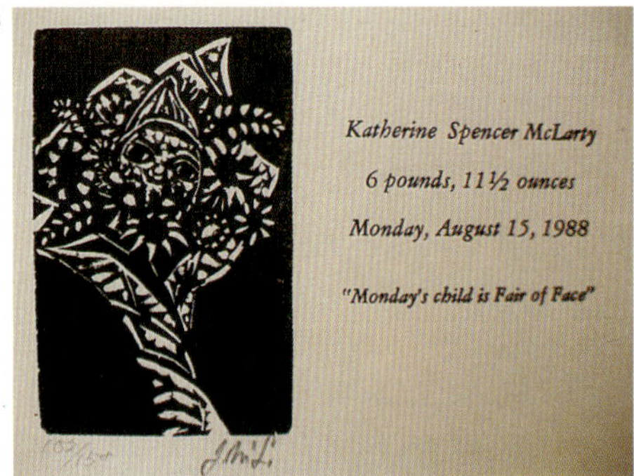

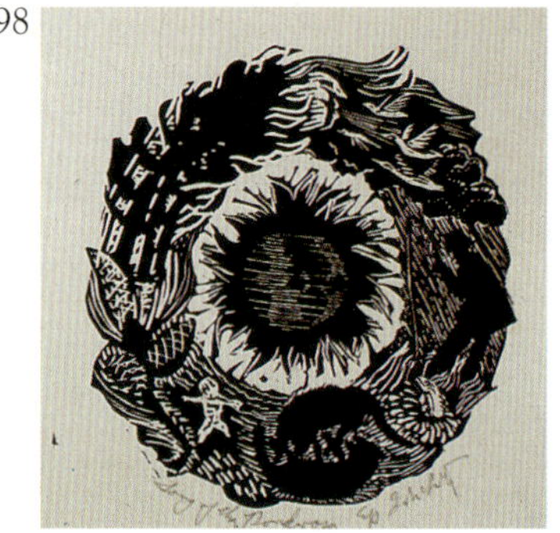

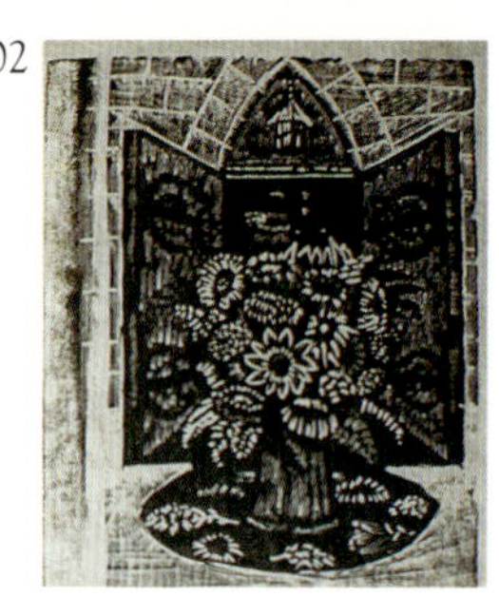

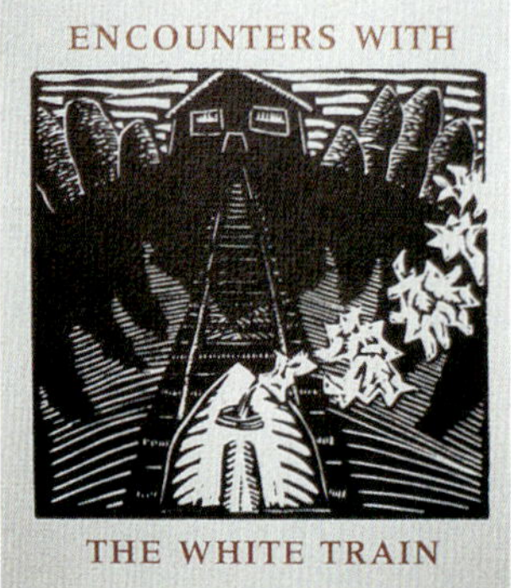

197. "Newt" (woodcut) 1986 2 x 2
198. "The Song of the Ponderosa" (woodcut for cover of a volume of poems by Russell Roberts) 1986 4 x 4
199. "Encounters with the White Train" (6 of 8 linocuts are shown including cover) 1986 all approximately 5 x 4
200. Noah (woodcut) 1988 19 x 14
201. Designed to Wear #1 (color woodcut) 1988 20 x 14½
   (*see page 106*)
202. Wedding Announcement: Dick Shoemaker (linocut) 1988 3¾ x 2½
203. Birth Announcement: Katherine Spencer McLarty (linocut) August 1988 3 x 2

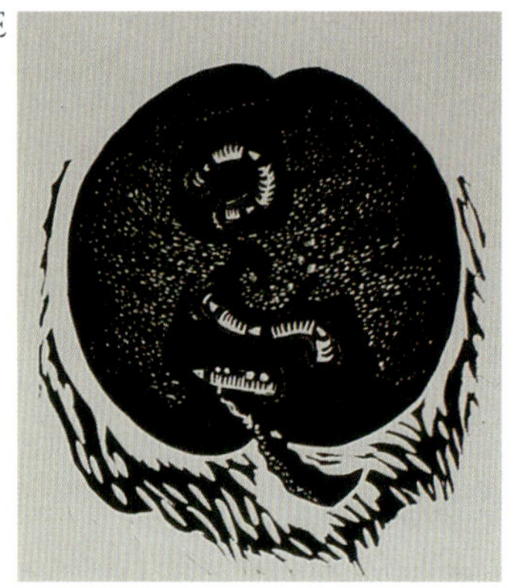

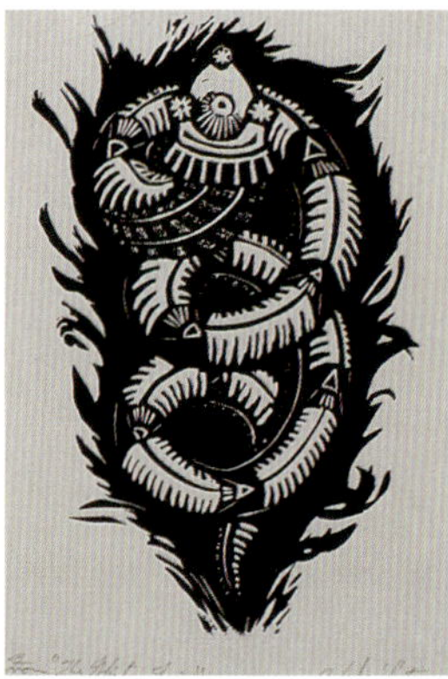

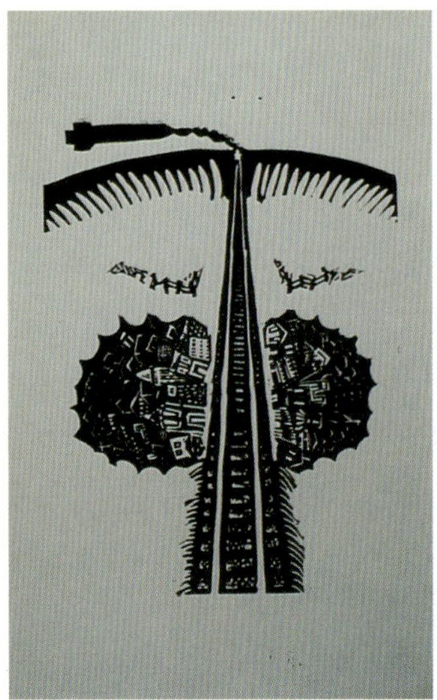

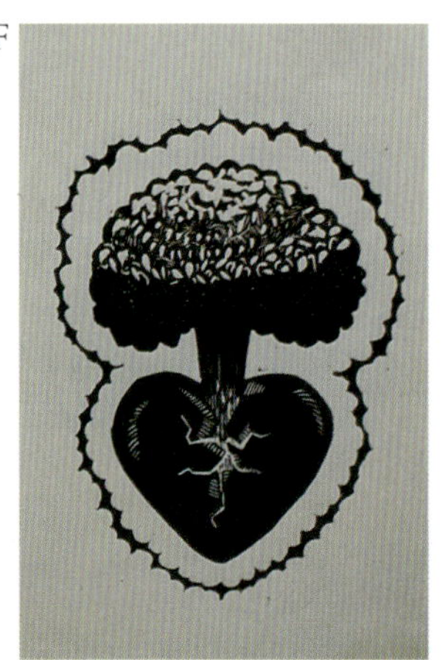

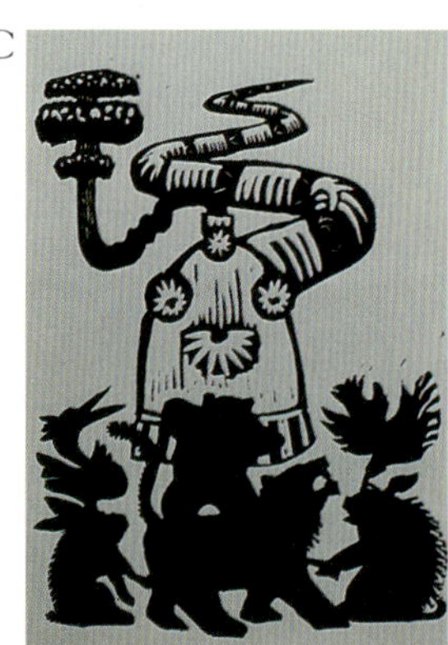

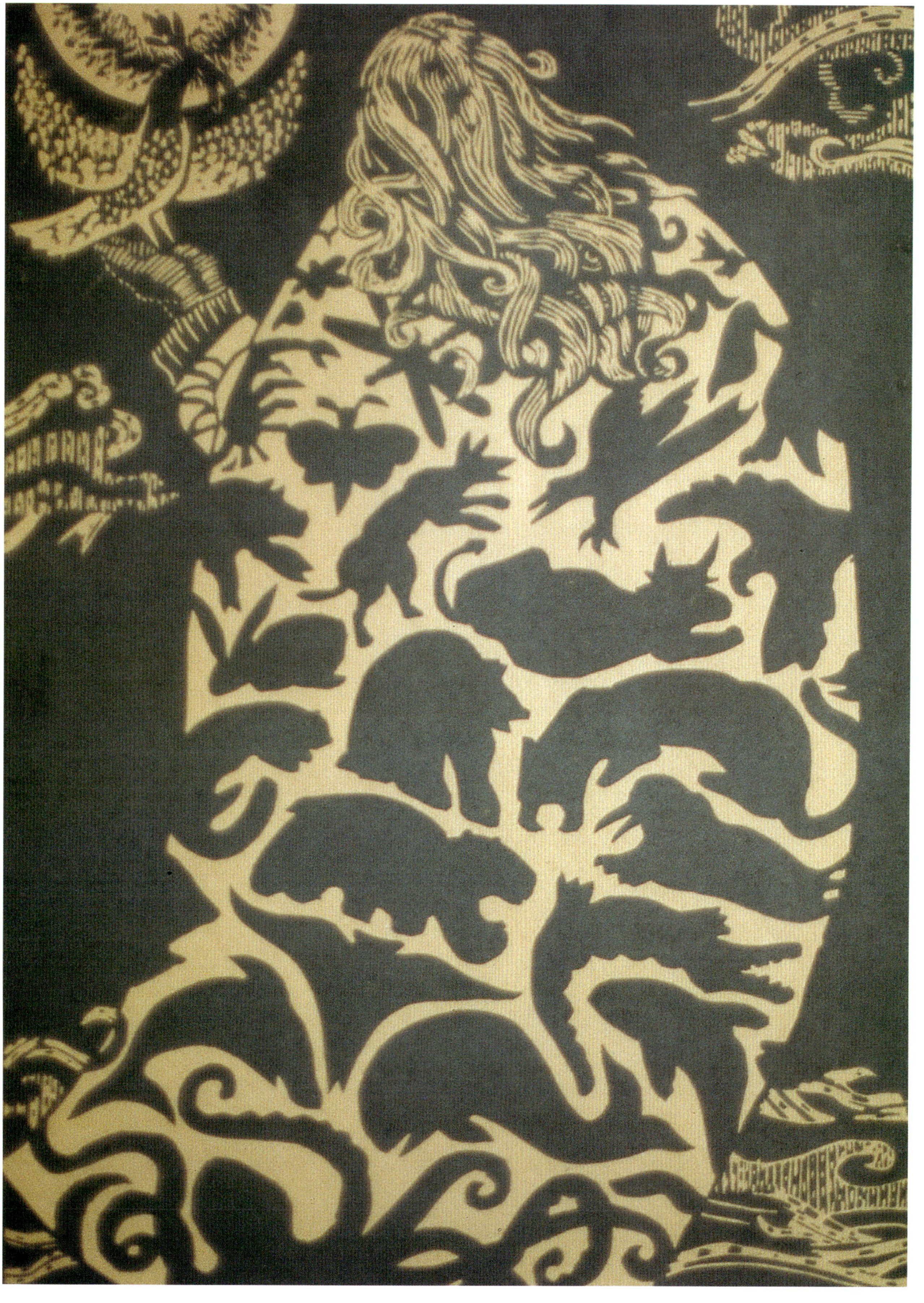

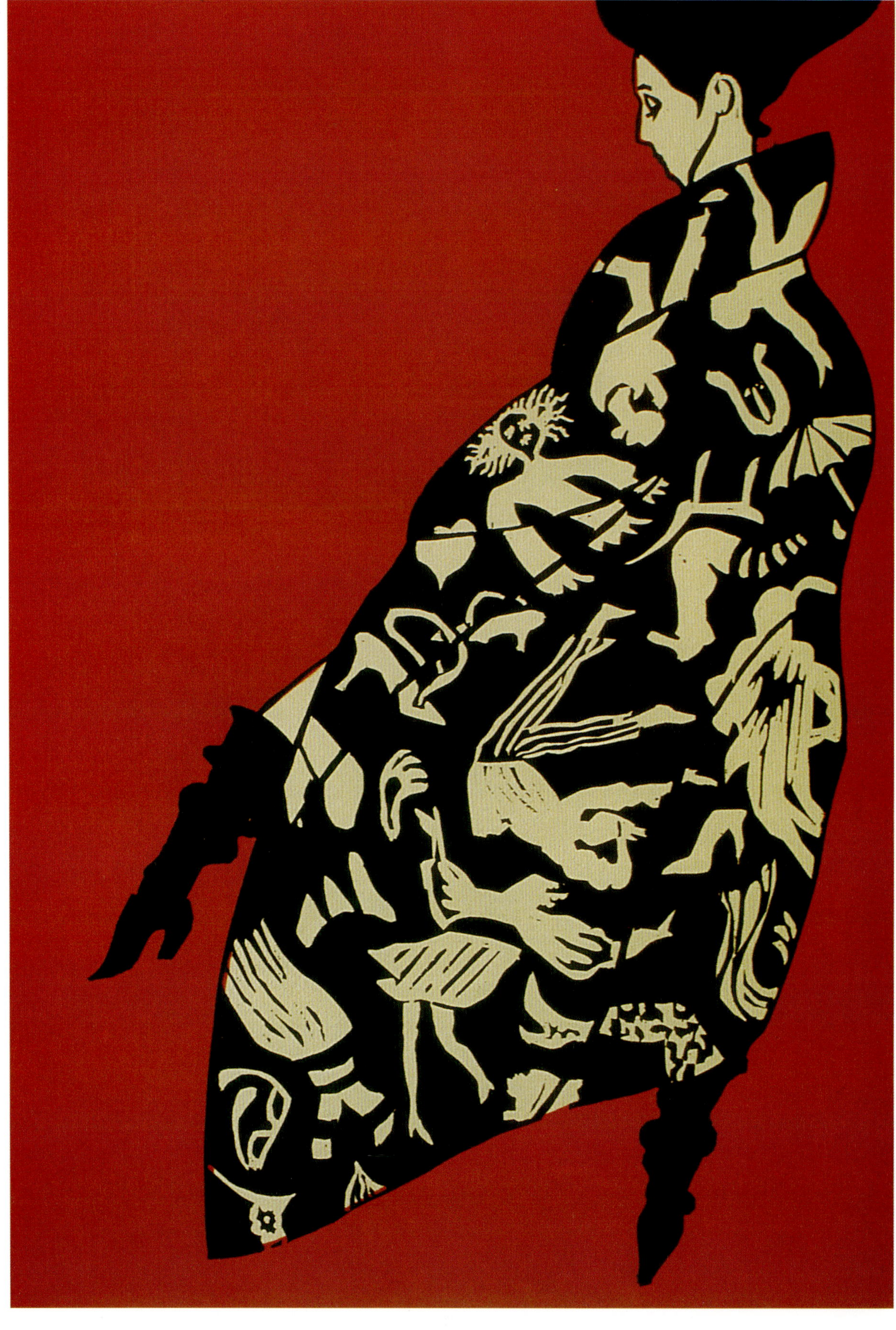

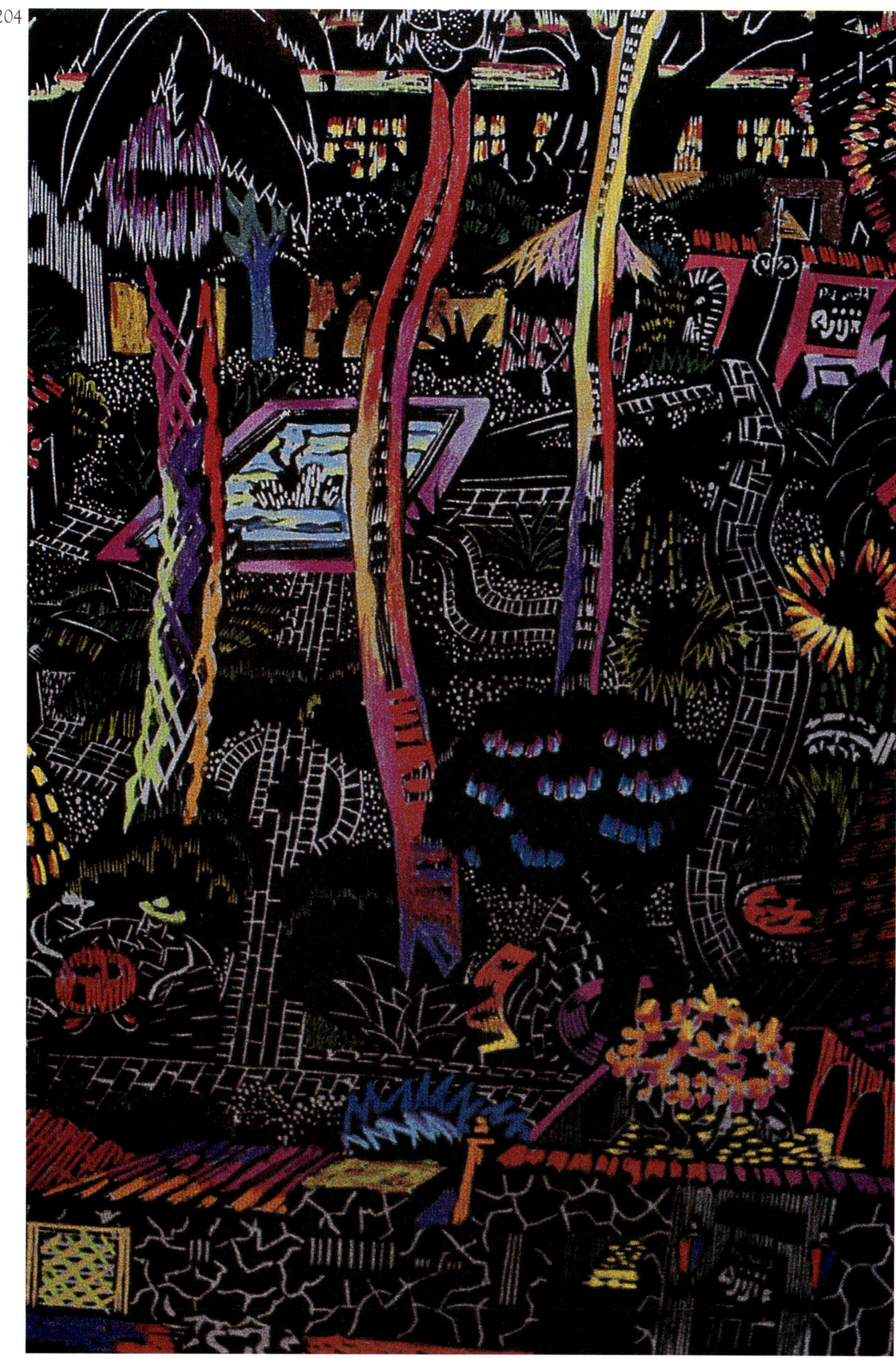

204. Posada Ajijic (hand-colored woodcut) 1989 18 x 12
    (*see page 107*)
205. Paper Flower Vendor (hand-colored woodcut) 1989 19 x 11
    (*see page 110*)
206. Designed to Wear #2 (color woodcut) 1990 20 x 14
    (*see page 111*)
207. Bonnard and Vuillard (color woodcuts from the series of 8
    portraits of artists included in "The Book of Color" of which we
    show 5) 1990 8 x 8 each
208. Gauguin (color woodcut from "The Book of Color") 1990 8 x 8
209. Delacroix (color woodcut from "The Book of Color") 1990
    8 x 8
210. Whistler (color woodcut from "The Book of Color") 1990 8 x 8
211. Easels of Famous Artists (color woodcut) 1990 6½ x 15
212. Cat-Man-Do (linocut) 1990 10 x 8

208
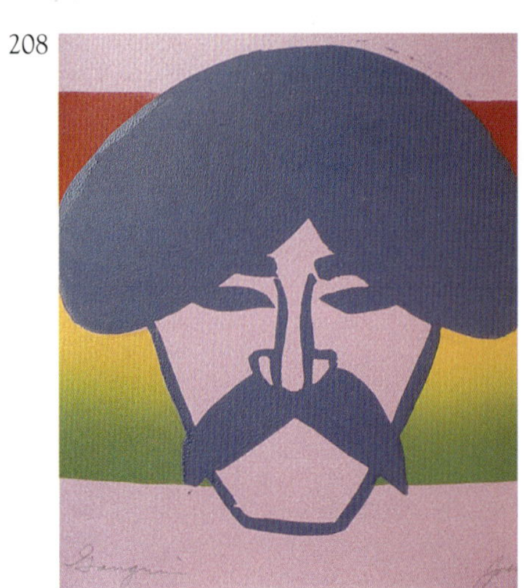

209
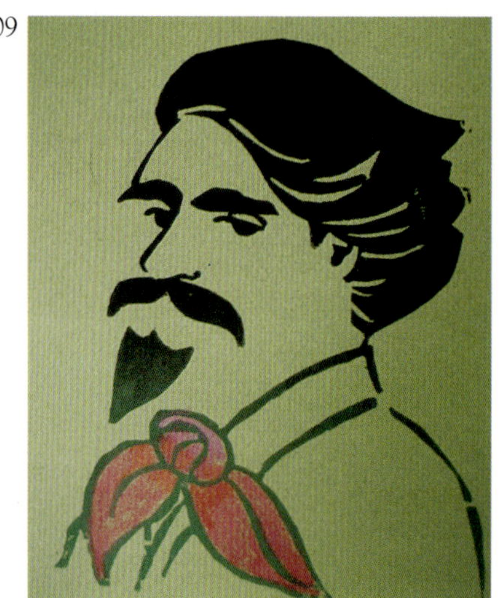

210
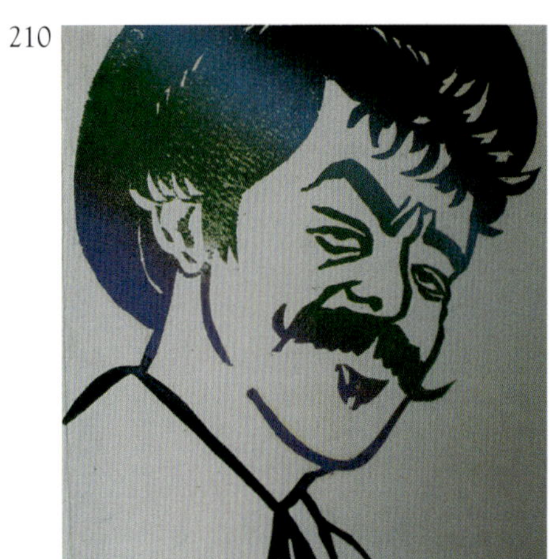

207
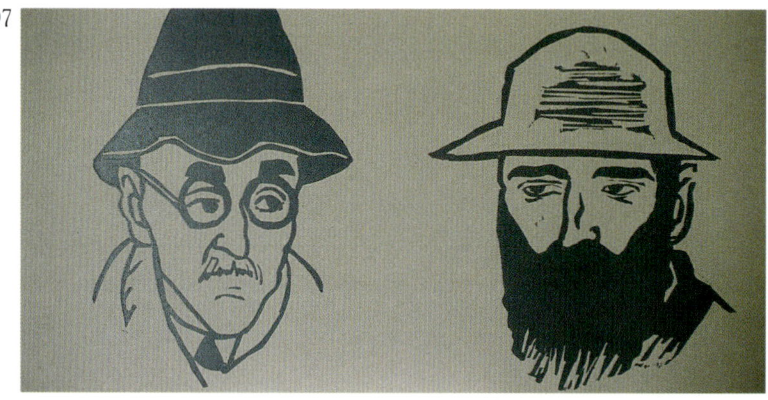

THE BOOK OF COLOR "Color and I are one—I am a painter" —Paul
Klee from *The Diaries*

A beautiful handbound book of forty pages, published in 1990 by Art
Advocates, Inc., Portland, Oregon. It contains eight color woodcuts by
Jack McLarty, printed from the original blocks, and is a limited edition
of sixty signed, numbered copies. Design was by Nancy Norman Ramsay. Printing was by Ash Creek Press, Portland, Oregon, in Optima
types on Teton paper.

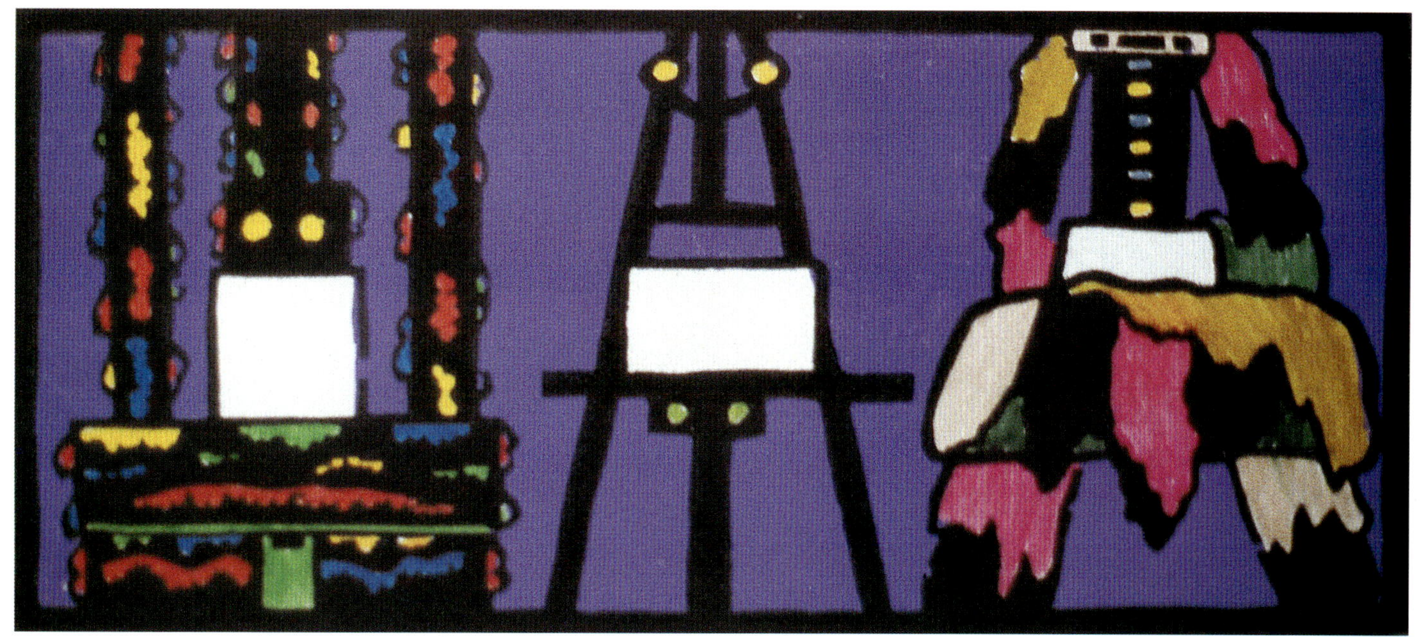

211

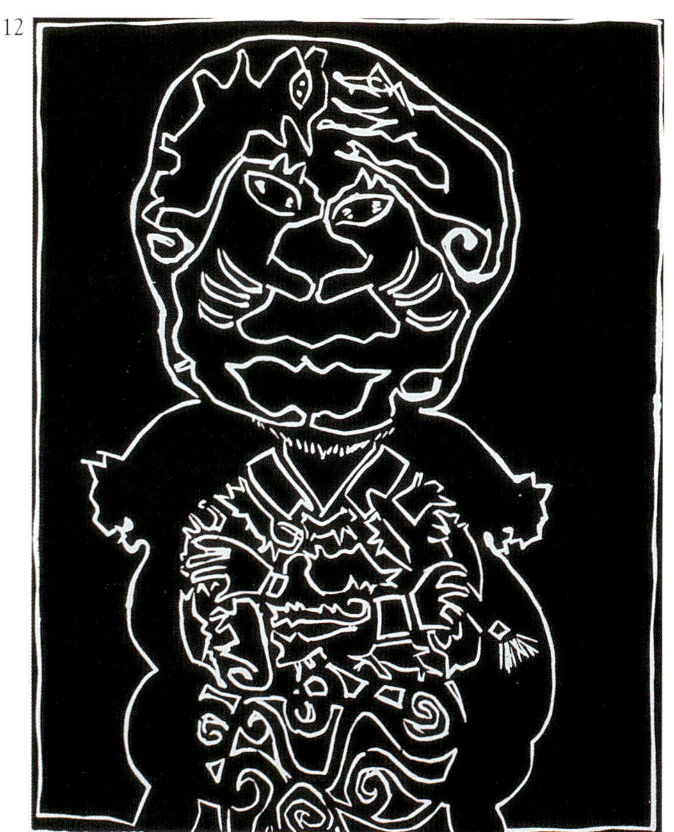

212

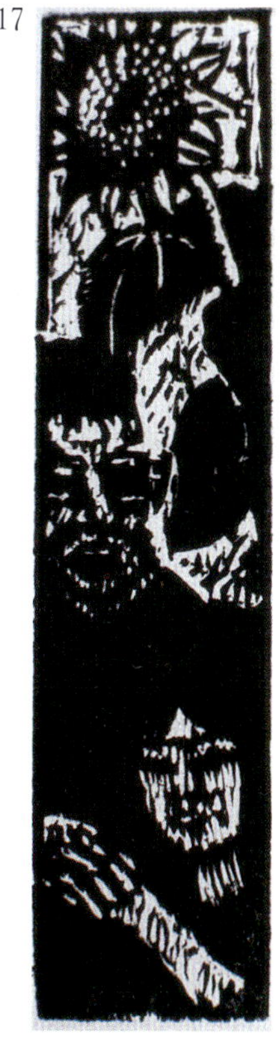

217

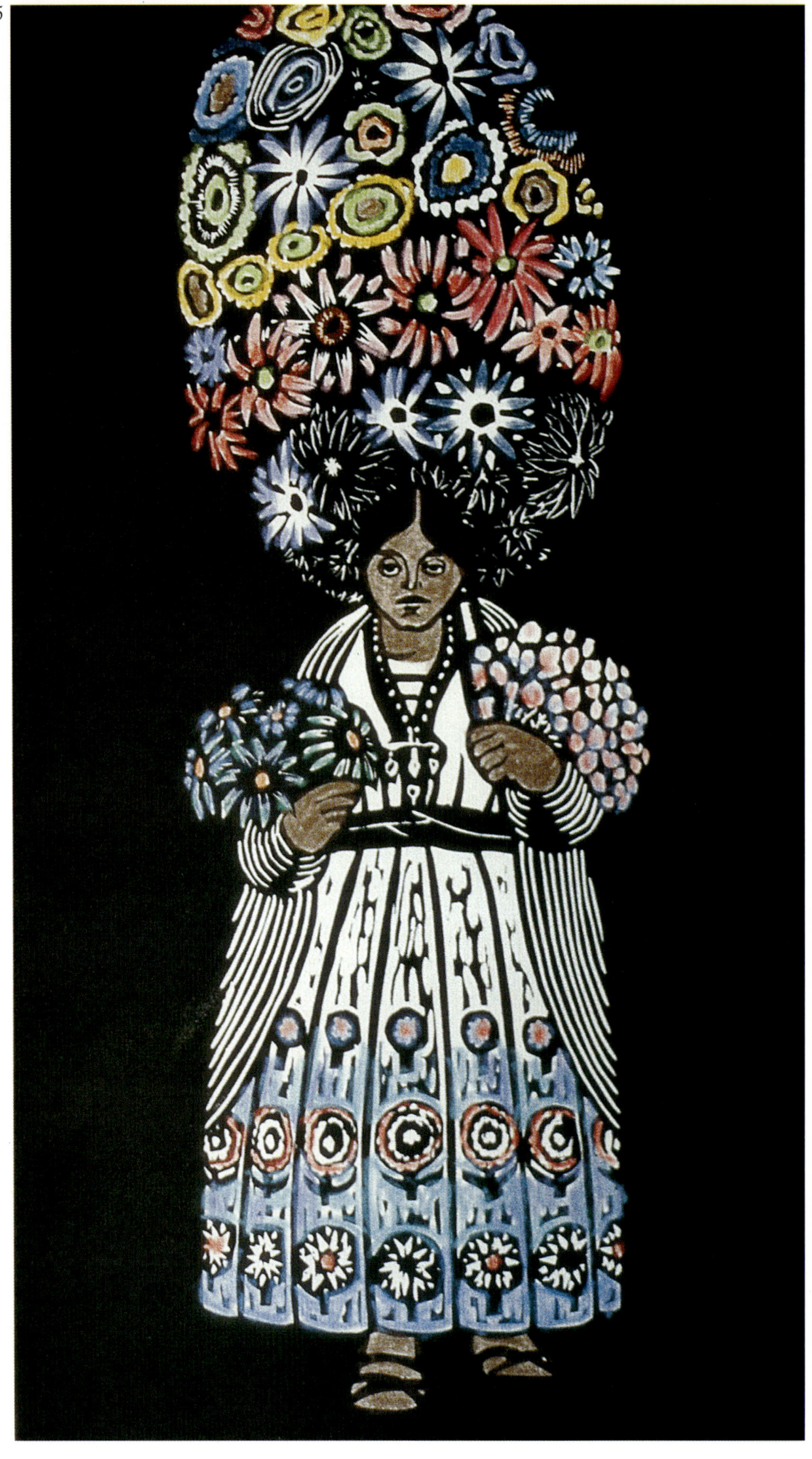

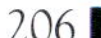

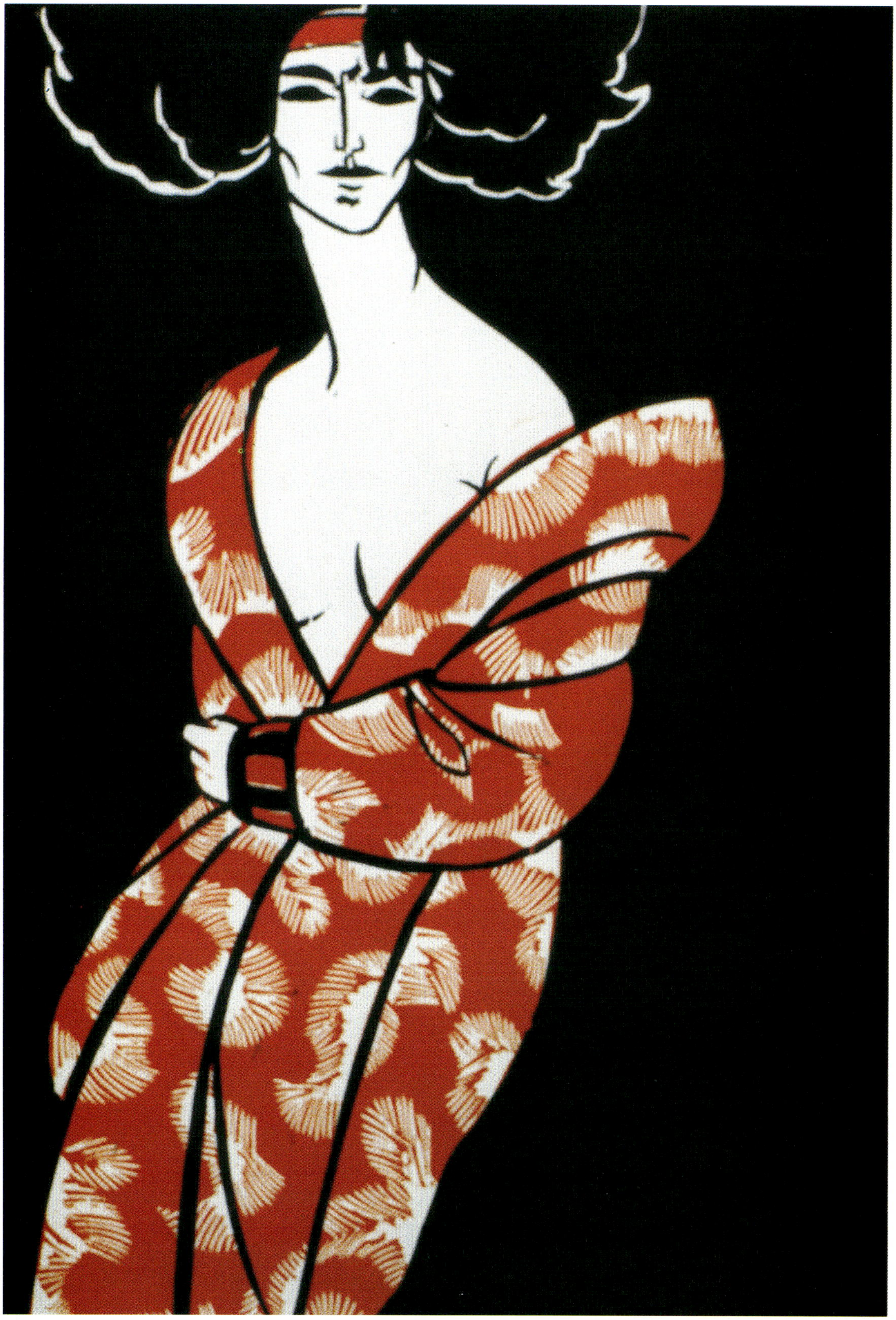

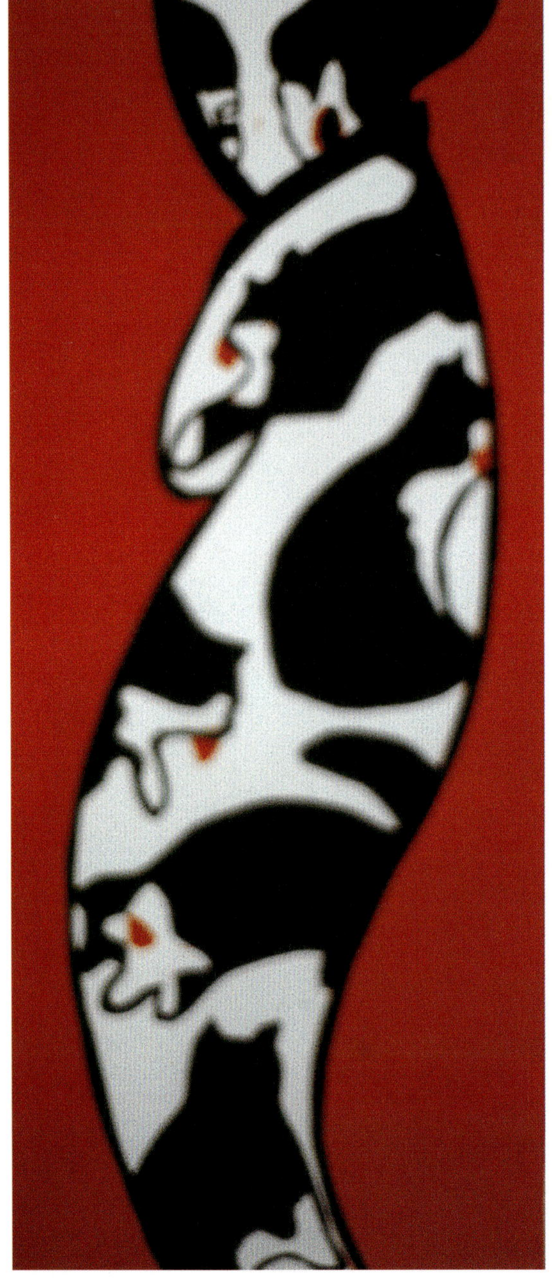

213

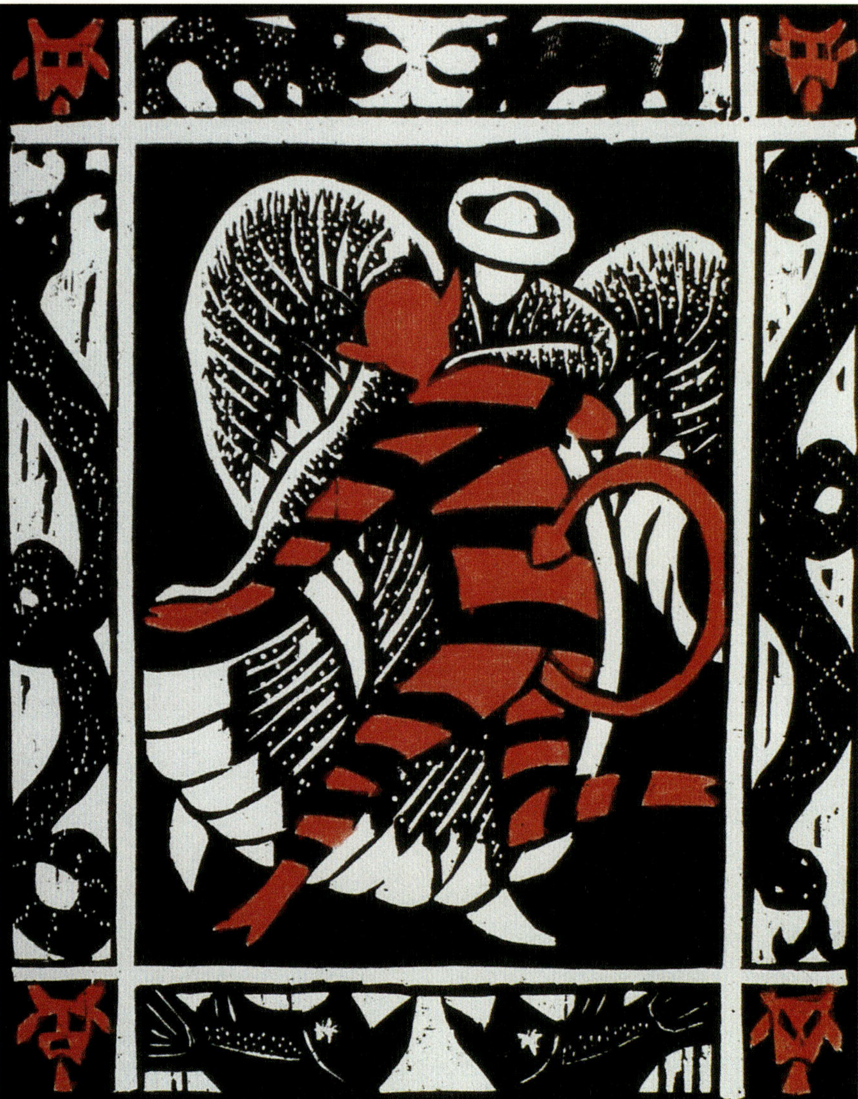

213. Designed to Wear #3 (color woodcut) 1991 14 x 6
214. The Striped Robe (color woodcut) 1991 10½ x 14½
215. Designed to Wear #4 (also titled "The Moth") (color woodcut)
1992 14 x 7 (*see page 114*)
216. The Sugar Angel (color woodcut) 1992 11 x 9
217. Wedding Announcement: Charles McLarty/Hiromi Watanabe
(woodcut) 1992 5 x 1⅛ (*see page 109*)
218. Walter and the Boys (woodcut) 1993 17¼ x 11½
219. Powell's (woodcut) 1993 18 x 24 (*see page 115*)
220. Dance of the One-Armed Bandit (hand-colored woodcut) 1993
15 x 12 (*see page 116*)
221. Baby Game (hand-colored woodcut) 1994 15½ x 12
(*see page 117*)

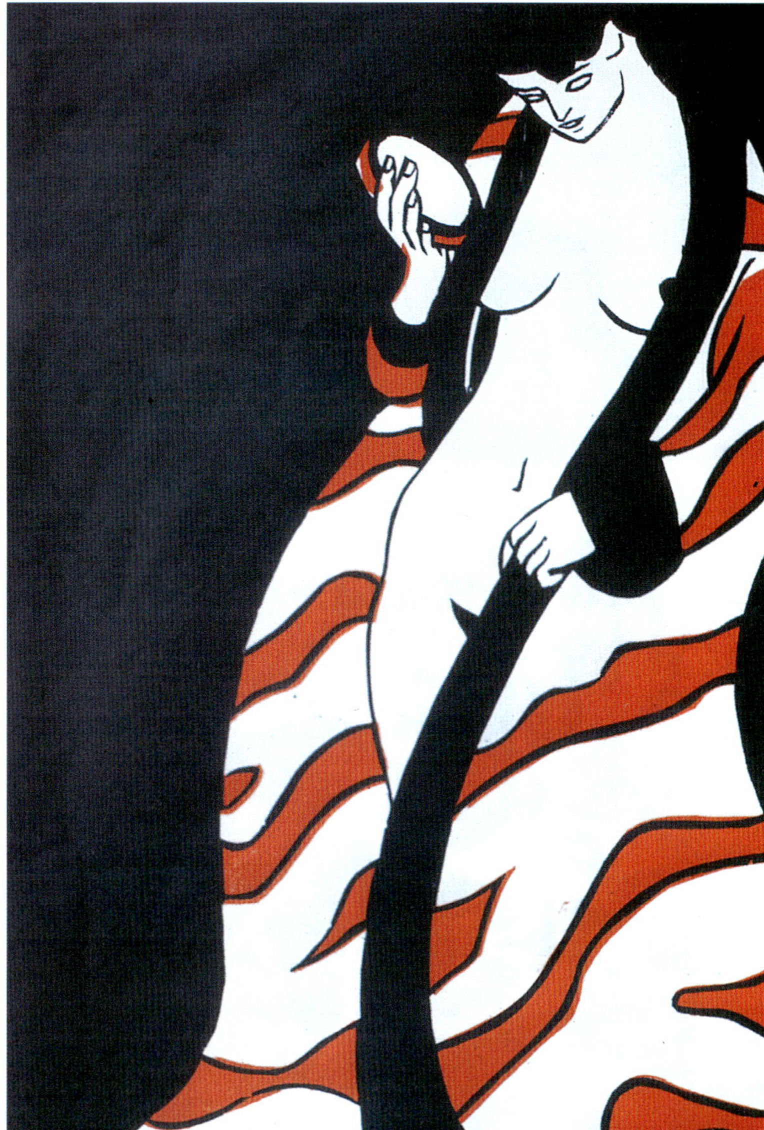

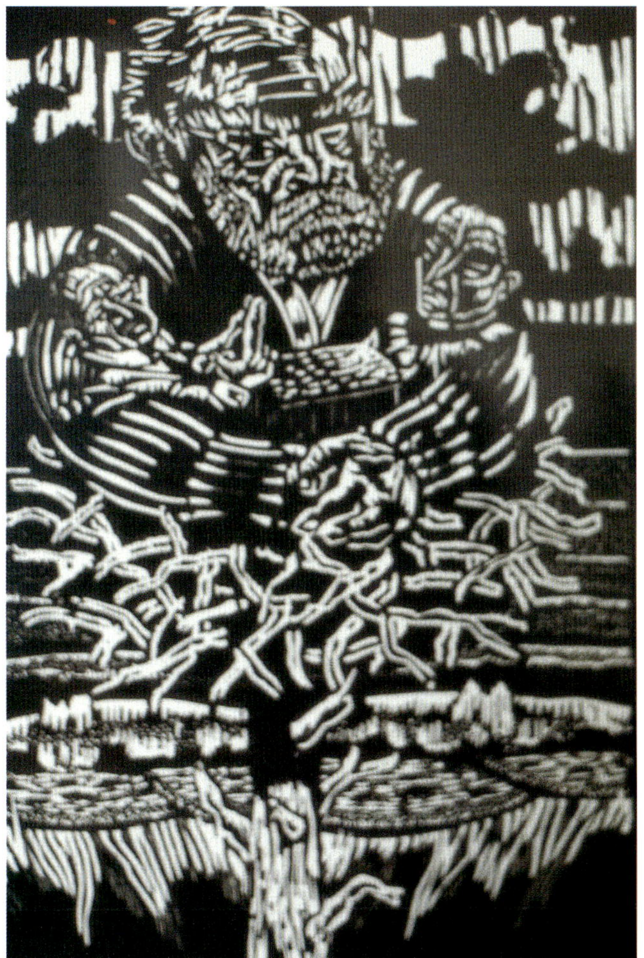

Dear Jack and Barbara:

I wanted to go to Bay City to see your show . . . but I wasn't going to go until I learned from Marge Hammond Farness that your portrait of me was there. I had to see that, dead or alive. . . . I was flattered. I'm glad it wasn't a photographic likeness which brings out the inner meanness. Please keep on making portraits (I might become famous, vicariously). I very much like the print portrait you made earlier. . . .

Walter Gordon, Newport, Oregon, 9 August 1995

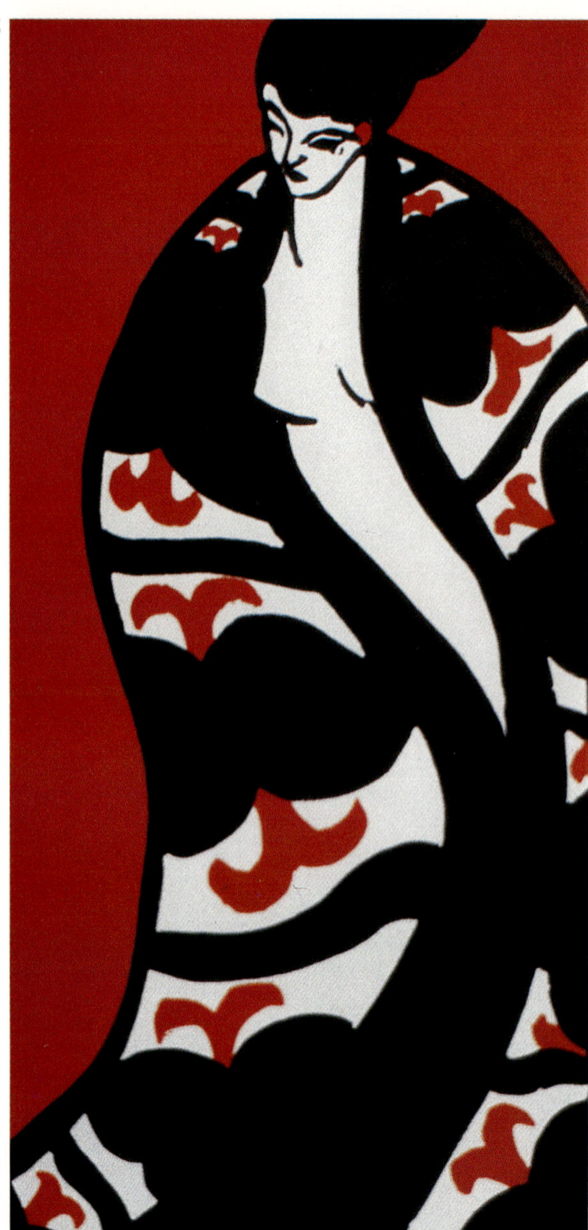

Jack and I are so happy with the McLarty paintings and prints on our walls, and they are so familiar to us, that we have never fussed about why we chose them, or what their place in the art world may be, or what they "mean." I have been inhibited from considering the meaning of art ever since Lloyd Reynolds read Archibald MacLeish's "Ars Poetica" to his writing class when I was a sophomore at Reed. It ends:

> A poem should not mean
> but be.

All these years I have been saved from art criticism I didn't want to hear by holding fast to that standard and applying it to all art forms. Jack McLarty's work "is," and each piece has its own unique and organic character, from the pure precision of the prints to the swirling shapes and colors of the paintings, yet they are always recognizably his.

As Jack's work has been written about through the years, there is one element left out of the discussion that we find most intriguing, and that is the mythic and magical references that occur everywhere. We see those frightening green babies as right out of the Grimm's folktales, a bit pitiful because they can't help being ogres, but to blame, anyway, for their selfish behavior. Every frame is the boundary of an enchanted world, a trip underground, a leap into space, automobiles that are alive—floating dream-beds, weightless ribbons in the air, a moonstruck parking lot—and often the Artist himself in hat and shades peering out . . . curious? amused? judgmental? With all the lovely, rich colors, even a sinking civilization is beautiful.

Janet W. Witter, Milwaukie, Oregon, 16 January 1996

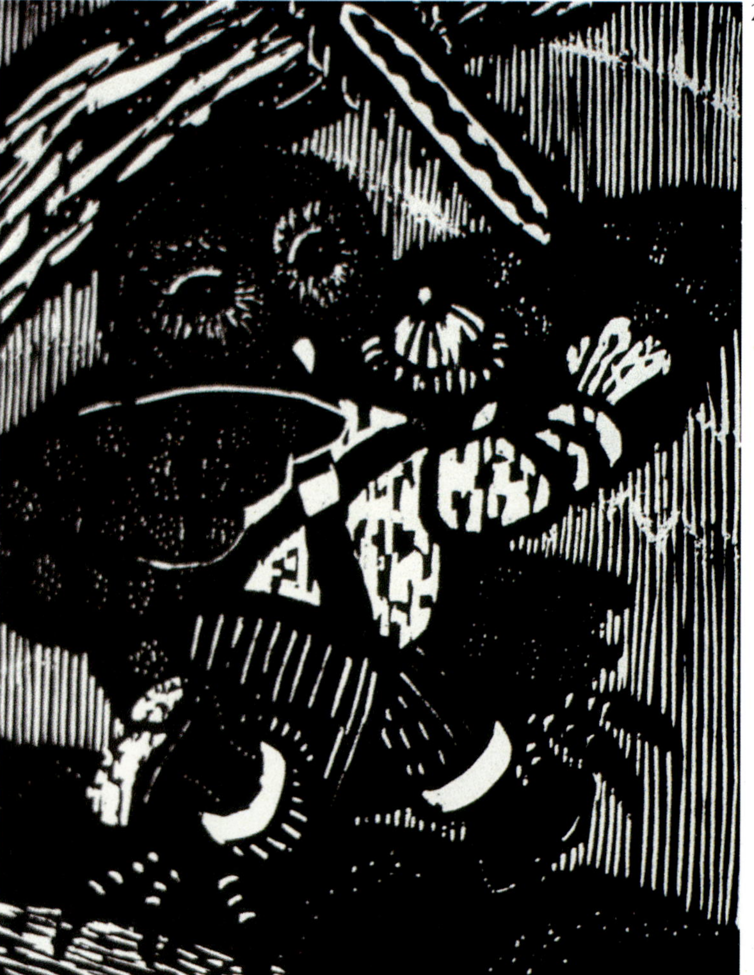

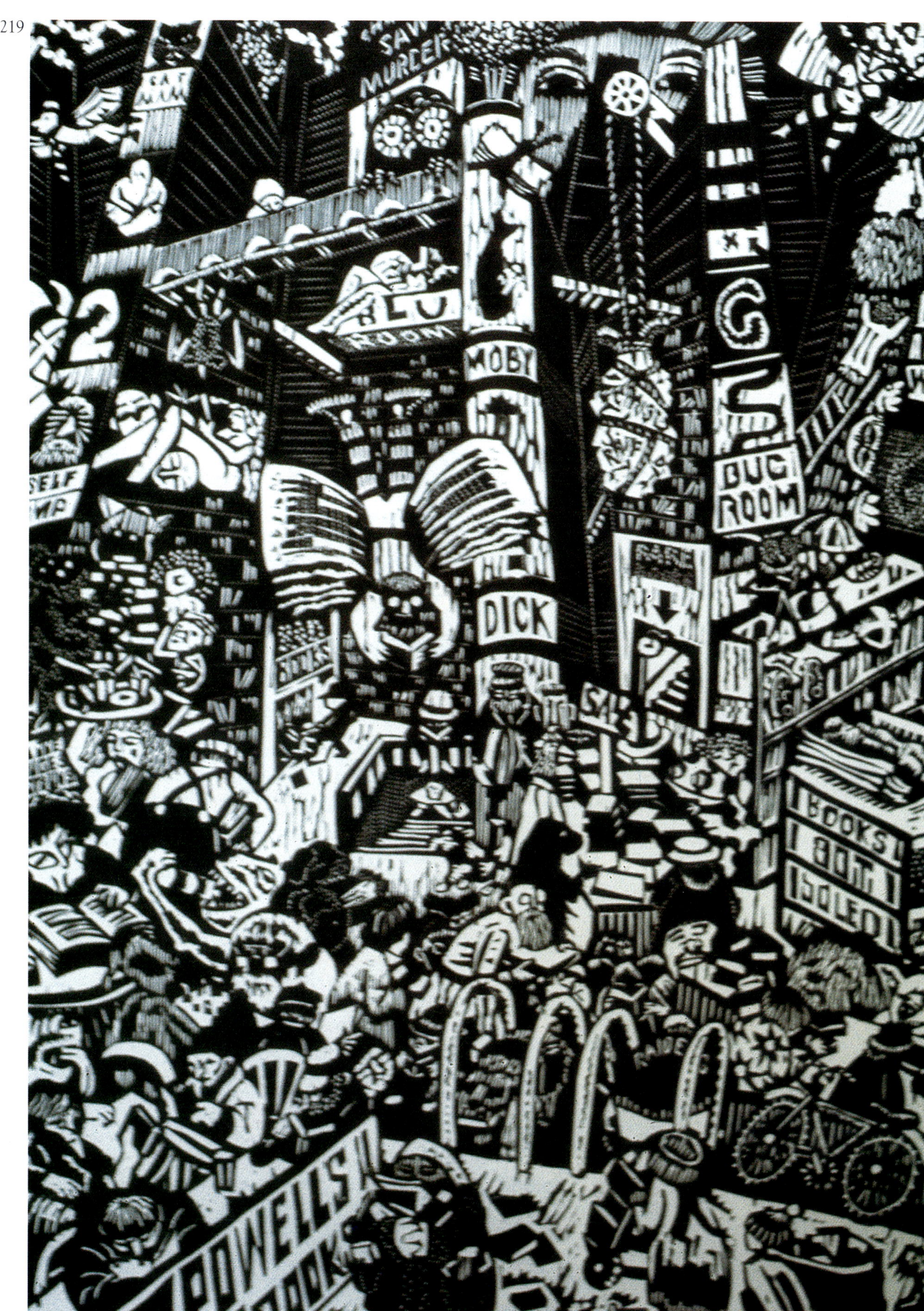
SAV
MURDER
x2
SELF
HELP
BLU
ROOM
MOBY
DICK
RARE
BUG
ROOM
BOOKS
BOT
SOLD
POWELLS
BOOKS

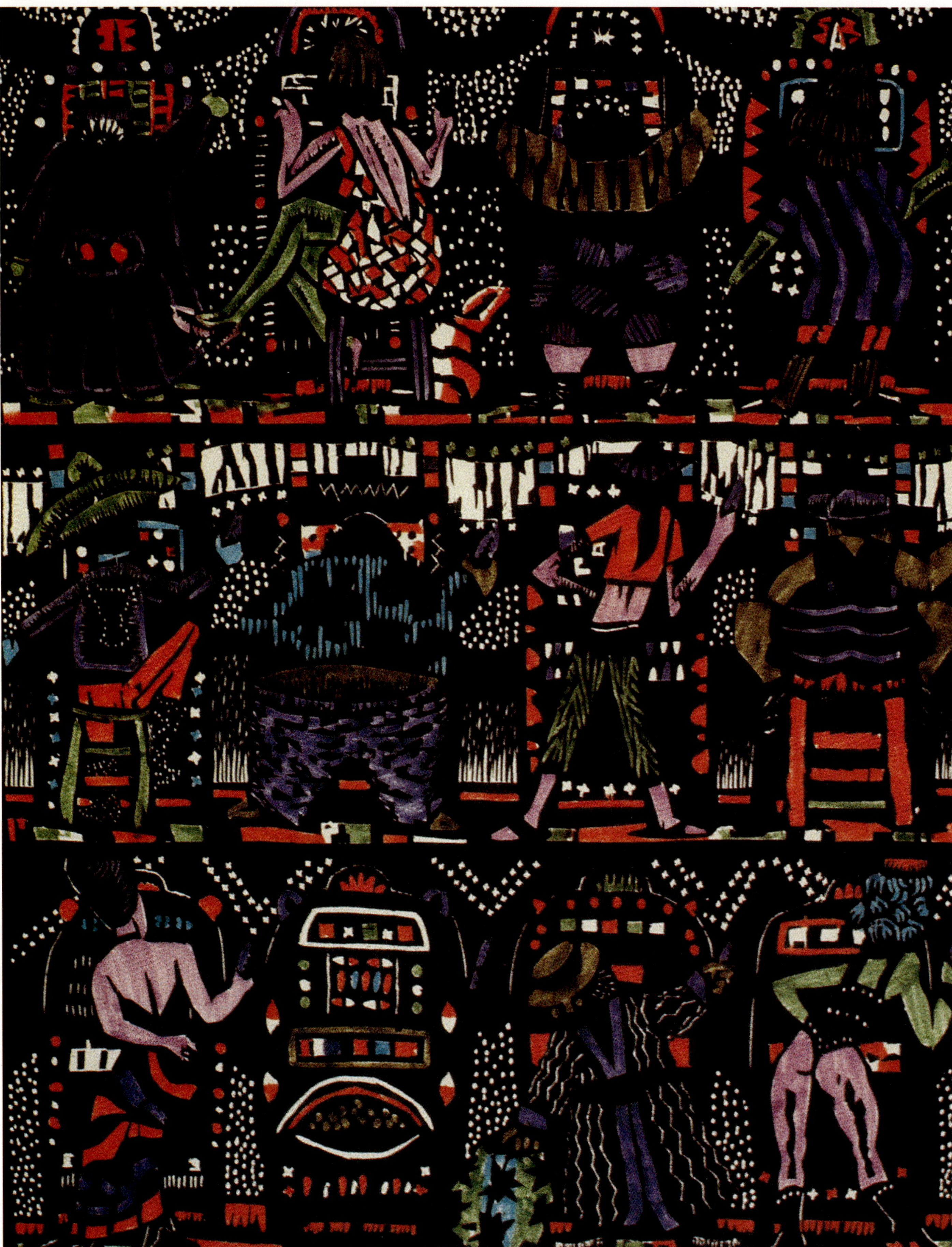

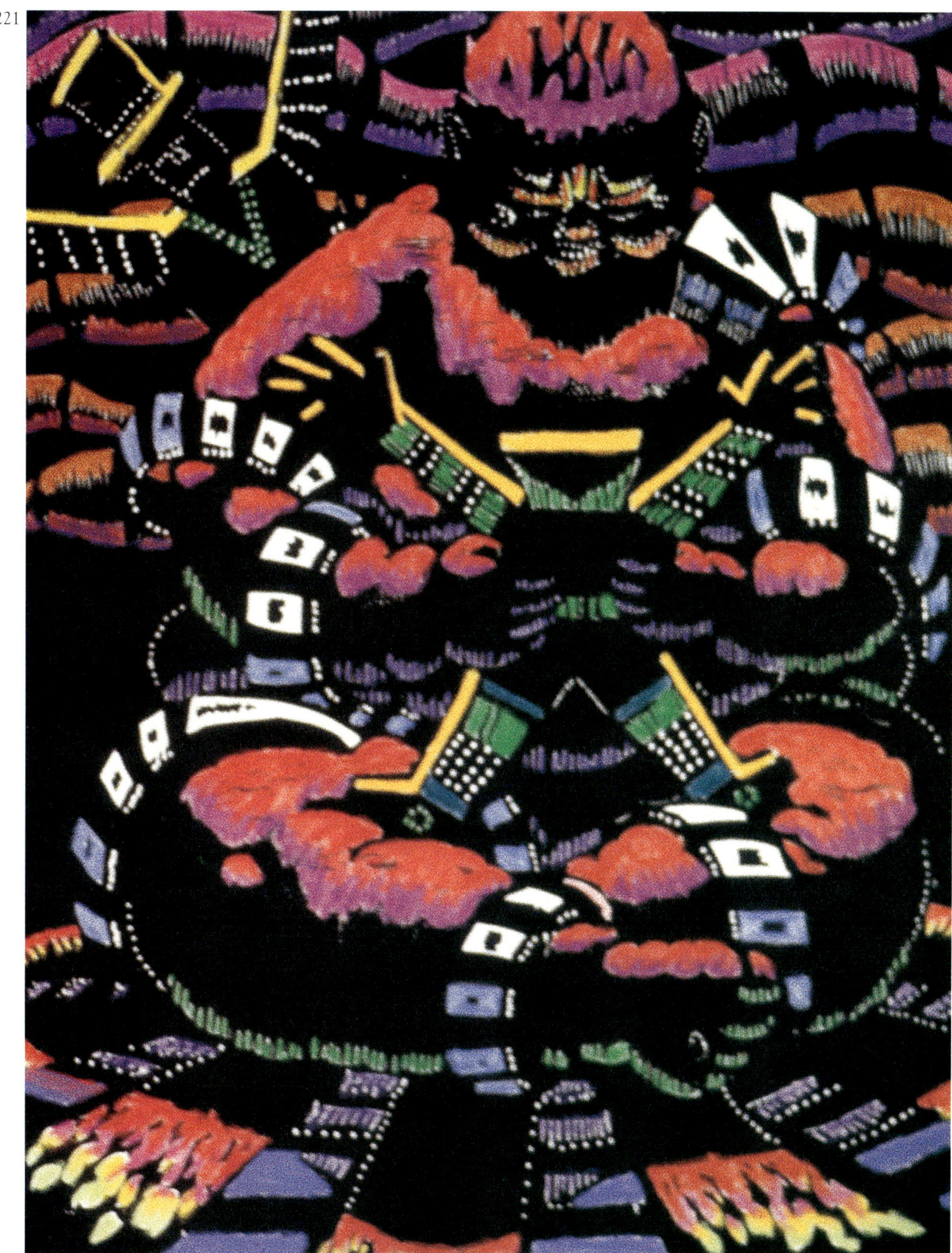

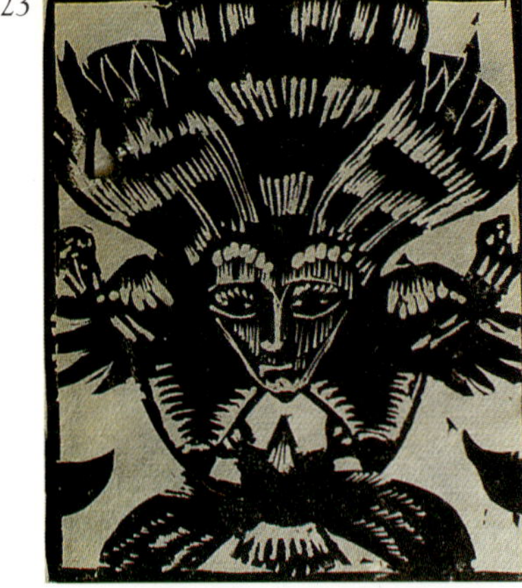

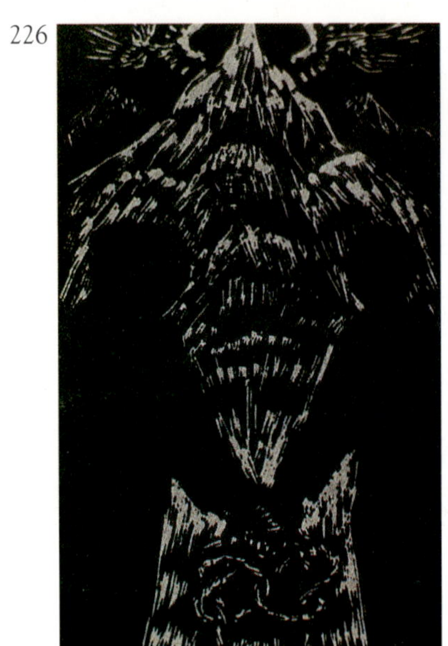

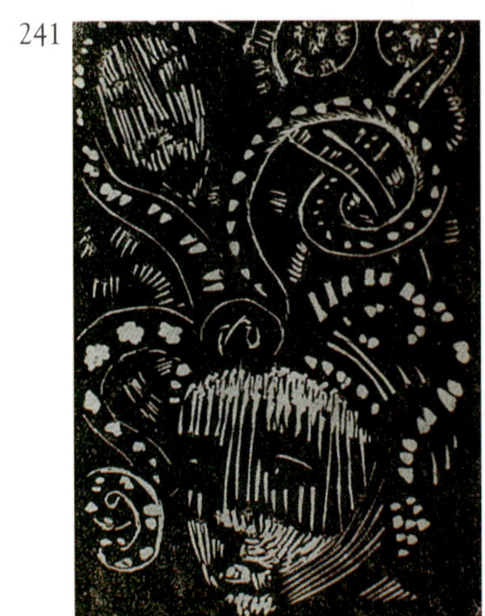

222. Dream Rider (hand-colored woodcut) 1994 15¾ x 12
223. Janesbonnets (woodengraving created to illustrate a poem by
    Casey Bush) 1995 2⅜ x 3¾
224. Mexican Tapestry (woodcut) 1995 15 x 21
225. Mexico (woodcut) 1995 9¾ x 29½ (*see page 120*)

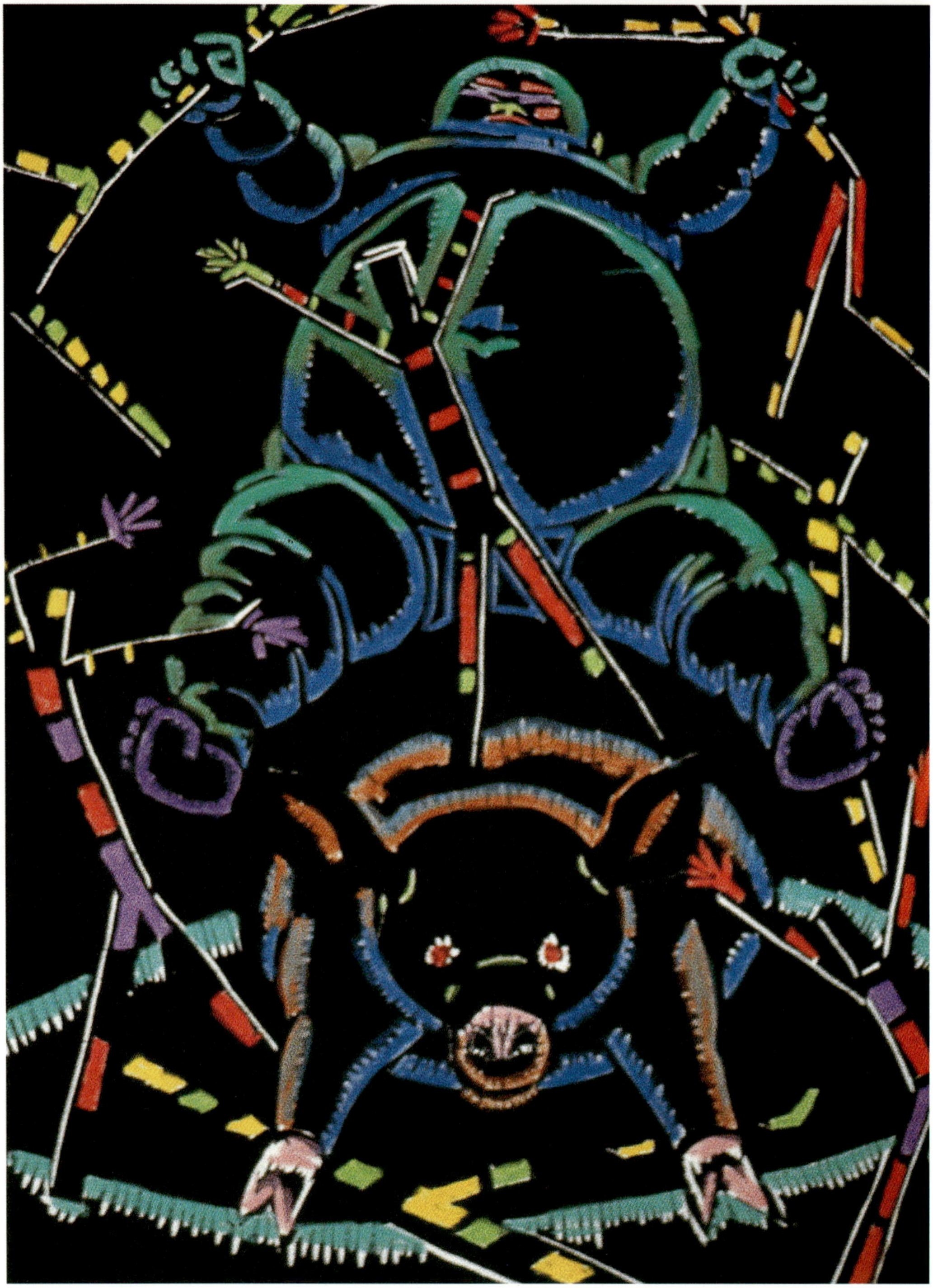

118

224

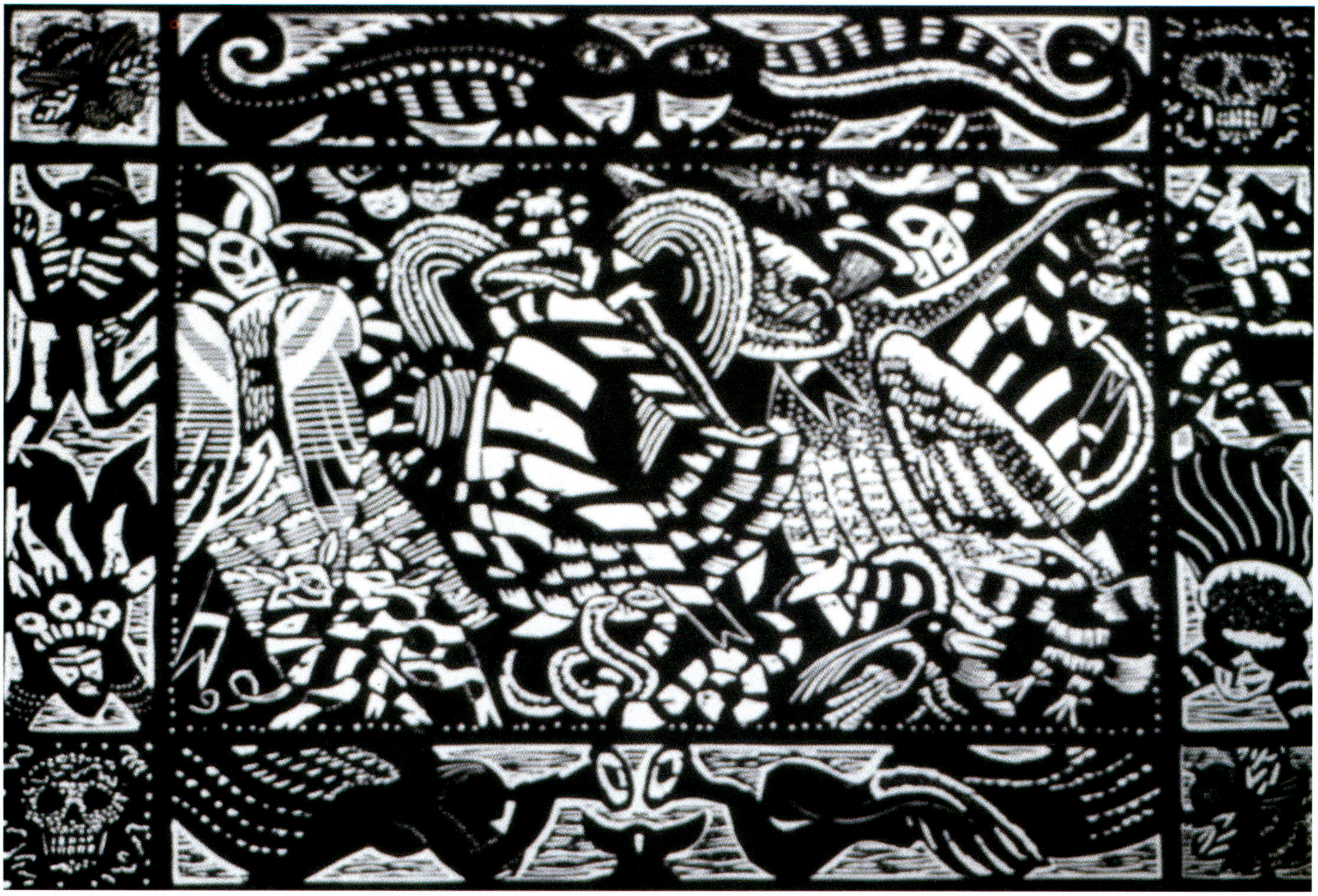

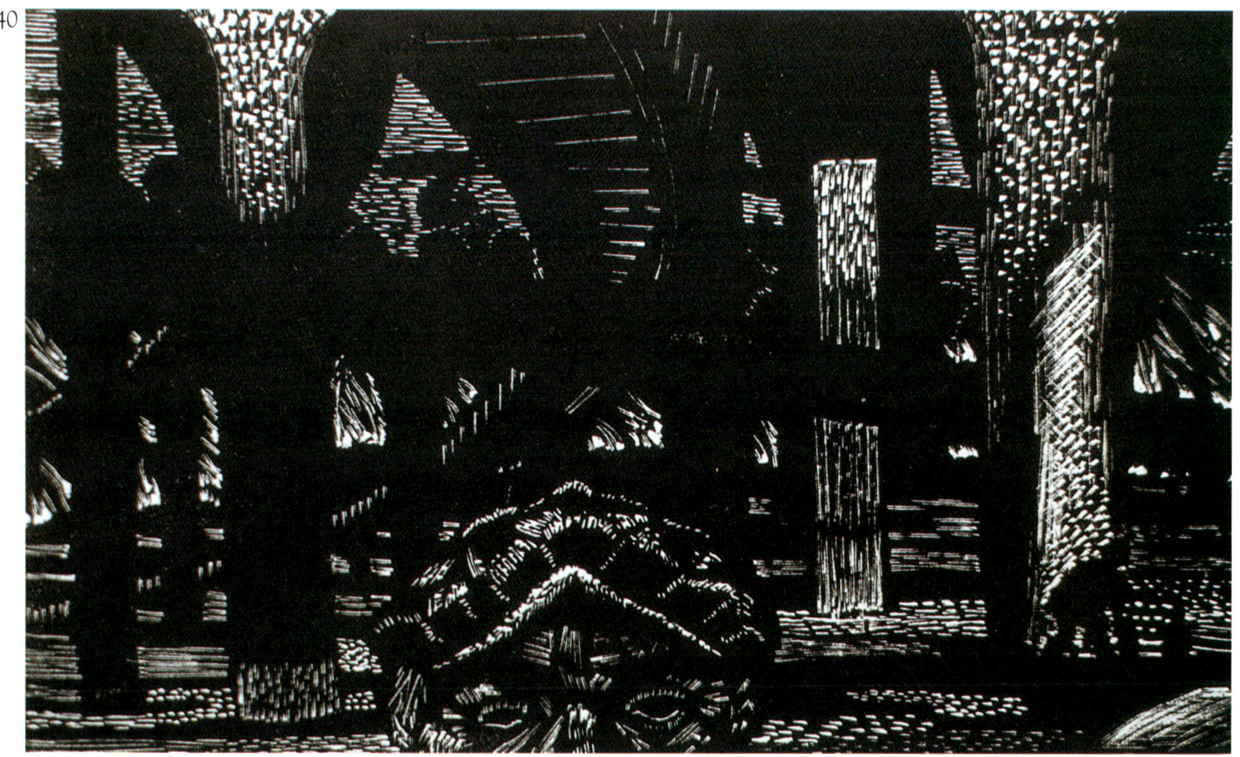

240

225

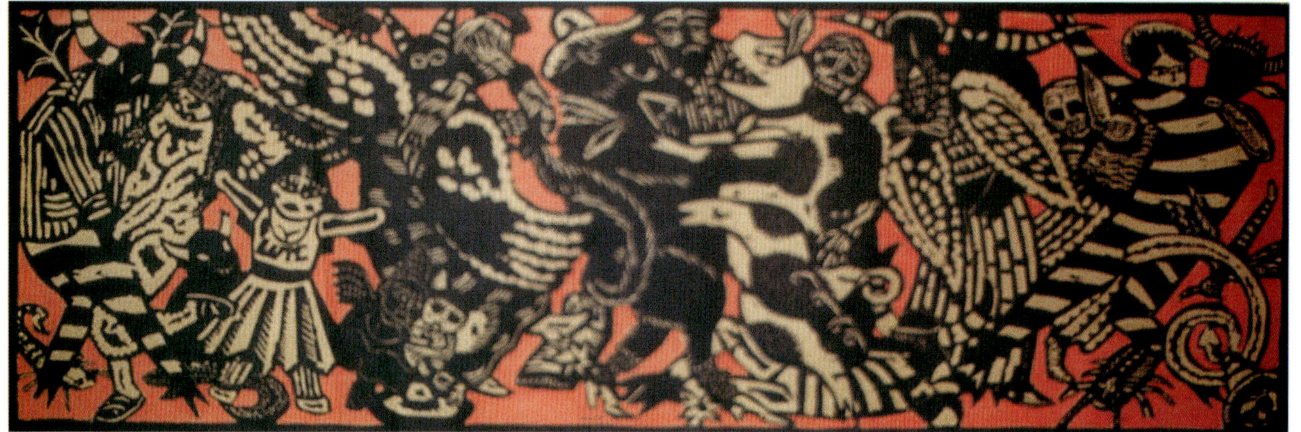

228

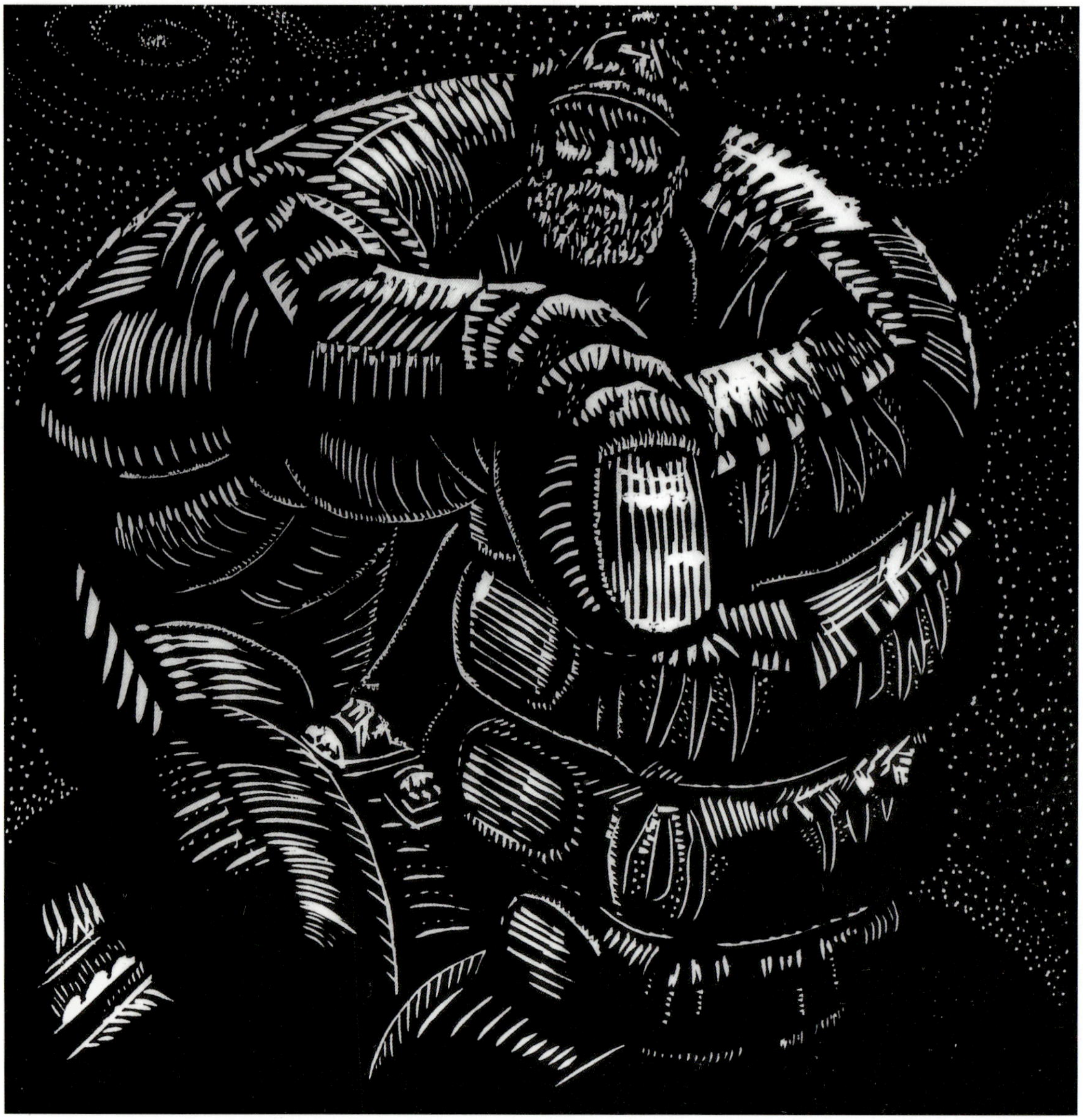

229

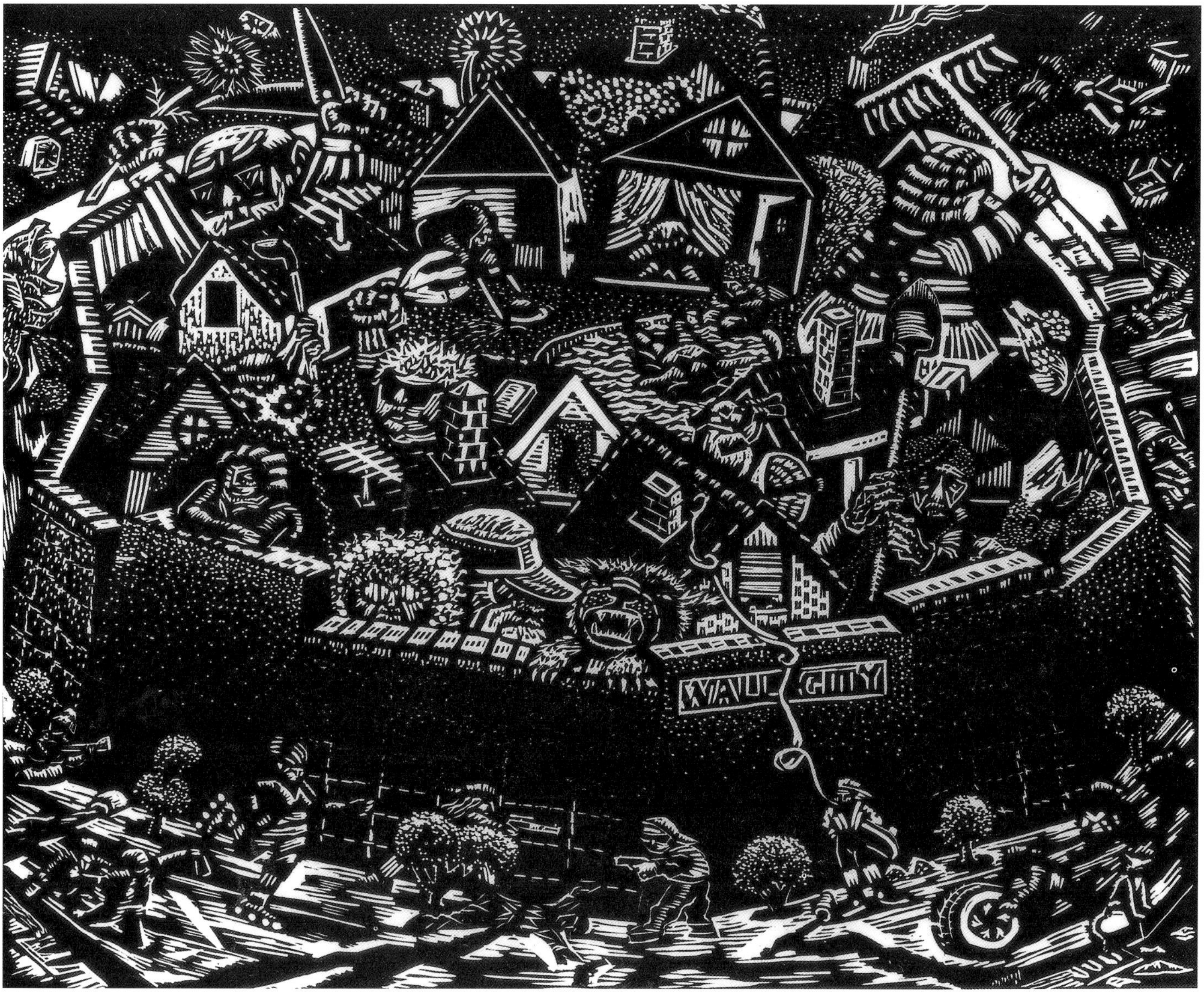

226. The Love Knot (woodengraving) 1996 3 x 2 (*see page 118*)
227. The Hand of God (woodcut) 1996 4 x 4
228. The Left Hand of God (woodcut) 1996 16 x 16
229. The Wall City (woodcut) 1996 16 x 20
230. The Rain Beast (hand-colored woodcut) 1996 12 x 9
   (*see page 122*)
231. The Owl Dance (woodcut) 1996 10 x 8 (*see page 114*)

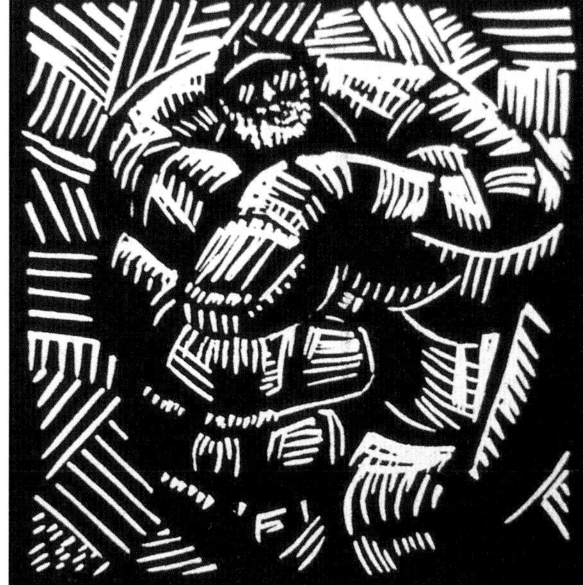

227

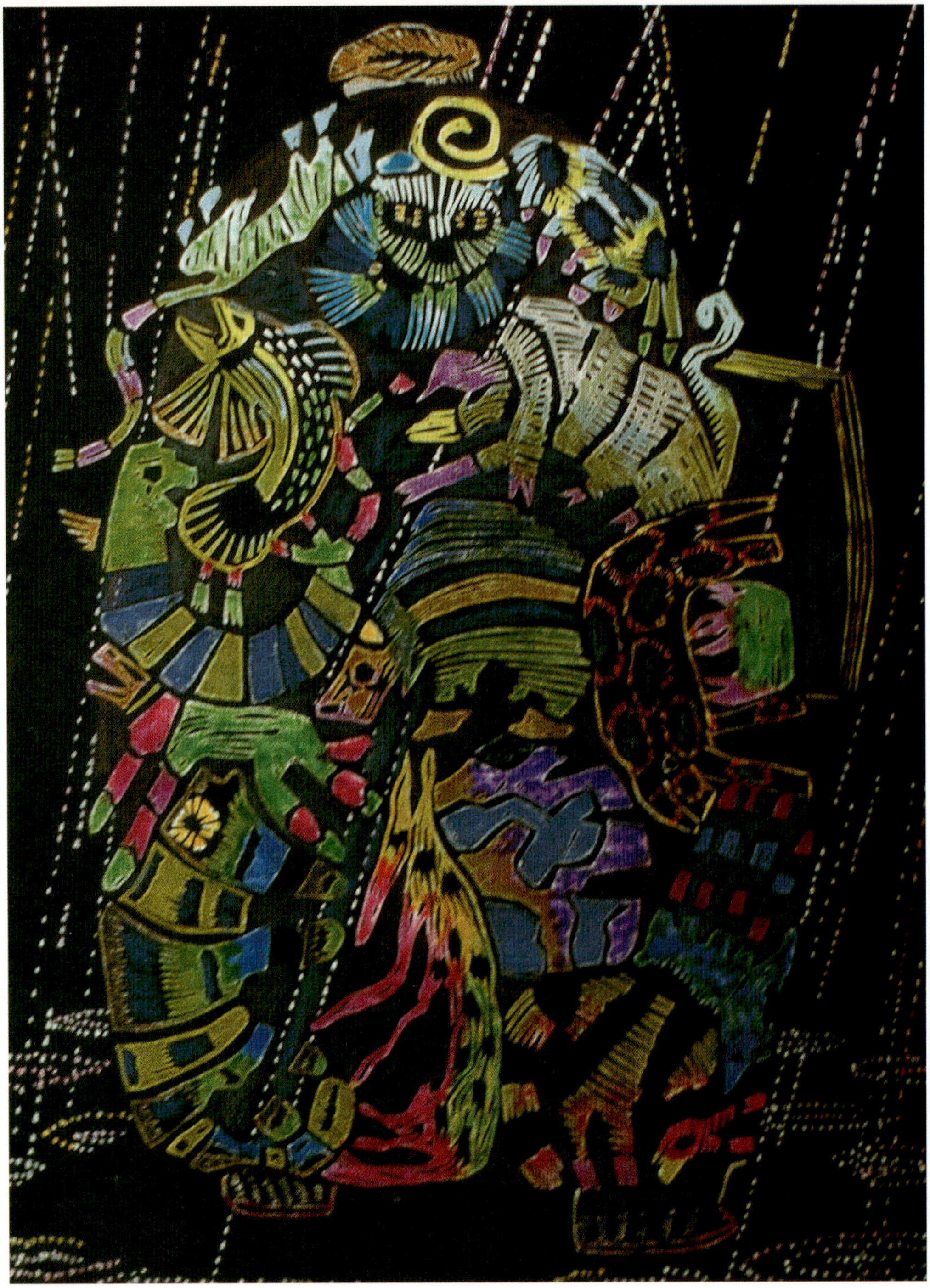

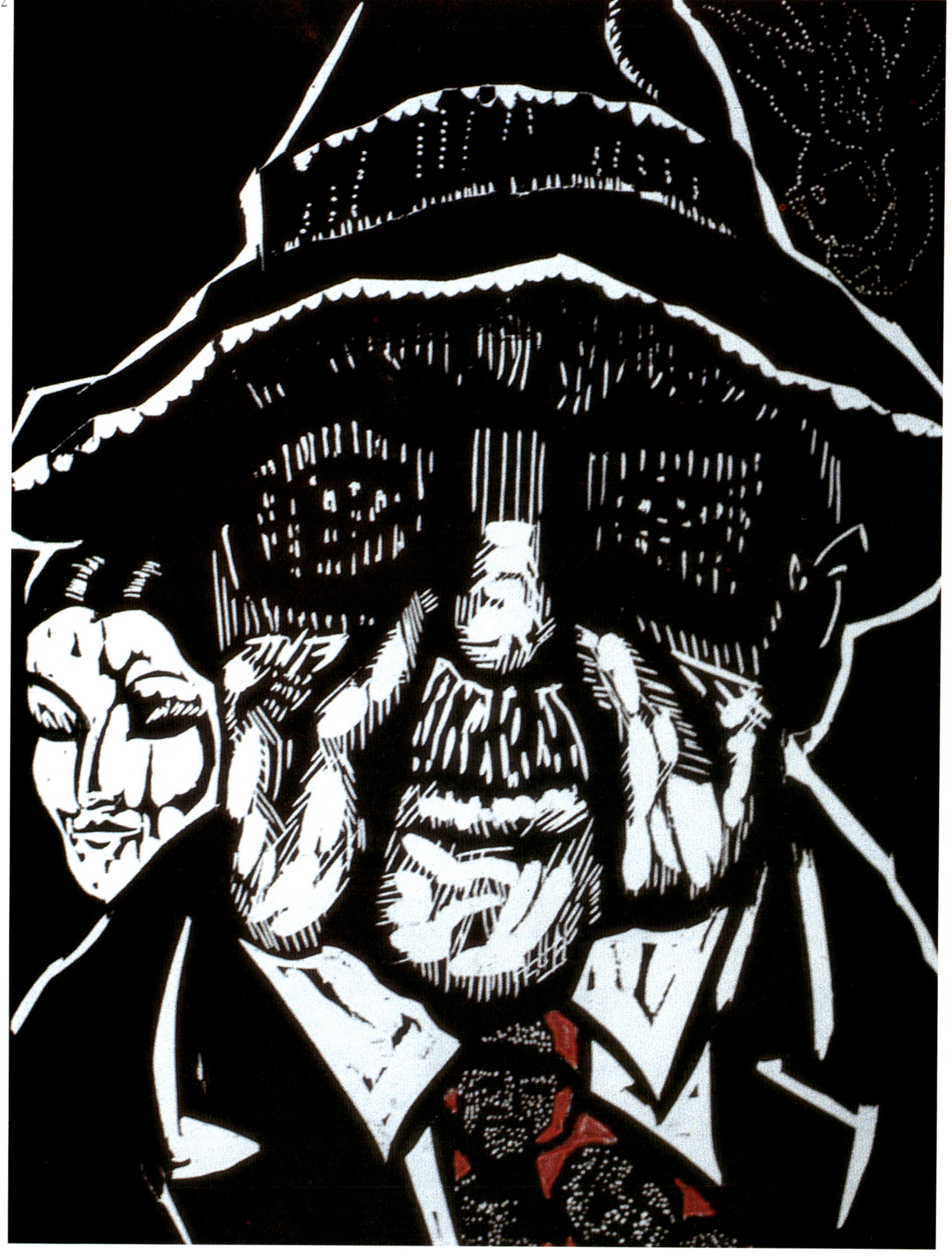

232. Gordon and Vivian (color woodcut) 1996 18 x 14
    (*see page 123*)
233. C. S. Price (woodcut) 1996 18 x 14
234. Charles Heaney (woodcut) 1996 18 x 14
235. George Johanson (woodcut) 1996 18 x 14
236. A. C. and Arthur Runquist (woodcut) 1996 18 x 14
237. Bill Givler (woodcut) 1996 18 x 14
238. Charles Voorhies (woodcut) 1996 18 x 14
239. Jack and Barbara McLarty (woodcut) 1996 18 x 14
240. Underworld (woodengraving) 1996 5 x 8 (*see page 119*)

234

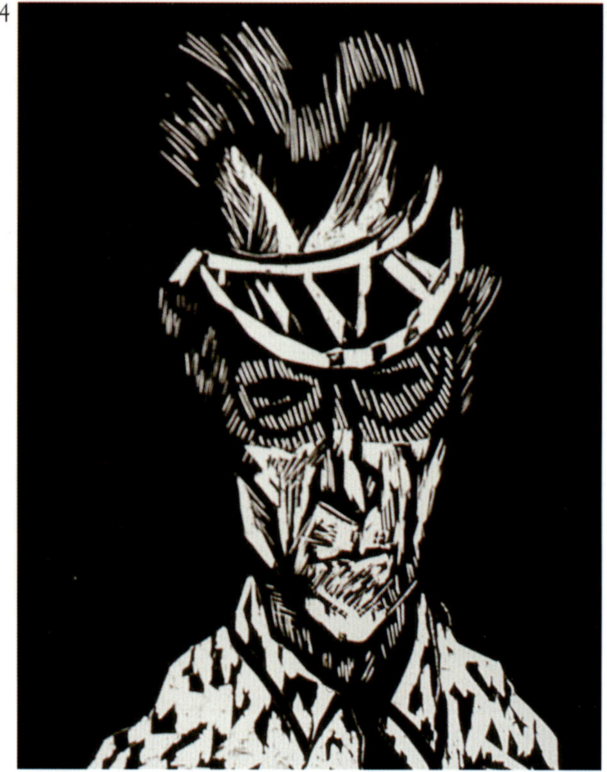

233

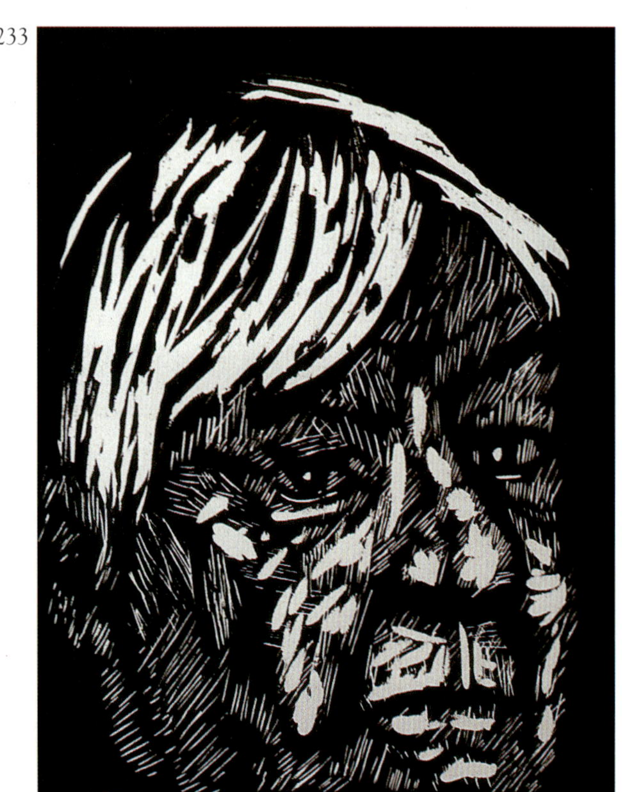

235

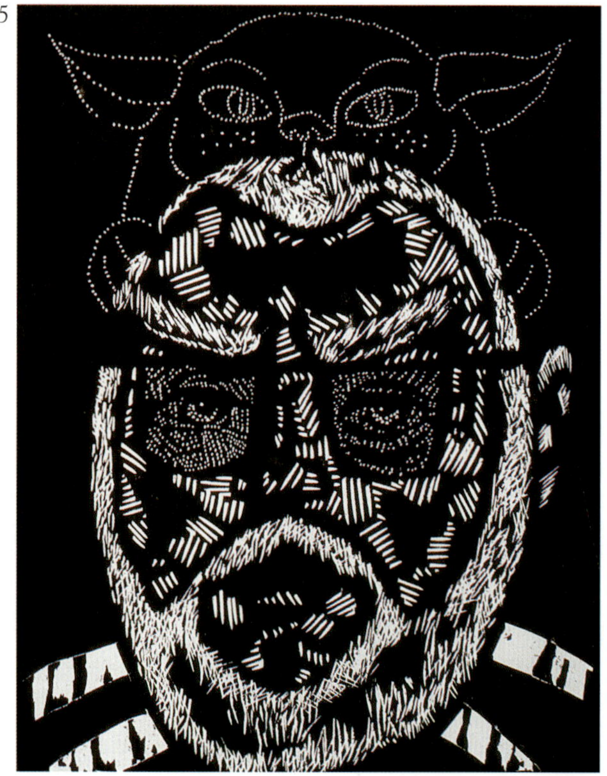

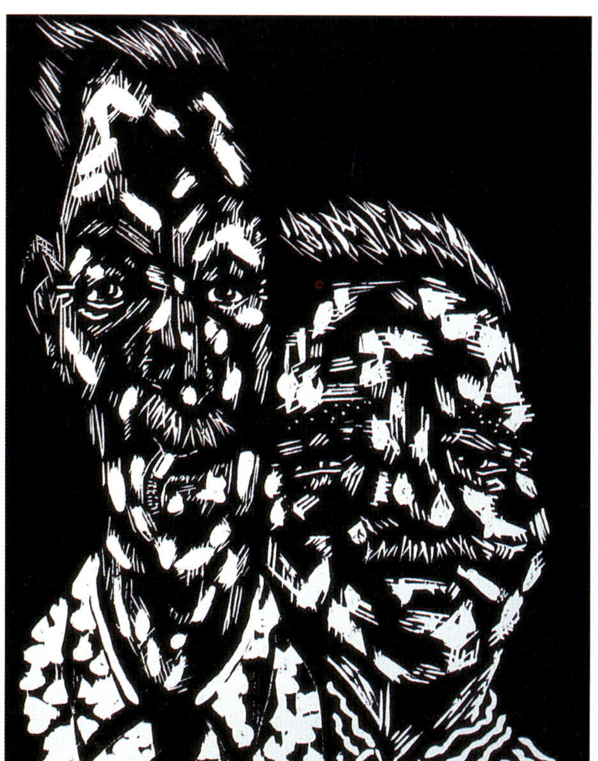

236

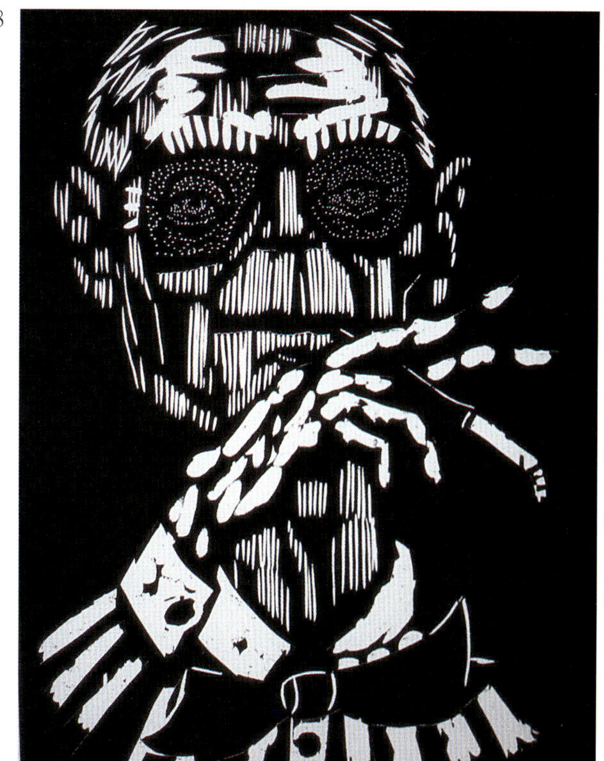

238

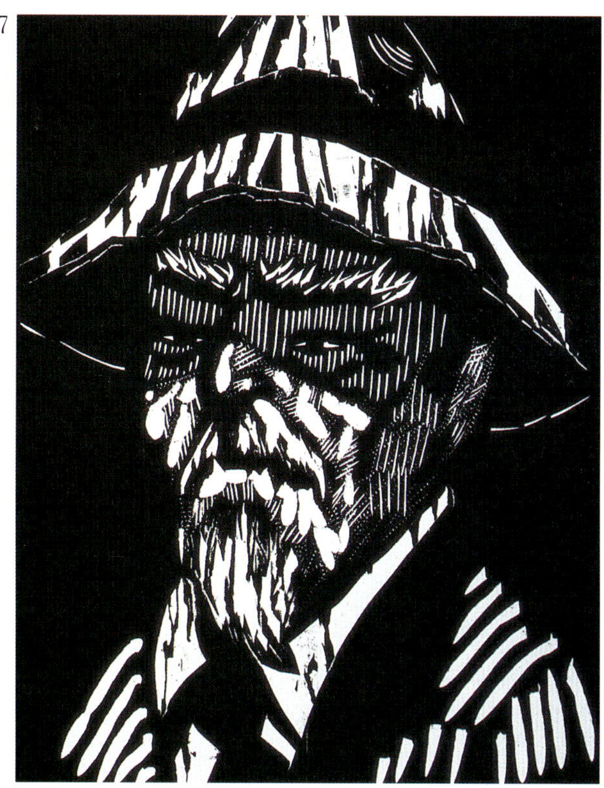

237

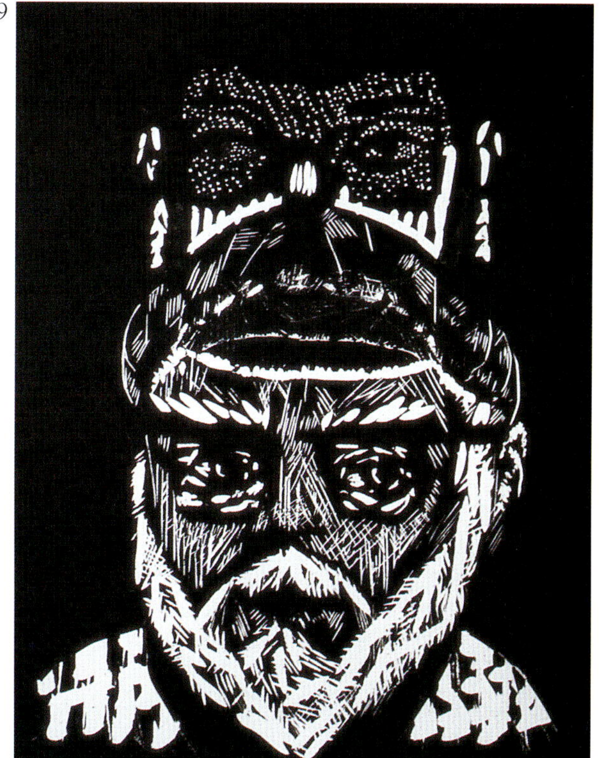

239

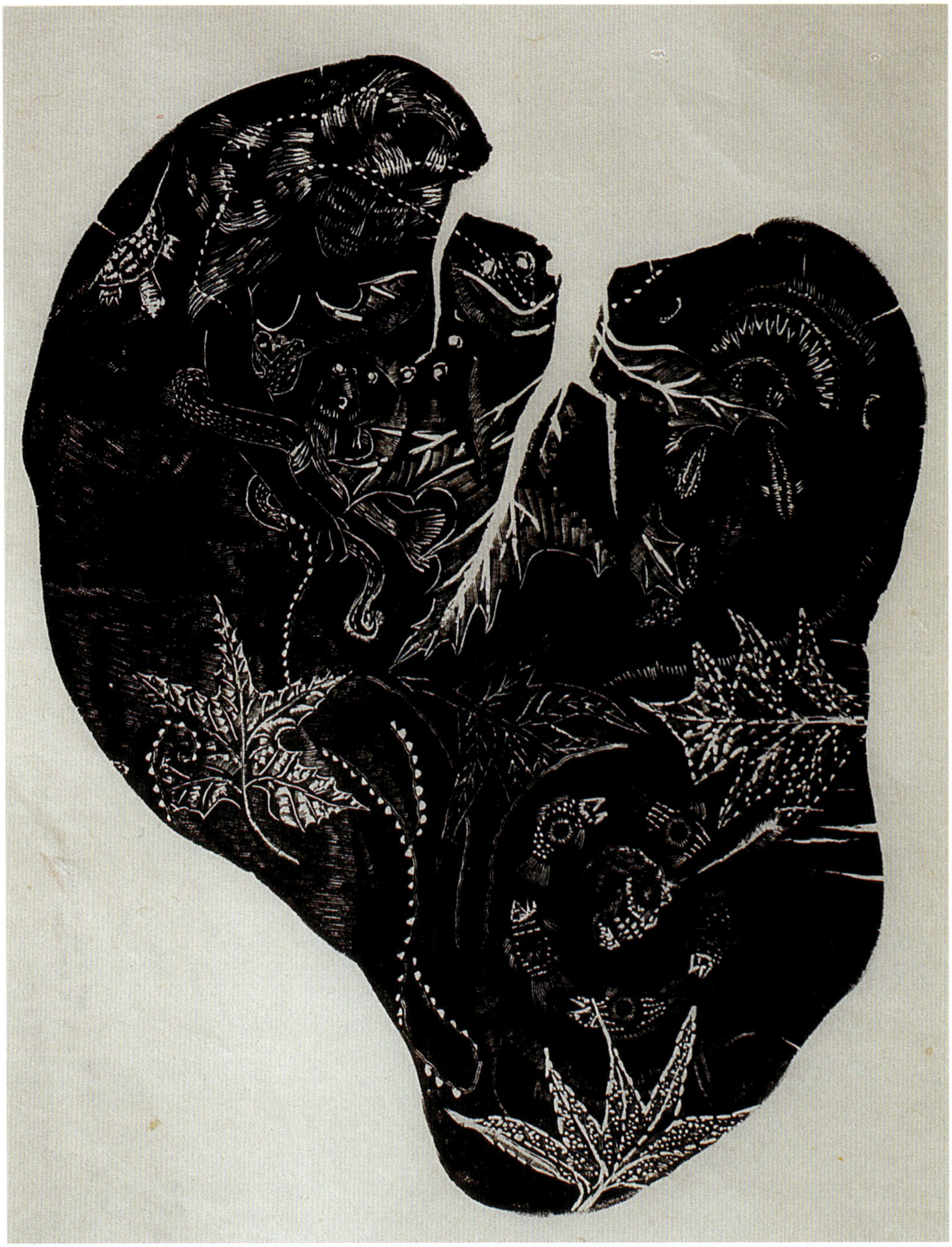

241. Strange Travels (woodengraving) 1996 3 x 2 (*see page 118*)
242. The Pond (woodengraving) 1996 11 x 9
243. A Walk Through the Woods (color woodcut) 1996 14 x 18

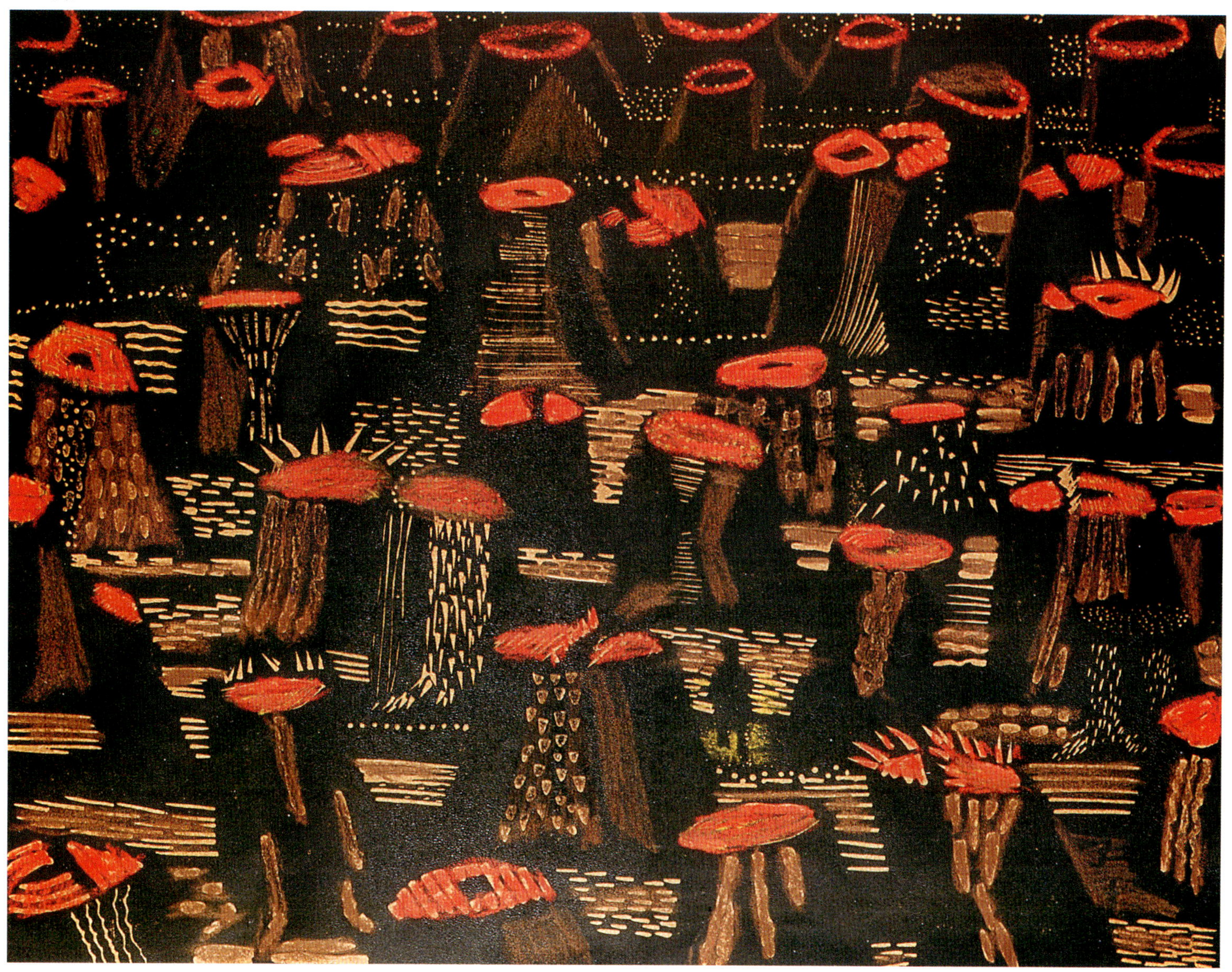

. . . Viewing 'Gordon and Vivian' and 'Powell's Books' reminds me that it is an uplifting experience to see and to respond to work made by a 'grown-up' artist—sure, honest and heartfelt work that comes from a tried-and-true commitment to making art. Our collections are richer for your thoughtful and generous gift. . . . When Ivins wrote *Prints and Visual Communication*, he could have had your prints in mind. Both these woodcuts vividly convey a feeling of personality and place, with an energy and directness that suggest the spirit of the maker as well. To my great pleasure, these prints also bring back memories of my recent stay in Portland by conjuring up two of Portland's national treasures: Powell's Books and Gordon Gilkey. . . .

Roberta Waddell, Curator of Prints, The New York Public Library, April 4, 1997

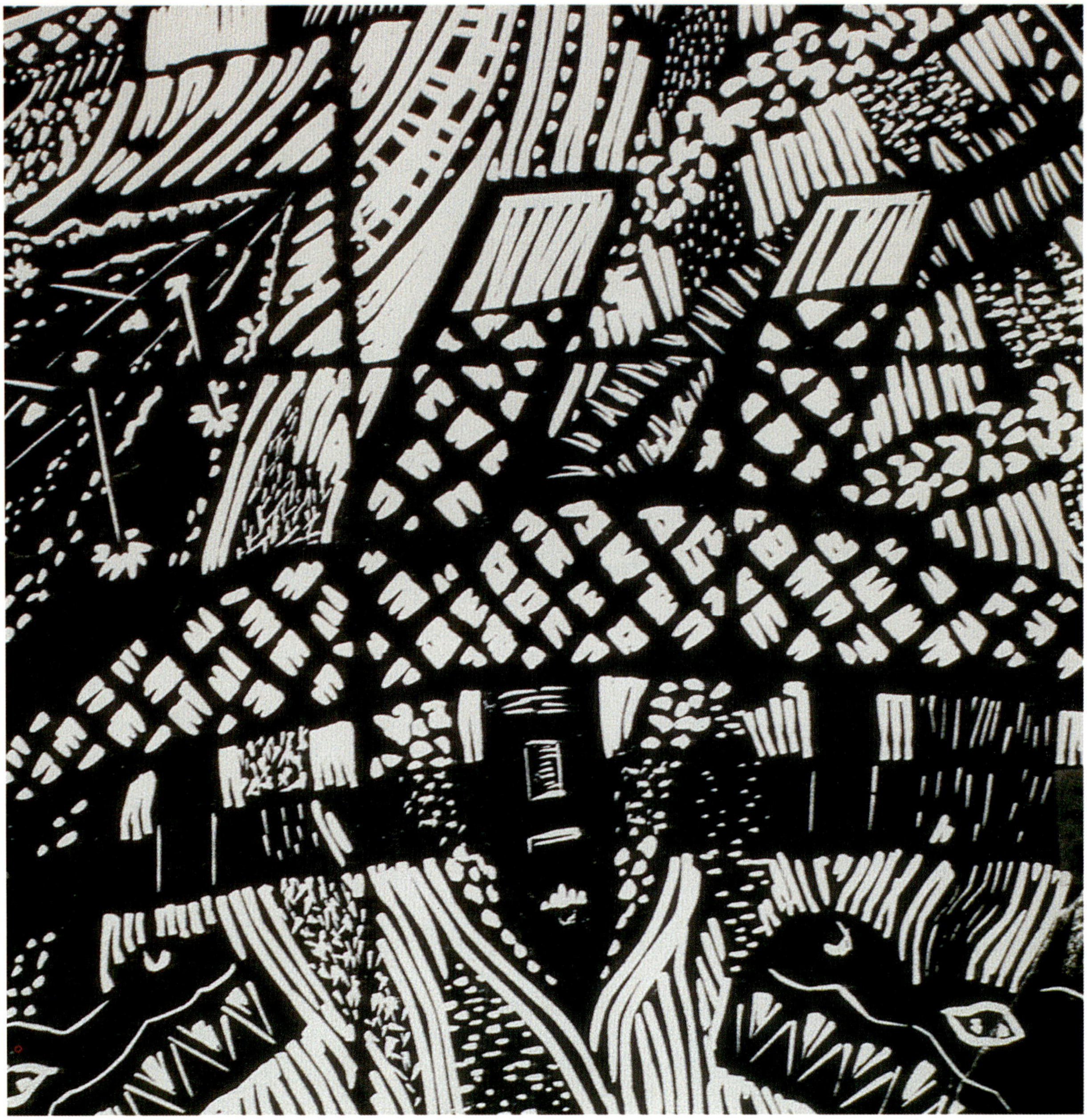

244. Detail of McLarty Woodcut Mural designed for City Hall, Portland 1997
245. Detail of The Pond #242 from page 126
246. Detail of Late Travelers #112 from page 49 (*see page 130*)
247. Detail of the Giant Tree #165 from page 85 (*see page 130*)
248. Detail of Ottos #188 from page 96 (*see page 131*)
249. Detail of Red Passage #125 from pages 64 and 65 (*see page 131*)
250. Detail of Butterfly Dogs #145 from page 71 (*see page 132*)
251. Detail of The Devil Lives Under Ocumicho #196 from page 103 (*see page 132*)
252. Detail of Powell's #219 from page 115 (*see page 133*)
253. Detail of The Doll Collector #190 from page 98 (*see page 133*)

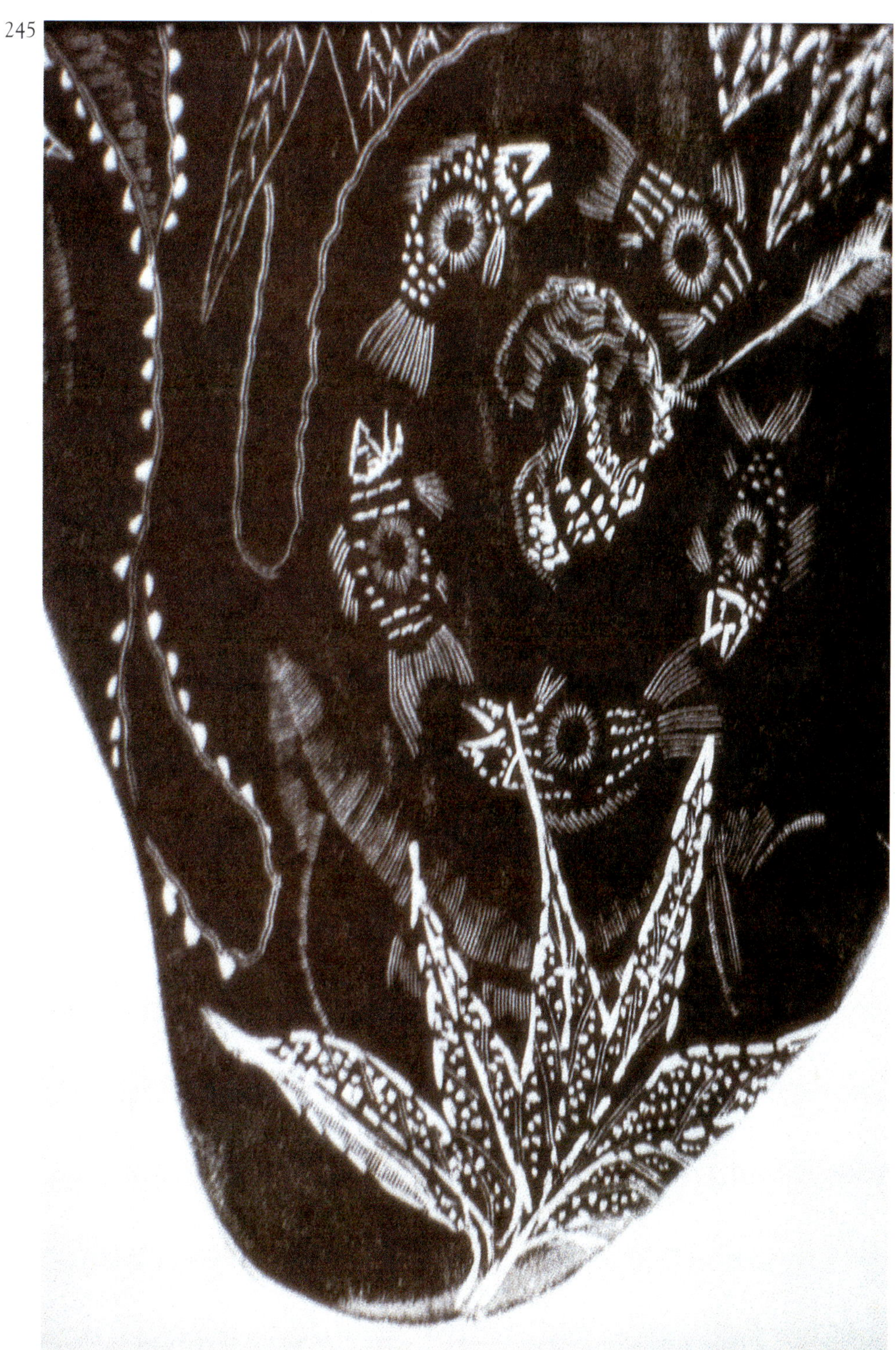

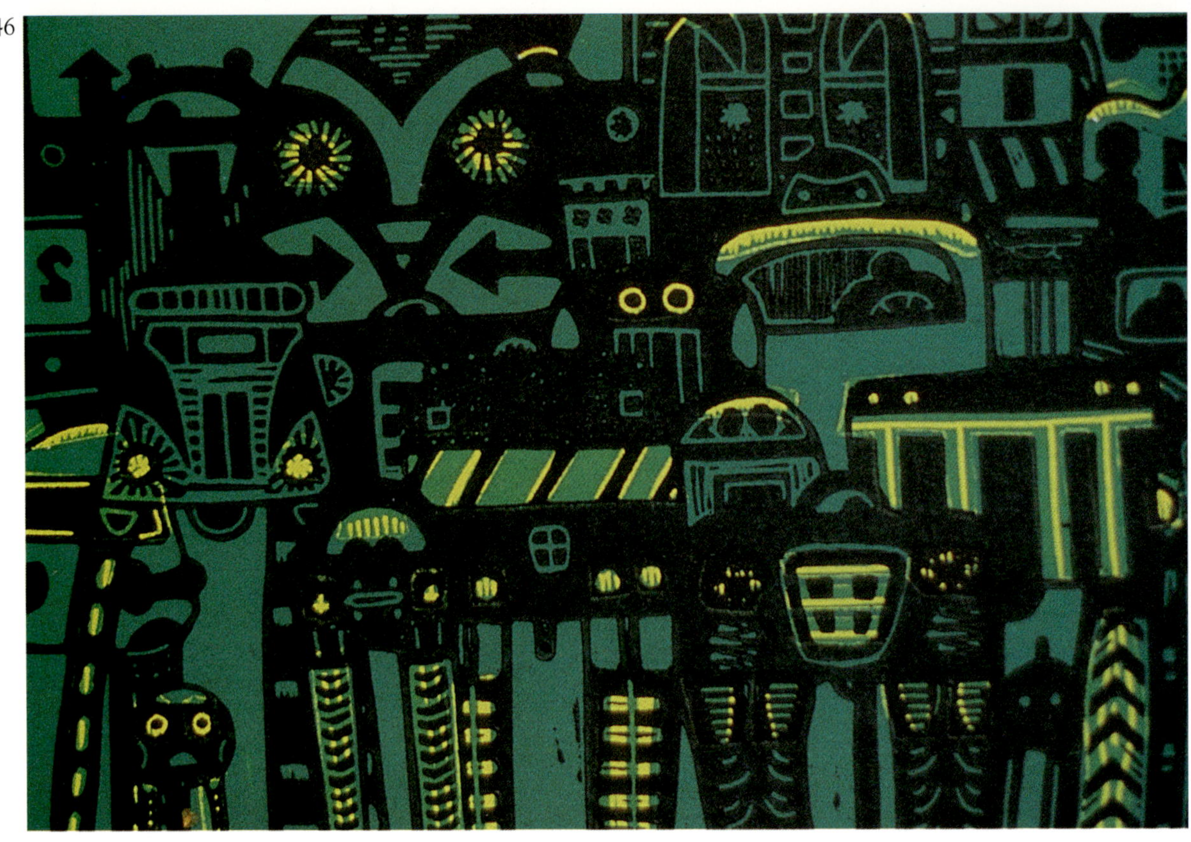

246

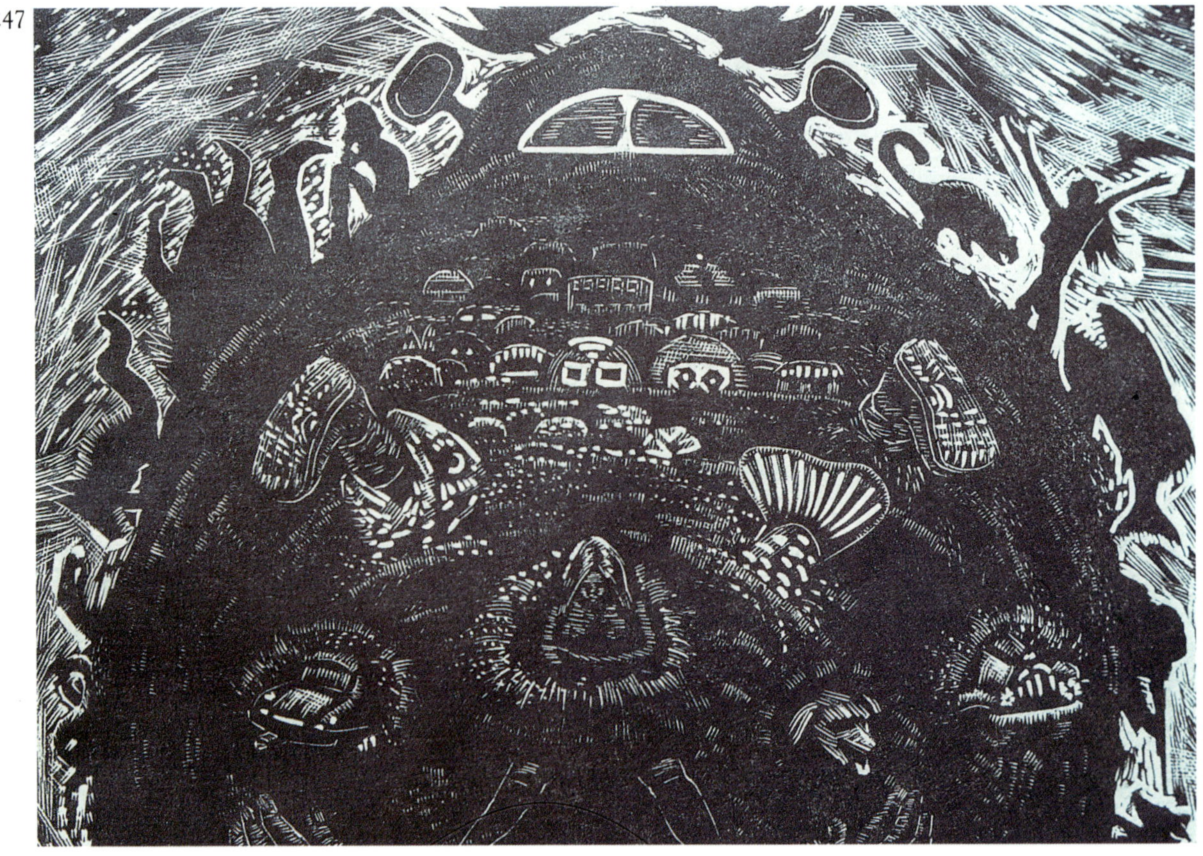

247

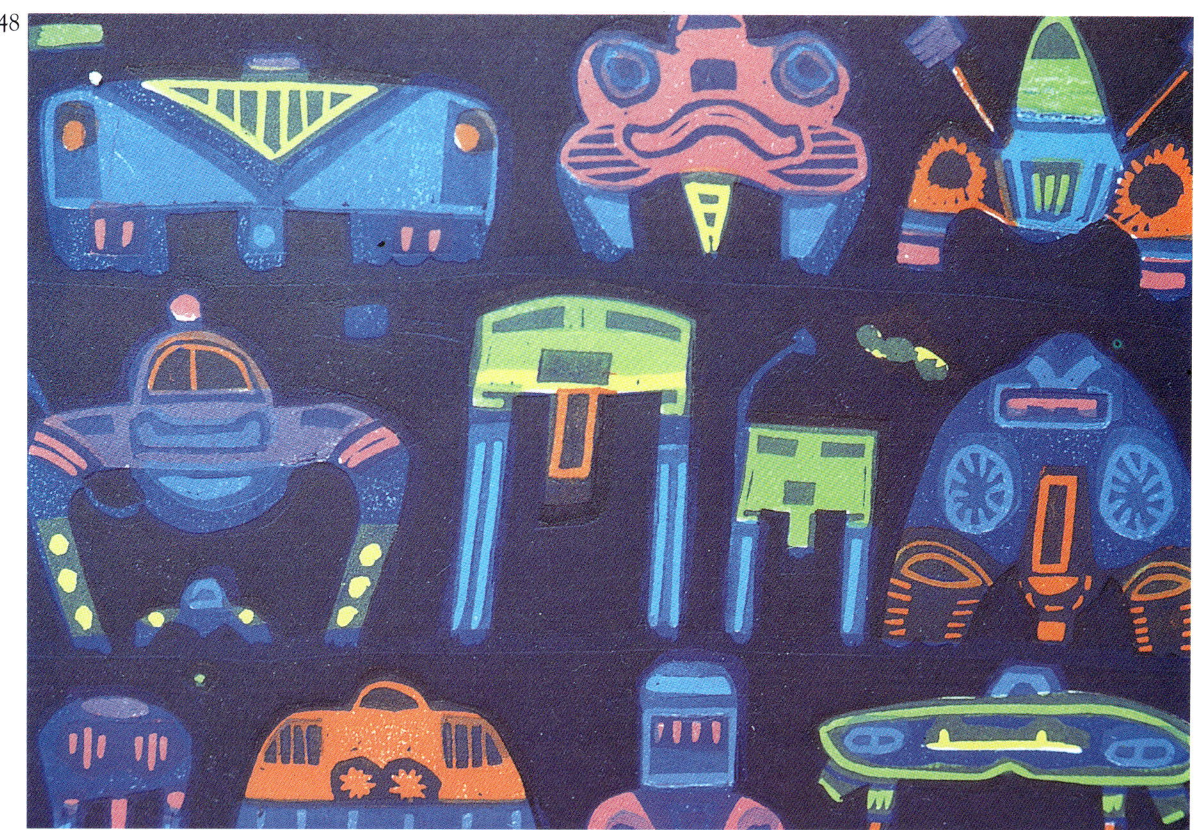

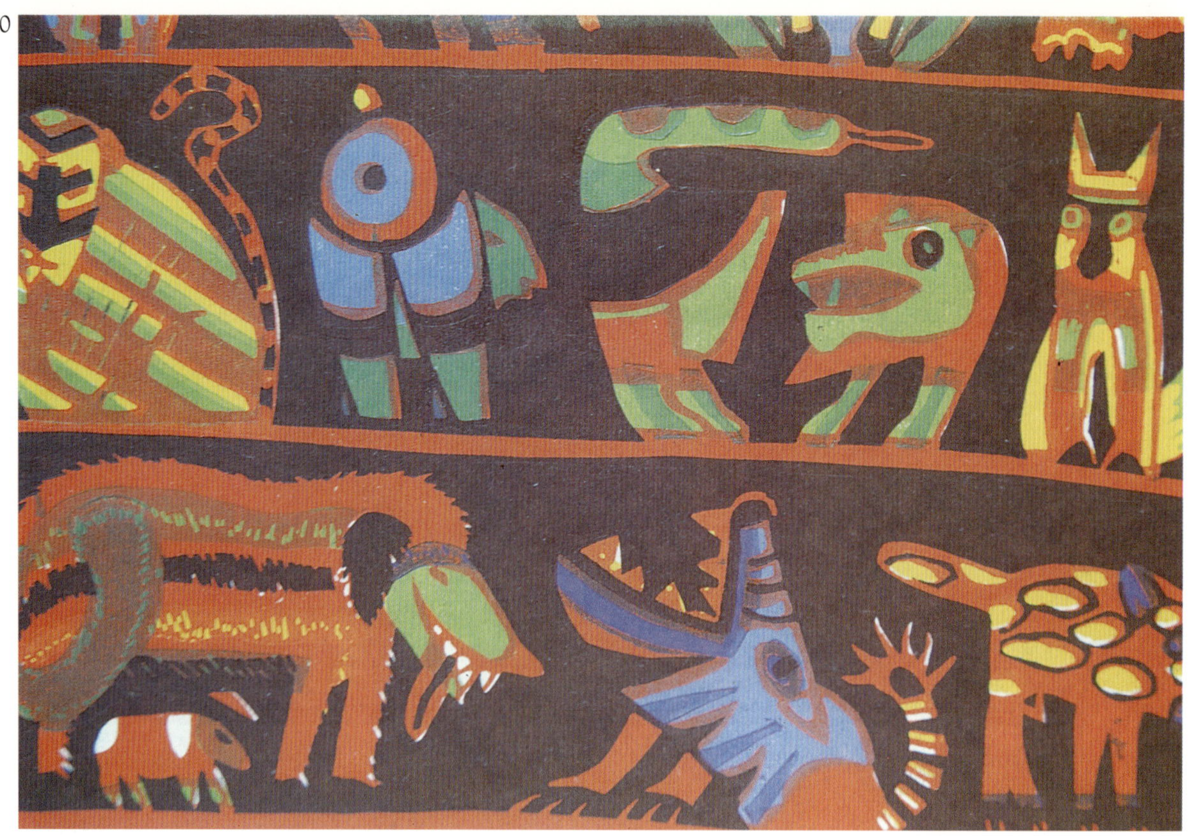

250

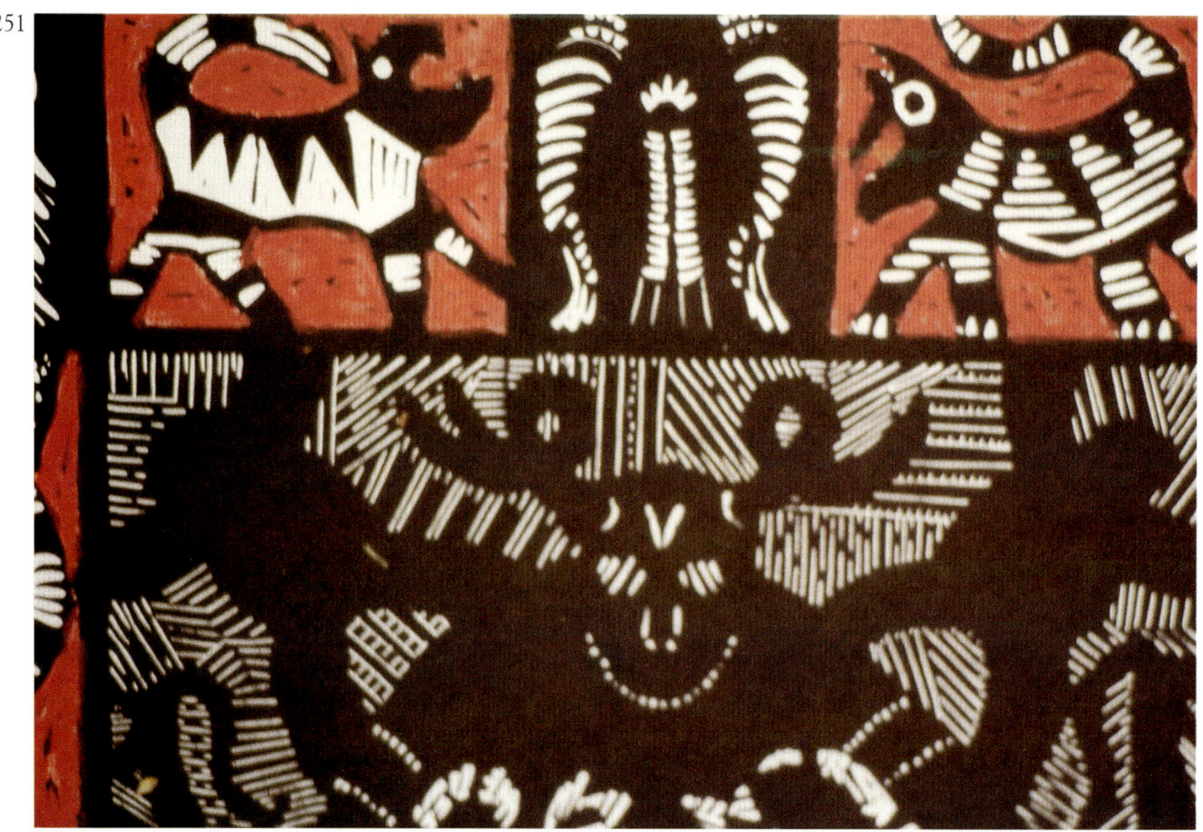

251

252

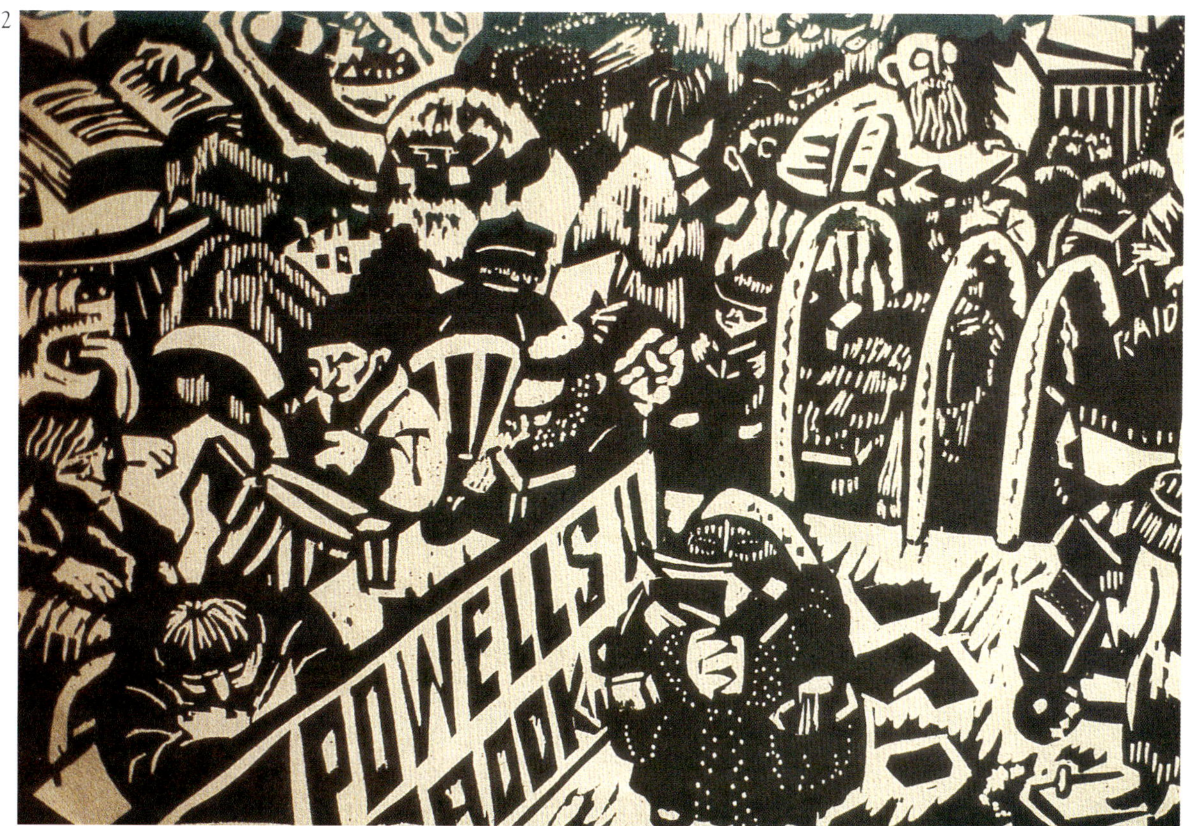

253

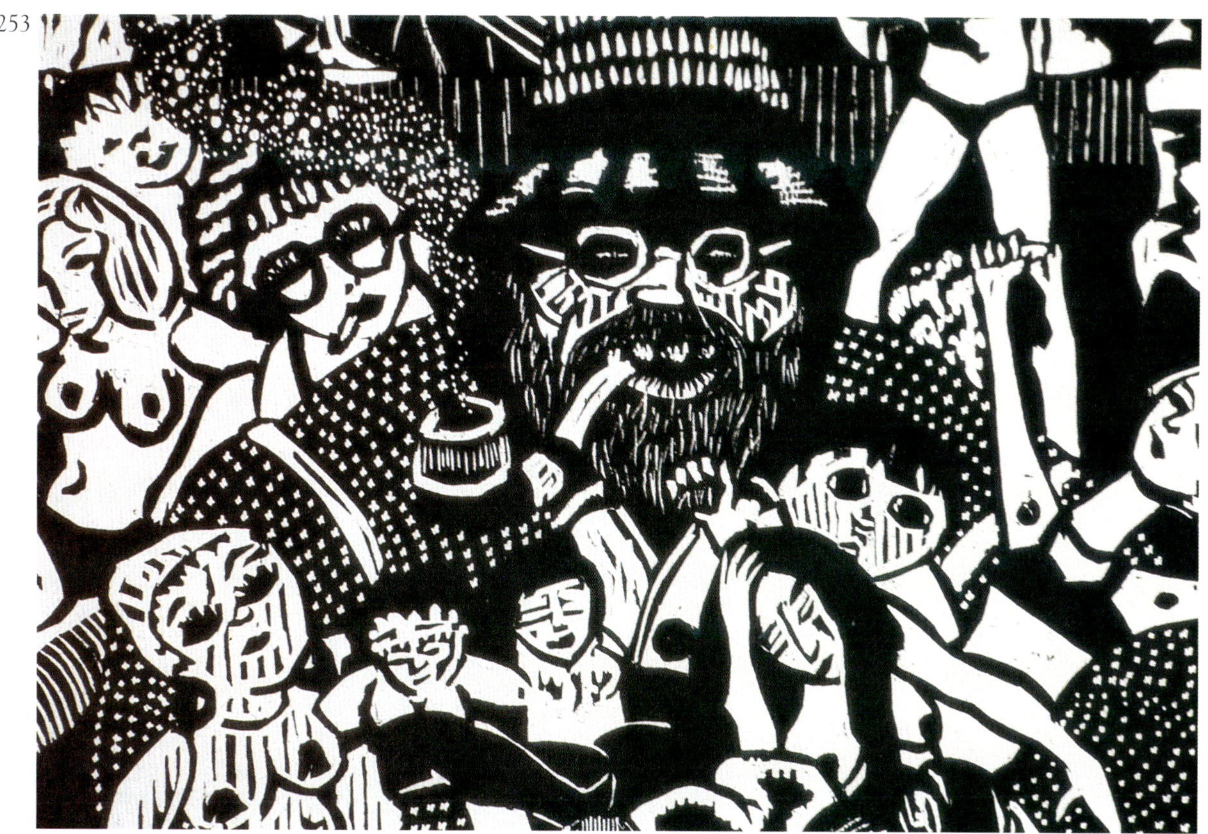

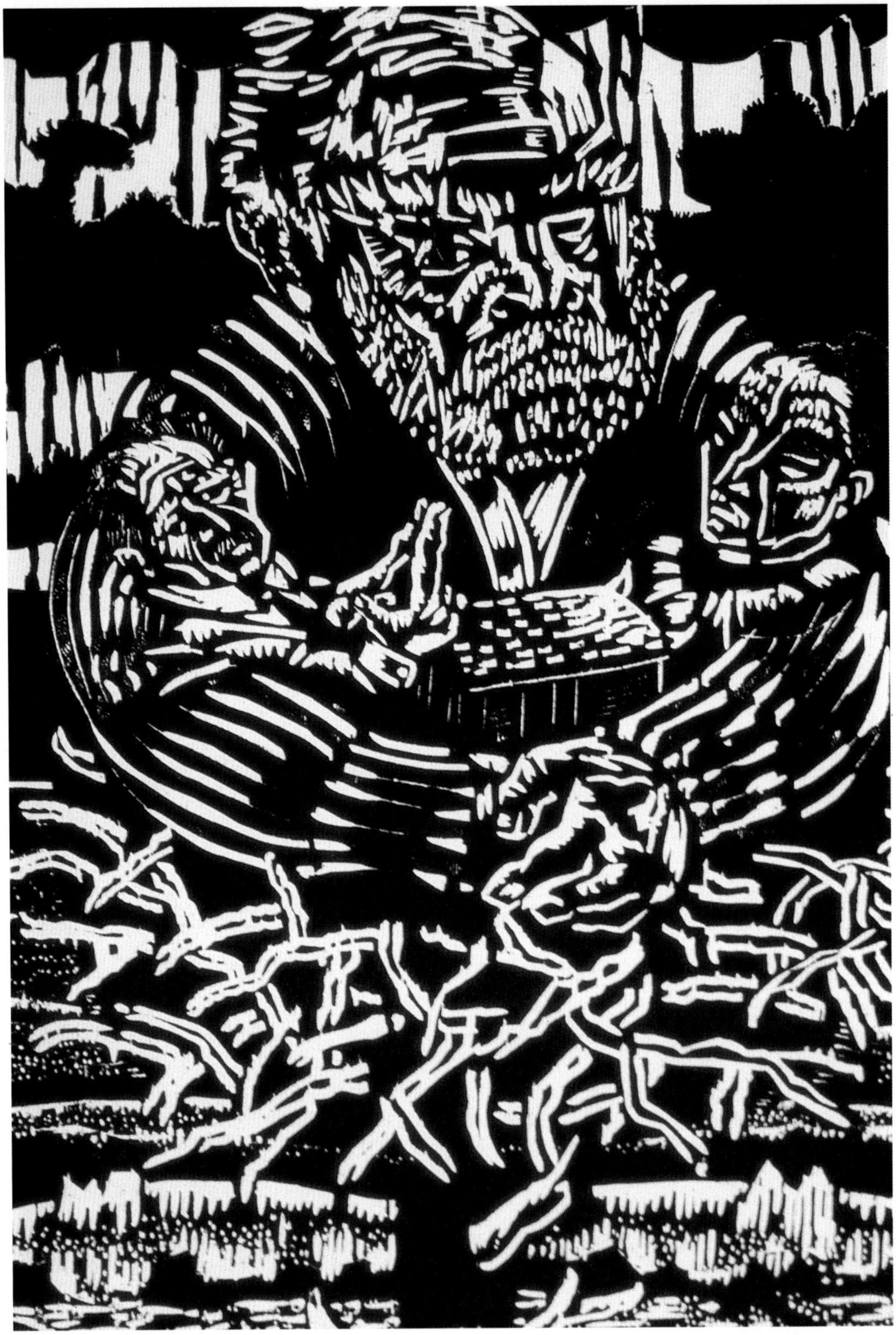

254. Detail of Walter and the Boys #218 from page 113
255. Detail of Some Dogs in the Fountain #155 from pages 78 and 79
256. Detail of Some Dogs in the Fountain #155 from pages 78 and 79

255

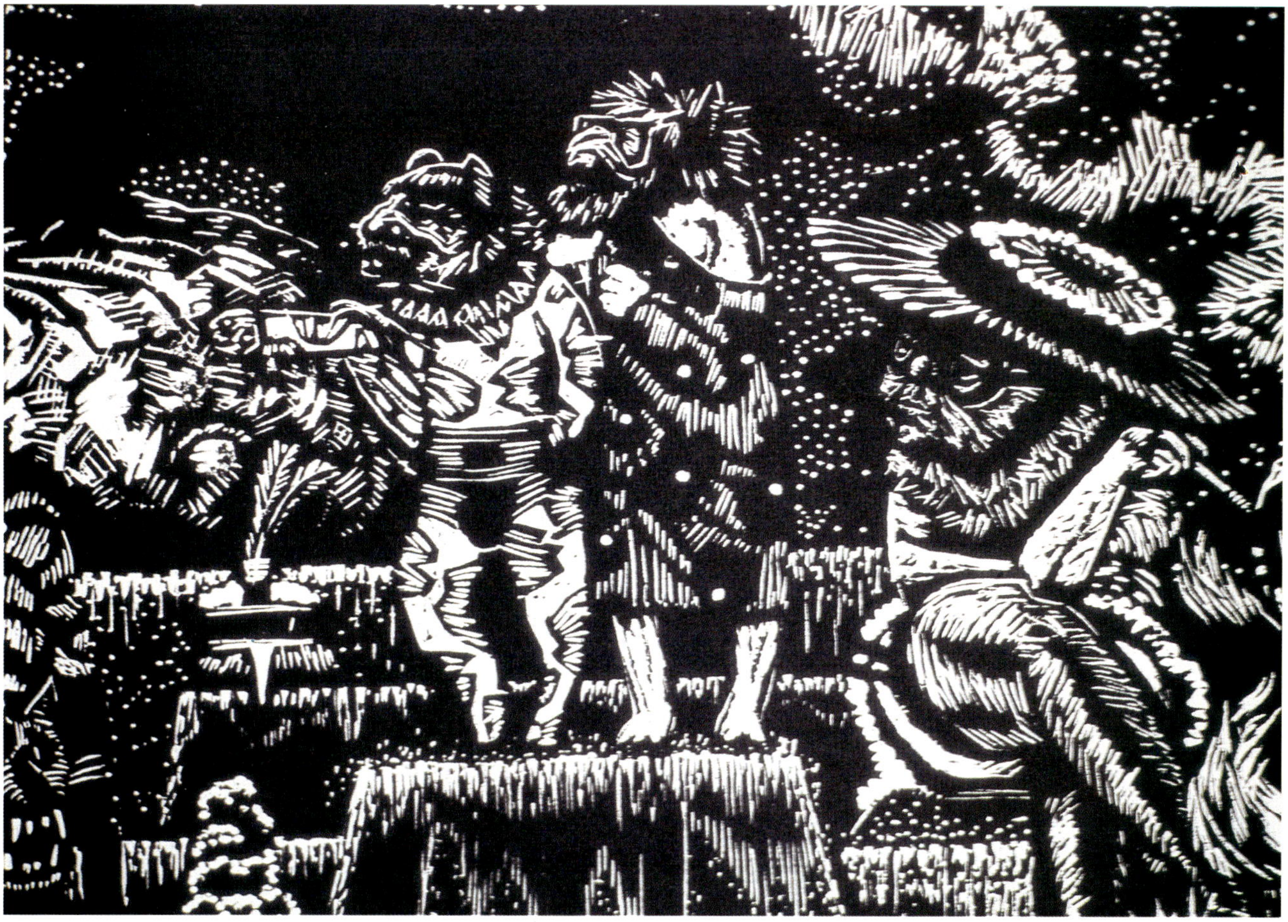

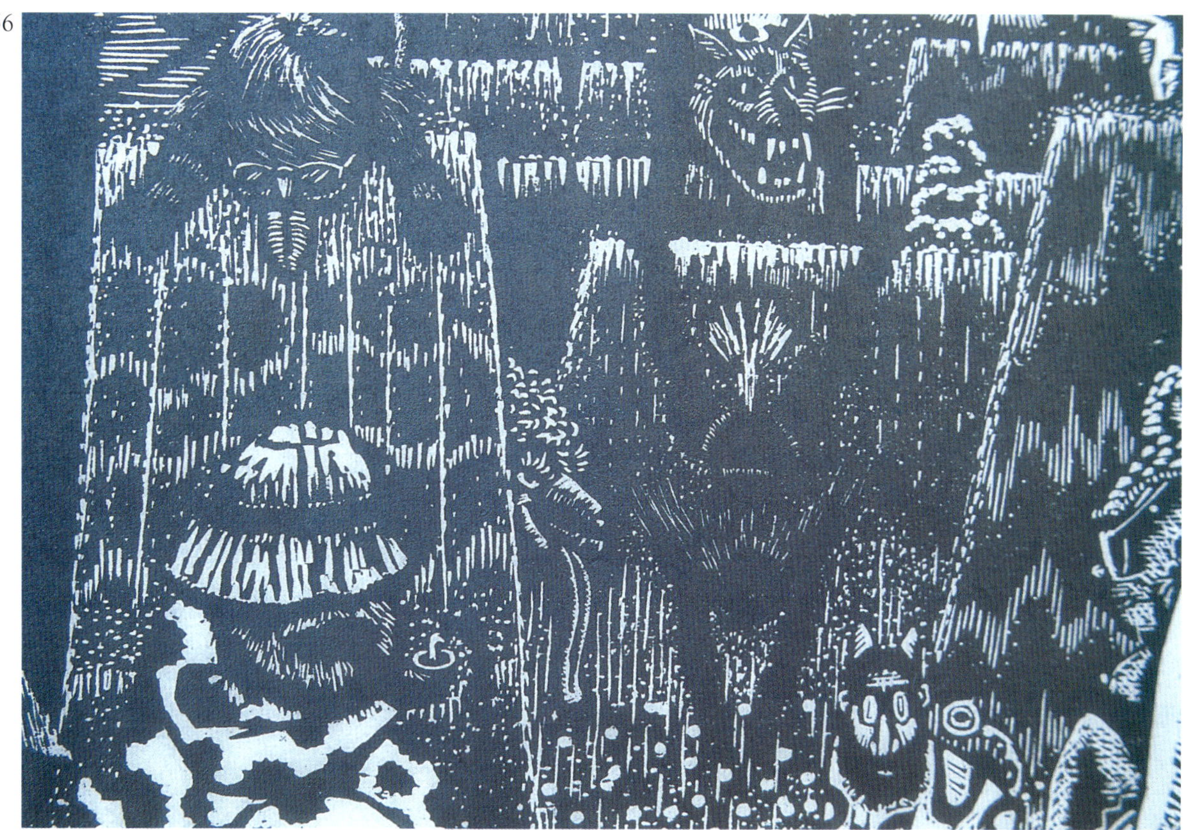

256

ABOUT THE EDITOR

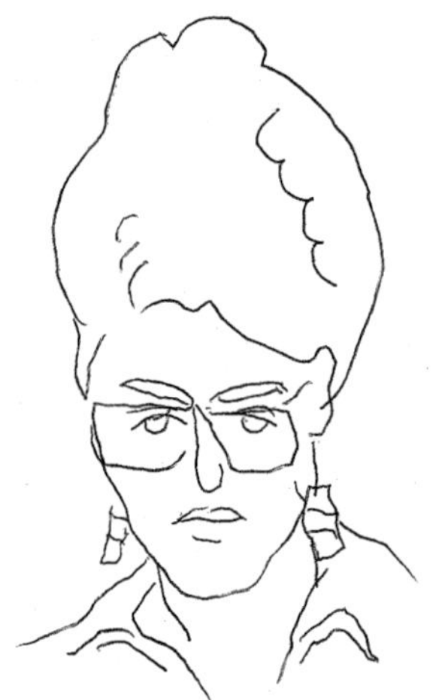

Barbara Lever McLarty was born in 1919 in Alberta, Canada, and has lived in Oregon since the tender age of two.

Co-founder and Director of the highly esteemed Image Gallery from its opening in fall 1961 until mid-1986, she was a leading spirit behind the energetic and unusual exhibition program of the gallery. Because she believed the role of art dealer should be the role of an educator, she served as an important community resource, offering a multitude of mostly unsung and totally unpaid services: lectures and artists' talks, school tours, packaged shows for small downstate art centers without resources.

During her 25 years at the Image, she issued a consistent stream of often handsome, always informative publications that were unprecedented: brochures, newsletters, monographs documenting the work of the artists she represented. Some names of note from the roster of the Image during the sixties and seventies are: James Castle, William Cumming, Byron Gardner, William Givler, Robert Hanson, Tom Hardy, Charles Heaney, Frederick Heidel, Manuel Izquierdo, George Johanson, Hank Kowert, Alden Mason, Richard Muller, Albert and Arthur Runquist, René Rickabaugh, Charles Voorhies, Harry Widman.

In 1966 the Image began to distinguish itself in the field of fine, handbound books with original prints. Much of the impetus for this came from Clyde Van Cleve, who was then designing Image publications. His fine touch is shown in "17 Love Poems" and in "Wind and Pines." Ms. McLarty was to serve both as inspiration and practical muse for six exceptional volumes in all. Involved in the early planning, she helped to determine content, organized the sponsorship/financial backing, handled all details of editing, and managed the mailing and distribution. Her editorial credits include:

"17 Love Poems," Image Gallery (1966)

"To His Coy Mistress," Image Gallery (1972)

"Wind and Pines," Art Advocates/Image Gallery (1977)

"Charles Heaney: Master of the Oregon Scene," Art Advocates/Image Gallery (1980)

"The Book of Color," Art Advocates (1990)

"Worldwatcher: Jack McLarty Fifty Years (1943–1993)," McLartys' Choice (1995)

PHOTOGRAPHY CREDITS:

All slides of the embossments from "Wind and Pines" were done by Brian Lincoln. These include catalog numbers 131 through 136. His credits also include the following: #38, Girl with a Scarf; #40, Moon Chair; #45, The Flute; #90, The White Sea; #97, New Orleans Street Band; #122, Jazz Shadows. #228 and #229 are by PhotoArt Studios. All other slides/photographs in the catalog were shot by the Artist except for the Back Cover Photo, which was shot by George Johanson.

COLOPHON

This book is set in Goudy Oldstyle Roman and Italic (Frederic W. Goudy, 1915) by Irish Setter, Portland, Oregon, and lithographed and bound by Sung In Printing, Inc., in Korea.